SGT. FROG™

KERORO GUNSOU

VOL. #10 BY MINE YOSHIZAKI

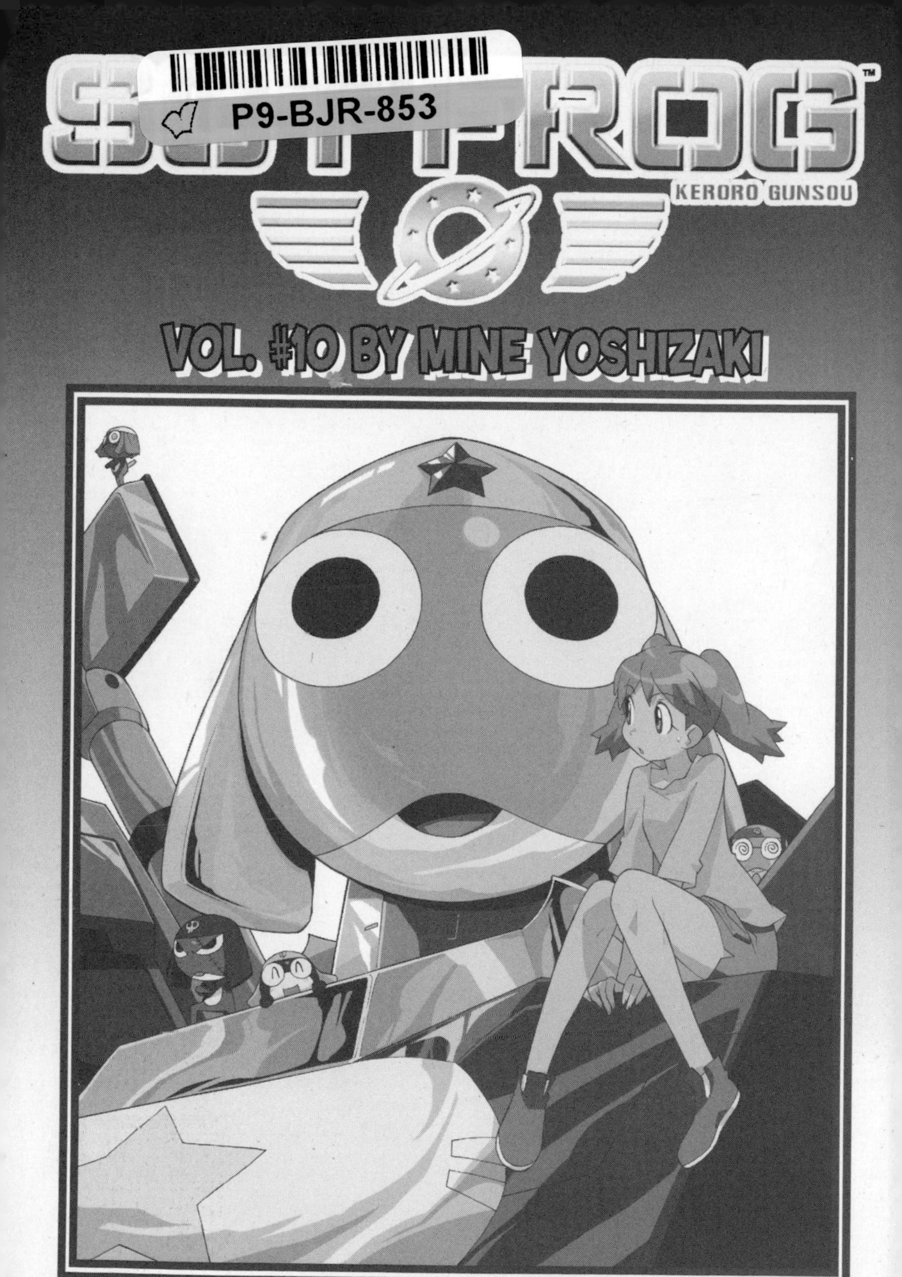

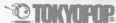

TOKYOPOP®

HAMBURG // LONDON // LOS ANGELES // TOKYO

SERGEANT-KERORO 2005

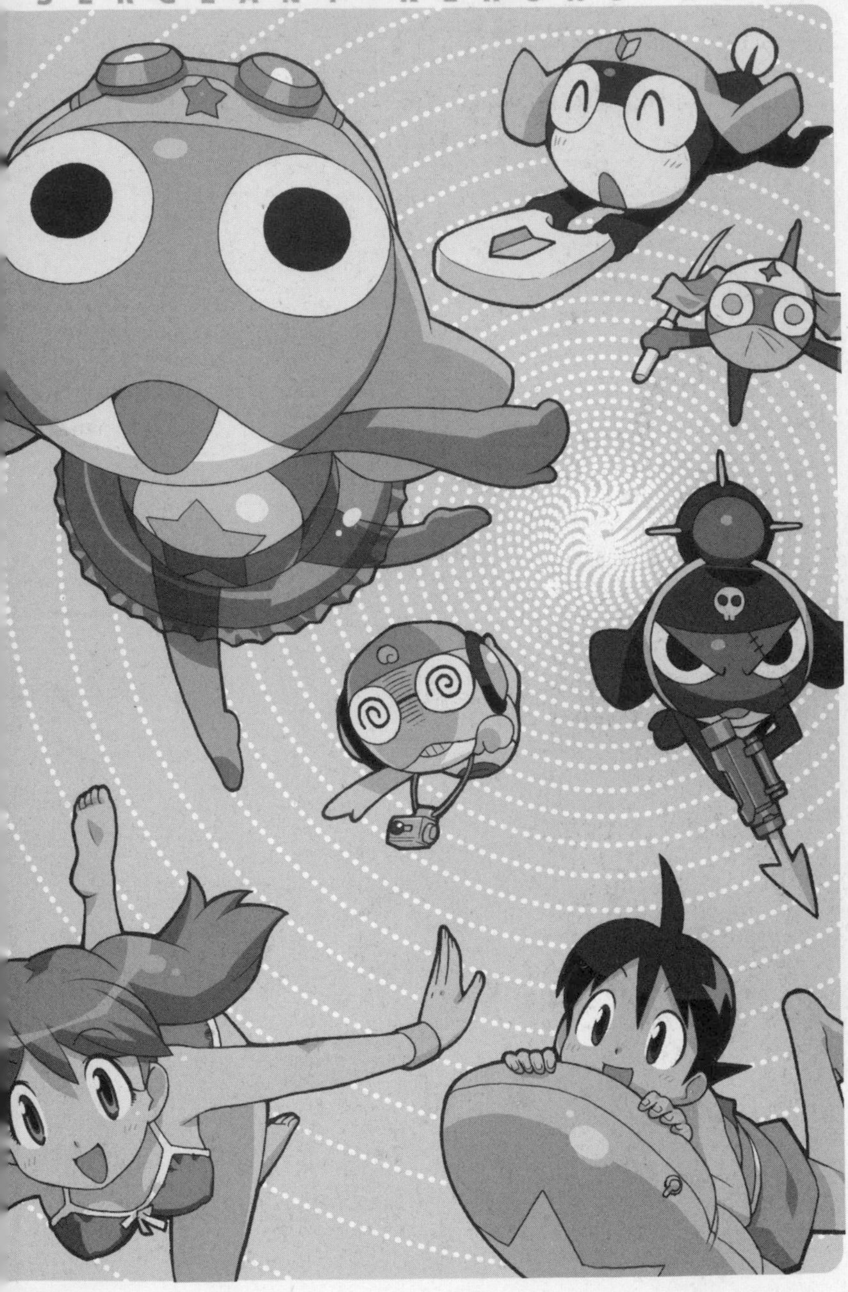

KERORO PIN-UP

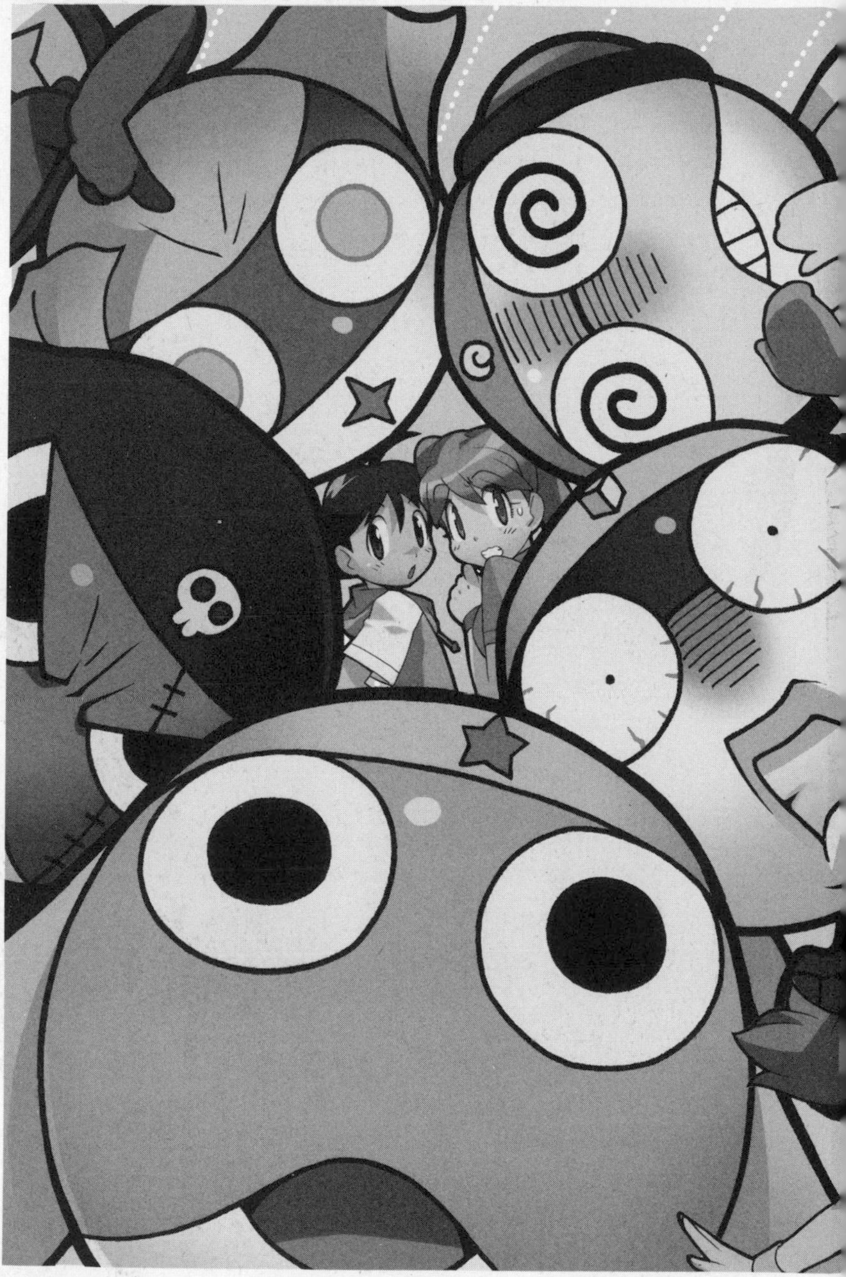

SGT. FROG 10 · TABLE OF CONTENTS

KERORO GUNSOU

VOLUME #10

BY
MINE YOSHIZAKI

HAMBURG // LONDON // LOS ANGELES // TOKYO

SGT. Frog Vol. 10
Created by Mine Yoshizaki

Translation - Yuko Fukami
English Adaptation - Carol Fox
Copy Editor - Eric Althoff
Retouch and Lettering - Jose Macasocol, Jr.
Production Artist - Jose Macasocol, Jr.
Cover Design - Raymond Makowski

Editor - Paul Morrissey
Digital Imaging Manager - Chris Buford
Production Managers - Jennifer Miller and Mutsumi Miyazaki
Managing Editor - Lindsey Johnston
VP of Production - Ron Klamert
Publisher and E.I.C. - Mike Kiley
President and C.O.O. - John Parker
C.E.O. - Stuart Levy

A **TOKYOPOP** Manga

TOKYOPOP Inc.
5900 Wilshire Blvd. Suite 2000
Los Angeles, CA 90036

E-mail: info@TOKYOPOP.com
Come visit us online at www.TOKYOPOP.com

ISBN: 1-59182-344-7

First TOKYOPOP printing: December 2005
10 9 8 7 6 5 4 3 2 1
Printed in the USA

CHARACTER RELATIONSHIPS AND THE STORY SO FAR

(FACT-CHECKING PERFORMED BY SHONEN ACE MAGAZINE)

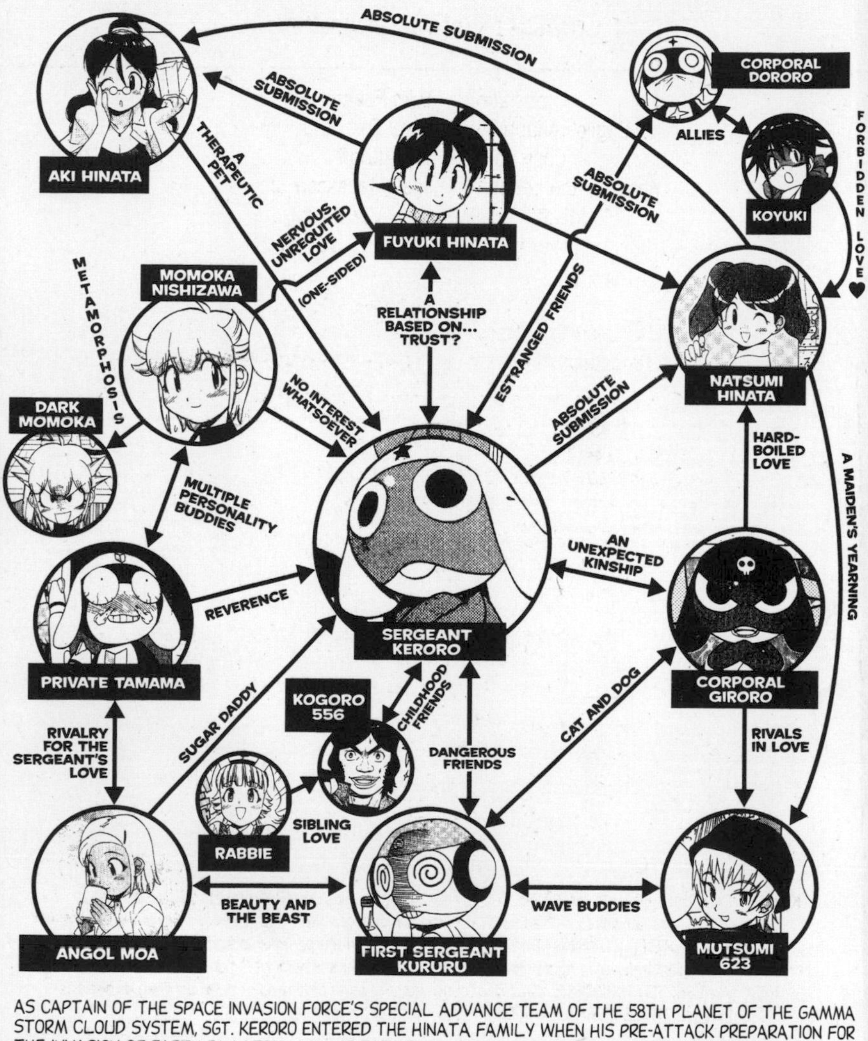
ABSOLUTE SUBMISSION
AKI HINATA
ABSOLUTE SUBMISSION
A THERAPEUTIC PET
FUYUKI HINATA
CORPORAL DORORO
ALLIES
KOYUKI
FORBIDDEN LOVE♥
ABSOLUTE SUBMISSION
NERVOUS, UNREQUITED LOVE
(ONE-SIDED)
MOMOKA NISHIZAWA
METAMORPHOSIS
A RELATIONSHIP BASED ON... TRUST?
ESTRANGED FRIENDS
NATSUMI HINATA
DARK MOMOKA
NO INTEREST WHATSOEVER
ABSOLUTE SUBMISSION
HARD-BOILED LOVE
A MAIDEN'S YEARNING
MULTIPLE PERSONALITY BUDDIES
AN UNEXPECTED KINSHIP
REVERENCE
SERGEANT KERORO
PRIVATE TAMAMA
CORPORAL GIRORO
SUGAR DADDY
KOGORO 556
CHILDHOOD FRIENDS
CAT AND DOG
RIVALRY FOR THE SERGEANT'S LOVE
DANGEROUS FRIENDS
RIVALS IN LOVE
SIBLING LOVE
RABBIE
BEAUTY AND THE BEAST
WAVE BUDDIES
ANGOL MOA
FIRST SERGEANT KURURU
MUTSUMI 623

AS CAPTAIN OF THE SPACE INVASION FORCE'S SPECIAL ADVANCE TEAM OF THE 58TH PLANET OF THE GAMMA STORM CLOUD SYSTEM, SGT. KERORO ENTERED THE HINATA FAMILY WHEN HIS PRE-ATTACK PREPARATION FOR THE INVASION OF EARTH RAN AFOUL VIA HIS EASY CAPTURE BY THE HINATA CHILDREN, FUYUKI AND NATSUMI. THANKS TO FUYUKI'S KINDNESS, OR AT LEAST HIS CURIOSITY, SGT. KERORO QUICKLY BECAME A BONA FIDE MEMBER OF THE HINATA FAMILY...IN OTHER WORDS, A TOTAL FREELOADER. THE SERGEANT'S SUBORDINATES--"DUAL PERSONALITY" PRIVATE TAMAMA; "BLAZING MILITARY MAN" CORPORATE GIRORO; THE "WAVISH" SERGEANT MAJOR KURURU; AND THE MUCH-HERALDED "LORD OF TERROR," ANGOL MOA--SOON JOINED HIM TO REFORM THE KERORO PLATOON, WHICH DOES AS IT PLEASES IN A TOP-SECRET BASE BENEATH THE HINATA HOME. AND WITH THE APPEARANCE OF ITS LONG-AWAITED FIFTH MEMBER, "ASSASSIN" CORPORAL DORORO, KERORO PLATOON IS COMPLETE, AND A FULL-SCALE INVASION OF POKOPEN IS ABOUT TO BEGIN...MAYBE? ONE THING'S FOR SURE--THEIR OPERATIONS WILL CONTINUE TO IRRITATE THE EARTH ON AN INTERGALACTIC SCALE!

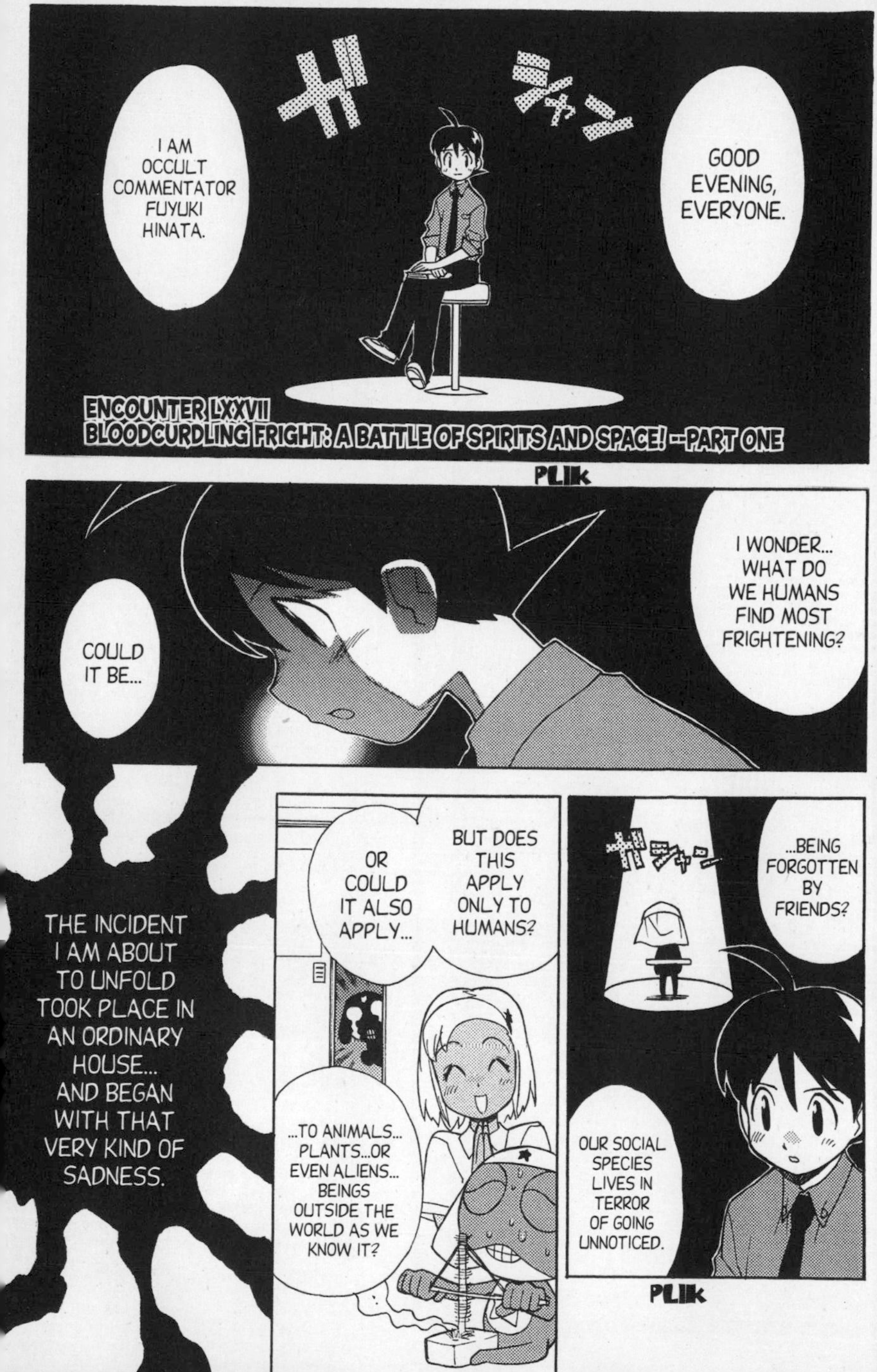
ガシャン
GOOD EVENING, EVERYONE.
I AM OCCULT COMMENTATOR FUYUKI HINATA.
ENCOUNTER LXXVII
BLOODCURDLING FRIGHT: A BATTLE OF SPIRITS AND SPACE! --PART ONE
PLIK
I WONDER... WHAT DO WE HUMANS FIND MOST FRIGHTENING?
COULD IT BE...
...BEING FORGOTTEN BY FRIENDS?
OUR SOCIAL SPECIES LIVES IN TERROR OF GOING UNNOTICED.
PLIK
BUT DOES THIS APPLY ONLY TO HUMANS?
OR COULD IT ALSO APPLY...
...TO ANIMALS... PLANTS...OR EVEN ALIENS... BEINGS OUTSIDE THE WORLD AS WE KNOW IT?
THE INCIDENT I AM ABOUT TO UNFOLD TOOK PLACE IN AN ORDINARY HOUSE... AND BEGAN WITH THAT VERY KIND OF SADNESS.

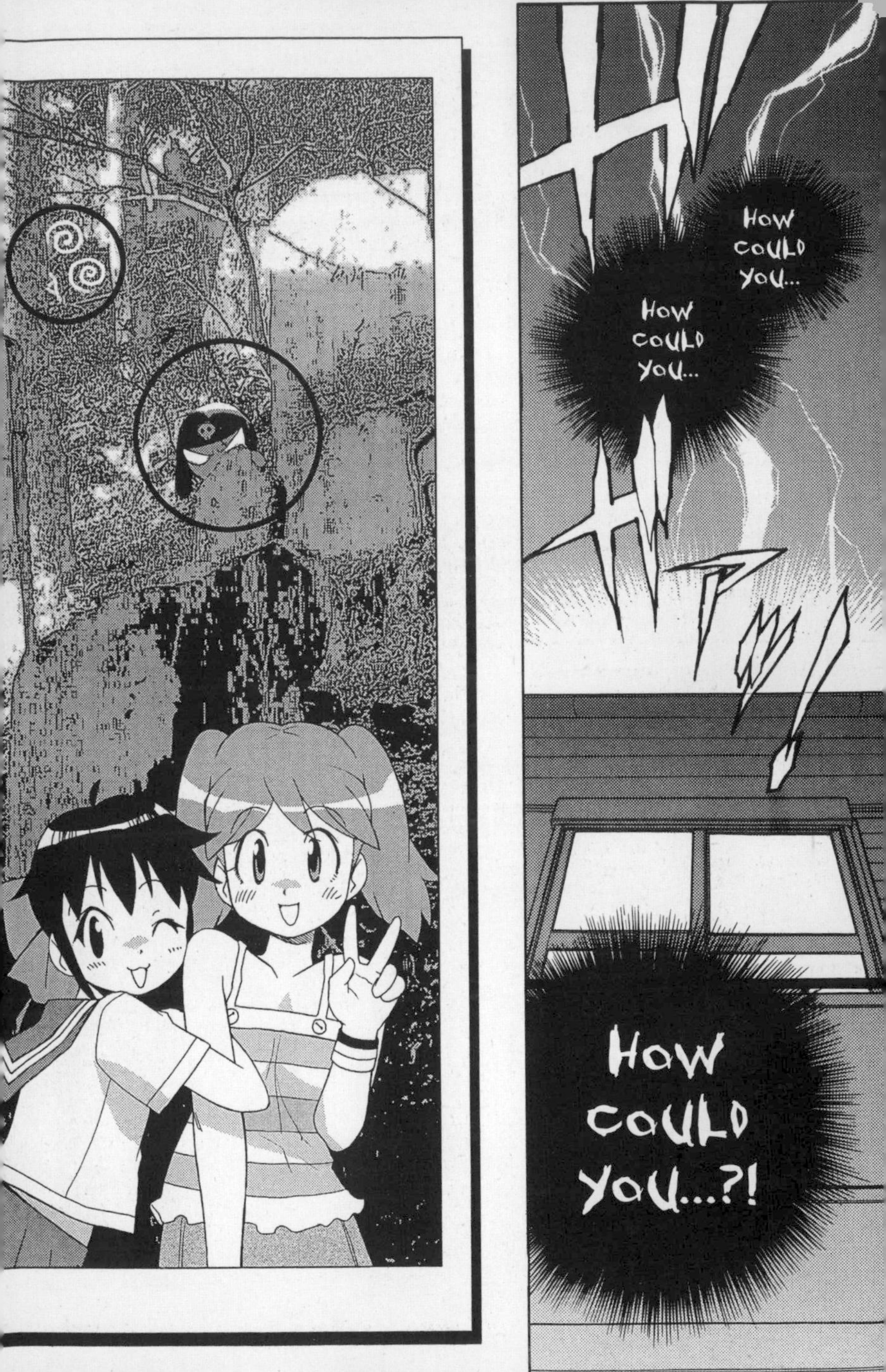
HOW COULD YOU...
HOW COULD YOU...
HOW COULD YOU...?!

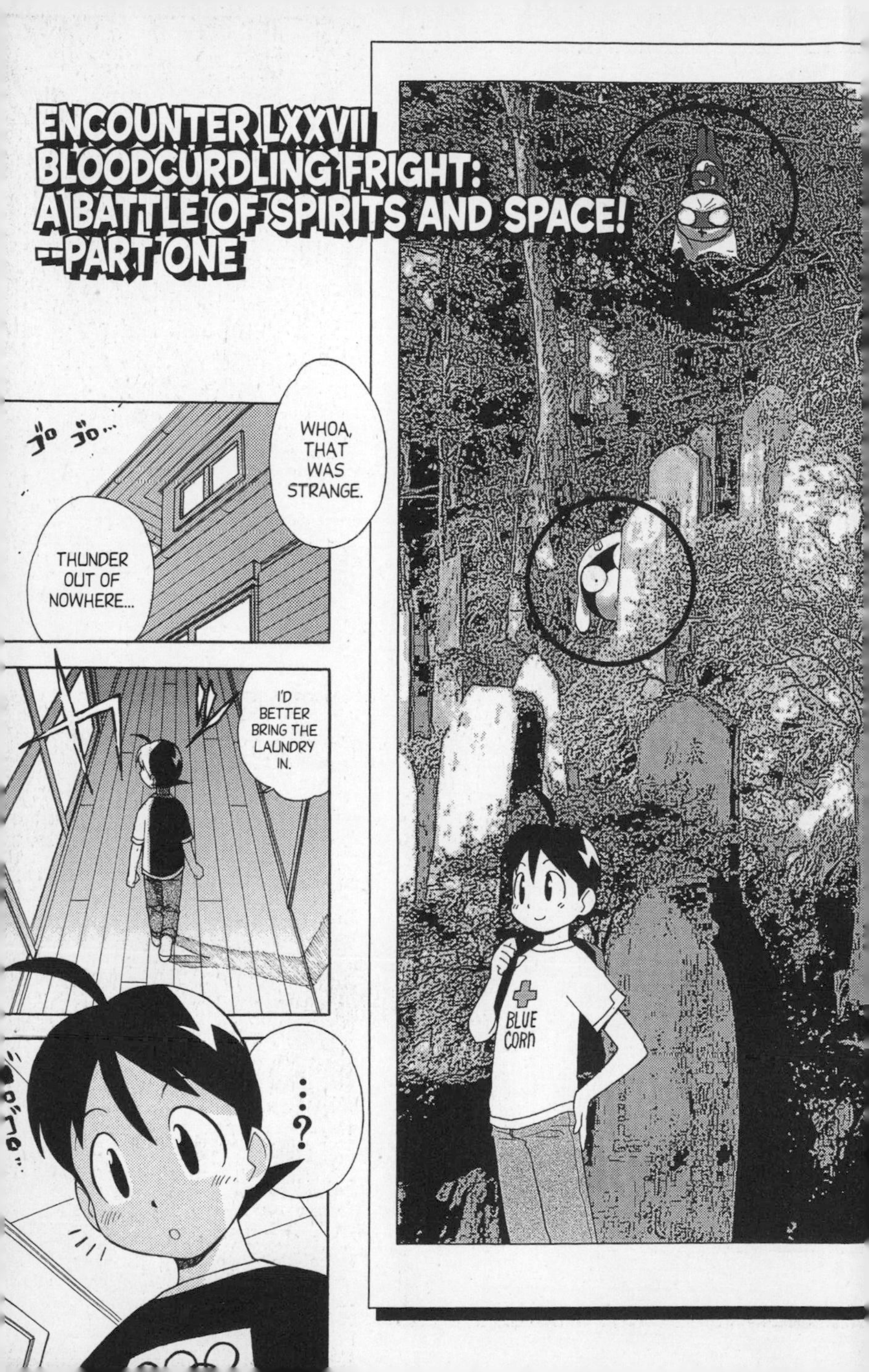
ENCOUNTER LXXVII
BLOODCURDLING FRIGHT:
A BATTLE OF SPIRITS AND SPACE!
--PART ONE
ゴロ ゴロ…
WHOA, THAT WAS STRANGE.
THUNDER OUT OF NOWHERE...
I'D BETTER BRING THE LAUNDRY IN.
...?
BLUE CORN

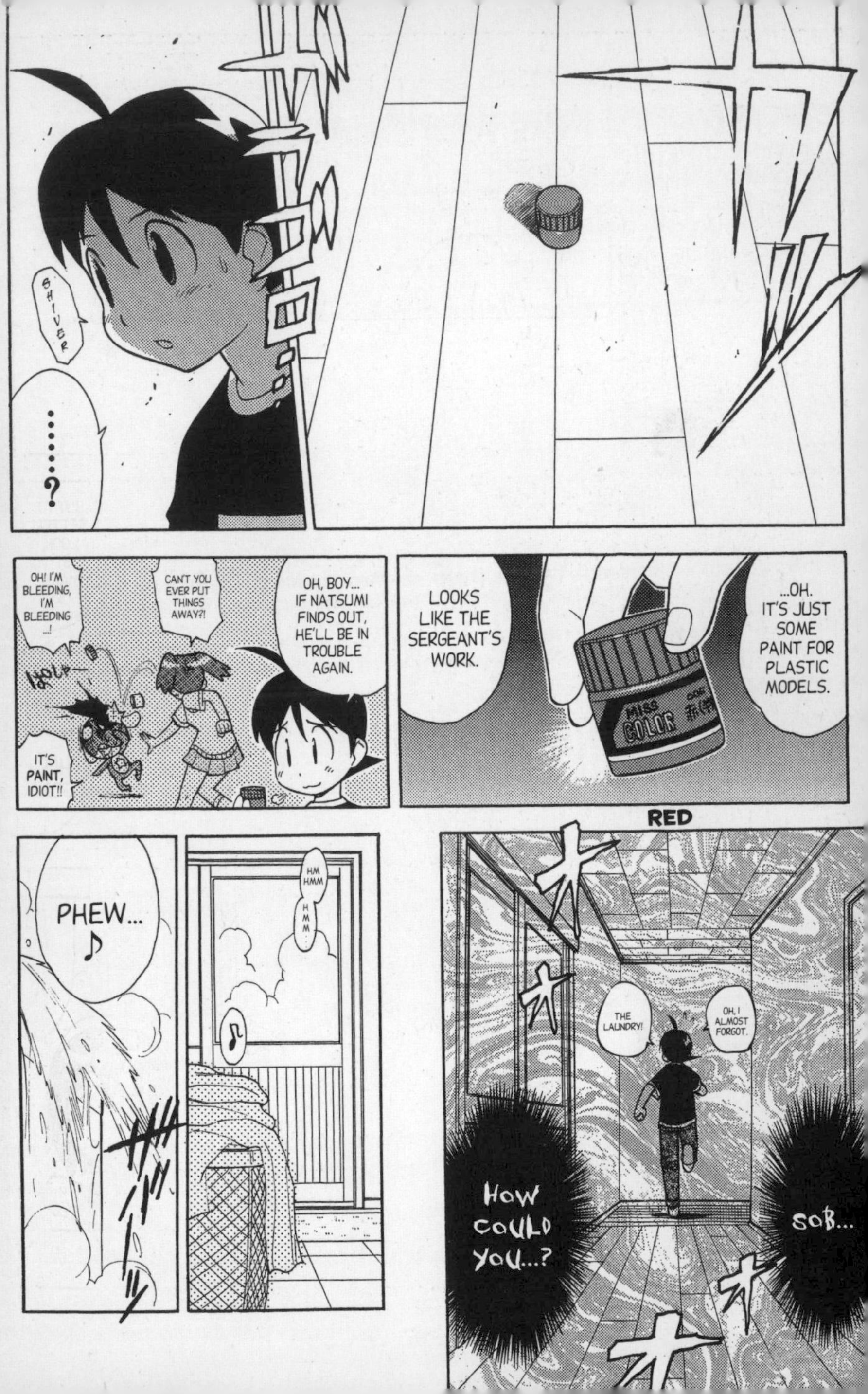
SHIVER
......?
...OH. IT'S JUST SOME PAINT FOR PLASTIC MODELS.
LOOKS LIKE THE SERGEANT'S WORK.
MISS COLOR
RED
OH, BOY... IF NATSUMI FINDS OUT, HE'LL BE IN TROUBLE AGAIN.
CAN'T YOU EVER PUT THINGS AWAY?!
OH! I'M BLEEDING, I'M BLEEDING ...!
IT'S PAINT, IDIOT!!
OH, I ALMOST FORGOT.
THE LAUNDRY!
SOB...
HOW COULD YOU...?
HM HMM HMM...
♪
PHEW... ♪

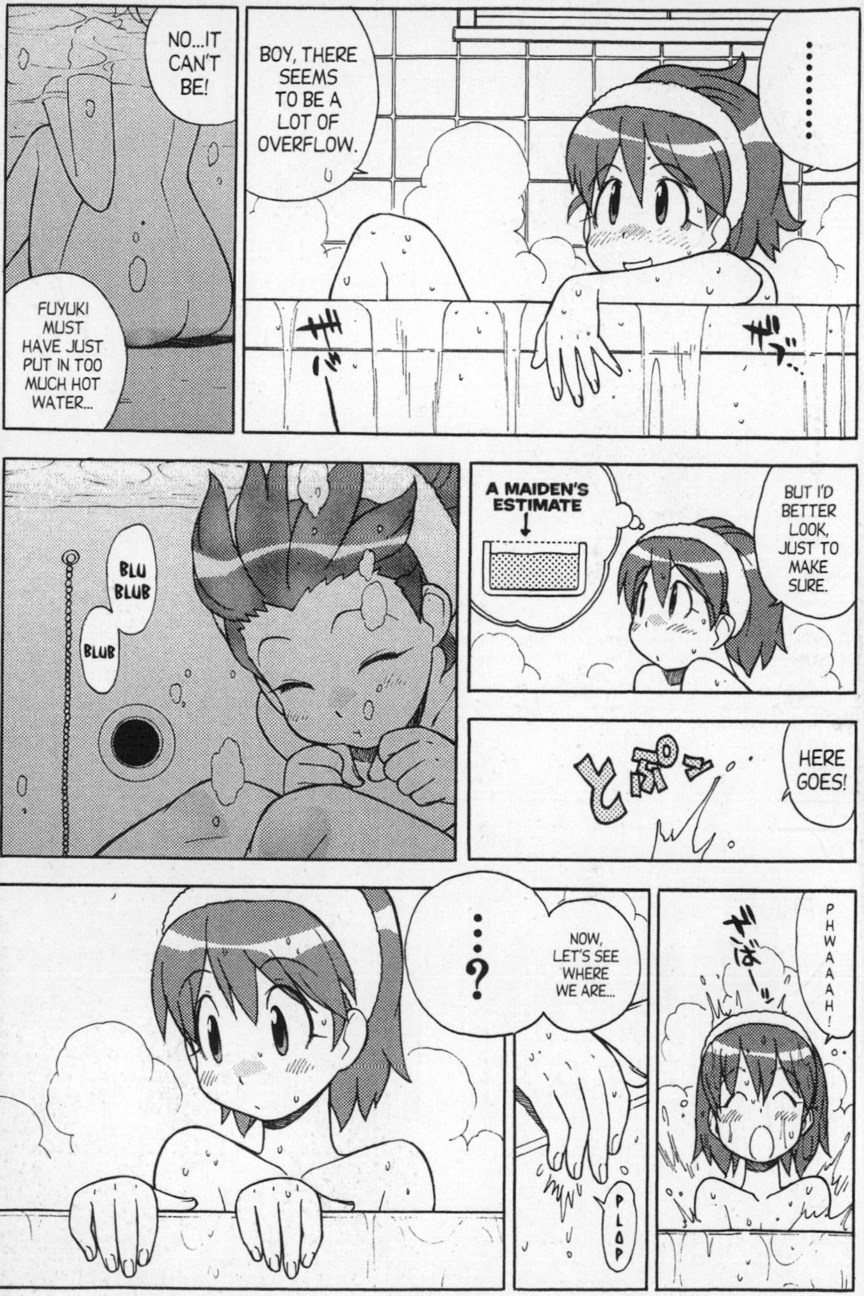
......
BOY, THERE SEEMS TO BE A LOT OF OVERFLOW.
NO...IT CAN'T BE!
FUYUKI MUST HAVE JUST PUT IN TOO MUCH HOT WATER...
BUT I'D BETTER LOOK, JUST TO MAKE SURE.
A MAIDEN'S ESTIMATE
HERE GOES!
BLU BLUB
BLUB
PHWAAAH!
NOW, LET'S SEE WHERE WE ARE...
PLOP
...?

......
PLOP PLOP
....
ぱしゃっ
PLOP
GYAAAAAH!
AAARGH!
PLOP
KYAAAAH!!
KYAAAAH!!
FUYU... FUYU... FUYU...
H-H-H-H-HAND...
GET SOME CLOTHES ON, NATSUMI!
AND CALM DOWN!!
Yaaaaaa!
HEEEEEEE!

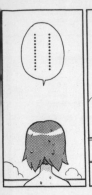

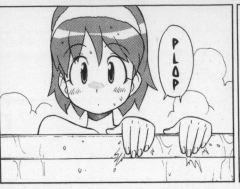

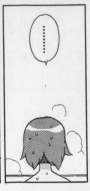

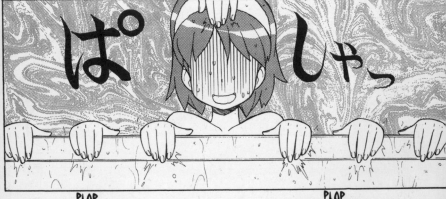

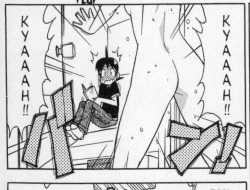

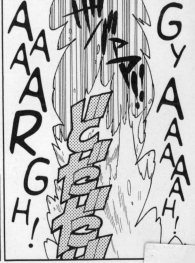

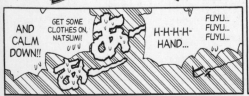

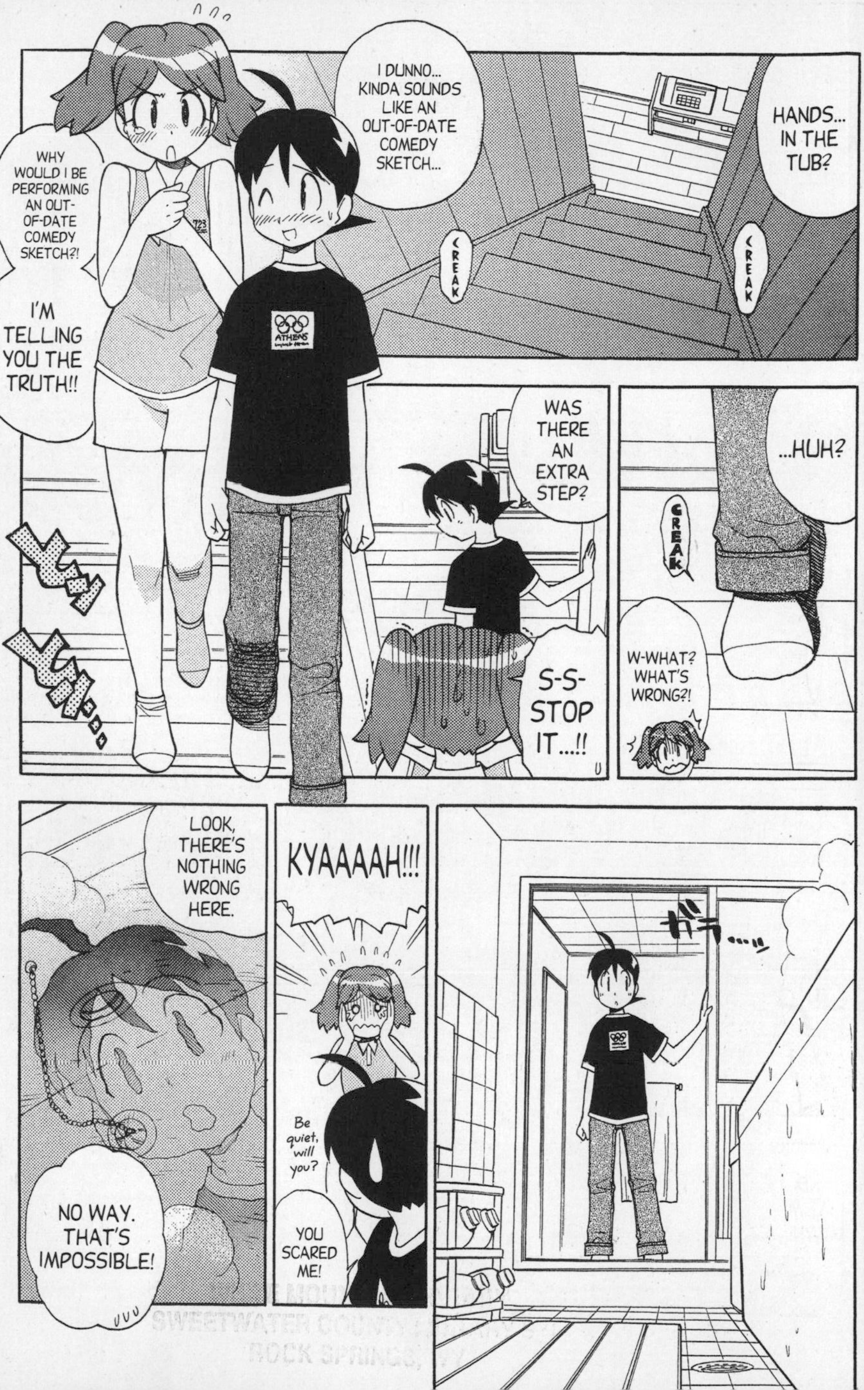
HANDS... IN THE TUB?
CREAK
CREAK
I DUNNO... KINDA SOUNDS LIKE AN OUT-OF-DATE COMEDY SKETCH...
WHY WOULD I BE PERFORMING AN OUT-OF-DATE COMEDY SKETCH?!
I'M TELLING YOU THE TRUTH!!
...HUH?
CREAK
W-WHAT? WHAT'S WRONG?!
WAS THERE AN EXTRA STEP?
S-S-STOP IT...!!
KYAAAAH!!!
Be quiet, will you?
YOU SCARED ME!
LOOK, THERE'S NOTHING WRONG HERE.
NO WAY. THAT'S IMPOSSIBLE!

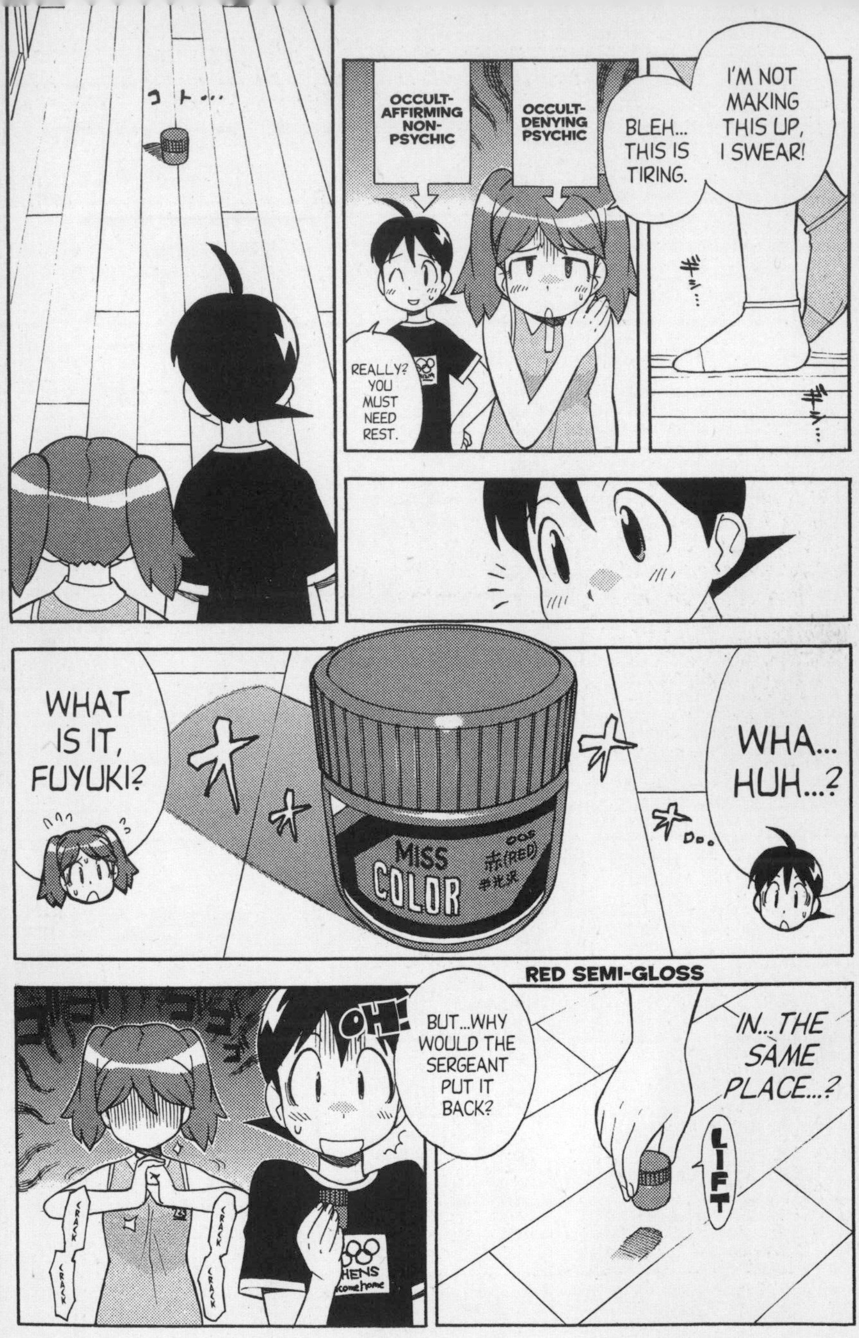
I'M NOT MAKING THIS UP, I SWEAR!
ギシ…
ギシ…
OCCULT-DENYING PSYCHIC
OCCULT-AFFIRMING NON-PSYCHIC
BLEH... THIS IS TIRING.
REALLY? YOU MUST NEED REST.
コト…
WHA... HUH...?
Doo...
MISS COLOR
赤(RED)
WHAT IS IT, FUYUKI?
RED SEMI-GLOSS
IN...THE SAME PLACE...?
LIFT
OH!
BUT...WHY WOULD THE SERGEANT PUT IT BACK?
CRACK
CRACK
CRACK
CRACK

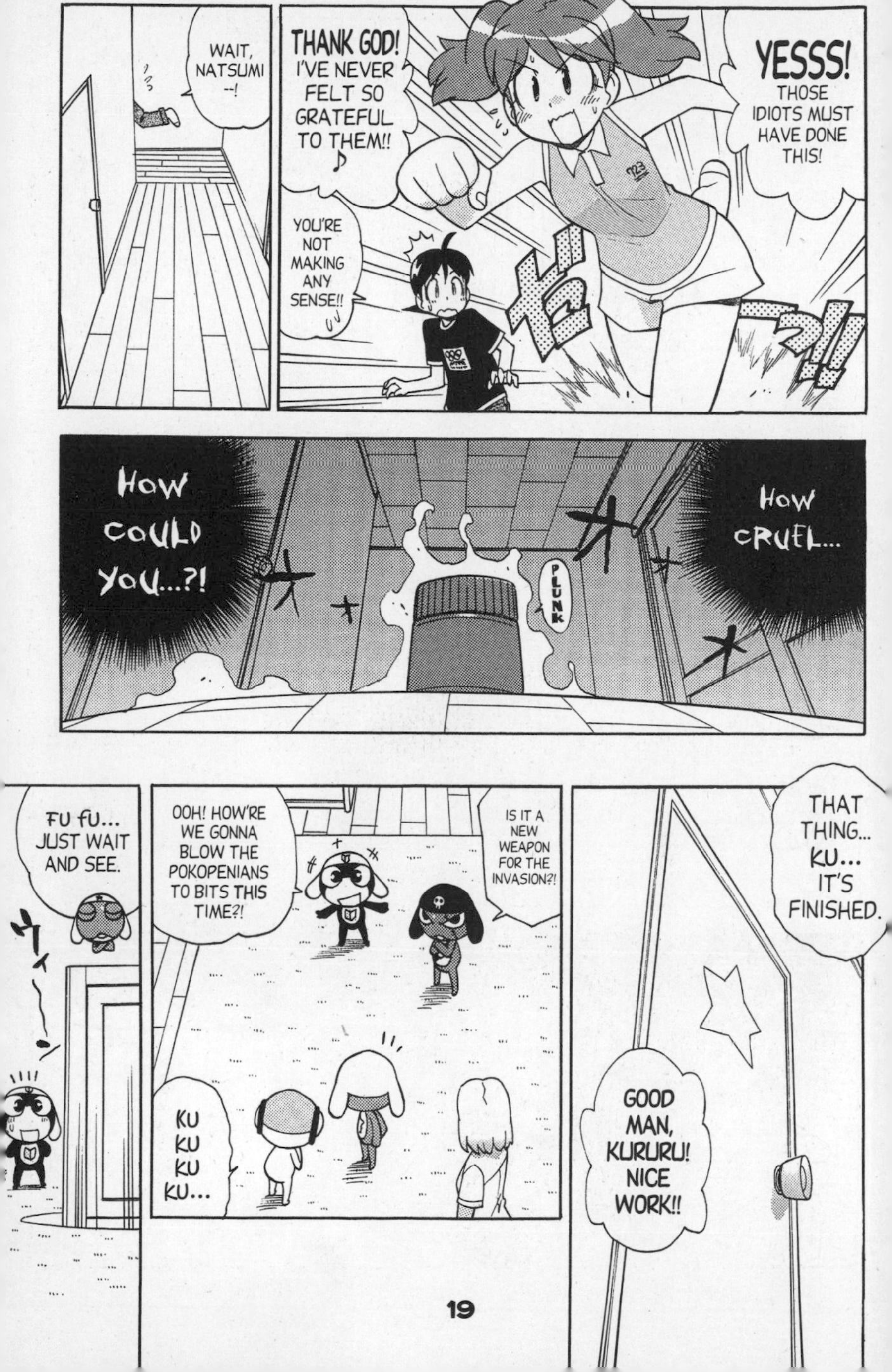
YESSS! THOSE IDIOTS MUST HAVE DONE THIS!
THANK GOD! I'VE NEVER FELT SO GRATEFUL TO THEM!! ♪
YOU'RE NOT MAKING ANY SENSE!!
WAIT, NATSUMI --!
HOW CRUEL...
PLUNK
HOW COULD YOU...?!
THAT THING... KU... IT'S FINISHED.
GOOD MAN, KURURU! NICE WORK!!
IS IT A NEW WEAPON FOR THE INVASION?!
OOH! HOW'RE WE GONNA BLOW THE POKOPENIANS TO BITS THIS TIME?!
KU KU KU KU...
FU FU... JUST WAIT AND SEE.

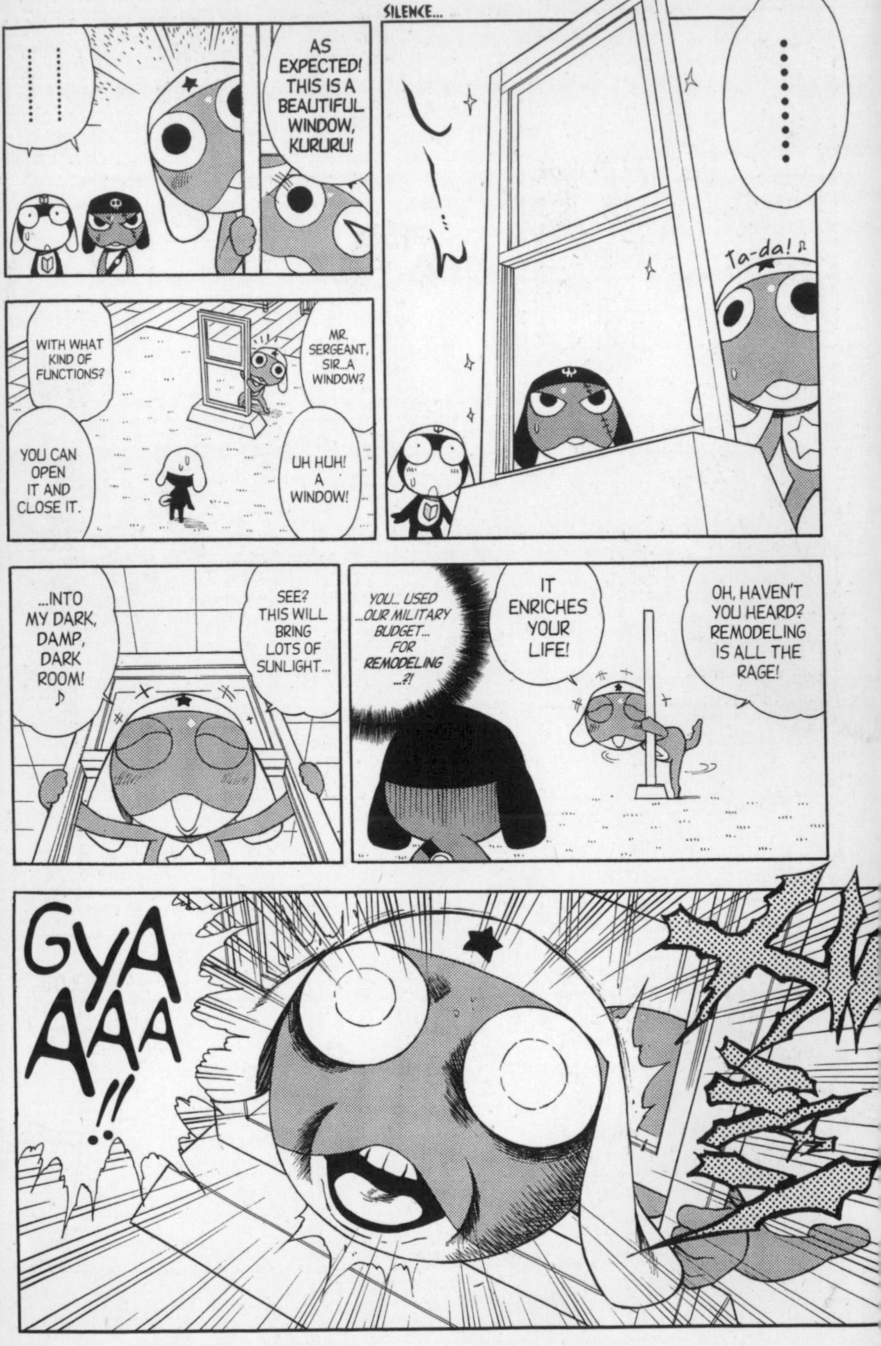
SILENCE...
......
Ta-da! ♪
AS EXPECTED! THIS IS A BEAUTIFUL WINDOW, KURURU!
......
MR. SERGEANT, SIR...A WINDOW?
UH HUH! A WINDOW!
WITH WHAT KIND OF FUNCTIONS?
YOU CAN OPEN IT AND CLOSE IT.
OH, HAVEN'T YOU HEARD? REMODELING IS ALL THE RAGE!
IT ENRICHES YOUR LIFE!
YOU... USED ...OUR MILITARY BUDGET... FOR REMODELING ...?!
SEE? THIS WILL BRING LOTS OF SUNLIGHT...
...INTO MY DARK, DAMP, DARK ROOM! ♪
GYAAAA!!

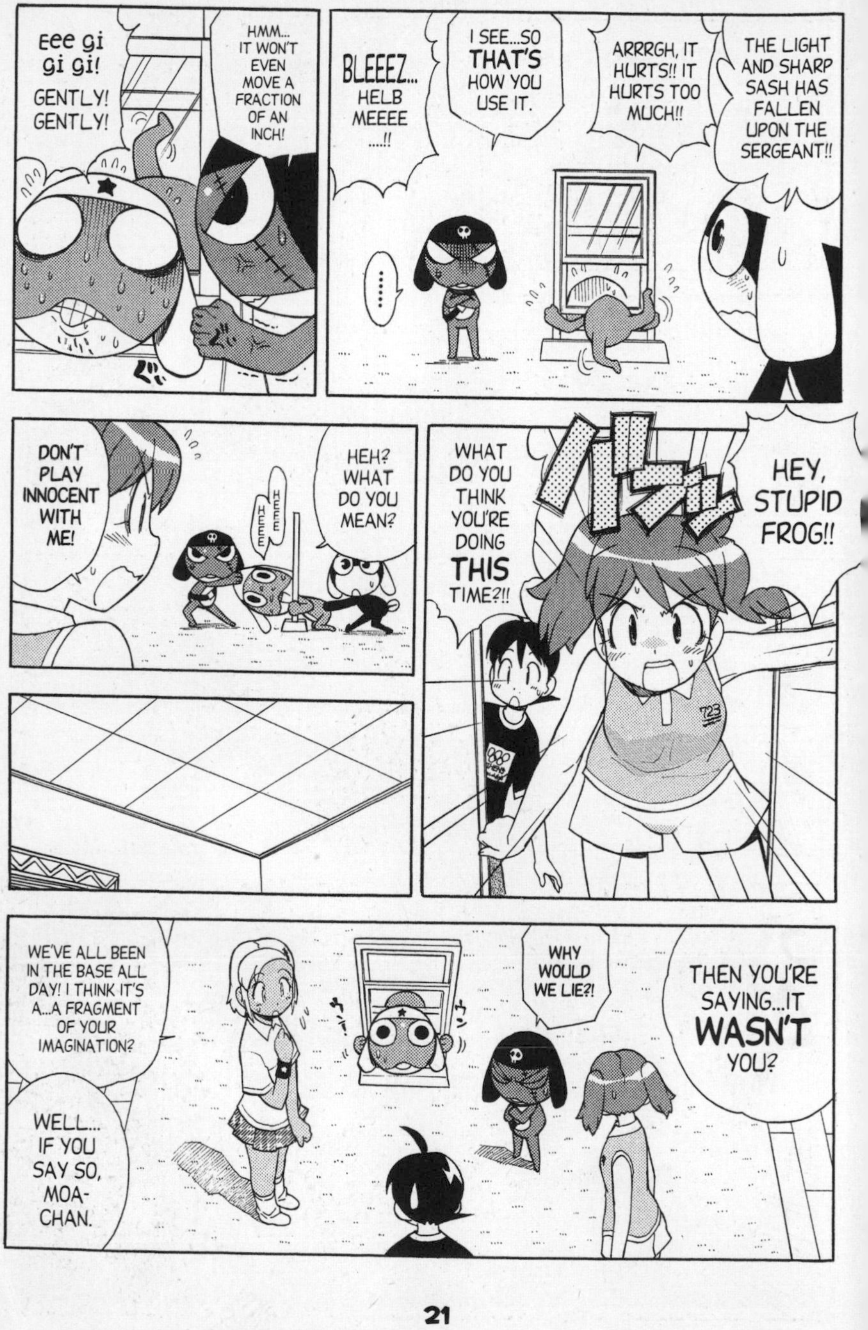
THE LIGHT AND SHARP SASH HAS FALLEN UPON THE SERGEANT!!
ARRRGH, IT HURTS!! IT HURTS TOO MUCH!!
I SEE...SO THAT'S HOW YOU USE IT.
BLEEEZ... HELB MEEEE ....!!
......
HMM... IT WON'T EVEN MOVE A FRACTION OF AN INCH!
Eee gi gi gi! GENTLY! GENTLY!
HEY, STUPID FROG!!
WHAT DO YOU THINK YOU'RE DOING THIS TIME?!!
HEH? WHAT DO YOU MEAN?
HEEE HEEE
DON'T PLAY INNOCENT WITH ME!
THEN YOU'RE SAYING...IT WASN'T YOU?
WHY WOULD WE LIE?!
WE'VE ALL BEEN IN THE BASE ALL DAY! I THINK IT'S A...A FRAGMENT OF YOUR IMAGINATION?
WELL... IF YOU SAY SO, MOA-CHAN.

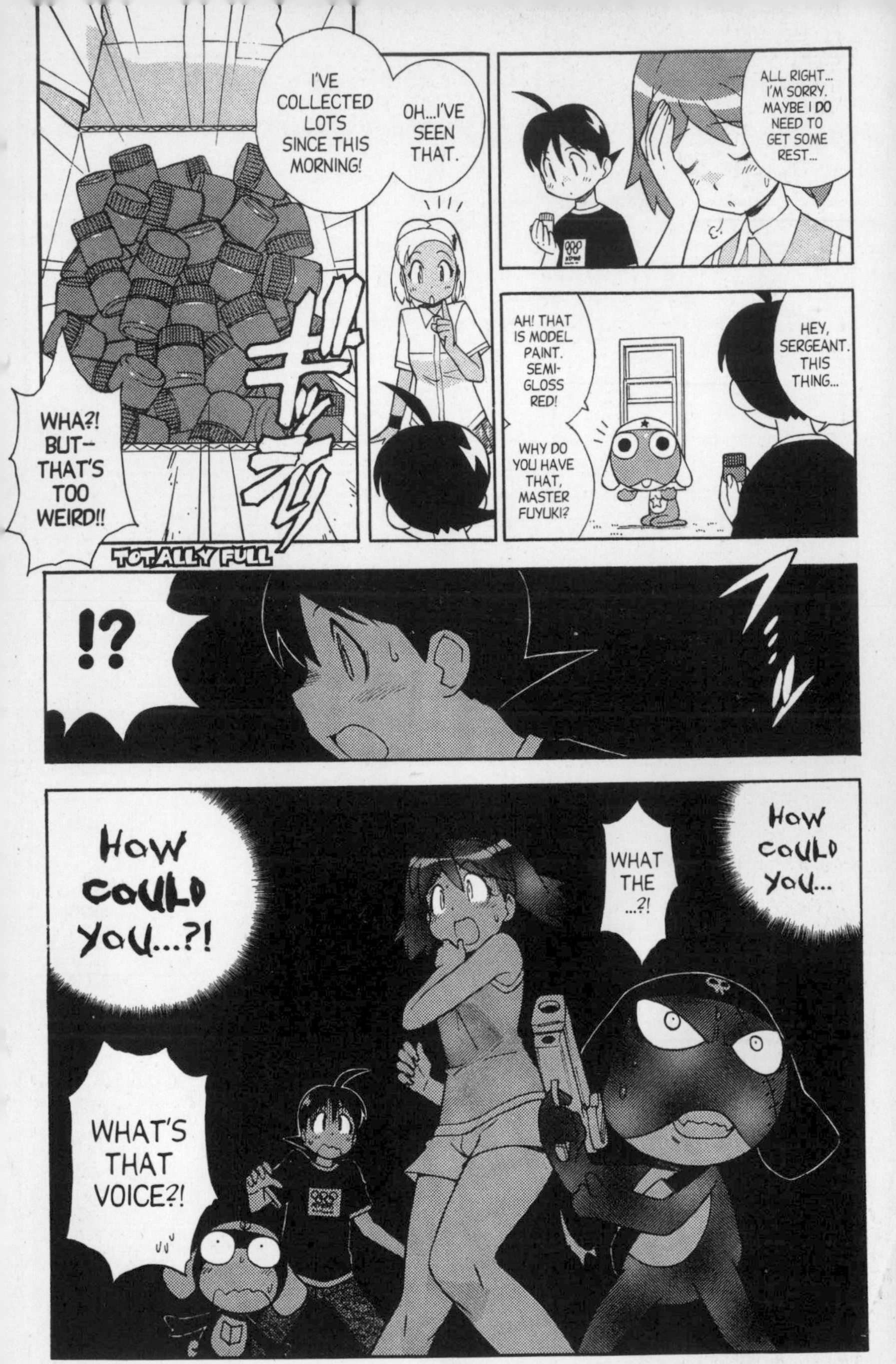
ALL RIGHT... I'M SORRY. MAYBE I DO NEED TO GET SOME REST...
HEY, SERGEANT. THIS THING...
AH! THAT IS MODEL PAINT. SEMI-GLOSS RED!
WHY DO YOU HAVE THAT, MASTER FUYUKI?
I'VE COLLECTED LOTS SINCE THIS MORNING!
OH...I'VE SEEN THAT.
WHA?! BUT-- THAT'S TOO WEIRD!!
TOTALLY FULL
!?
How could you...
WHAT THE ...?!
How could you...?!
WHAT'S THAT VOICE?!

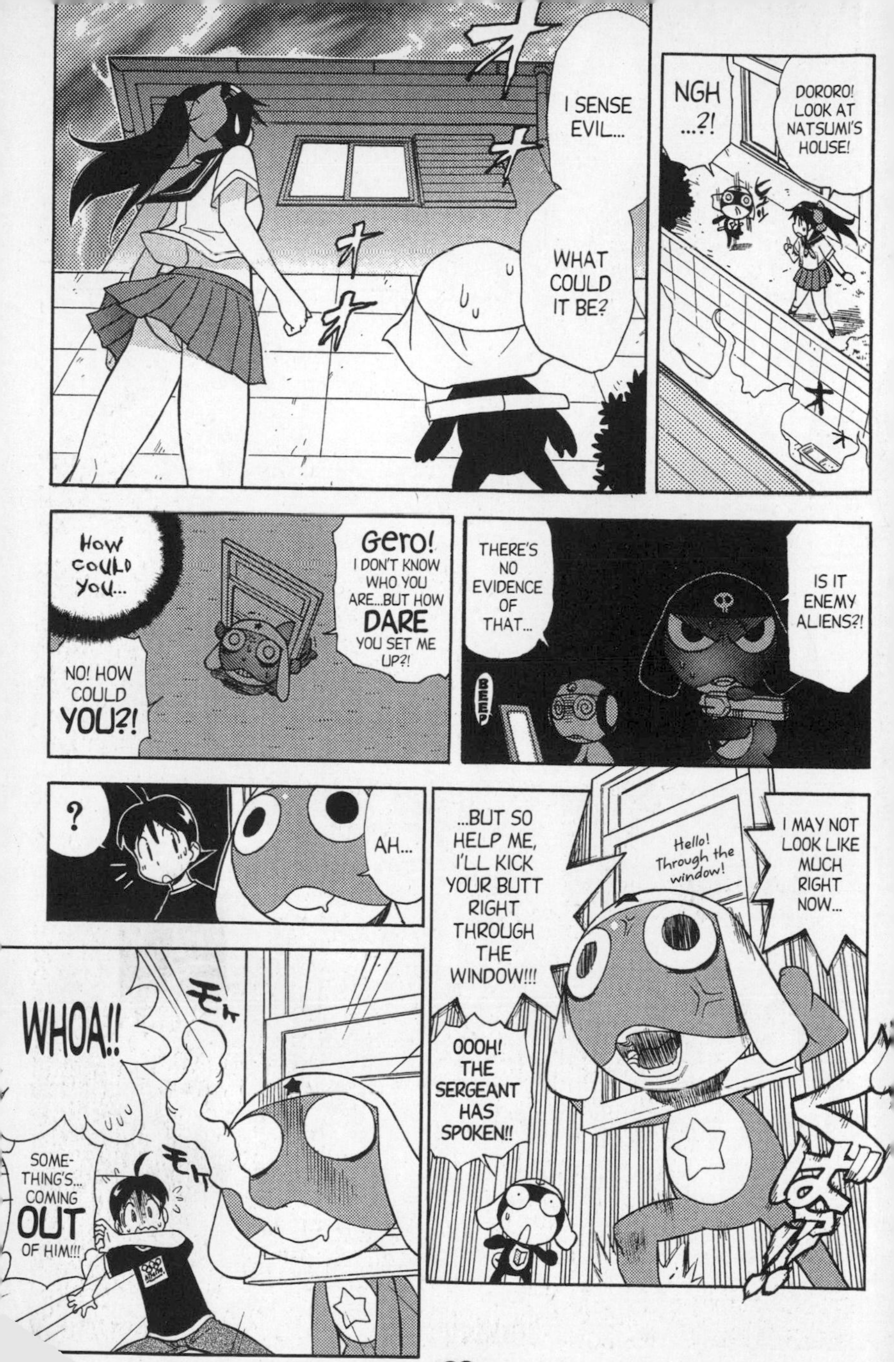
DORORO! LOOK AT NATSUMI'S HOUSE!
NGH ...?!
I SENSE EVIL...
WHAT COULD IT BE?
IS IT ENEMY ALIENS?!
THERE'S NO EVIDENCE OF THAT...
BEEP
Gero! I DON'T KNOW WHO YOU ARE...BUT HOW DARE YOU SET ME UP?!
How could you...
NO! HOW COULD YOU?!
I MAY NOT LOOK LIKE MUCH RIGHT NOW...
Hello! Through the window!
...BUT SO HELP ME, I'LL KICK YOUR BUTT RIGHT THROUGH THE WINDOW!!!
OOOH! THE SERGEANT HAS SPOKEN!!
AH...
?
WHOA!!
SOME-THING'S... COMING OUT OF HIM!!!

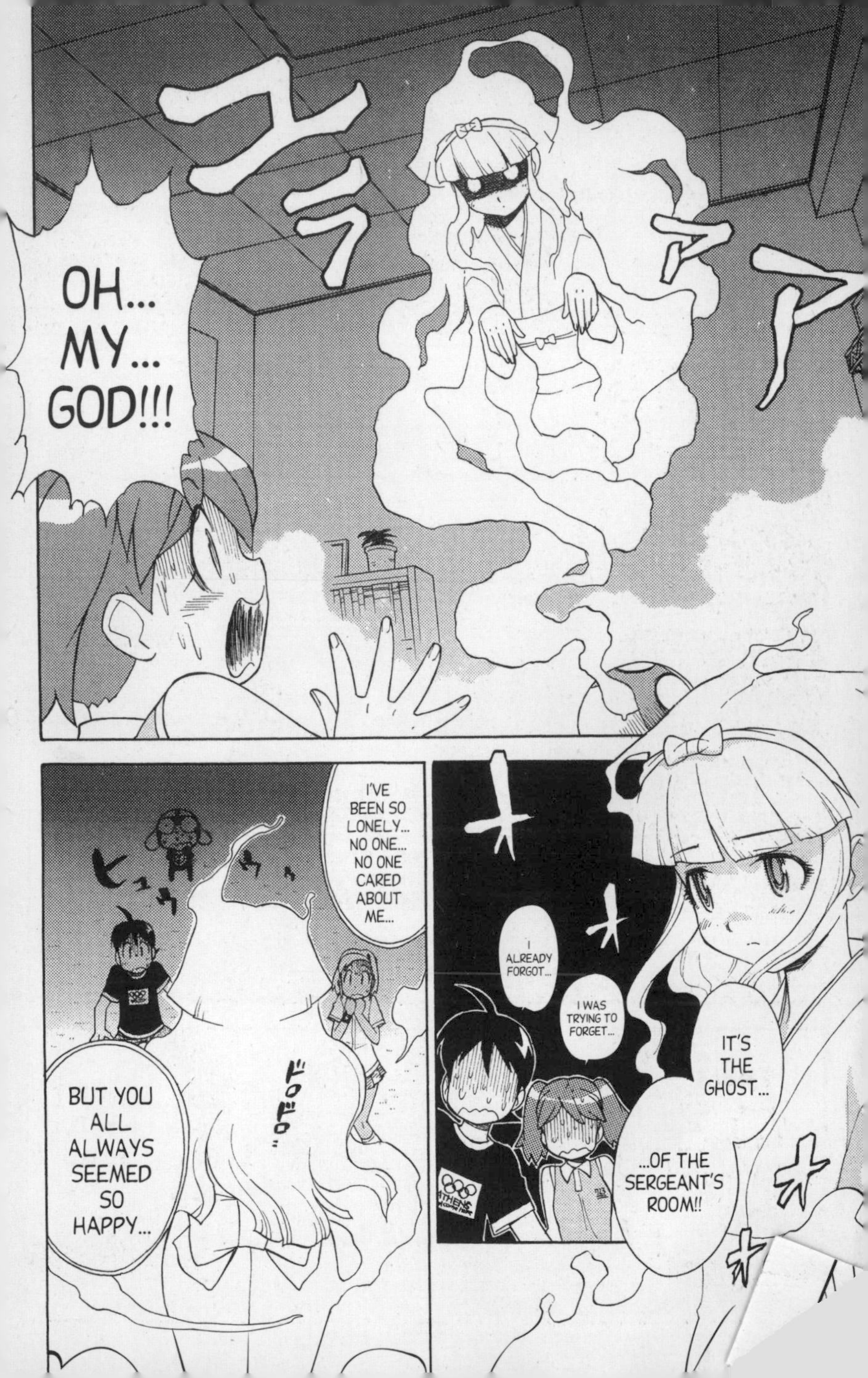
OH... MY... GOD!!!
IT'S THE GHOST...
...OF THE SERGEANT'S ROOM!!
I ALREADY FORGOT...
I WAS TRYING TO FORGET...
I'VE BEEN SO LONELY... NO ONE... NO ONE CARED ABOUT ME...
BUT YOU ALL ALWAYS SEEMED SO HAPPY...
ドロドロ

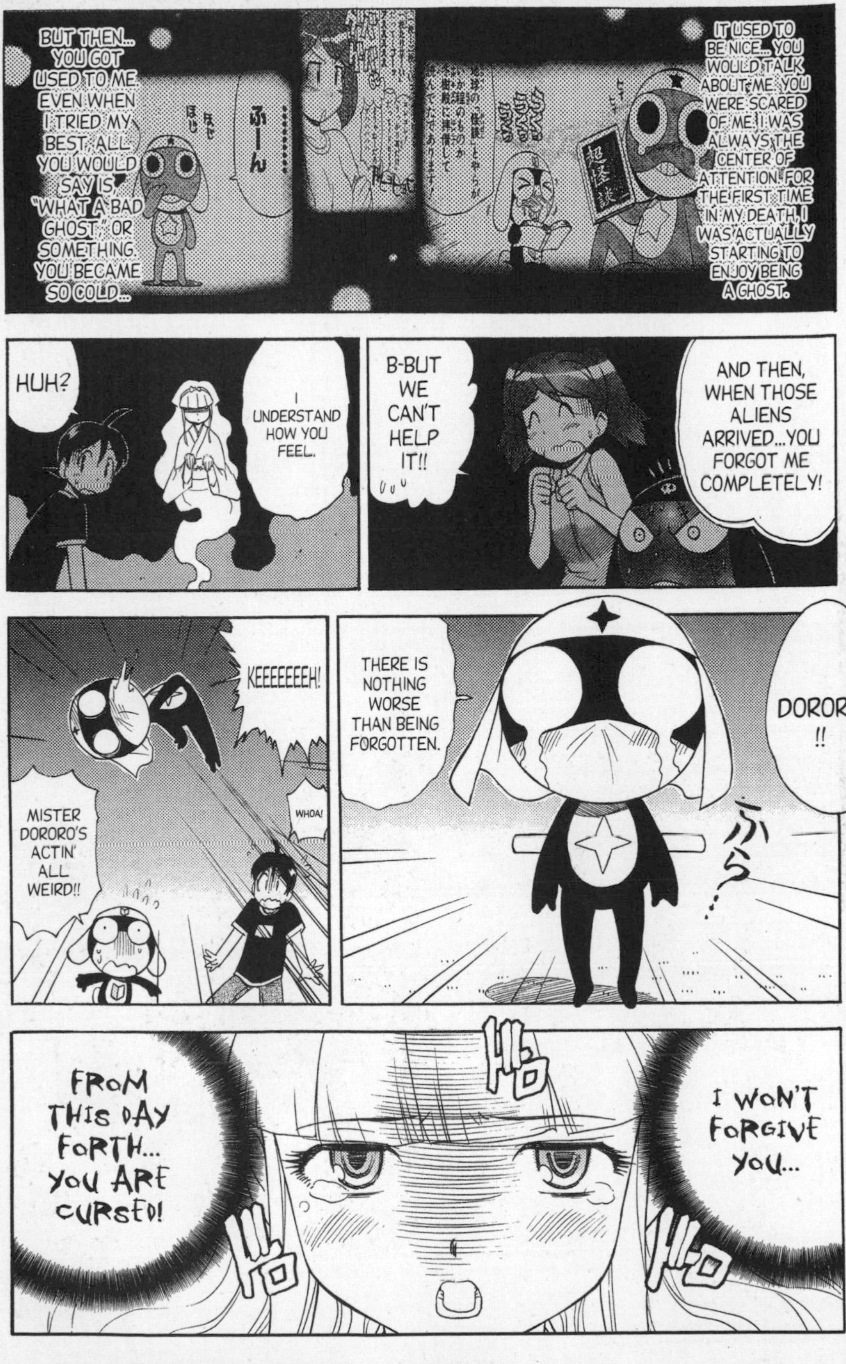
IT USED TO BE NICE... YOU WOULD TALK ABOUT ME. YOU WERE SCARED OF ME. I WAS ALWAYS THE CENTER OF ATTENTION. FOR THE FIRST TIME IN MY DEATH, I WAS ACTUALLY STARTING TO ENJOY BEING A GHOST.
超怪談
ふーん
ほじ ほじ
BUT THEN... YOU GOT USED TO ME. EVEN WHEN I TRIED MY BEST, ALL YOU WOULD SAY IS, "WHAT A BAD GHOST," OR SOMETHING. YOU BECAME SO COLD...
AND THEN, WHEN THOSE ALIENS ARRIVED...YOU FORGOT ME COMPLETELY!
B-BUT WE CAN'T HELP IT!!
I UNDERSTAND HOW YOU FEEL.
HUH?
DORORO !!
THERE IS NOTHING WORSE THAN BEING FORGOTTEN.
ふら…
KEEEEEEEH!
WHOA!
MISTER DORORO'S ACTIN' ALL WEIRD!!
I WON'T FORGIVE YOU...
FROM THIS DAY FORTH... YOU ARE CURSED!

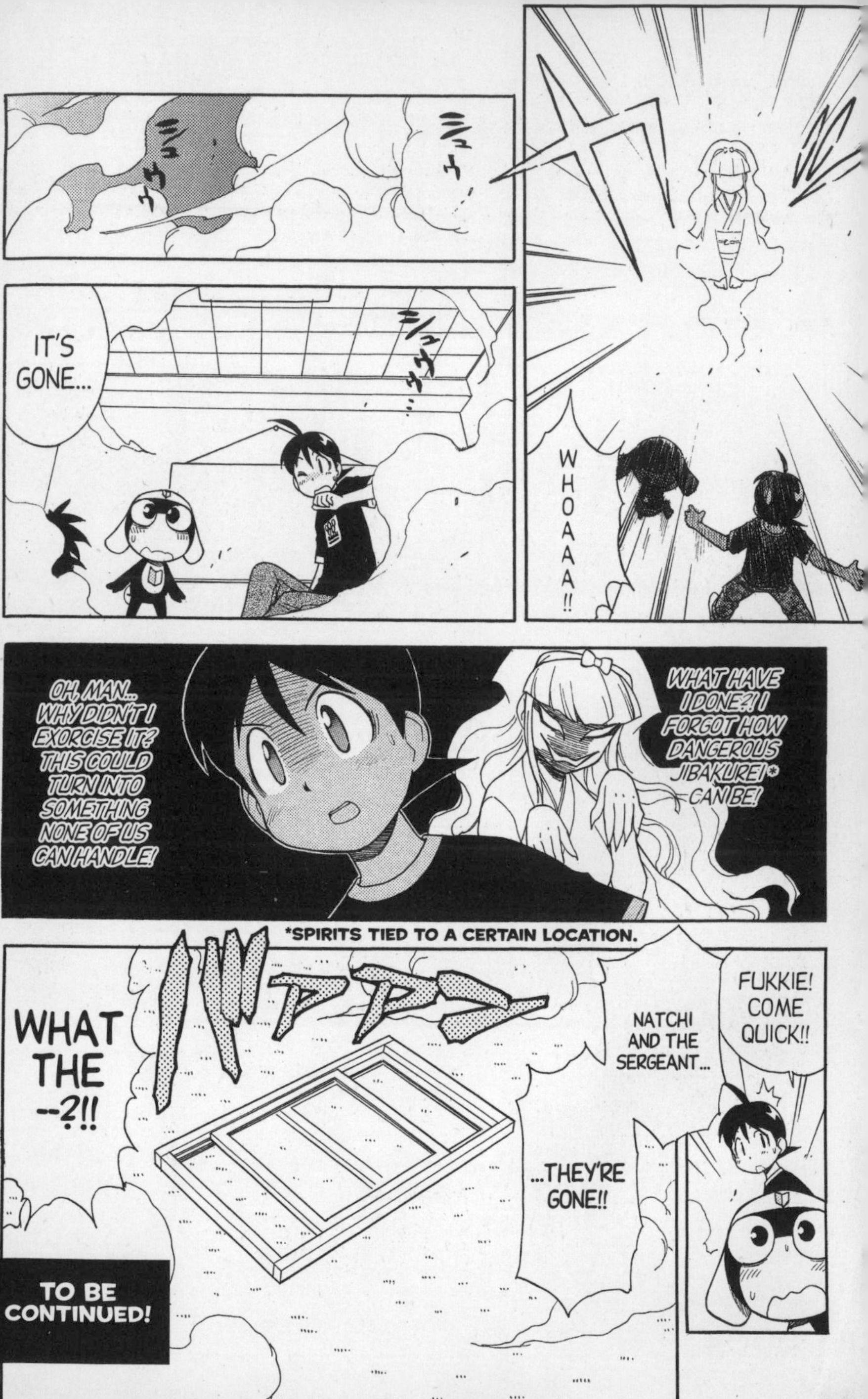
WHOAAAA!!
IT'S GONE...
WHAT HAVE I DONE?! I FORGOT HOW DANGEROUS JIBAKUREI* CAN BE!
OH, MAN... WHY DIDN'T I EXORCISE IT? THIS COULD TURN INTO SOMETHING NONE OF US CAN HANDLE!
*SPIRITS TIED TO A CERTAIN LOCATION.
FUKKIE! COME QUICK!!
NATCHI AND THE SERGEANT...
...THEY'RE GONE!!
WHAT THE --?!!
TO BE CONTINUED!

ENCOUNTER LXXVIII
BLOODCURDLING FRIGHT: A BATTLE OF SPIRITS AND SPACE!--PART TWO

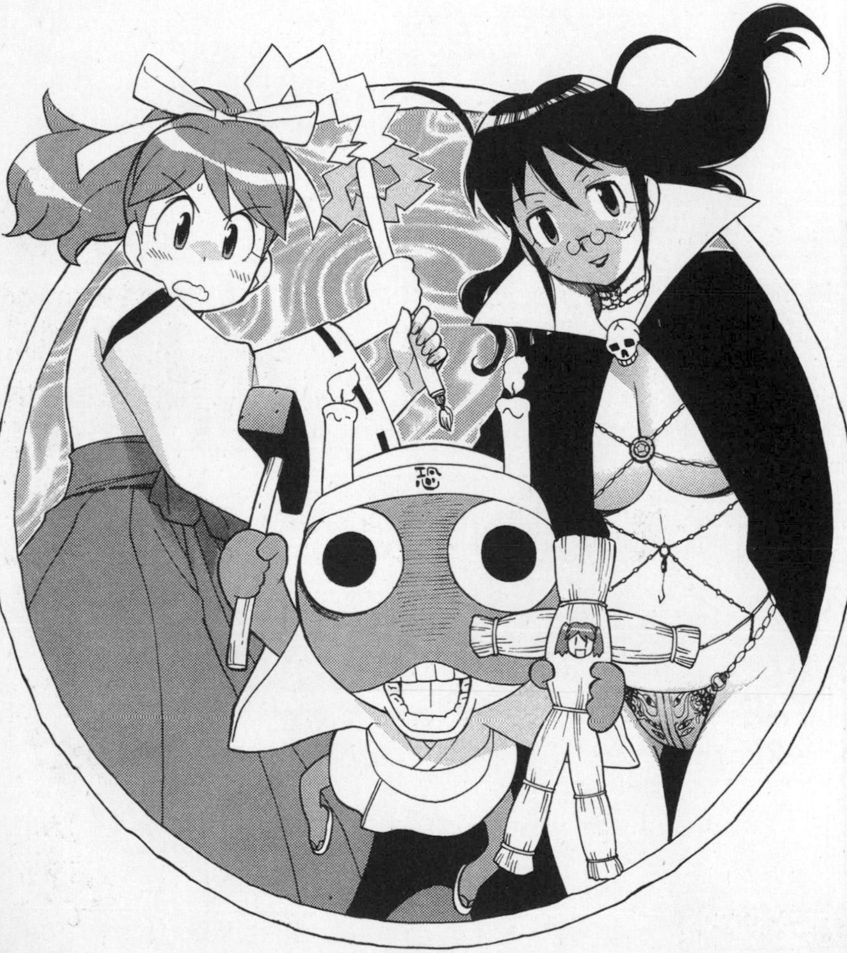

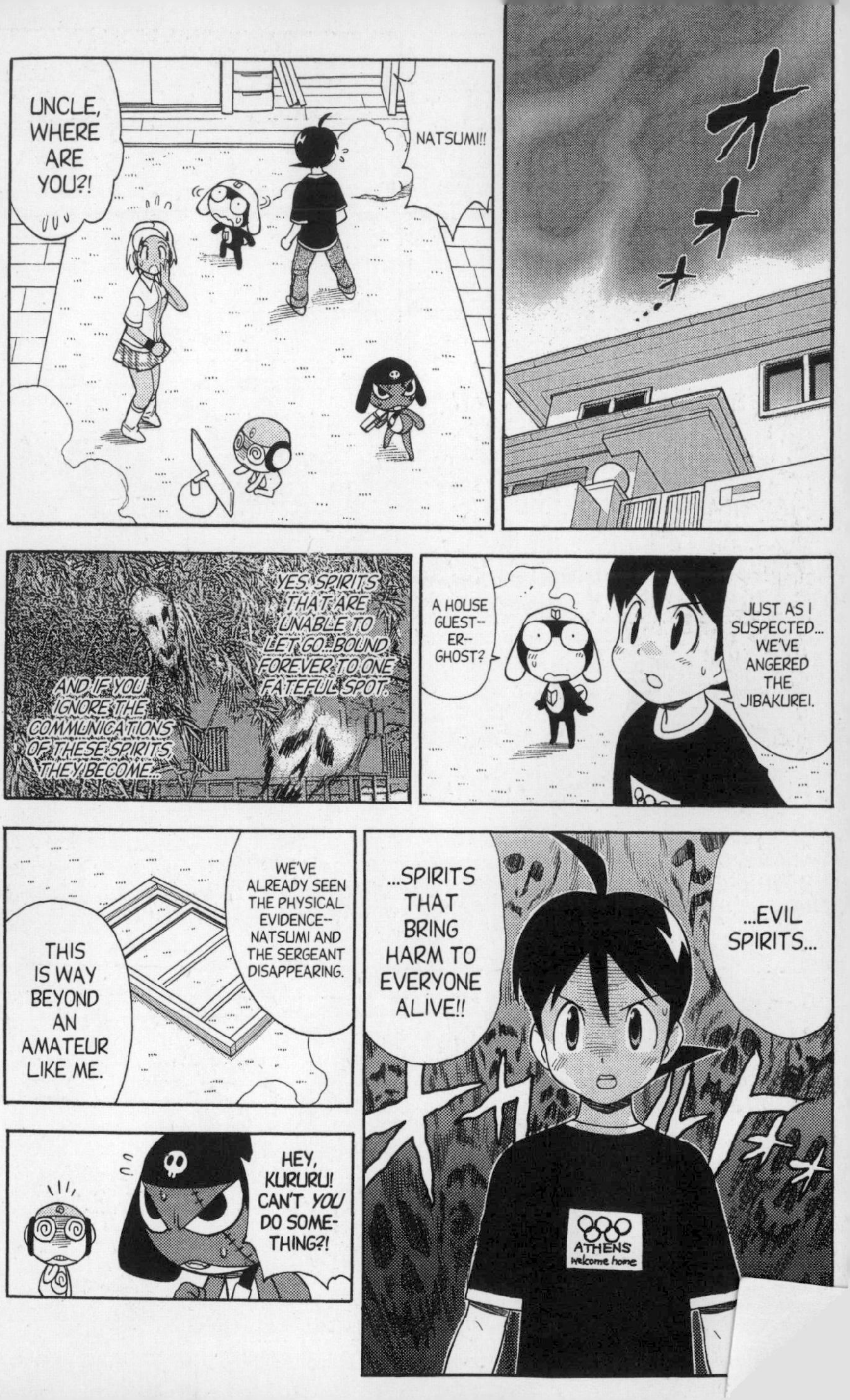
NATSUMI!!
UNCLE, WHERE ARE YOU?!
JUST AS I SUSPECTED... WE'VE ANGERED THE JIBAKUREI.
A HOUSE GUEST-- ER-- GHOST?
YES. SPIRITS THAT ARE UNABLE TO LET GO...BOUND FOREVER TO ONE FATEFUL SPOT.
AND IF YOU IGNORE THE COMMUNICATIONS OF THESE SPIRITS, THEY BECOME...
...EVIL SPIRITS...
...SPIRITS THAT BRING HARM TO EVERYONE ALIVE!!
ATHENS
welcome home
WE'VE ALREADY SEEN THE PHYSICAL EVIDENCE-- NATSUMI AND THE SERGEANT DISAPPEARING.
THIS IS WAY BEYOND AN AMATEUR LIKE ME.
HEY, KURURU! CAN'T *YOU* DO SOME-THING?!

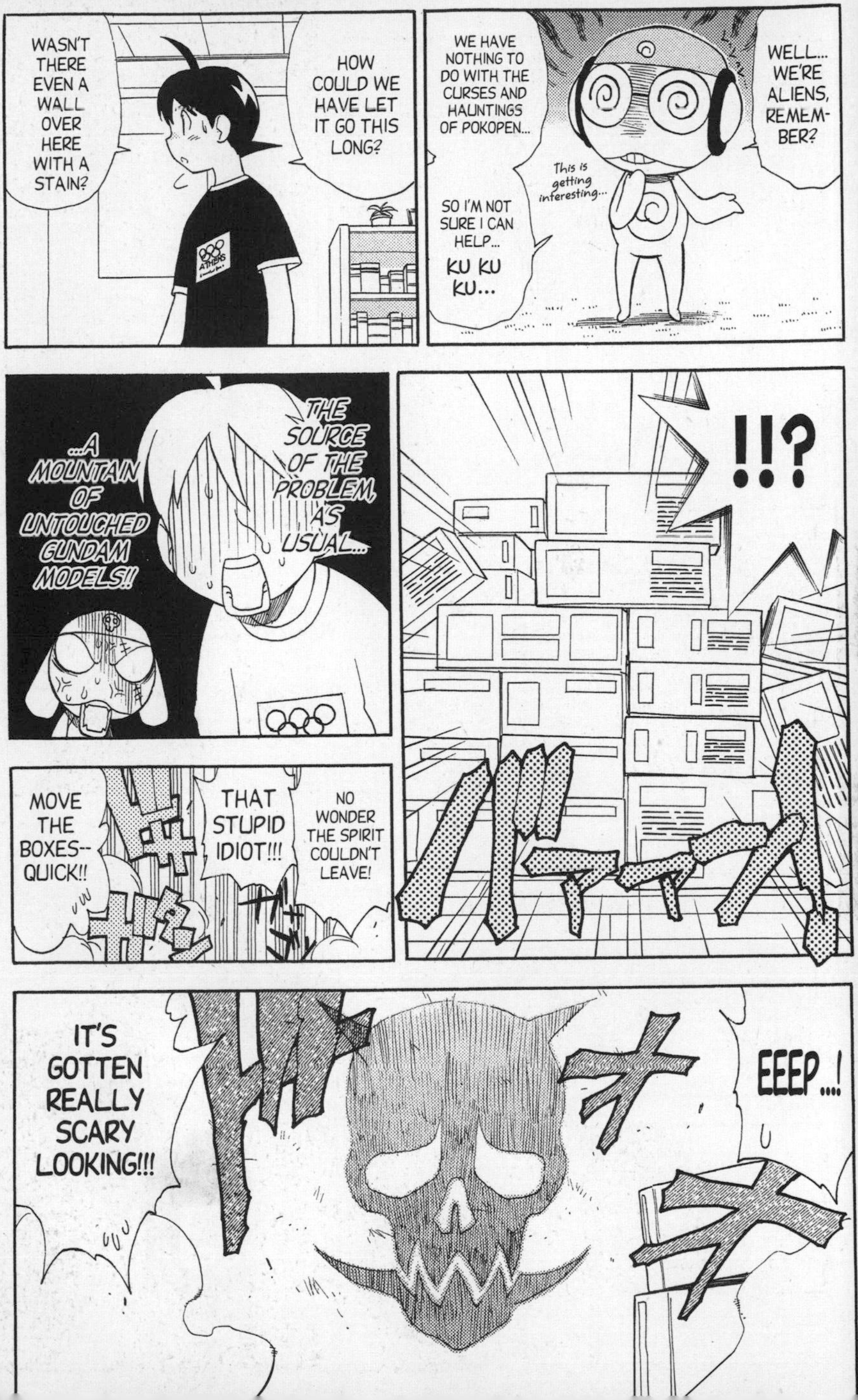
WELL... WE'RE ALIENS, REMEMBER?
WE HAVE NOTHING TO DO WITH THE CURSES AND HAUNTINGS OF POKOPEN...
This is getting interesting...
SO I'M NOT SURE I CAN HELP...
KU KU KU...
HOW COULD WE HAVE LET IT GO THIS LONG?
WASN'T THERE EVEN A WALL OVER HERE WITH A STAIN?
!!?
THE SOURCE OF THE PROBLEM, AS USUAL...
...A MOUNTAIN OF UNTOUCHED GUNDAM MODELS!!
NO WONDER THE SPIRIT COULDN'T LEAVE!
THAT STUPID IDIOT!!!
MOVE THE BOXES--QUICK!!
EEEP...!
IT'S GOTTEN REALLY SCARY LOOKING!!!

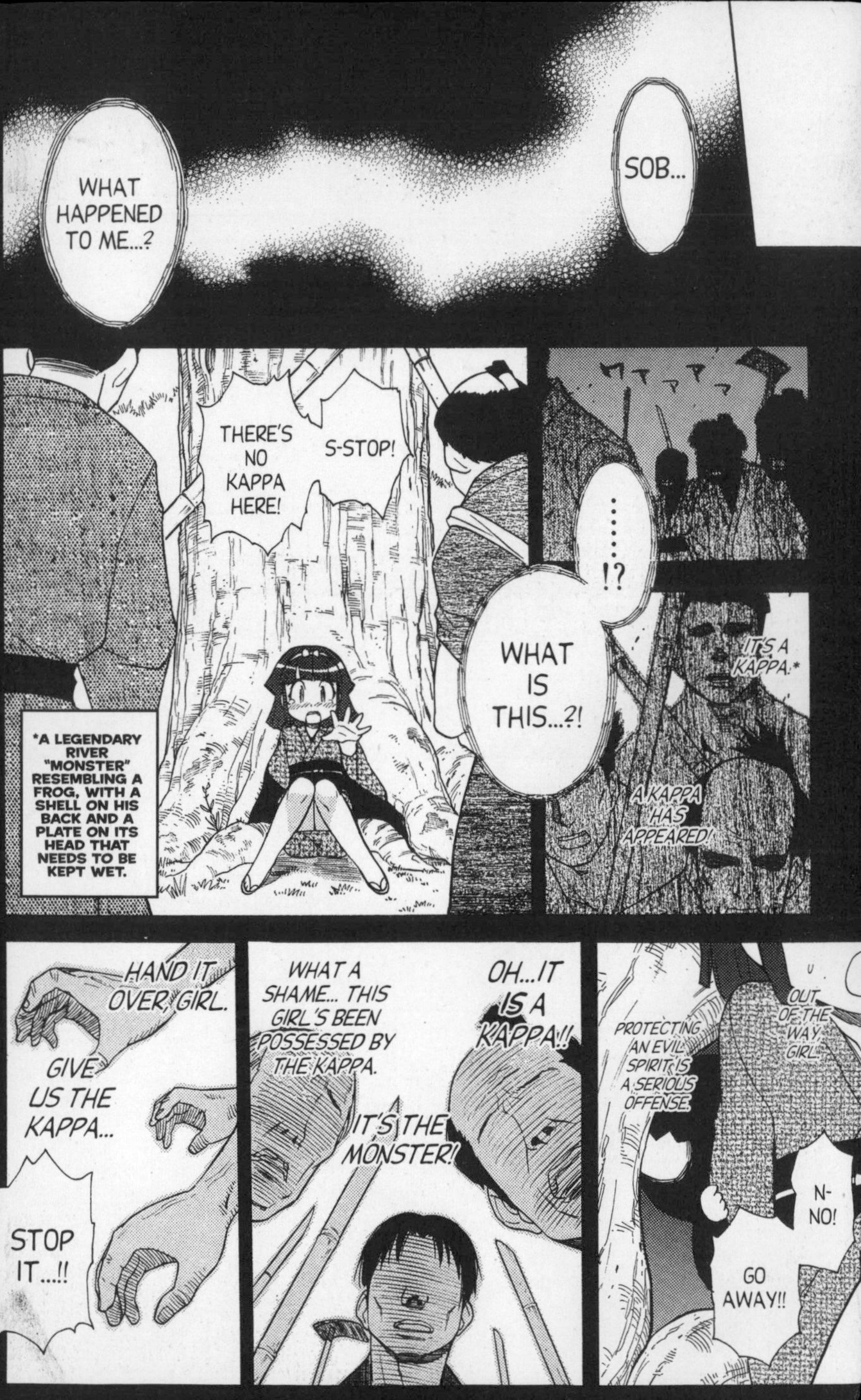
SOB...
WHAT HAPPENED TO ME...?
......
!?
IT'S A KAPPA.*
A KAPPA HAS APPEARED!
WHAT IS THIS...?!
S-STOP!
THERE'S NO KAPPA HERE!
*A LEGENDARY RIVER "MONSTER" RESEMBLING A FROG, WITH A SHELL ON HIS BACK AND A PLATE ON ITS HEAD THAT NEEDS TO BE KEPT WET.
OUT OF THE WAY, GIRL.
PROTECTING AN EVIL SPIRIT IS A SERIOUS OFFENSE.
N-NO!
GO AWAY!!
OH...IT IS A KAPPA!!
WHAT A SHAME... THIS GIRL'S BEEN POSSESSED BY THE KAPPA.
IT'S THE MONSTER!
HAND IT OVER, GIRL.
GIVE US THE KAPPA...
STOP IT...!!

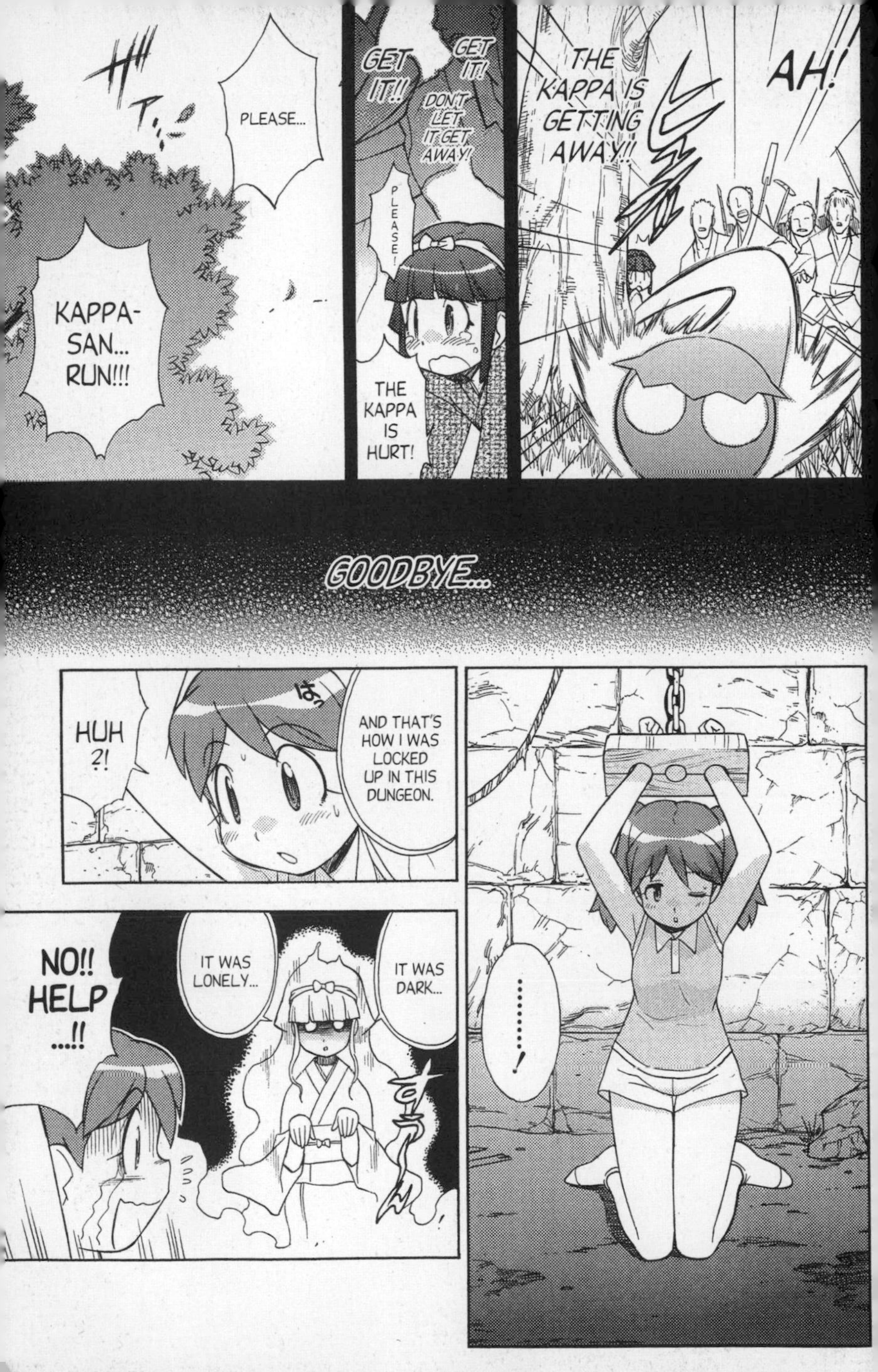
AH!
THE KAPPA IS GETTING AWAY!!
GET IT!
GET IT!!
DON'T LET IT GET AWAY!
PLEASE!
THE KAPPA IS HURT!
PLEASE...
KAPPA-SAN... RUN!!!
GOODBYE...
......!
AND THAT'S HOW I WAS LOCKED UP IN THIS DUNGEON.
HUH ?!
IT WAS DARK...
IT WAS LONELY...
NO!! HELP ...!!

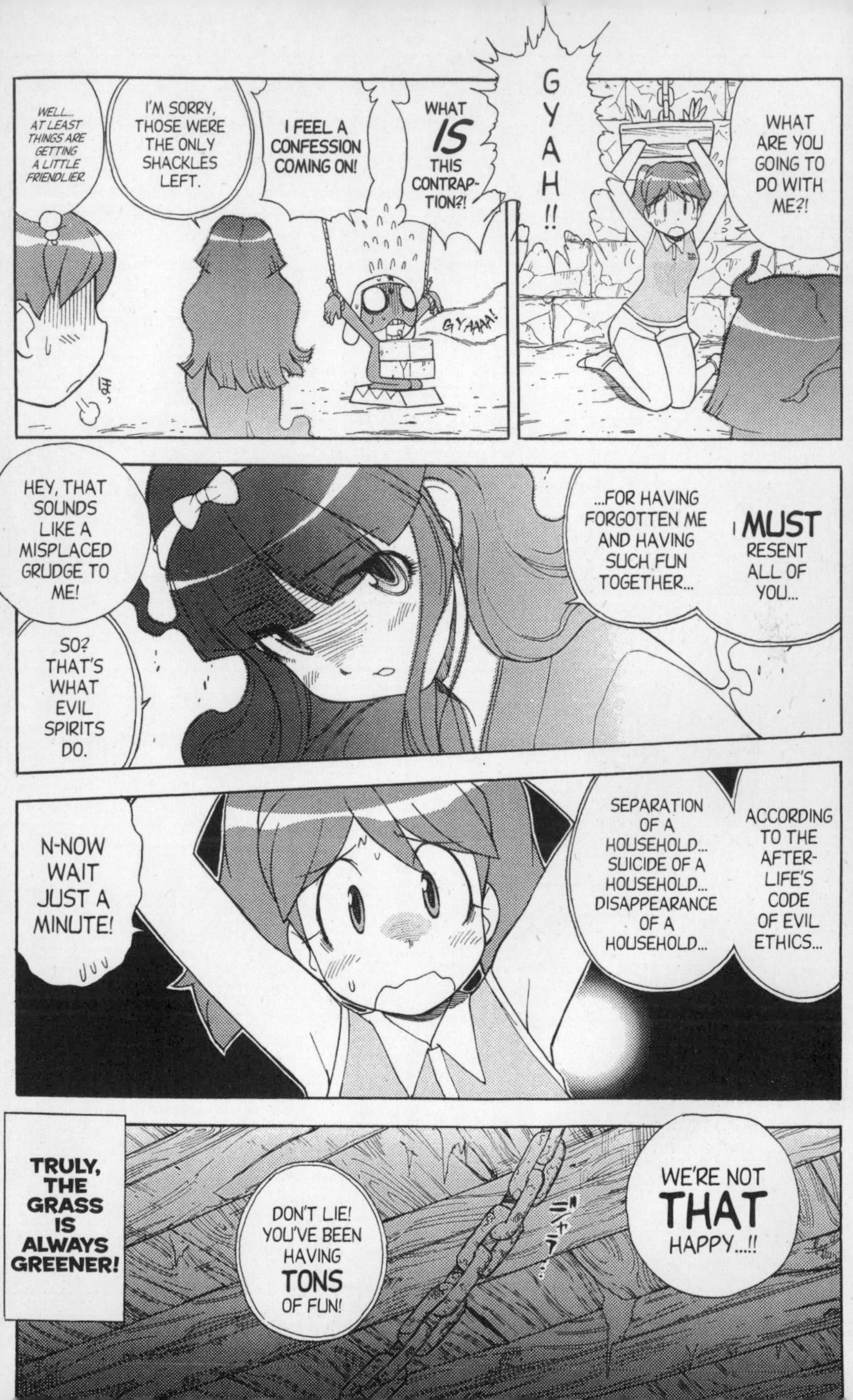
WHAT ARE YOU GOING TO DO WITH ME?!
GYAH!!
WHAT IS THIS CONTRAPTION?!
I FEEL A CONFESSION COMING ON!
GYAAAA!
I'M SORRY, THOSE WERE THE ONLY SHACKLES LEFT.
WELL... AT LEAST THINGS ARE GETTING A LITTLE FRIENDLIER.
I MUST RESENT ALL OF YOU...
...FOR HAVING FORGOTTEN ME AND HAVING SUCH FUN TOGETHER...
HEY, THAT SOUNDS LIKE A MISPLACED GRUDGE TO ME!
SO? THAT'S WHAT EVIL SPIRITS DO.
ACCORDING TO THE AFTER-LIFE'S CODE OF EVIL ETHICS...
SEPARATION OF A HOUSEHOLD... SUICIDE OF A HOUSEHOLD... DISAPPEARANCE OF A HOUSEHOLD...
N-NOW WAIT JUST A MINUTE!
WE'RE NOT THAT HAPPY...!!
DON'T LIE! YOU'VE BEEN HAVING TONS OF FUN!
TRULY, THE GRASS IS ALWAYS GREENER!

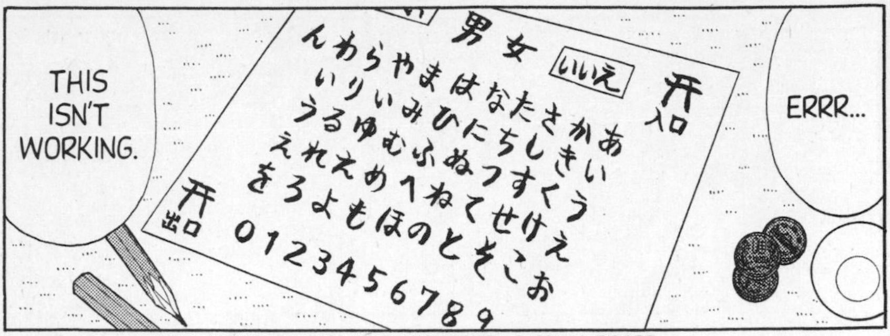
ERRR...
男 女
いいえ
入口
んわらやまはなたさかあ
いりいみひにちしきい
うるゆむふぬつすくう
えれえめへねてせけえ
をろよもほのとそこお
出口
0123456789
THIS ISN'T WORKING.

THE JAPANESE SYLLABIC ALPHABET--A OUIJA BOARD

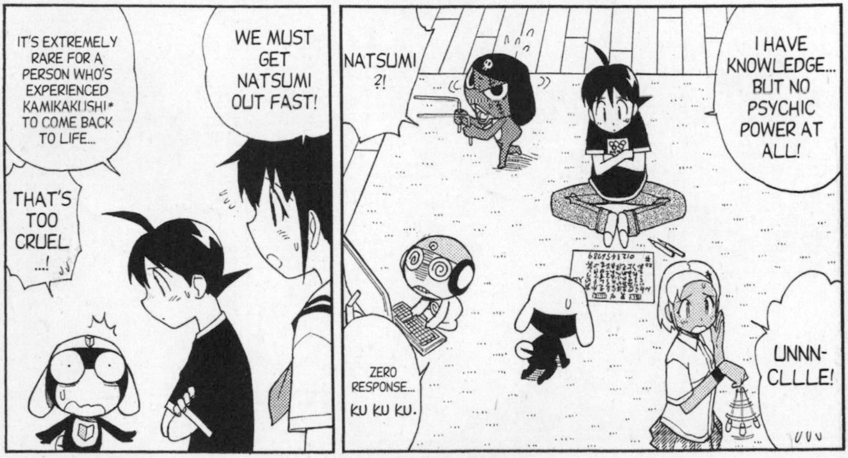
I HAVE KNOWLEDGE... BUT NO PSYCHIC POWER AT ALL!
NATSUMI ?!
UNNN-CLLLE!
ZERO RESPONSE... KU KU KU.
WE MUST GET NATSUMI OUT FAST!
IT'S EXTREMELY RARE FOR A PERSON WHO'S EXPERIENCED KAMIKAKUSHI* TO COME BACK TO LIFE...
THAT'S TOO CRUEL ...!

*LITERALLY, "HIDDEN BY GOD"--A SUPERNATURAL DISAPPEARANCE.

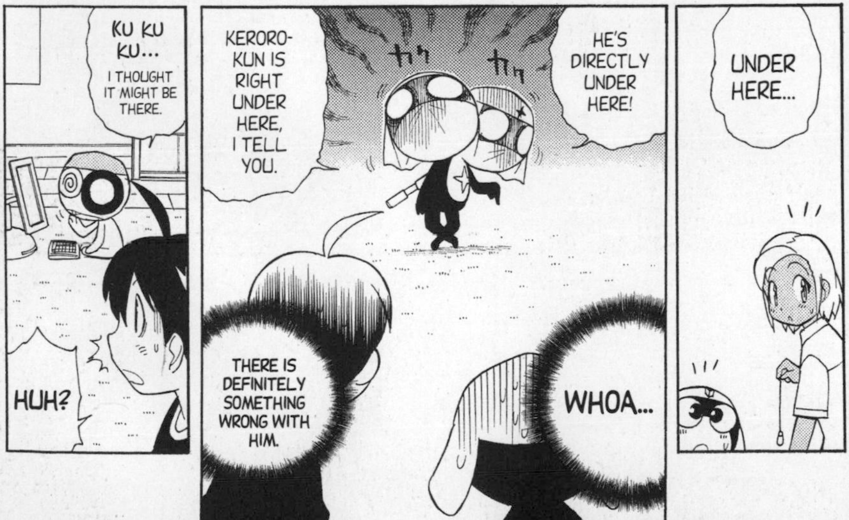
UNDER HERE...
HE'S DIRECTLY UNDER HERE!
KERORO-KUN IS RIGHT UNDER HERE, I TELL YOU.
WHOA...
THERE IS DEFINITELY SOMETHING WRONG WITH HIM.
KU KU KU... I THOUGHT IT MIGHT BE THERE.
HUH?

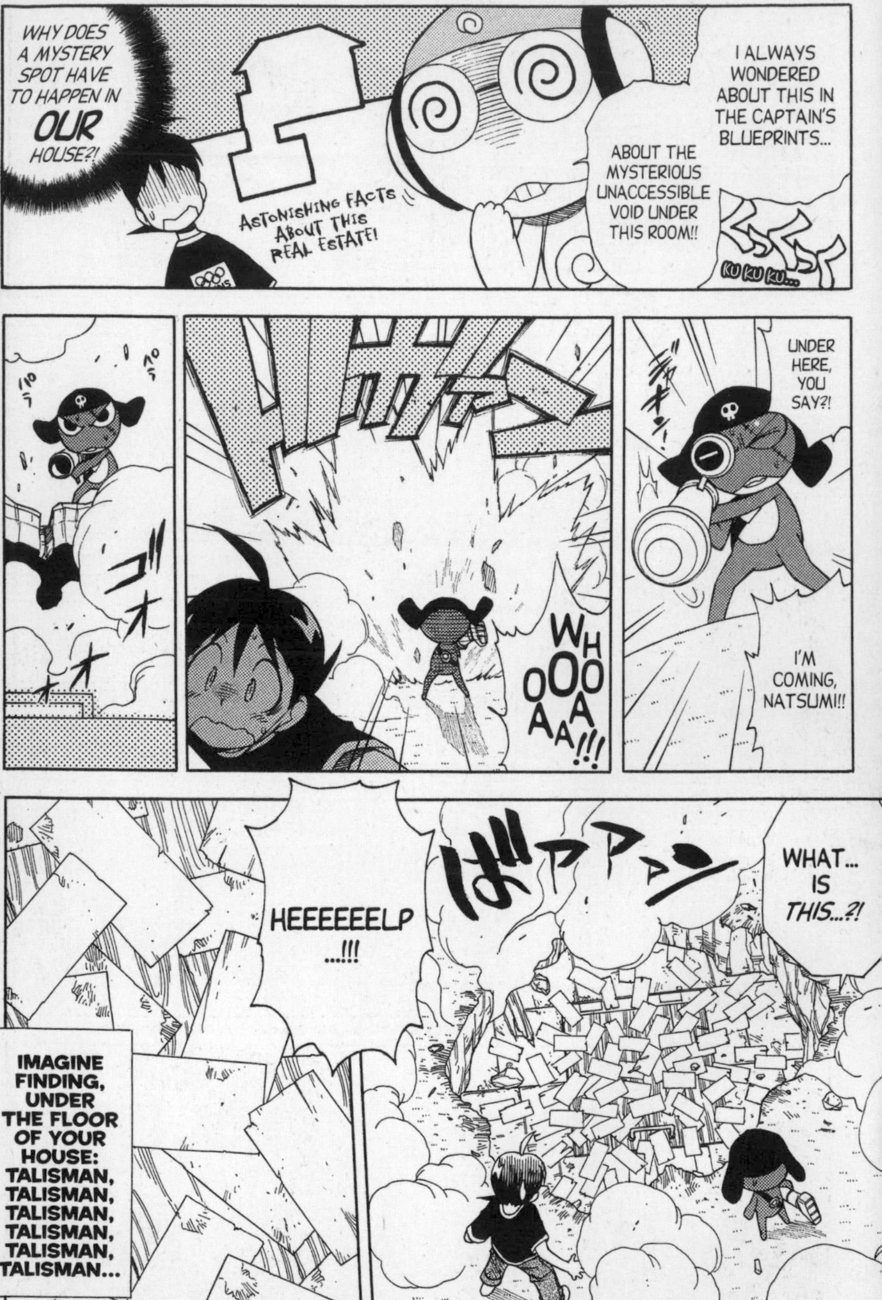
I ALWAYS WONDERED ABOUT THIS IN THE CAPTAIN'S BLUEPRINTS...
KU KU KU...
ABOUT THE MYSTERIOUS UNACCESSIBLE VOID UNDER THIS ROOM!!
ASTONISHING FACTS ABOUT THIS REAL ESTATE!
WHY DOES A MYSTERY SPOT HAVE TO HAPPEN IN OUR HOUSE?!
UNDER HERE, YOU SAY?!
I'M COMING, NATSUMI!!
WHOOOAAA!!!
WHAT... IS THIS...?!
HEEEEEEELP ...!!!
IMAGINE FINDING, UNDER THE FLOOR OF YOUR HOUSE: TALISMAN, TALISMAN, TALISMAN, TALISMAN, TALISMAN, TALISMAN...

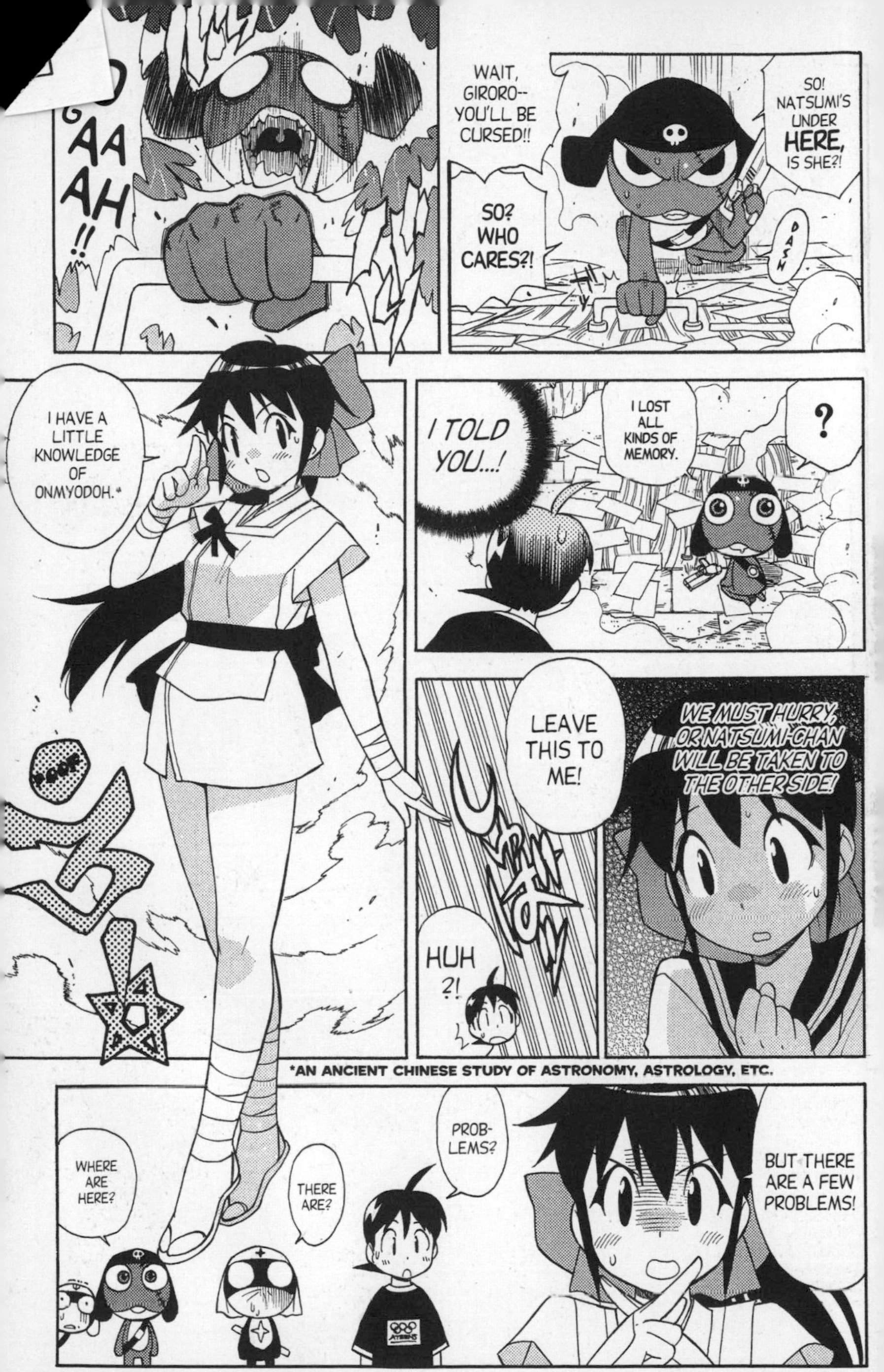
SO! NATSUMI'S UNDER HERE, IS SHE?!
WAIT, GIRORO-- YOU'LL BE CURSED!!
SO? WHO CARES?!
DASH
GAAAH!!
?
I LOST ALL KINDS OF MEMORY.
I TOLD YOU...!
WE MUST HURRY, OR NATSUMI-CHAN WILL BE TAKEN TO THE OTHER SIDE!
LEAVE THIS TO ME!
HUH?!
I HAVE A LITTLE KNOWLEDGE OF ONMYODOH.*
BUT THERE ARE A FEW PROBLEMS!
PROBLEMS?
THERE ARE?
WHERE ARE HERE?

*AN ANCIENT CHINESE STUDY OF ASTRONOMY, ASTROLOGY, ETC.

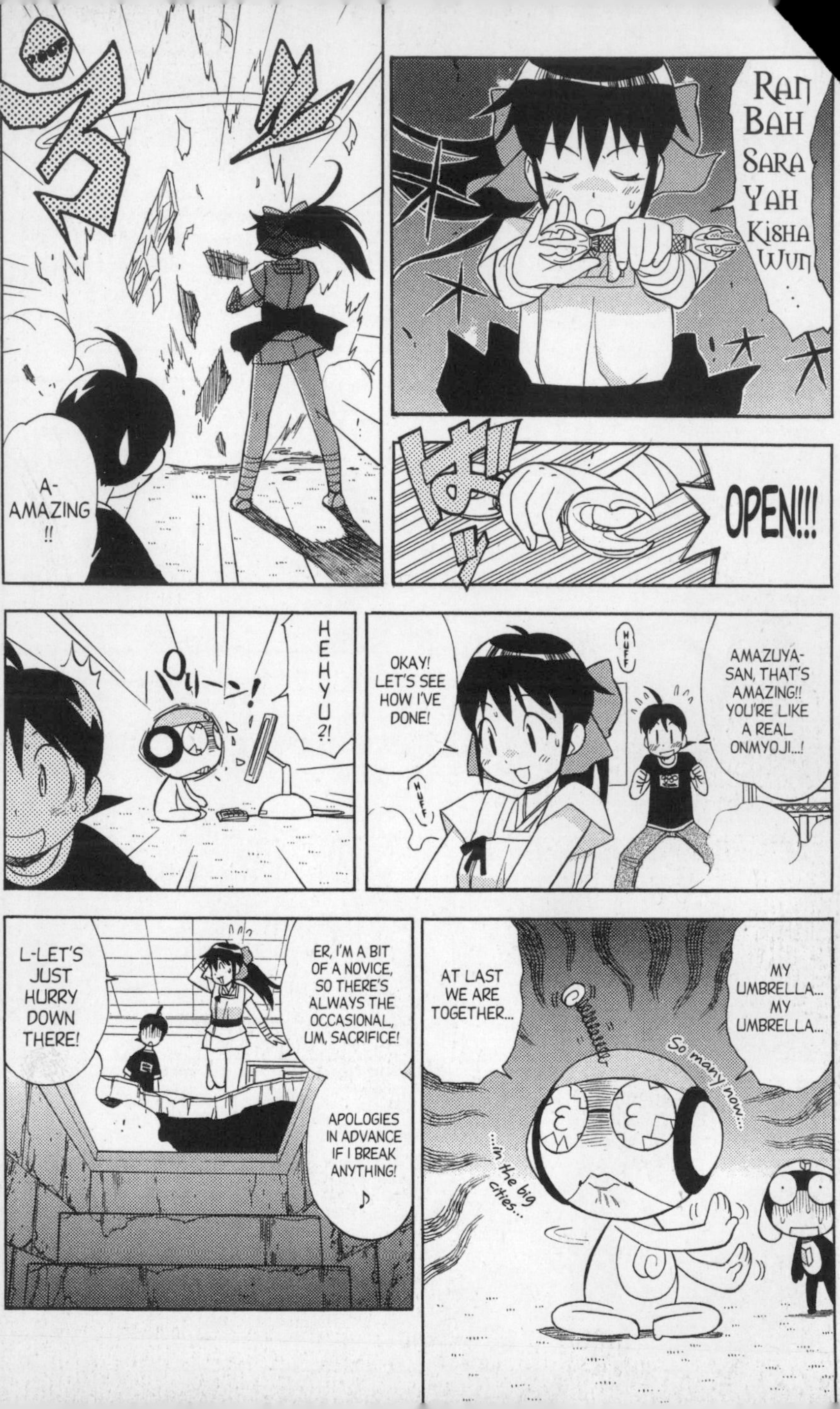
RAN BAH SARA YAH KISHA WUN
OPEN!!!
A-AMAZING!!
AMAZUYA-SAN, THAT'S AMAZING!! YOU'RE LIKE A REAL ONMYOJI...!
HUFF
OKAY! LET'S SEE HOW I'VE DONE!
HUFF
HEHYU?!
MY UMBRELLA... MY UMBRELLA...
AT LAST WE ARE TOGETHER...
So many now...
...in the big cities...
ER, I'M A BIT OF A NOVICE, SO THERE'S ALWAYS THE OCCASIONAL, UM, SACRIFICE!
L-LET'S JUST HURRY DOWN THERE!
APOLOGIES IN ADVANCE IF I BREAK ANYTHING! ♪

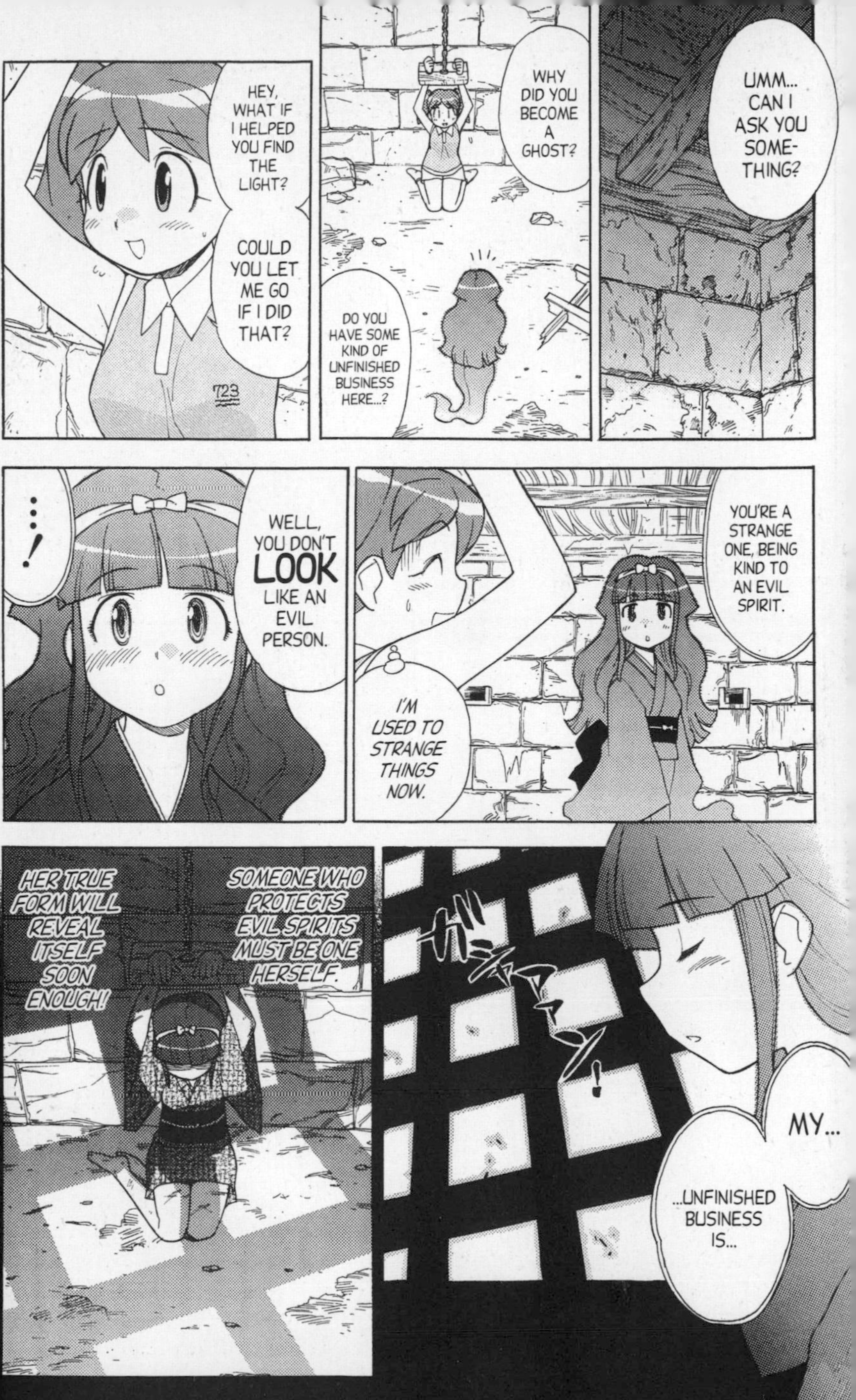
UMM... CAN I ASK YOU SOME-THING?
WHY DID YOU BECOME A GHOST?
DO YOU HAVE SOME KIND OF UNFINISHED BUSINESS HERE...?
HEY, WHAT IF I HELPED YOU FIND THE LIGHT?
COULD YOU LET ME GO IF I DID THAT?
YOU'RE A STRANGE ONE, BEING KIND TO AN EVIL SPIRIT.
I'M USED TO STRANGE THINGS NOW.
...!
WELL, YOU DON'T LOOK LIKE AN EVIL PERSON.
MY...
...UNFINISHED BUSINESS IS...
SOMEONE WHO PROTECTS EVIL SPIRITS MUST BE ONE HERSELF.
HER TRUE FORM WILL REVEAL ITSELF SOON ENOUGH!

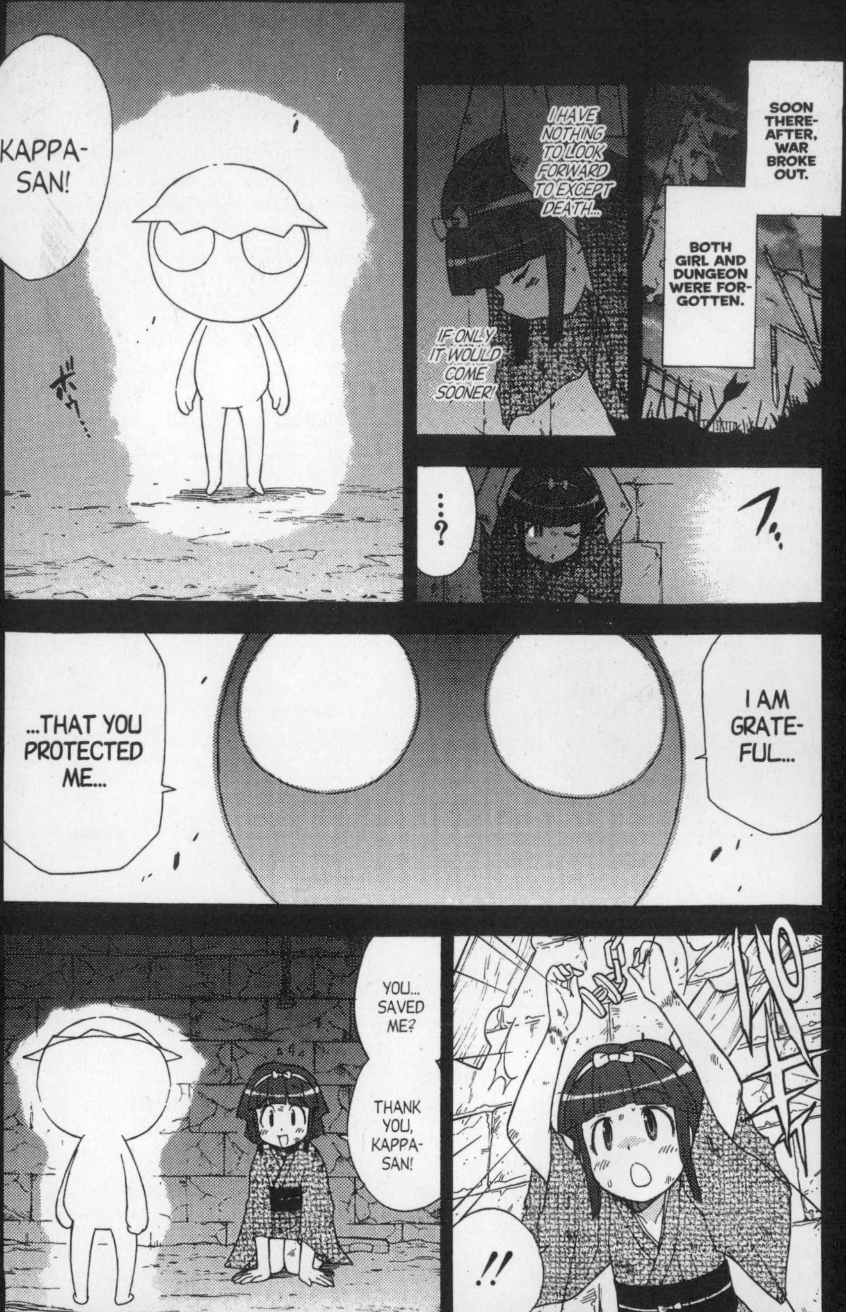
SOON THERE-AFTER, WAR BROKE OUT.
BOTH GIRL AND DUNGEON WERE FOR-GOTTEN.
I HAVE NOTHING TO LOOK FORWARD TO EXCEPT DEATH...
IF ONLY IT WOULD COME SOONER!
...?
KAPPA-SAN!
I AM GRATE-FUL...
...THAT YOU PROTECTED ME...
!!
YOU... SAVED ME?
THANK YOU, KAPPA-SAN!

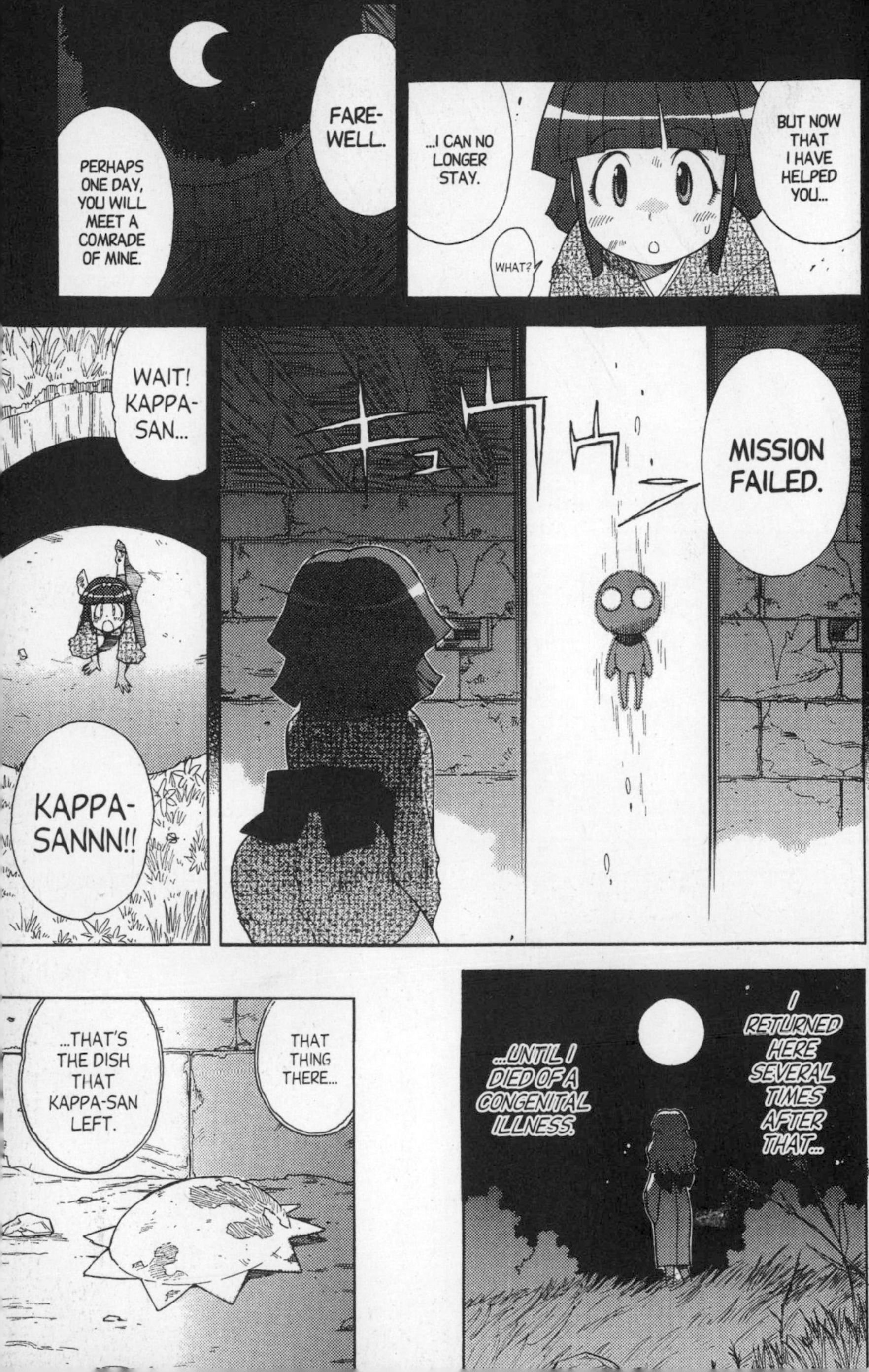
BUT NOW THAT I HAVE HELPED YOU...
...I CAN NO LONGER STAY.
WHAT?
FARE-WELL.
PERHAPS ONE DAY, YOU WILL MEET A COMRADE OF MINE.
MISSION FAILED.
WAIT! KAPPA-SAN...
KAPPA-SANNN!!
I RETURNED HERE SEVERAL TIMES AFTER THAT...
...UNTIL I DIED OF A CONGENITAL ILLNESS.
THAT THING THERE...
...THAT'S THE DISH THAT KAPPA-SAN LEFT.

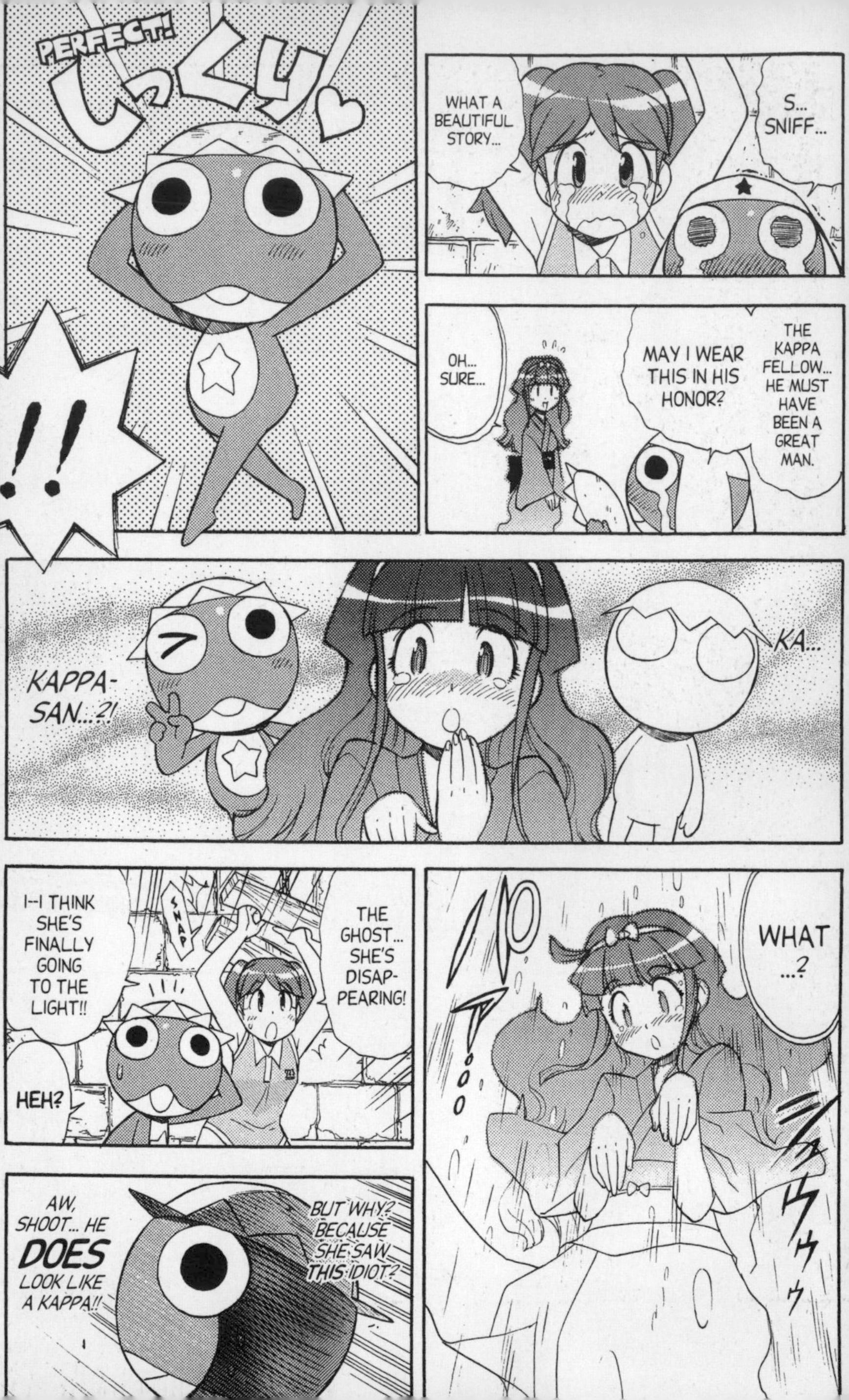
S... SNIFF...
WHAT A BEAUTIFUL STORY...
THE KAPPA FELLOW... HE MUST HAVE BEEN A GREAT MAN.
MAY I WEAR THIS IN HIS HONOR?
OH... SURE...
PERFECT!
じっくり
!!
KA...
KAPPA-SAN...?!
WHAT ...?
THE GHOST... SHE'S DISAPPEARING!
SNAP
I--I THINK SHE'S FINALLY GOING TO THE LIGHT!!
HEH?
BUT WHY? BECAUSE SHE SAW THIS IDIOT?
AW, SHOOT... HE **DOES** LOOK LIKE A KAPPA!!

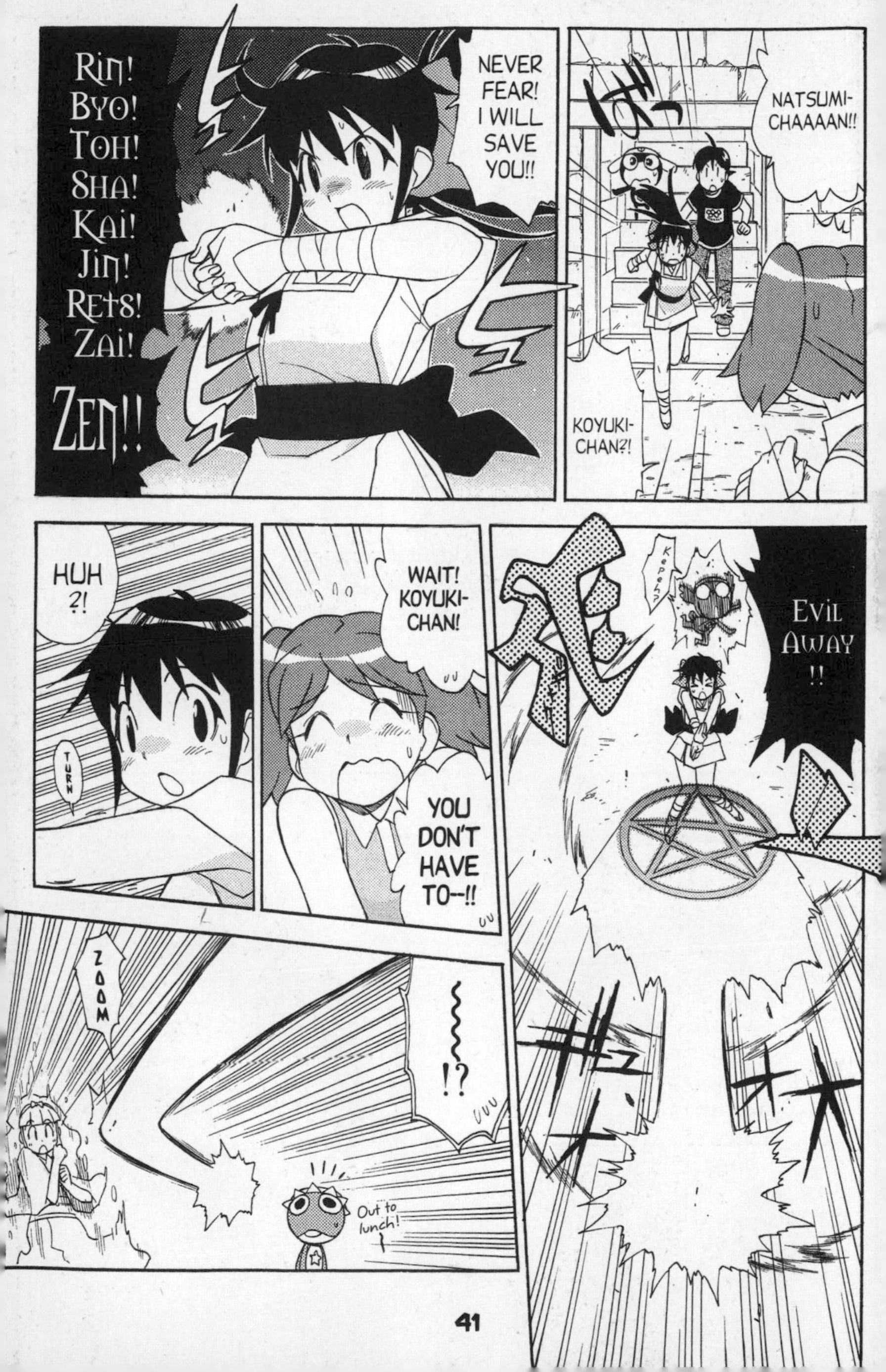
NATSUMI-CHAAAAN!!
ぱっ
KOYUKI-CHAN?!
NEVER FEAR! I WILL SAVE YOU!!
RIN! BYO! TOH! SHA! KAI! JIN! RETS! ZAI!
ZEN!!
EVIL AWAY!!
Kepeh?
WAIT! KOYUKI-CHAN!
YOU DON'T HAVE TO--!!
HUH?!
TURN
~~~!?
ZOOM
Out to lunch!
~~~

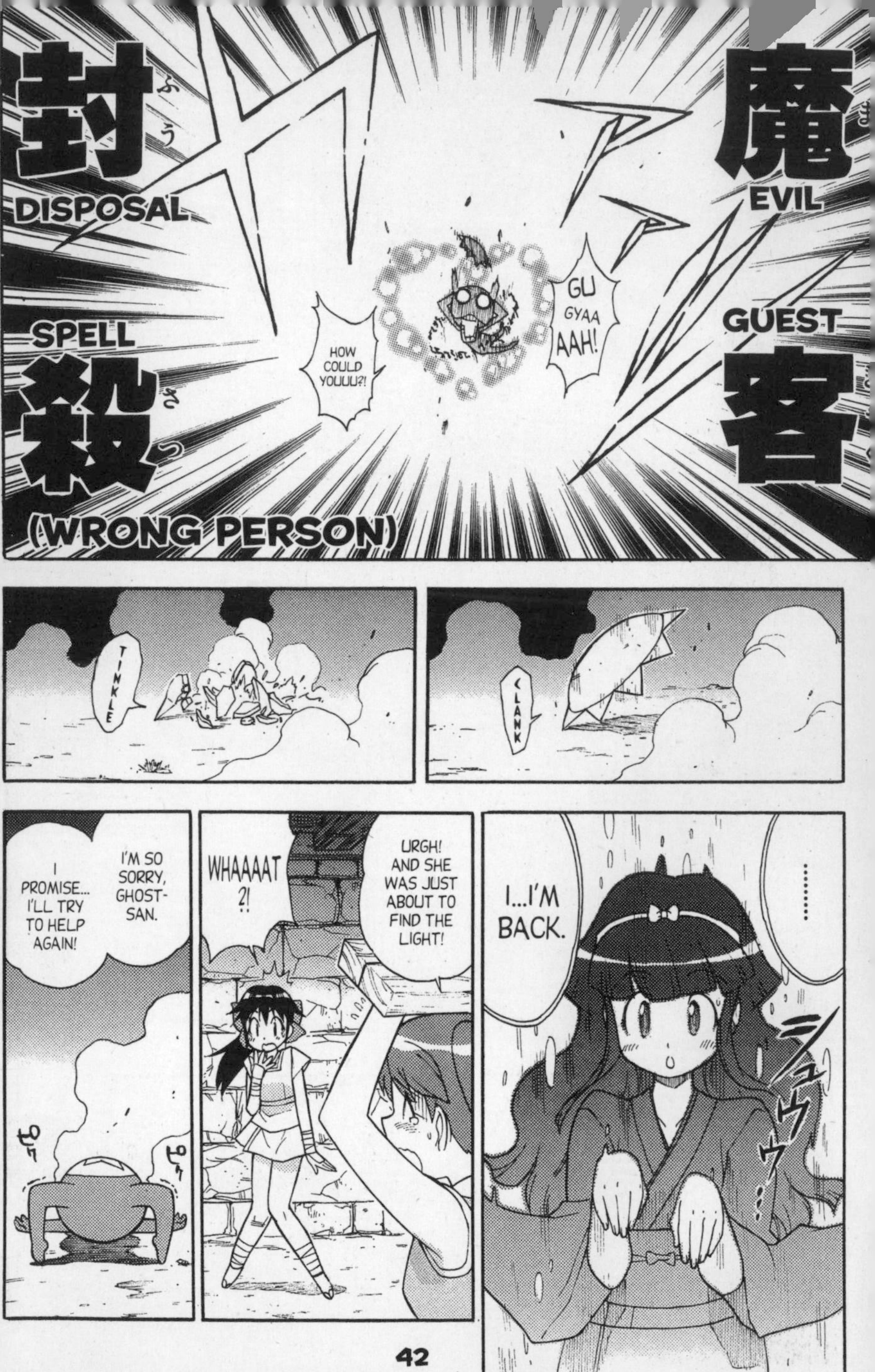
魔
EVIL
GUEST
客
封
DISPOSAL
SPELL
殺
(WRONG PERSON)
GU GYAA AAH!
HOW COULD YOUUU?!
CLANK
TINKLE
......
I...I'M BACK.
URGH! AND SHE WAS JUST ABOUT TO FIND THE LIGHT!
WHAAAAT?!
I'M SO SORRY, GHOST-SAN.
I PROMISE... I'LL TRY TO HELP AGAIN!

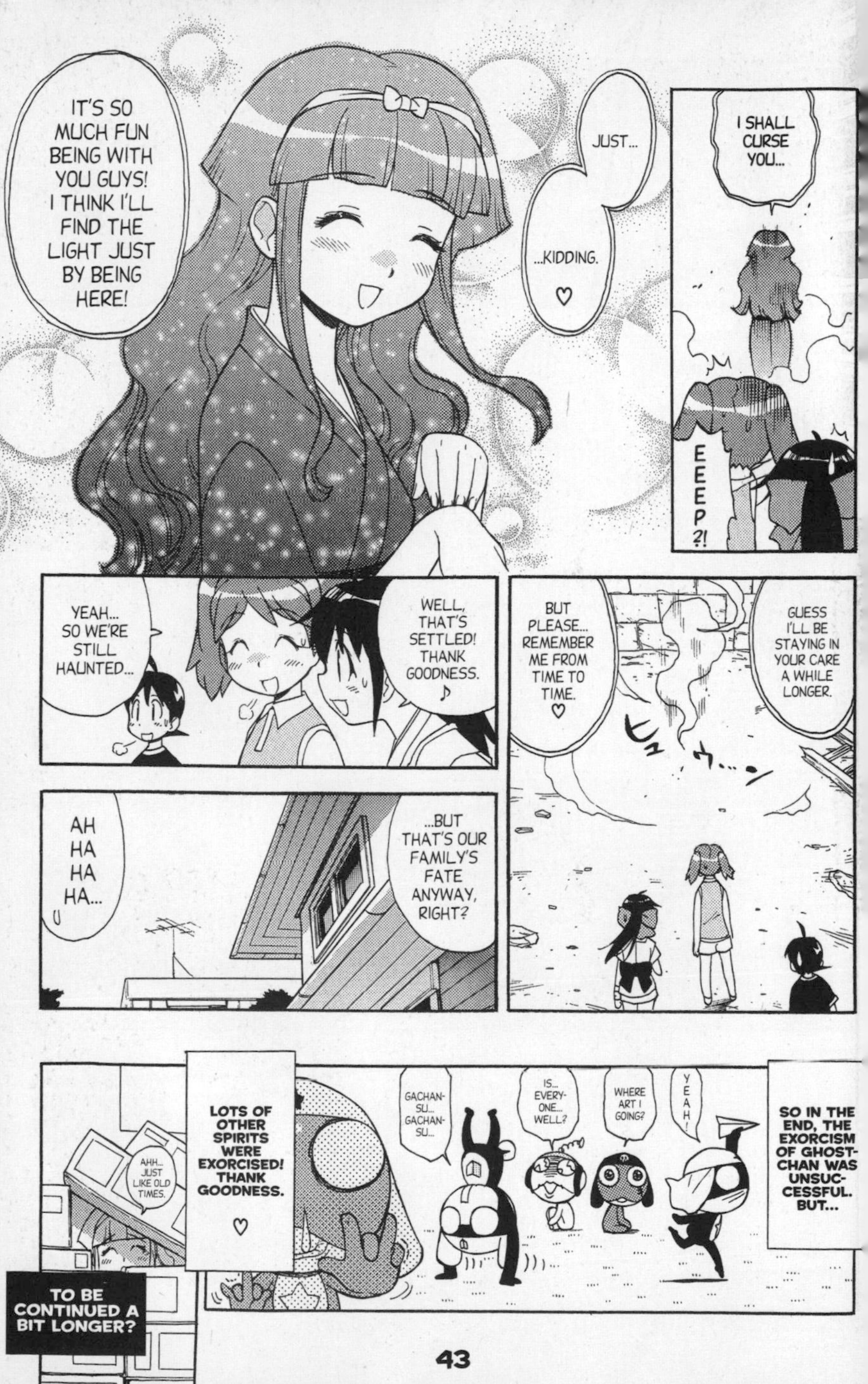
I SHALL CURSE YOU...
EEEP?!
JUST...
...KIDDING. ♡
IT'S SO MUCH FUN BEING WITH YOU GUYS! I THINK I'LL FIND THE LIGHT JUST BY BEING HERE!
GUESS I'LL BE STAYING IN YOUR CARE A WHILE LONGER.
BUT PLEASE... REMEMBER ME FROM TIME TO TIME. ♡
WELL, THAT'S SETTLED! THANK GOODNESS. ♪
YEAH... SO WE'RE STILL HAUNTED...
...BUT THAT'S OUR FAMILY'S FATE ANYWAY, RIGHT?
AH HA HA HA...
SO IN THE END, THE EXORCISM OF GHOST-CHAN WAS UNSUCCESSFUL. BUT...
YEAH!
WHERE ART I GOING?
IS... EVERY-ONE... WELL?
GACHAN-SU... GACHAN-SU...
LOTS OF OTHER SPIRITS WERE EXORCISED! THANK GOODNESS. ♡
AHH... JUST LIKE OLD TIMES.
TO BE CONTINUED A BIT LONGER?

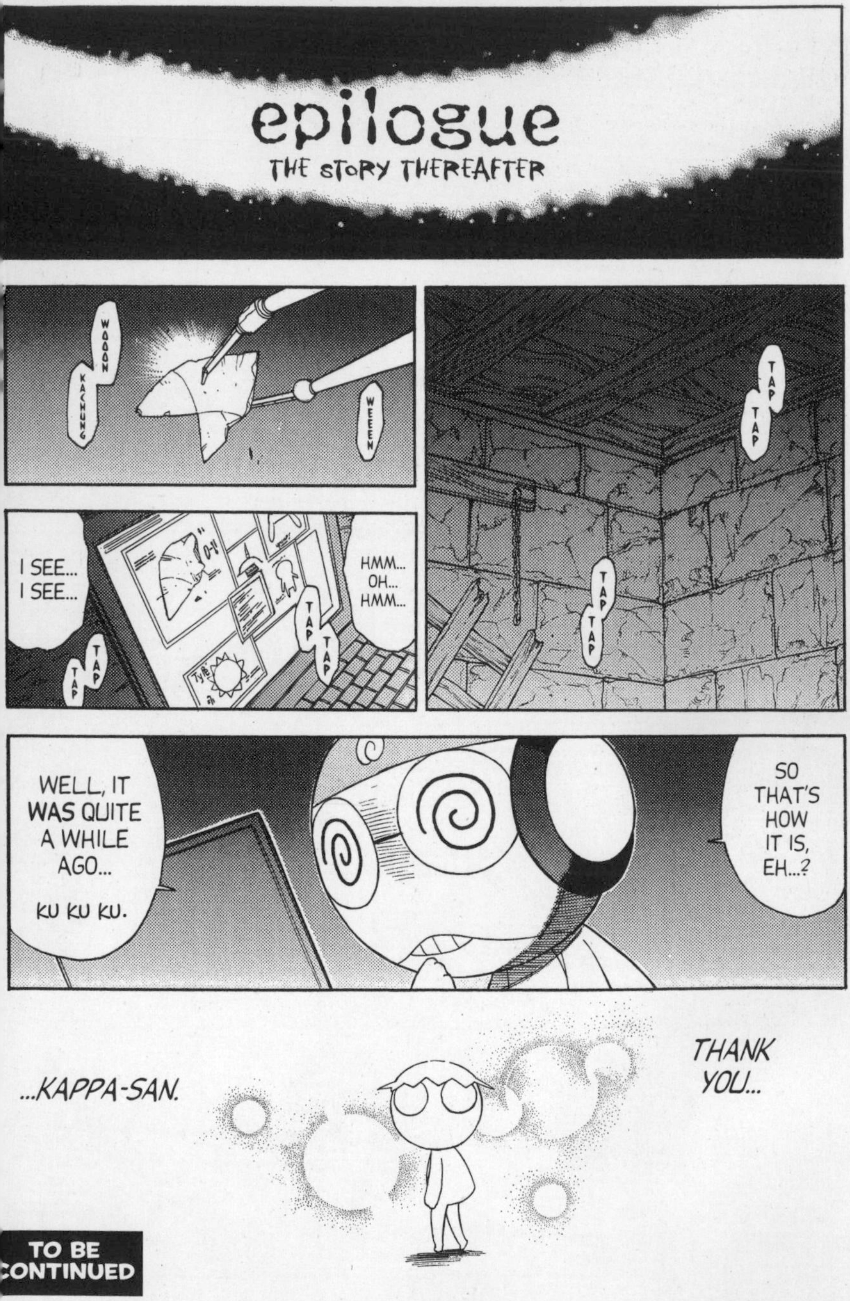
epilogue
THE STORY THEREAFTER
TAP TAP
TAP TAP TAP
WOOON
KACHUNG
WEEEN
HMM... OH... HMM...
TAP TAP
I SEE... I SEE...
TAP TAP
SO THAT'S HOW IT IS, EH...?
WELL, IT WAS QUITE A WHILE AGO...
KU KU KU.
THANK YOU...
...KAPPA-SAN.
TO BE CONTINUED

ENCOUNTER LXXIX
A LESSON IN ALIEN SAVOIR FAIRE!

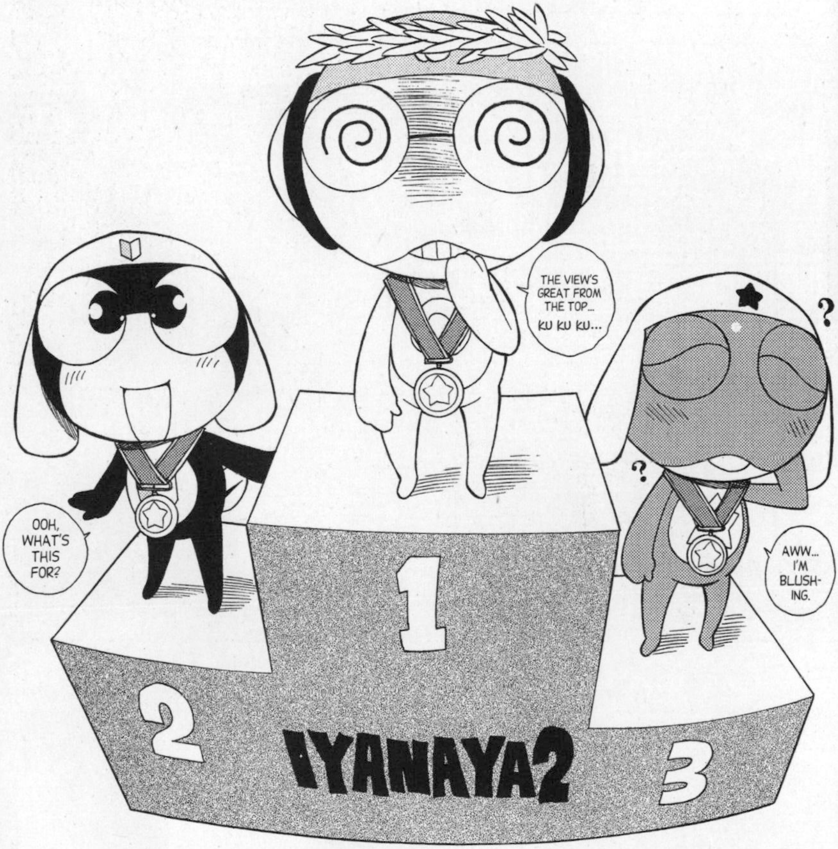
THE VIEW'S GREAT FROM THE TOP... KU KU KU...
AWW... I'M BLUSHING.
OOH, WHAT'S THIS FOR?
1
2
3
IYANAYA2

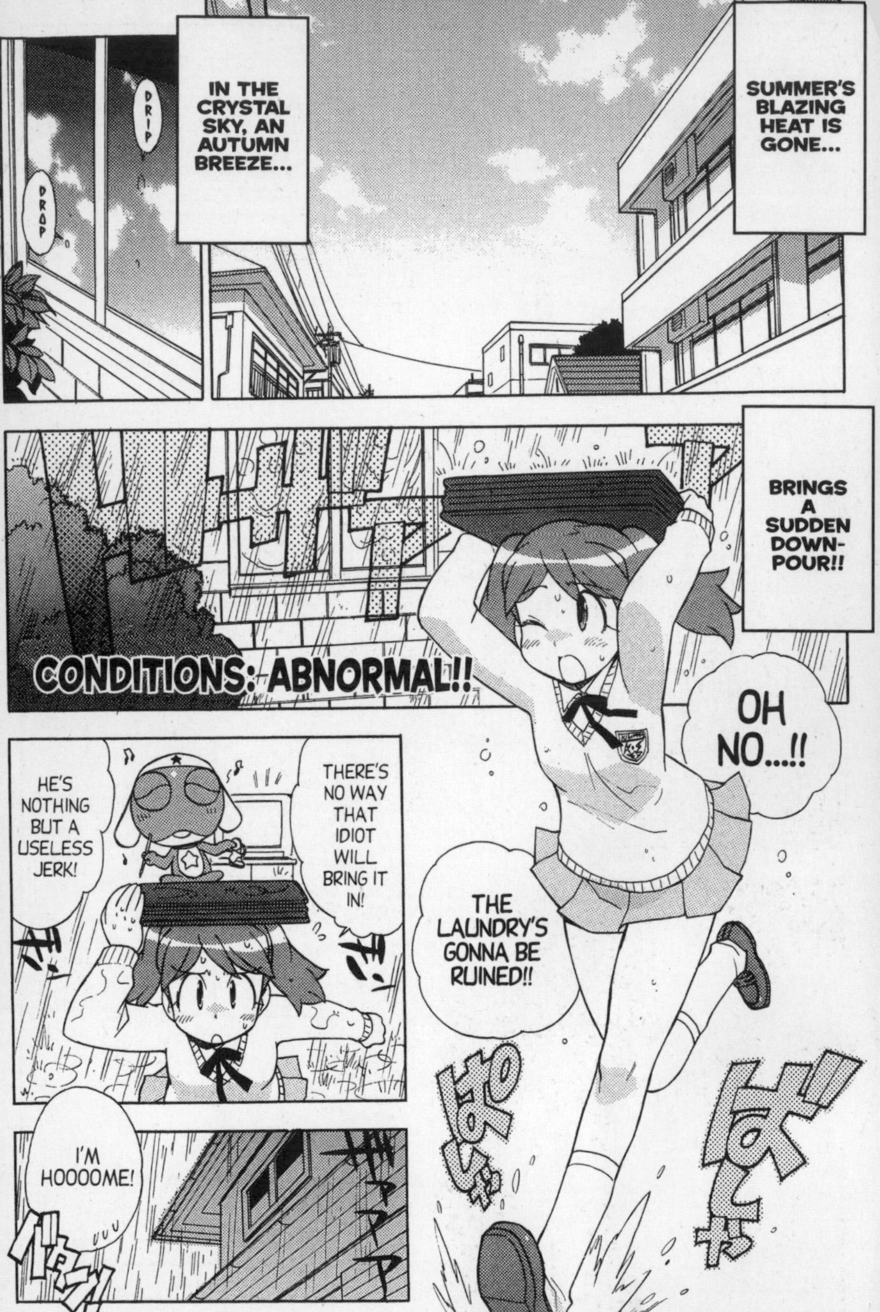
SUMMER'S BLAZING HEAT IS GONE...
IN THE CRYSTAL SKY, AN AUTUMN BREEZE...
DRIP
DROP
BRINGS A SUDDEN DOWN-POUR!!
CONDITIONS: ABNORMAL!!
OH NO...!!
THE LAUNDRY'S GONNA BE RUINED!!
THERE'S NO WAY THAT IDIOT WILL BRING IT IN!
HE'S NOTHING BUT A USELESS JERK!
I'M HOOOOME!

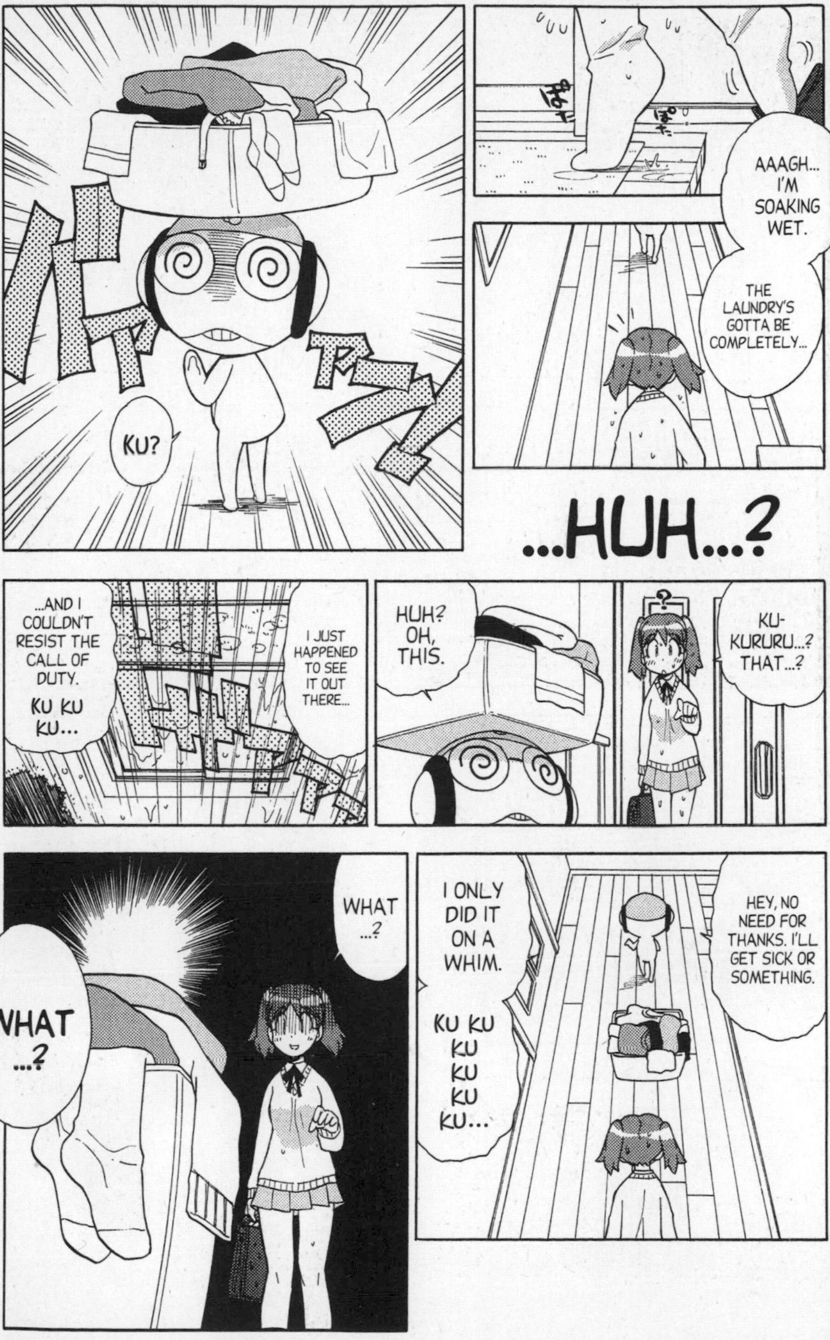

AAAGH... I'M SOAKING WET.
THE LAUNDRY'S GOTTA BE COMPLETELY...
KU?
...HUH...?
KU-KURURU...? THAT...?
HUH? OH, THIS.
I JUST HAPPENED TO SEE IT OUT THERE...
...AND I COULDN'T RESIST THE CALL OF DUTY.
KU KU KU...
HEY, NO NEED FOR THANKS. I'LL GET SICK OR SOMETHING.
I ONLY DID IT ON A WHIM.
KU KU KU KU KU KU...
WHAT ...?
WHAT ...?

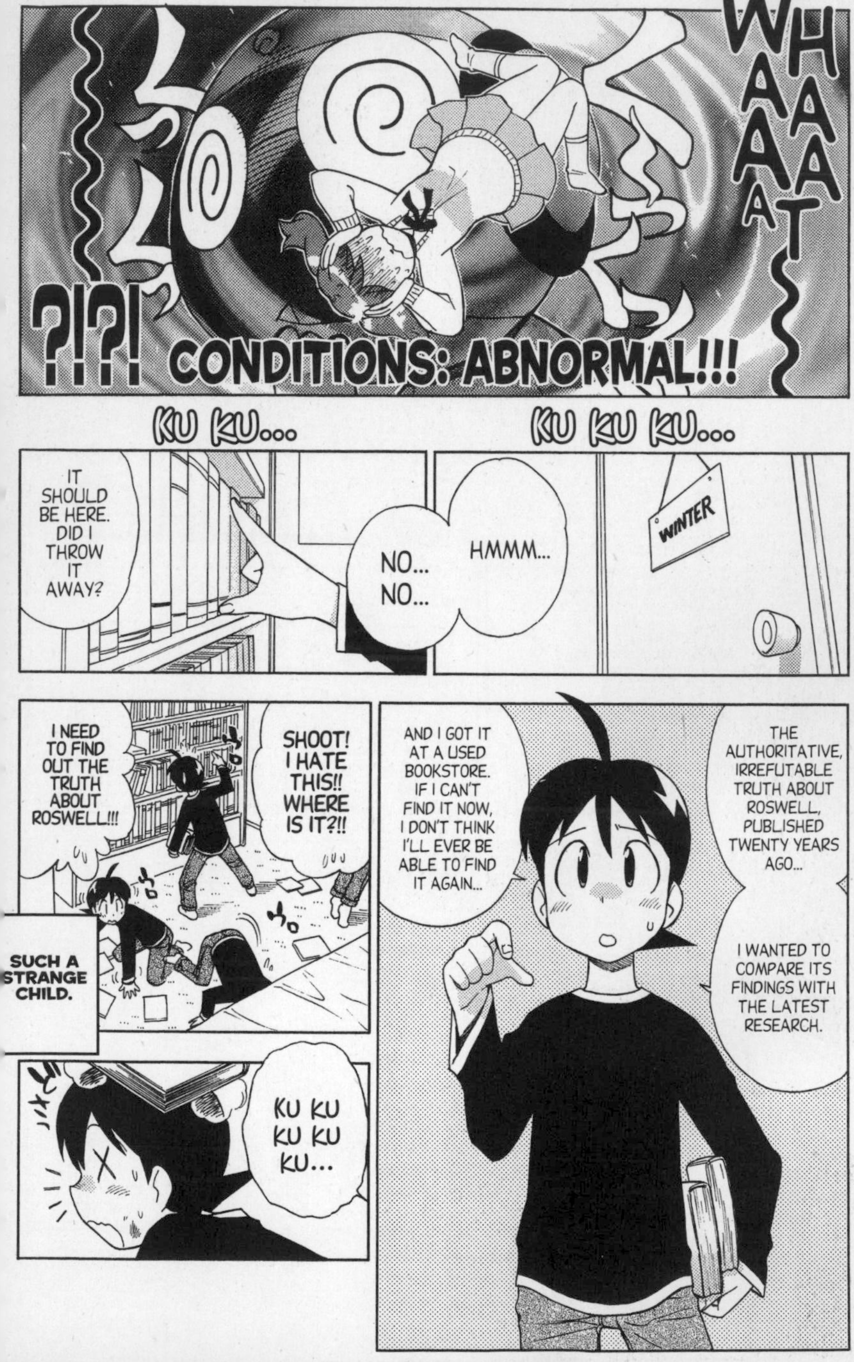
WHAAAAAAT~
CONDITIONS: ABNORMAL!!!
?!?!
KU KU KU...
KU KU...
HMMM...
NO... NO...
IT SHOULD BE HERE. DID I THROW IT AWAY?
THE AUTHORITATIVE, IRREFUTABLE TRUTH ABOUT ROSWELL, PUBLISHED TWENTY YEARS AGO...
I WANTED TO COMPARE ITS FINDINGS WITH THE LATEST RESEARCH.
AND I GOT IT AT A USED BOOKSTORE. IF I CAN'T FIND IT NOW, I DON'T THINK I'LL EVER BE ABLE TO FIND IT AGAIN...
SHOOT! I HATE THIS!! WHERE IS IT?!!
I NEED TO FIND OUT THE TRUTH ABOUT ROSWELL!!!
SUCH A STRANGE CHILD.
KU KU KU KU KU...

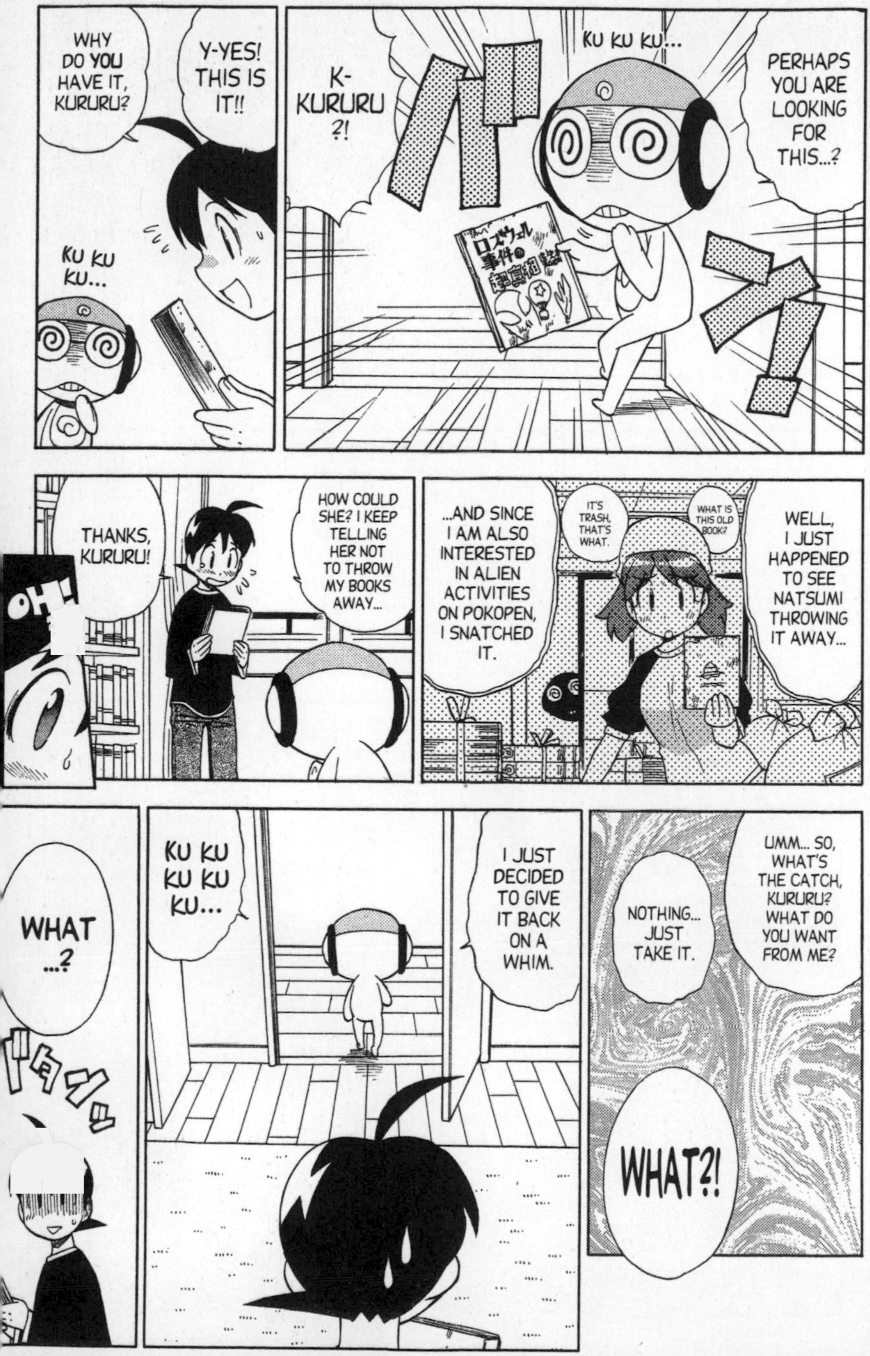
PERHAPS YOU ARE LOOKING FOR THIS...?
KU KU KU...
K-KURURU?!
Y-YES! THIS IS IT!!
WHY DO YOU HAVE IT, KURURU?
KU KU KU...
WELL, I JUST HAPPENED TO SEE NATSUMI THROWING IT AWAY...
WHAT IS THIS OLD BOOK?
IT'S TRASH, THAT'S WHAT.
...AND SINCE I AM ALSO INTERESTED IN ALIEN ACTIVITIES ON POKOPEN, I SNATCHED IT.
HOW COULD SHE? I KEEP TELLING HER NOT TO THROW MY BOOKS AWAY...
THANKS, KURURU!
OH!
UMM... SO, WHAT'S THE CATCH, KURURU? WHAT DO YOU WANT FROM ME?
NOTHING... JUST TAKE IT.
WHAT?!
I JUST DECIDED TO GIVE IT BACK ON A WHIM.
KU KU KU KU KU...
WHAT ...?

THAT WAS...
WHAAAAT
あの…
...KURURU???
クルルが
!?!?
CONDITIONS: ABNORMAL!!!
OKAY, EVERYBODY! WE NOW BRING TO ORDER ANOTHER FRUITFUL AND MEANINGFUL...
Keroro Platoon Healthy 'n' Refreshing Operation: Pokopen Invasion Strategy Meeting
...MEETING FOR THE INVASION, Y'ALL!
HERE GOES...
AH!?!
あ!!?
NO BUDGET!! NO IDEAS!!
AN INVASION IN THIS CONDITION?!! TELL ME ANOTHER ONE!!
I KNOW! MAYBE WE CAN MAKE THEM MAKE US DO IT!!
OH!?!
お!!?
WHAT THERE IS NONE OF IS YOUR MOTIVATION!!!
I KNOW! DO SOMETHING YOURSELF FOR ONCE, DAMMIT!!
HOW CAN YOU MAKE ANYONE DO ANYTHING?!!

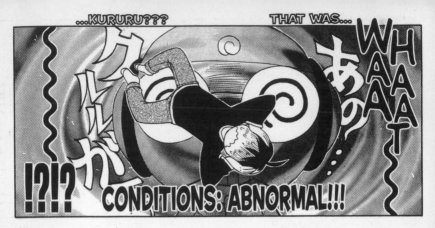

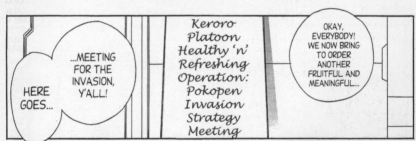

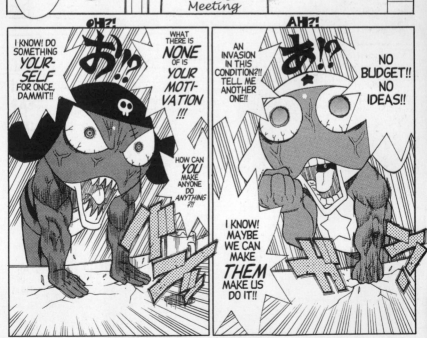

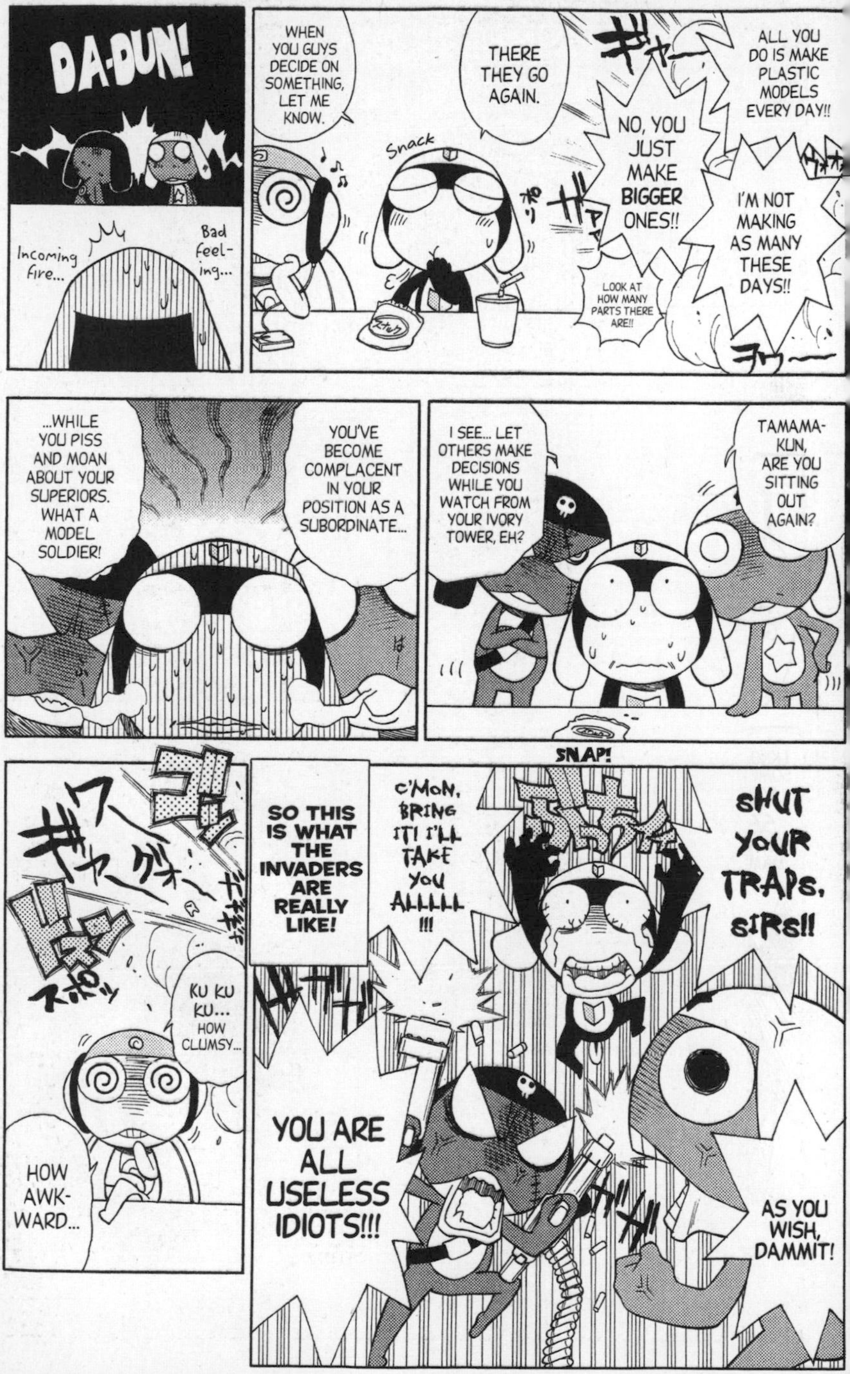
ALL YOU DO IS MAKE PLASTIC MODELS EVERY DAY!!
I'M NOT MAKING AS MANY THESE DAYS!!
NO, YOU JUST MAKE BIGGER ONES!!
LOOK AT HOW MANY PARTS THERE ARE!!
THERE THEY GO AGAIN.
WHEN YOU GUYS DECIDE ON SOMETHING, LET ME KNOW.
Snack
DA-DUN!
Bad feel-ing...
Incoming fire...
TAMAMA-KUN, ARE YOU SITTING OUT AGAIN?
I SEE... LET OTHERS MAKE DECISIONS WHILE YOU WATCH FROM YOUR IVORY TOWER, EH?
YOU'VE BECOME COMPLACENT IN YOUR POSITION AS A SUBORDINATE...
...WHILE YOU PISS AND MOAN ABOUT YOUR SUPERIORS. WHAT A MODEL SOLDIER!
SNAP!
SHUT YOUR TRAPS, SIRS!!
C'MON, BRING IT! I'LL TAKE YOU ALLLLL!!!
SO THIS IS WHAT THE INVADERS ARE REALLY LIKE!
AS YOU WISH, DAMMIT!
YOU ARE ALL USELESS IDIOTS!!!
KU KU KU... HOW CLUMSY...
HOW AWK-WARD...

SPARKS ON HOLD

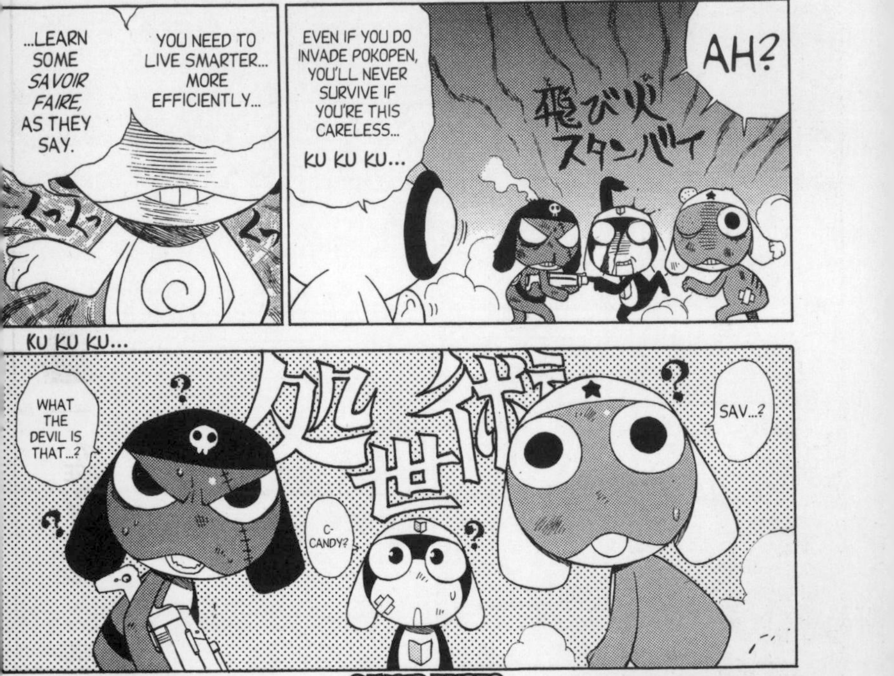
AH?
飛び火スタンバイ
EVEN IF YOU DO INVADE POKOPEN, YOU'LL NEVER SURVIVE IF YOU'RE THIS CARELESS...
KU KU KU...
YOU NEED TO LIVE SMARTER... MORE EFFICIENTLY...
...LEARN SOME *SAVOIR FAIRE,* AS THEY SAY.
くっくっ
KU KU KU...
処世術
SAV...?
WHAT THE DEVIL IS THAT...?
C-CANDY?

SAVOIR FAIRE?

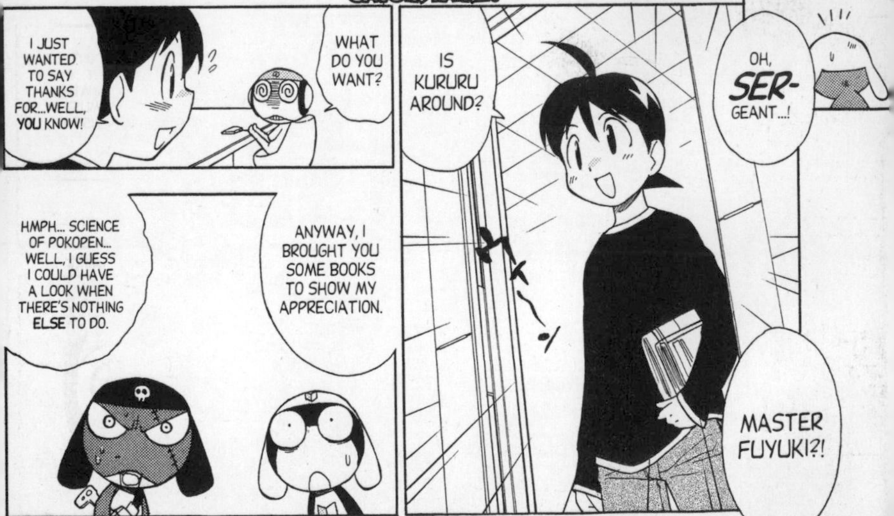
OH, SER-GEANT...!
MASTER FUYUKI?!
IS KURURU AROUND?
WHAT DO YOU WANT?
I JUST WANTED TO SAY THANKS FOR...WELL, YOU KNOW!
ANYWAY, I BROUGHT YOU SOME BOOKS TO SHOW MY APPRECIATION.
HMPH... SCIENCE OF POKOPEN... WELL, I GUESS I COULD HAVE A LOOK WHEN THERE'S NOTHING ELSE TO DO.

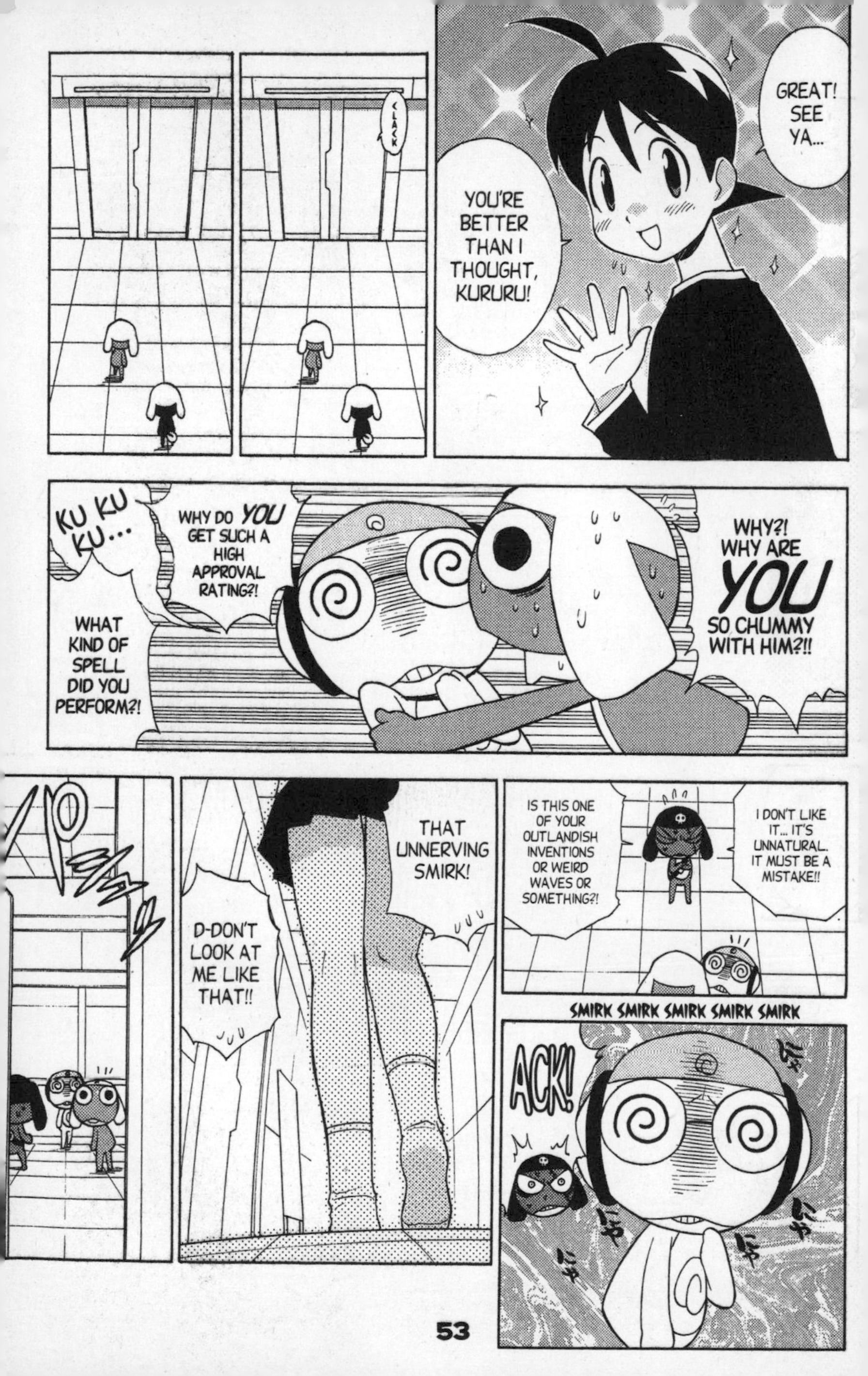
GREAT! SEE YA...
YOU'RE BETTER THAN I THOUGHT, KURURU!
CLACK
WHY?! WHY ARE YOU SO CHUMMY WITH HIM?!!
WHY DO YOU GET SUCH A HIGH APPROVAL RATING?!
WHAT KIND OF SPELL DID YOU PERFORM?!
KU KU KU...
I DON'T LIKE IT... IT'S UNNATURAL. IT MUST BE A MISTAKE!!
IS THIS ONE OF YOUR OUTLANDISH INVENTIONS OR WEIRD WAVES OR SOMETHING?!
SMIRK SMIRK SMIRK SMIRK SMIRK
ACK!
THAT UNNERVING SMIRK!
D-DON'T LOOK AT ME LIKE THAT!!

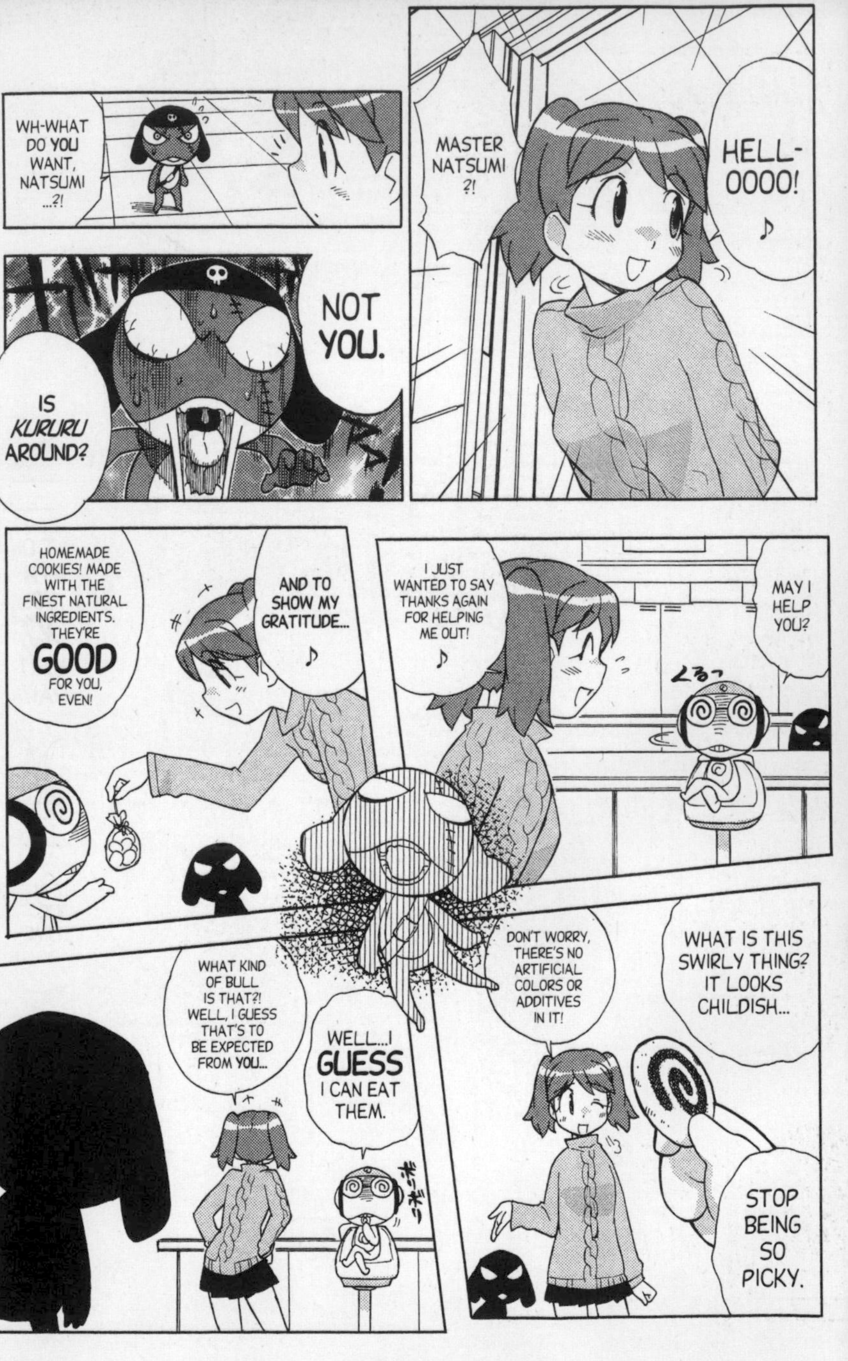
HELL-OOOO! ♪
MASTER NATSUMI ?!
WH-WHAT DO YOU WANT, NATSUMI ...?!
NOT YOU.
IS KURURU AROUND?
MAY I HELP YOU?
くるっ
I JUST WANTED TO SAY THANKS AGAIN FOR HELPING ME OUT! ♪
AND TO SHOW MY GRATITUDE... ♪
HOMEMADE COOKIES! MADE WITH THE FINEST NATURAL INGREDIENTS. THEY'RE GOOD FOR YOU, EVEN!
WHAT IS THIS SWIRLY THING? IT LOOKS CHILDISH...
DON'T WORRY, THERE'S NO ARTIFICIAL COLORS OR ADDITIVES IN IT!
STOP BEING SO PICKY.
WHAT KIND OF BULL IS THAT?! WELL, I GUESS THAT'S TO BE EXPECTED FROM YOU...
WELL...I GUESS I CAN EAT THEM.

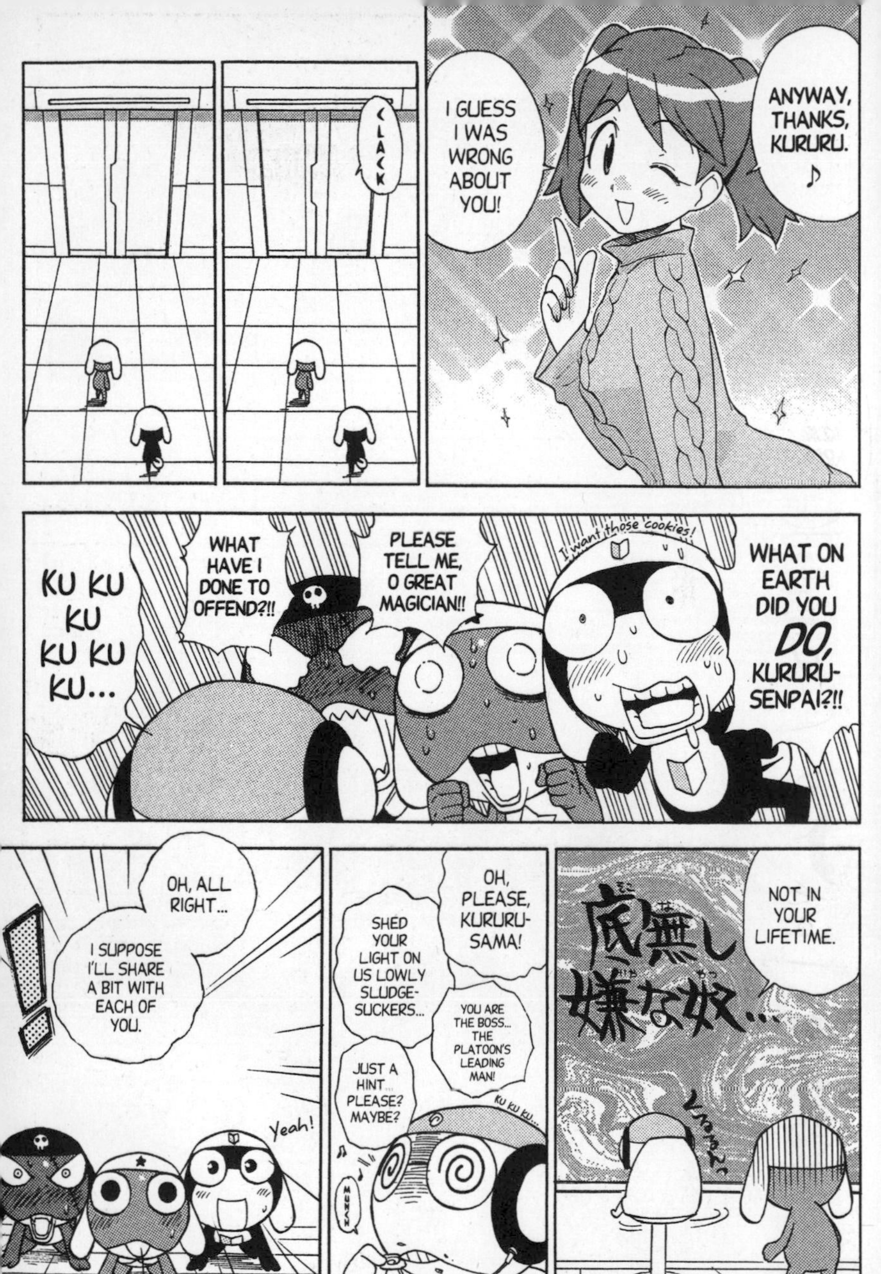
ANYWAY, THANKS, KURURU. ♪
I GUESS I WAS WRONG ABOUT YOU!
CLACK
WHAT ON EARTH DID YOU DO, KURURU-SENPAI?!!
I want those cookies!
PLEASE TELL ME, O GREAT MAGICIAN!!
WHAT HAVE I DONE TO OFFEND?!!
KU KU KU KU KU KU...
NOT IN YOUR LIFETIME.
底無し嫌な奴…
OH, PLEASE, KURURU-SAMA!
SHED YOUR LIGHT ON US LOWLY SLUDGE-SUCKERS...
YOU ARE THE BOSS... THE PLATOON'S LEADING MAN!
JUST A HINT... PLEASE? MAYBE?
KU KU KU...
OH, ALL RIGHT...
I SUPPOSE I'LL SHARE A BIT WITH EACH OF YOU.
!
Yeah!

BOTTOMLESS PIT OF A SCHMUCK...

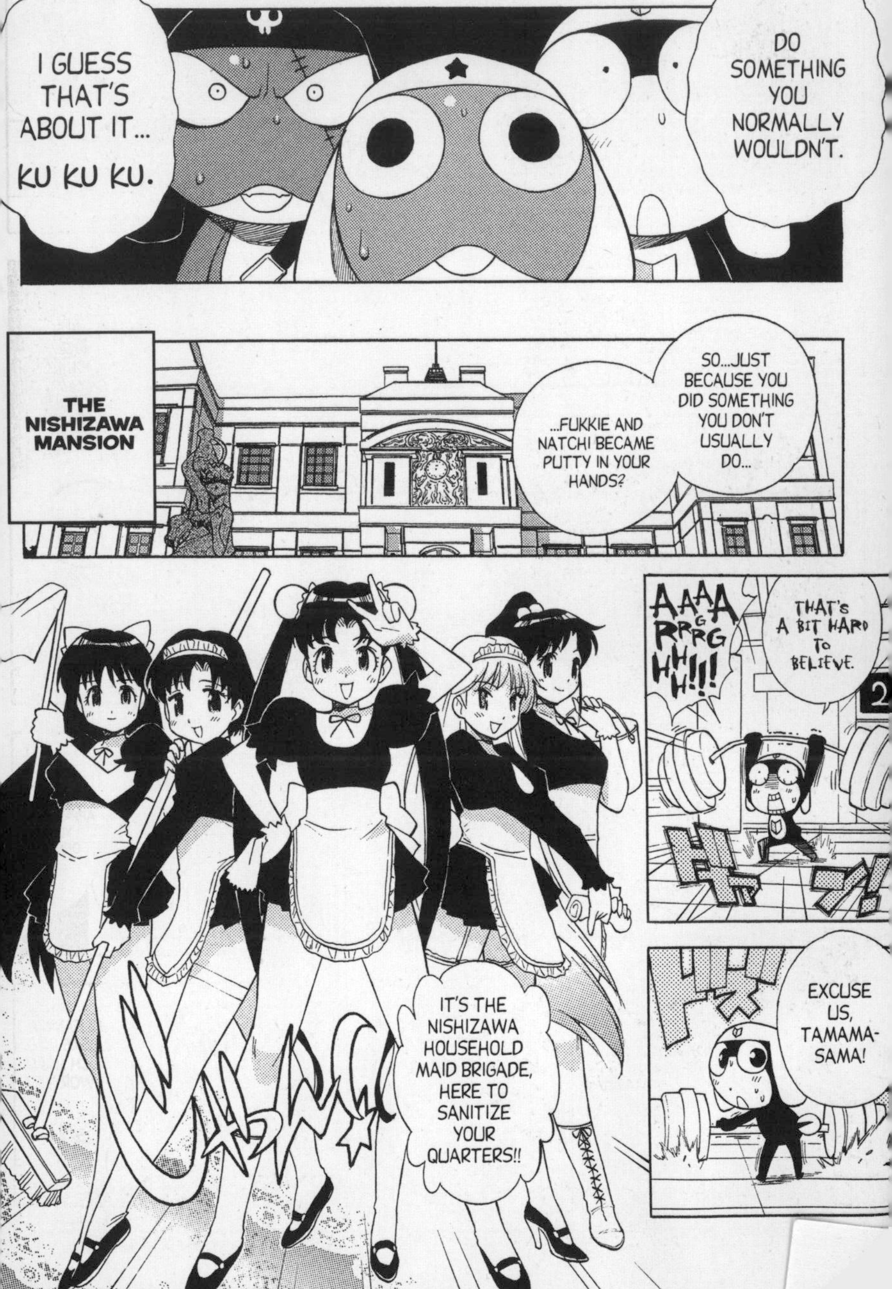
DO SOMETHING YOU NORMALLY WOULDN'T.
I GUESS THAT'S ABOUT IT... KU KU KU.
THE NISHIZAWA MANSION
SO...JUST BECAUSE YOU DID SOMETHING YOU DON'T USUALLY DO...
...FUKKIE AND NATCHI BECAME PUTTY IN YOUR HANDS?
THAT's A BIT HARD TO BELIEVE.
AAAARRRGGHHHH!!!
EXCUSE US, TAMAMA-SAMA!
IT'S THE NISHIZAWA HOUSEHOLD MAID BRIGADE, HERE TO SANITIZE YOUR QUARTERS!!

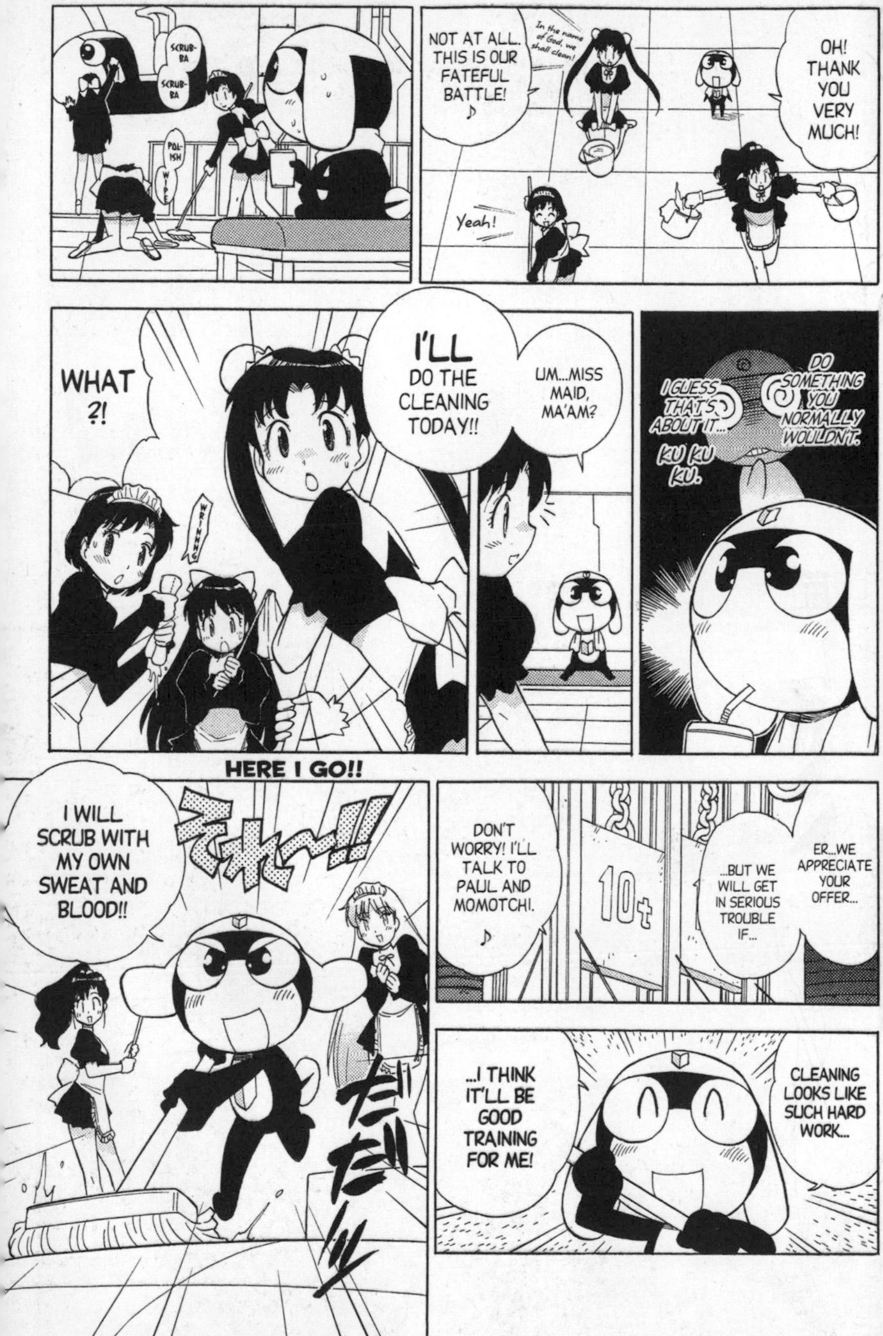
OH! THANK YOU VERY MUCH!
In the name of God, we shall clean!
NOT AT ALL. THIS IS OUR FATEFUL BATTLE! ♪
Yeah!
SCRUB-BA
SCRUB-BA
POL-ISH
WIPE
DO SOMETHING YOU NORMALLY WOULDN'T.
I GUESS THAT'S ABOUT IT...
KU KU KU.
UM...MISS MAID, MA'AM?
I'LL DO THE CLEANING TODAY!!
WHAT ?!
WRINNNG
ER...WE APPRECIATE YOUR OFFER...
...BUT WE WILL GET IN SERIOUS TROUBLE IF...
10t
DON'T WORRY! I'LL TALK TO PAUL AND MOMOTCHI. ♪
CLEANING LOOKS LIKE SUCH HARD WORK...
...I THINK IT'LL BE GOOD TRAINING FOR ME!
HERE I GO!!
それ〜!!
I WILL SCRUB WITH MY OWN SWEAT AND BLOOD!!

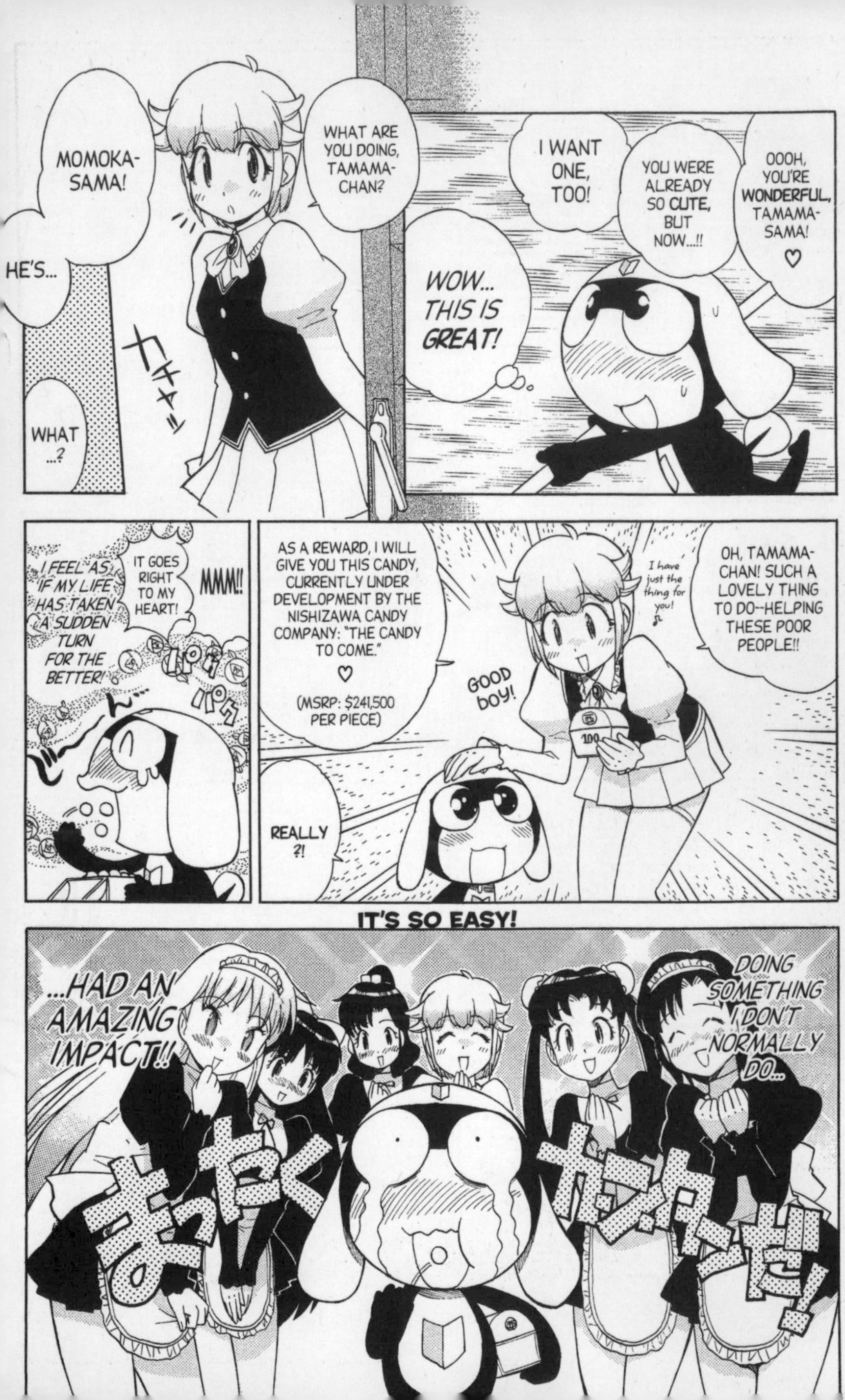
OOOH, YOU'RE WONDERFUL, TAMAMA-SAMA! ♡
YOU WERE ALREADY SO CUTE, BUT NOW...!!
I WANT ONE, TOO!
WOW... THIS IS GREAT!
WHAT ARE YOU DOING, TAMAMA-CHAN?
MOMOKA-SAMA!
HE'S...
WHAT ...?
OH, TAMAMA-CHAN! SUCH A LOVELY THING TO DO--HELPING THESE POOR PEOPLE!!
I have just the thing for you!
AS A REWARD, I WILL GIVE YOU THIS CANDY, CURRENTLY UNDER DEVELOPMENT BY THE NISHIZAWA CANDY COMPANY: "THE CANDY TO COME." ♡
(MSRP: $241,500 PER PIECE)
GOOD boy!
REALLY ?!
MMM!!
IT GOES RIGHT TO MY HEART!
I FEEL AS IF MY LIFE HAS TAKEN A SUDDEN TURN FOR THE BETTER!
IT'S SO EASY!
DOING SOMETHING I DON'T NORMALLY DO...
...HAD AN AMAZING IMPACT!!

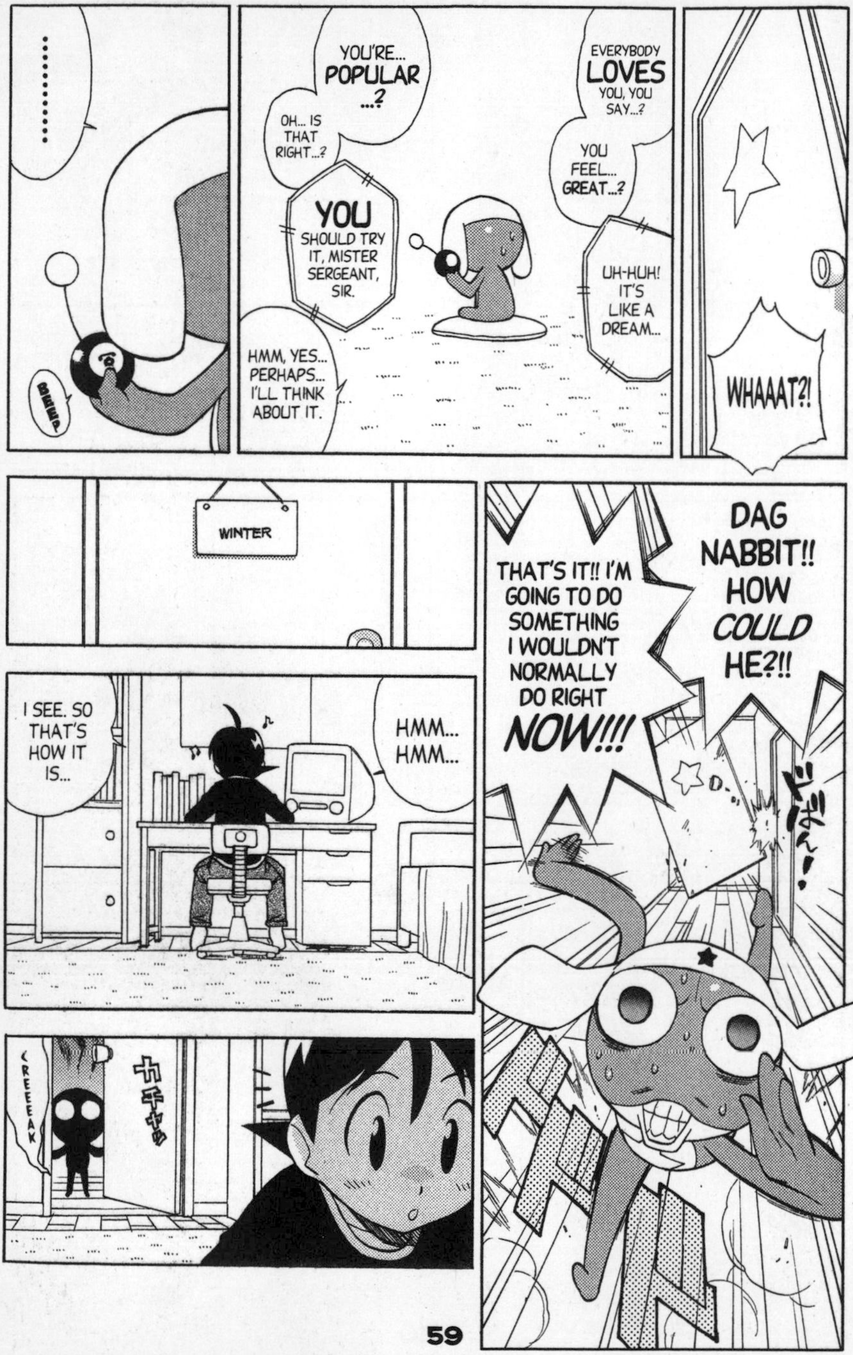
WHAAAT?!
EVERYBODY LOVES YOU, YOU SAY...?
YOU FEEL... GREAT...?
UH-HUH! IT'S LIKE A DREAM...
YOU'RE... POPULAR ...?
OH... IS THAT RIGHT...?
YOU SHOULD TRY IT, MISTER SERGEANT, SIR.
HMM, YES... PERHAPS... I'LL THINK ABOUT IT.
....
BEEP
DAG NABBIT!! HOW COULD HE?!!
THAT'S IT!! I'M GOING TO DO SOMETHING I WOULDN'T NORMALLY DO RIGHT NOW!!!
D...
WINTER
HMM... HMM...
I SEE. SO THAT'S HOW IT IS...
カチャ
CREEEAK

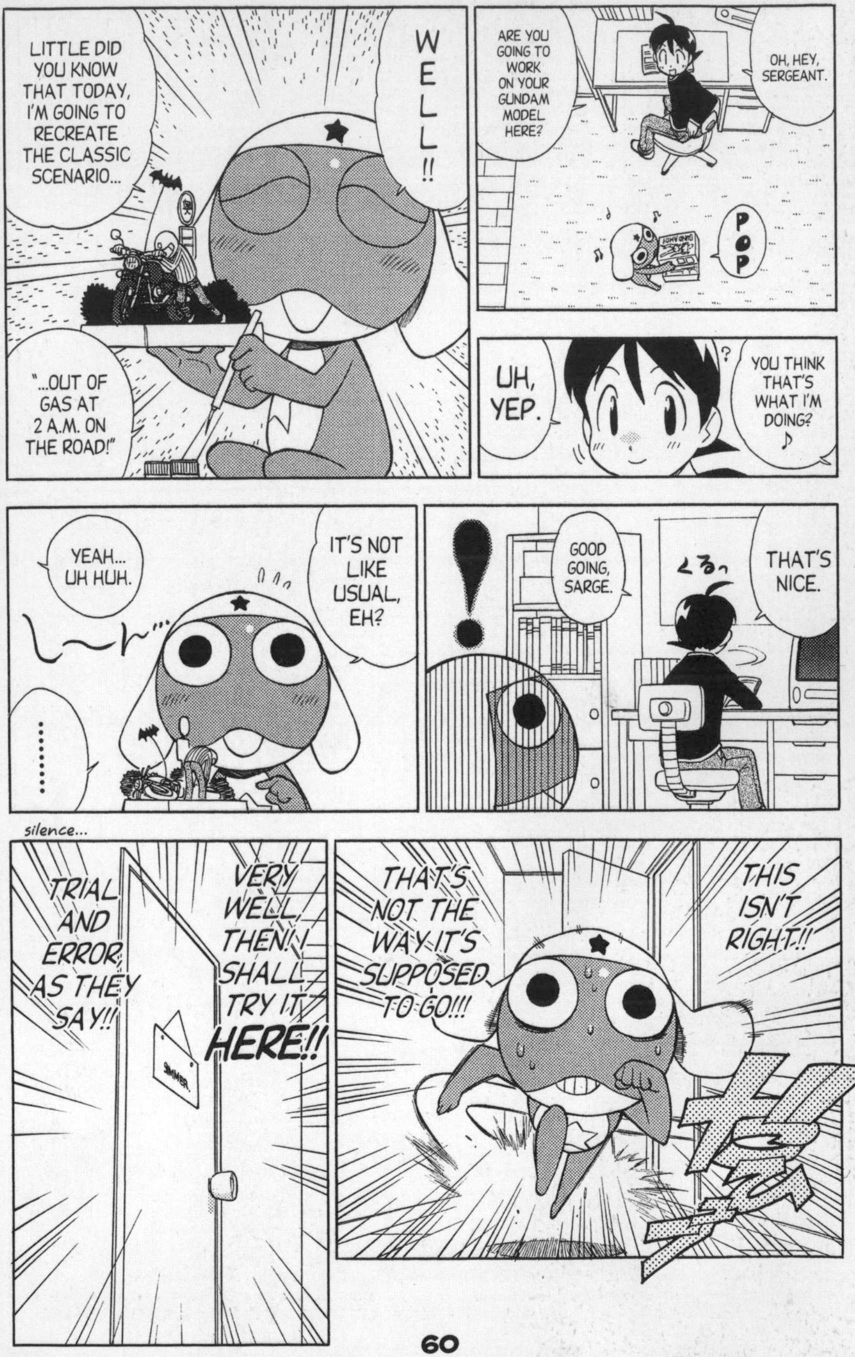
OH, HEY, SERGEANT.
ARE YOU GOING TO WORK ON YOUR GUNDAM MODEL HERE?
POP
YOU THINK THAT'S WHAT I'M DOING? ♪
UH, YEP.
WELL!!
LITTLE DID YOU KNOW THAT TODAY, I'M GOING TO RECREATE THE CLASSIC SCENARIO...
"...OUT OF GAS AT 2 A.M. ON THE ROAD!"
THAT'S NICE.
くるっ
GOOD GOING, SARGE.
!
IT'S NOT LIKE USUAL, EH?
YEAH... UH HUH.
し〜ん…
....
silence...
THIS ISN'T RIGHT!!
THAT'S NOT THE WAY IT'S SUPPOSED TO GO!!!
VERY WELL, THEN! I SHALL TRY IT HERE!!
TRIAL AND ERROR, AS THEY SAY!!

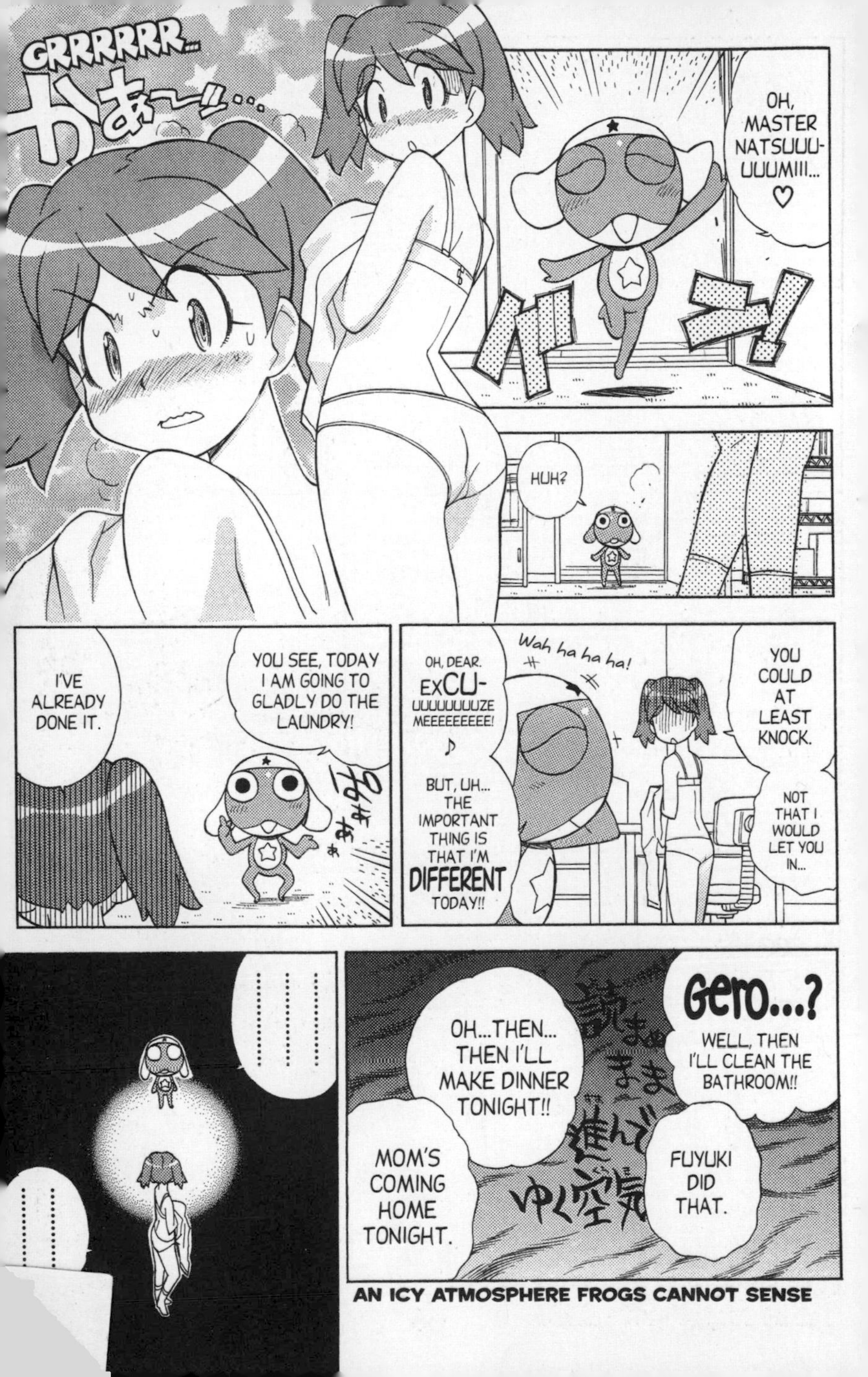
OH, MASTER NATSUUUU-UUUMIII... ♡
HUH?
GRRRRRR...
YOU COULD AT LEAST KNOCK.
NOT THAT I WOULD LET YOU IN...
Wah ha ha ha!
OH, DEAR. EXCU-UUUUUUUUZE MEEEEEEEEE! ♪
BUT, UH... THE IMPORTANT THING IS THAT I'M DIFFERENT TODAY!!
YOU SEE, TODAY I AM GOING TO GLADLY DO THE LAUNDRY!
I'VE ALREADY DONE IT.
Gero...?
WELL, THEN I'LL CLEAN THE BATHROOM!!
FUYUKI DID THAT.
OH...THEN... THEN I'LL MAKE DINNER TONIGHT!!
MOM'S COMING HOME TONIGHT.
......
......
AN ICY ATMOSPHERE FROGS CANNOT SENSE

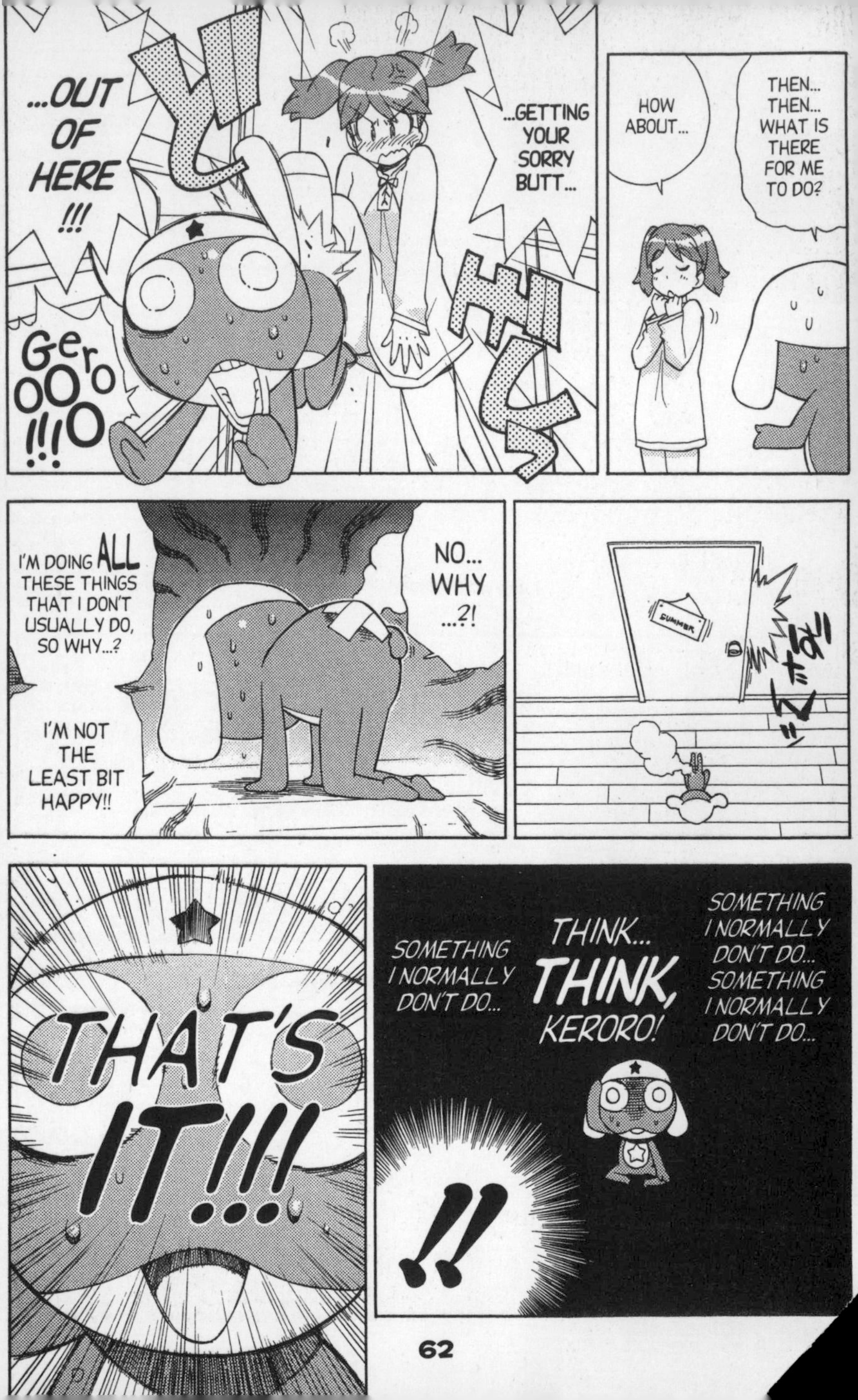
THEN... THEN... WHAT IS THERE FOR ME TO DO?
HOW ABOUT...
...GETTING YOUR SORRY BUTT...
...OUT OF HERE!!!
Gerooooo!!!
SUMMER
NO... WHY ...?!
I'M DOING ALL THESE THINGS THAT I DON'T USUALLY DO, SO WHY...?
I'M NOT THE LEAST BIT HAPPY!!
SOMETHING I NORMALLY DON'T DO... SOMETHING I NORMALLY DON'T DO...
THINK... THINK, KERORO!
SOMETHING I NORMALLY DON'T DO...
!!
THAT'S IT!!!

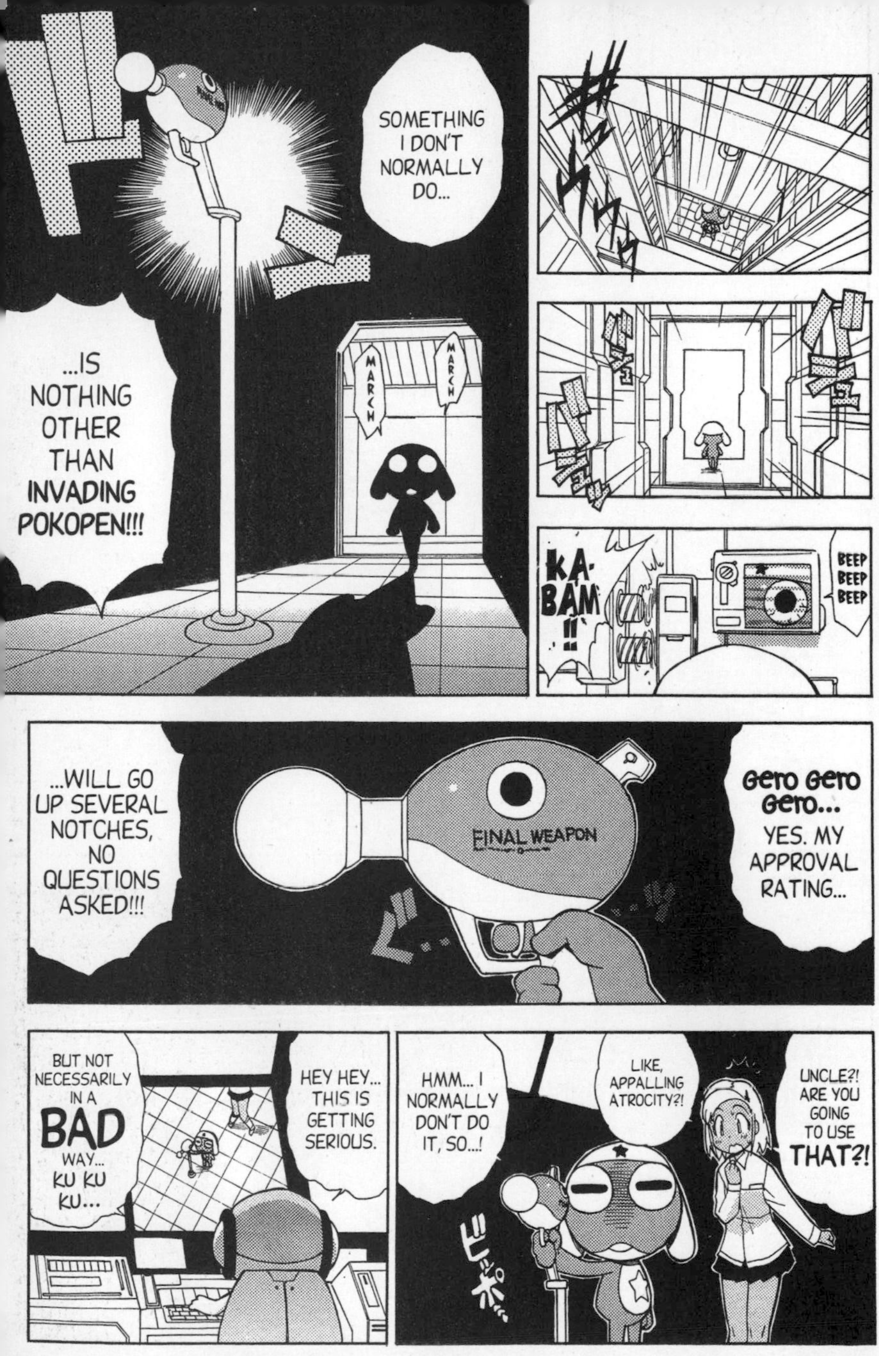
BEEP BEEP BEEP
KA-BAM!!
SOMETHING I DON'T NORMALLY DO...
MARCH
MARCH
...IS NOTHING OTHER THAN INVADING POKOPEN!!!
Gero Gero Gero... YES. MY APPROVAL RATING...
FINAL WEAPON
...WILL GO UP SEVERAL NOTCHES, NO QUESTIONS ASKED!!!
UNCLE?! ARE YOU GOING TO USE THAT?!
LIKE, APPALLING ATROCITY?!
HMM... I NORMALLY DON'T DO IT, SO...!
HEY HEY... THIS IS GETTING SERIOUS.
BUT NOT NECESSARILY IN A BAD WAY... KU KU KU...

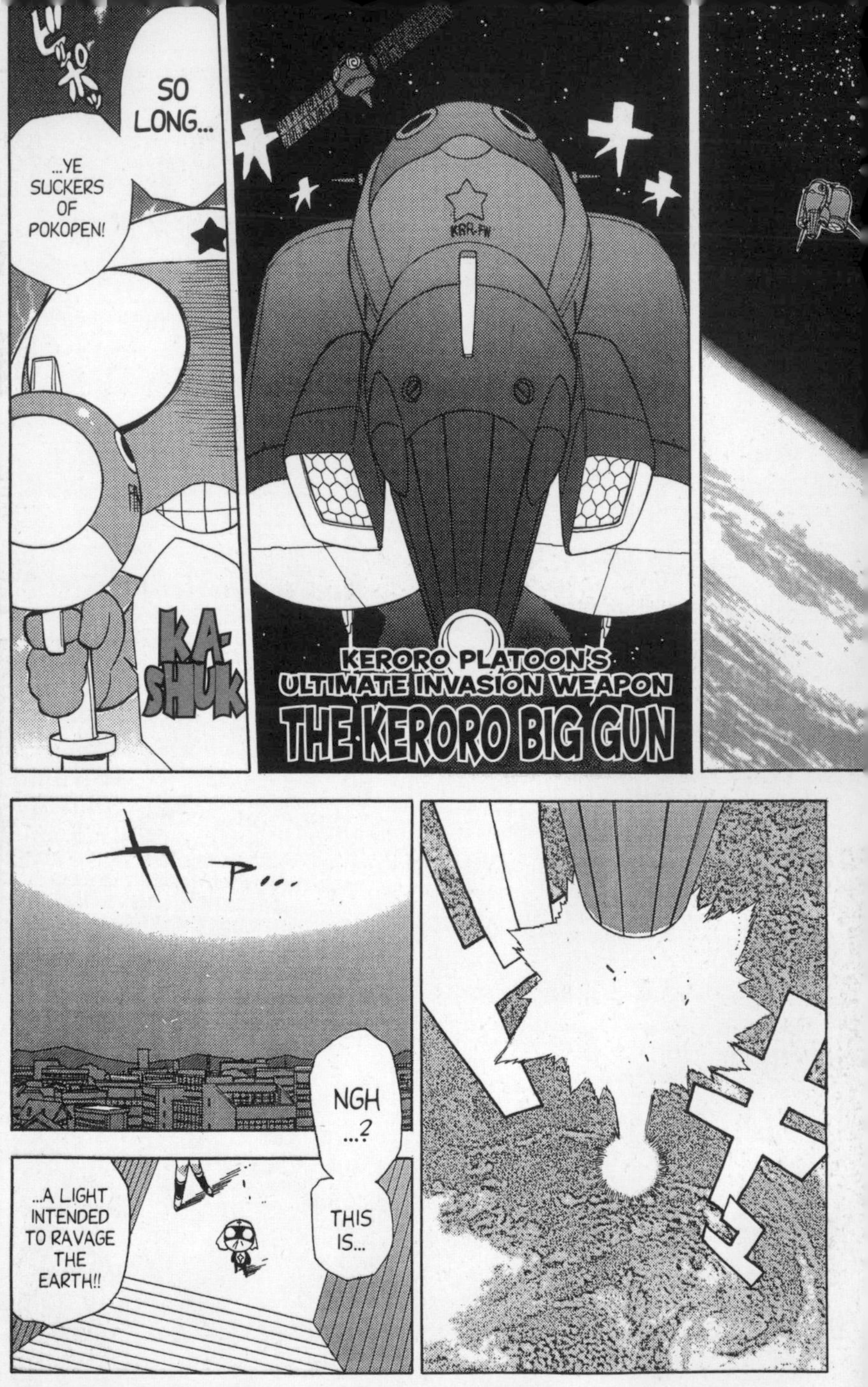
KERORO PLATOON'S
ULTIMATE INVASION WEAPON
THE KERORO BIG GUN
SO LONG...
...YE SUCKERS OF POKOPEN!
KA-SHUK
NGH ...?
THIS IS...
...A LIGHT INTENDED TO RAVAGE THE EARTH!!

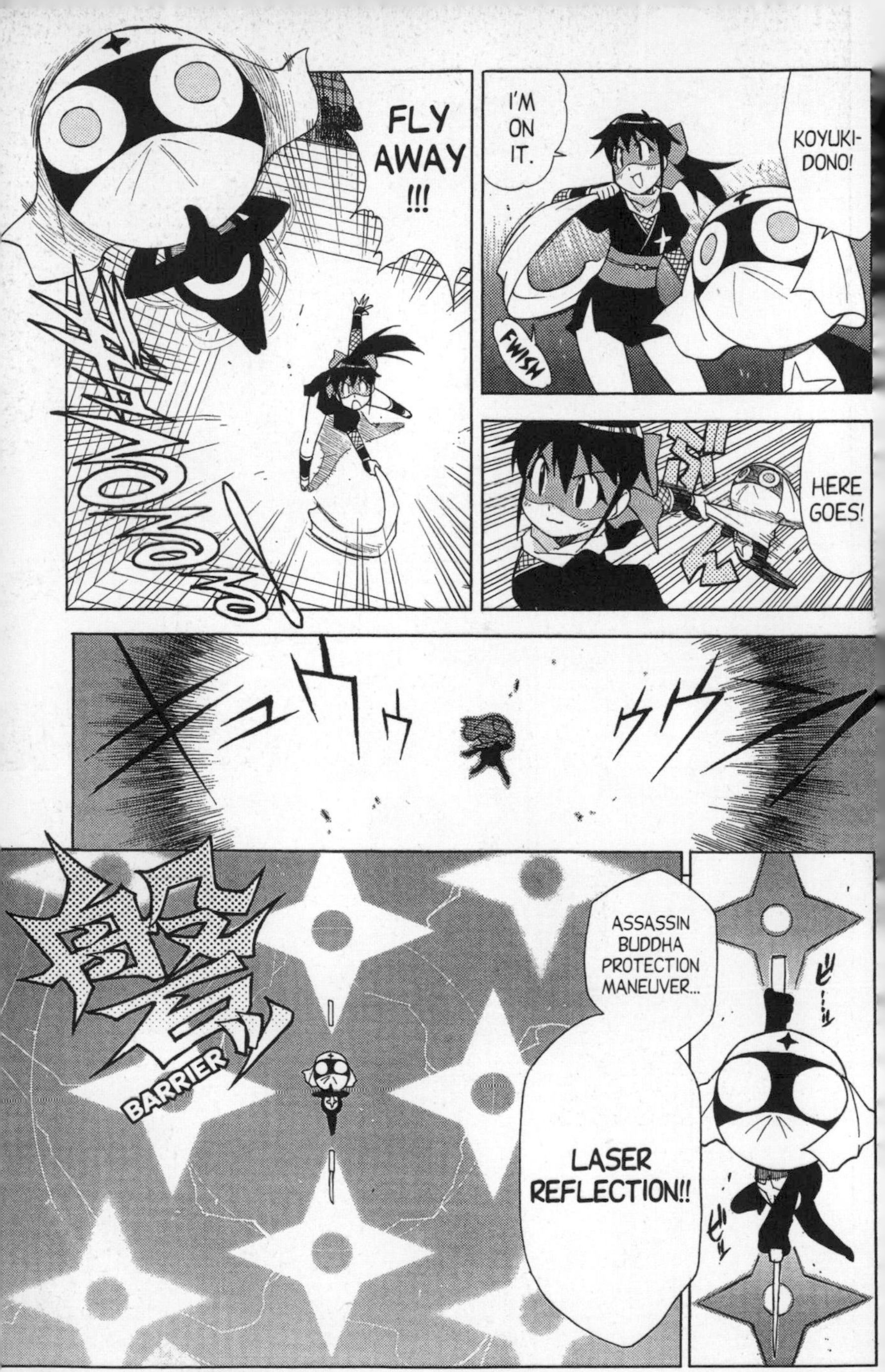
KOYUKI-DONO!
I'M ON IT.
FWISH
HERE GOES!
FLY AWAY!!!
ASSASSIN BUDDHA PROTECTION MANEUVER...
LASER REFLECTION!!
BARRIER

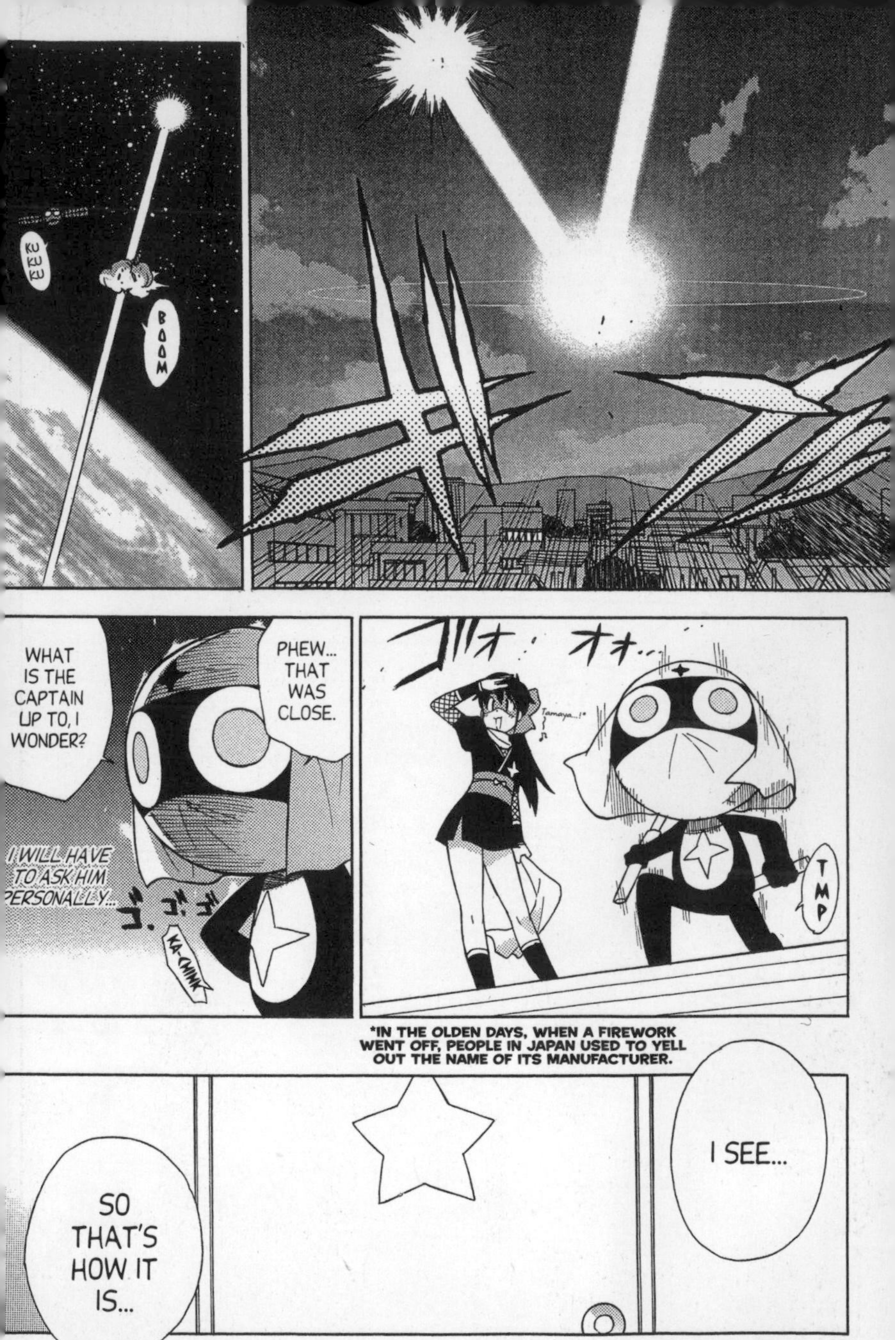
KU KU KU
BOOM
Tamaya...!*
TMP
PHEW... THAT WAS CLOSE.
WHAT IS THE CAPTAIN UP TO, I WONDER?
I WILL HAVE TO ASK HIM PERSONALLY...
KA-CHINK
*IN THE OLDEN DAYS, WHEN A FIREWORK WENT OFF, PEOPLE IN JAPAN USED TO YELL OUT THE NAME OF ITS MANUFACTURER.
I SEE...
SO THAT'S HOW IT IS...

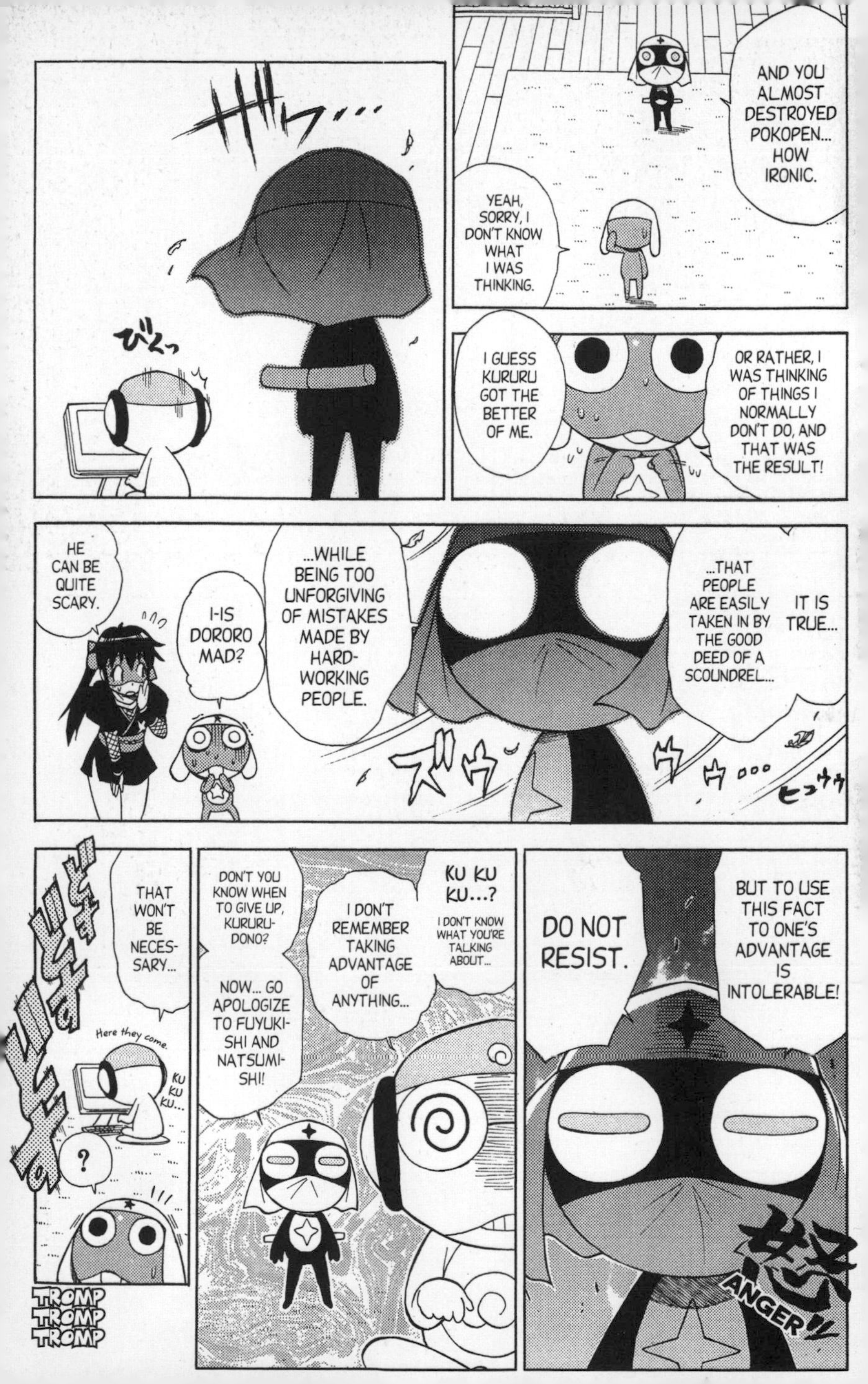
AND YOU ALMOST DESTROYED POKOPEN... HOW IRONIC.
YEAH, SORRY, I DON'T KNOW WHAT I WAS THINKING.
OR RATHER, I WAS THINKING OF THINGS I NORMALLY DON'T DO, AND THAT WAS THE RESULT!
I GUESS KURURU GOT THE BETTER OF ME.
IT IS TRUE...
...THAT PEOPLE ARE EASILY TAKEN IN BY THE GOOD DEED OF A SCOUNDREL...
...WHILE BEING TOO UNFORGIVING OF MISTAKES MADE BY HARD-WORKING PEOPLE.
I-IS DORORO MAD?
HE CAN BE QUITE SCARY.
BUT TO USE THIS FACT TO ONE'S ADVANTAGE IS INTOLERABLE!
DO NOT RESIST.
ANGER!!
KU KU KU...?
I DON'T KNOW WHAT YOU'RE TALKING ABOUT...
I DON'T REMEMBER TAKING ADVANTAGE OF ANYTHING...
DON'T YOU KNOW WHEN TO GIVE UP, KURURU-DONO?
NOW... GO APOLOGIZE TO FUYUKI-SHI AND NATSUMI-SHI!
THAT WON'T BE NECES-SARY...
Here they come.
KU KU KU...
?
TROMP TROMP TROMP

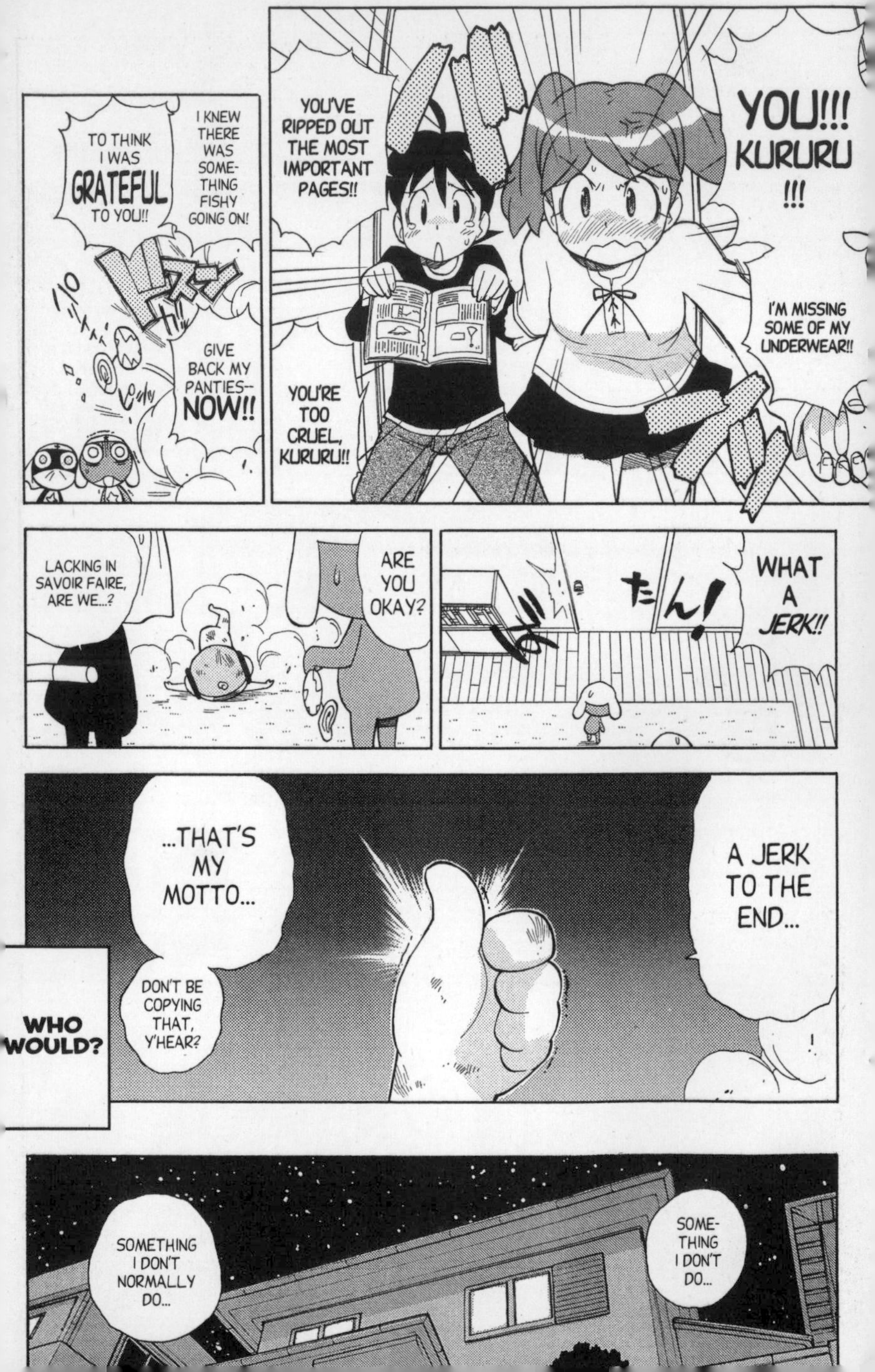
YOU!!! KURURU !!!
YOU'VE RIPPED OUT THE MOST IMPORTANT PAGES!!
I'M MISSING SOME OF MY UNDERWEAR!!
YOU'RE TOO CRUEL, KURURU!!
I KNEW THERE WAS SOME-THING FISHY GOING ON!
TO THINK I WAS GRATEFUL TO YOU!!
GIVE BACK MY PANTIES-- NOW!!
WHAT A JERK!!
たん!
ARE YOU OKAY?
LACKING IN SAVOIR FAIRE, ARE WE...?
A JERK TO THE END...
...THAT'S MY MOTTO...
DON'T BE COPYING THAT, Y'HEAR?
WHO WOULD?
SOME-THING I DON'T DO...
SOMETHING I DON'T NORMALLY DO...

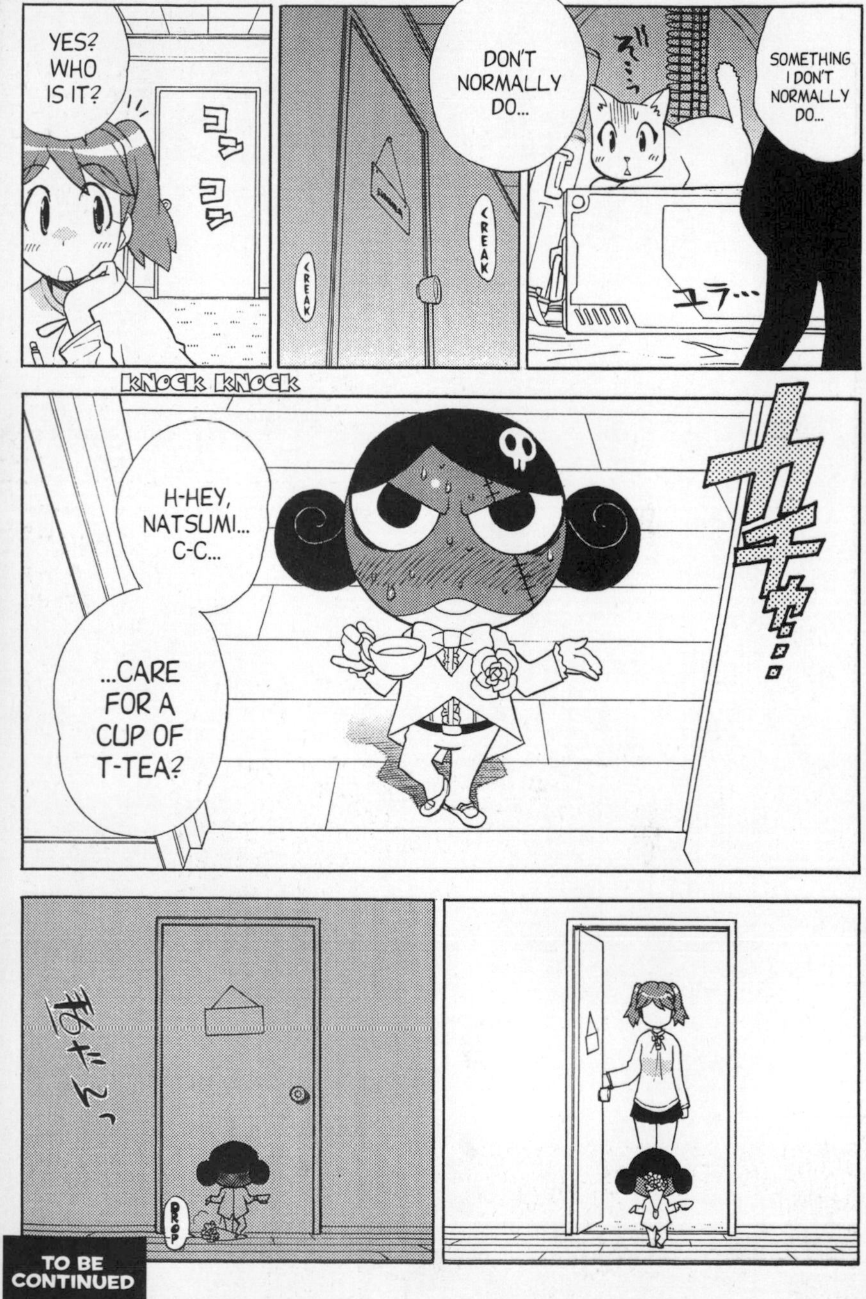
SOMETHING I DON'T NORMALLY DO...
ユラ…
DON'T NORMALLY DO...
CREAK
CREAK
YES? WHO IS IT?
コンコン
KNOCK KNOCK
H-HEY, NATSUMI... C-C...
...CARE FOR A CUP OF T-TEA?
DROP
TO BE CONTINUED

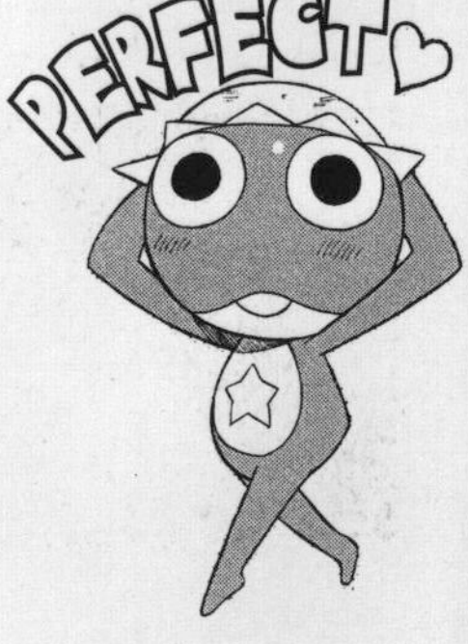
PERFECT♥

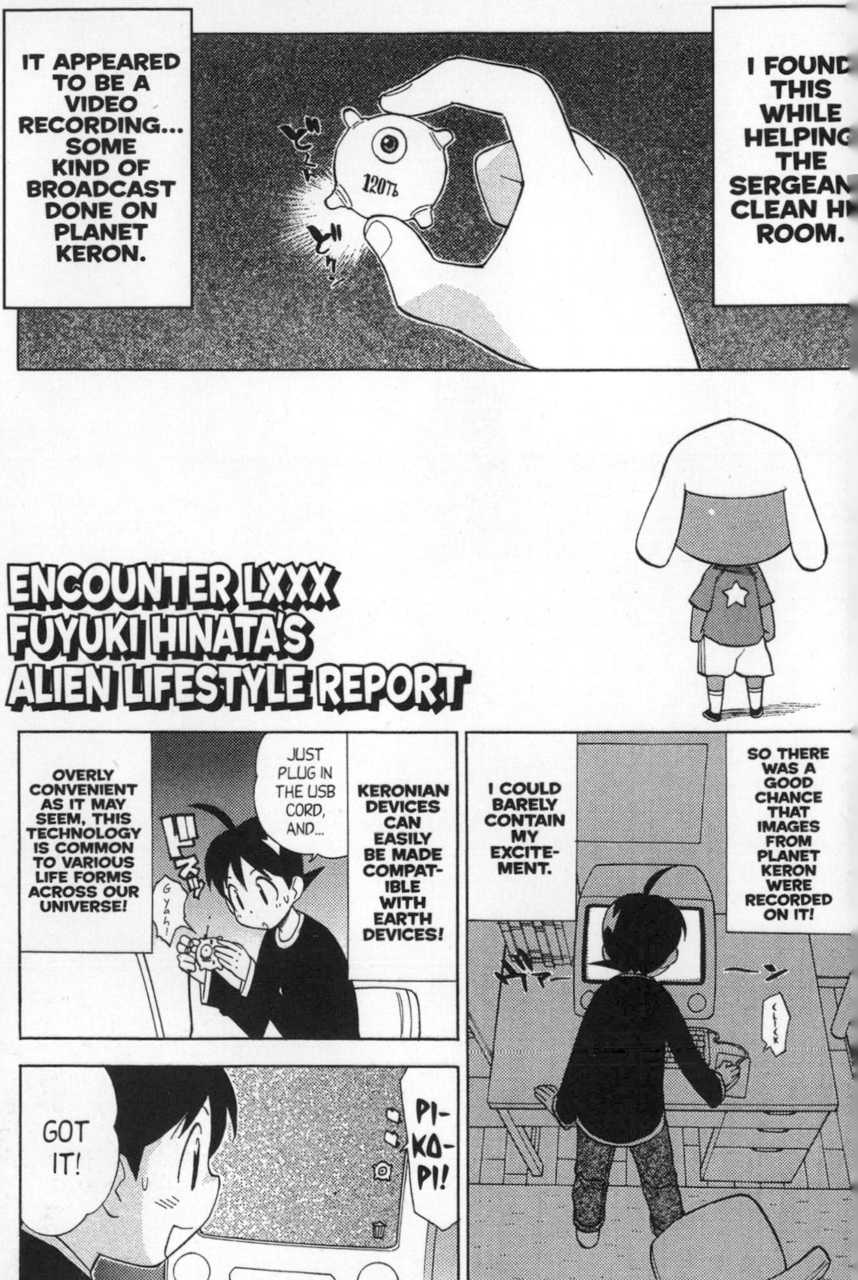
I FOUND THIS WHILE HELPING THE SERGEAN CLEAN H ROOM.
120Tb
IT APPEARED TO BE A VIDEO RECORDING... SOME KIND OF BROADCAST DONE ON PLANET KERON.
ENCOUNTER LXXX FUYUKI HINATA'S ALIEN LIFESTYLE REPORT
SO THERE WAS A GOOD CHANCE THAT IMAGES FROM PLANET KERON WERE RECORDED ON IT!
I COULD BARELY CONTAIN MY EXCITEMENT.
CLICK
KERONIAN DEVICES CAN EASILY BE MADE COMPATIBLE WITH EARTH DEVICES!
JUST PLUG IN THE USB CORD, AND...
Gyah!
OVERLY CONVENIENT AS IT MAY SEEM, THIS TECHNOLOGY IS COMMON TO VARIOUS LIFE FORMS ACROSS OUR UNIVERSE!
PI-KO-PI!
GOT IT!

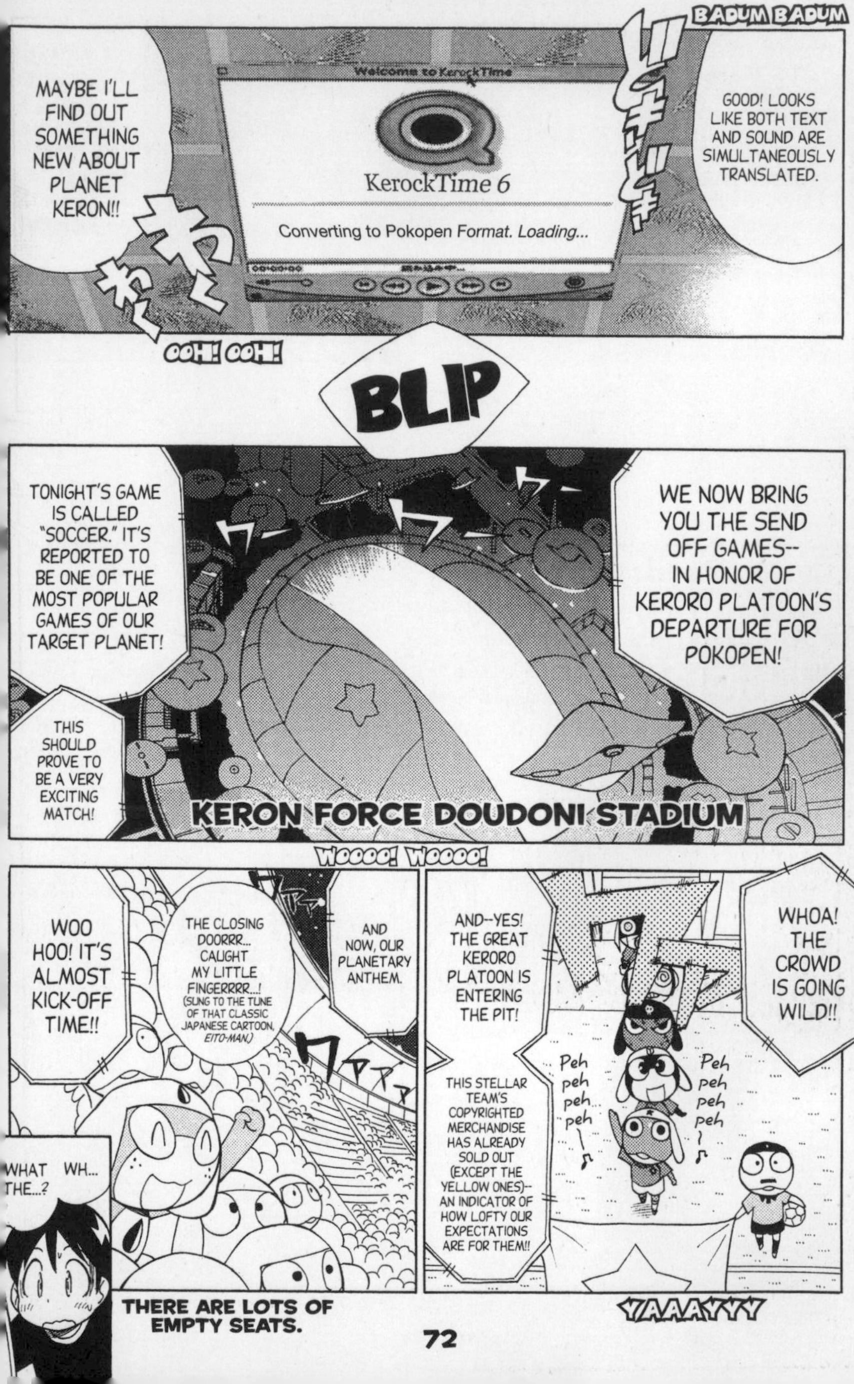
BADUM BADUM
GOOD! LOOKS LIKE BOTH TEXT AND SOUND ARE SIMULTANEOUSLY TRANSLATED.
Welcome to KerockTime
KerockTime 6
Converting to Pokopen Format. Loading...
MAYBE I'LL FIND OUT SOMETHING NEW ABOUT PLANET KERON!!
OOH! OOH!
BLIP
WE NOW BRING YOU THE SEND OFF GAMES-- IN HONOR OF KERORO PLATOON'S DEPARTURE FOR POKOPEN!
TONIGHT'S GAME IS CALLED "SOCCER." IT'S REPORTED TO BE ONE OF THE MOST POPULAR GAMES OF OUR TARGET PLANET!
THIS SHOULD PROVE TO BE A VERY EXCITING MATCH!
KERON FORCE DOUDONI STADIUM
WOOOO! WOOOO!
WHOA! THE CROWD IS GOING WILD!!
AND--YES! THE GREAT KERORO PLATOON IS ENTERING THE PIT!
THIS STELLAR TEAM'S COPYRIGHTED MERCHANDISE HAS ALREADY SOLD OUT (EXCEPT THE YELLOW ONES)-- AN INDICATOR OF HOW LOFTY OUR EXPECTATIONS ARE FOR THEM!!
Peh peh peh peh
Peh peh peh peh
YAAAYYY
AND NOW, OUR PLANETARY ANTHEM.
THE CLOSING DOORRR... CAUGHT MY LITTLE FINGERRRR...! (SUNG TO THE TUNE OF THAT CLASSIC JAPANESE CARTOON, EITO-MAN.)
WOO HOO! IT'S ALMOST KICK-OFF TIME!!
WH...
WHAT THE...?
THERE ARE LOTS OF EMPTY SEATS.

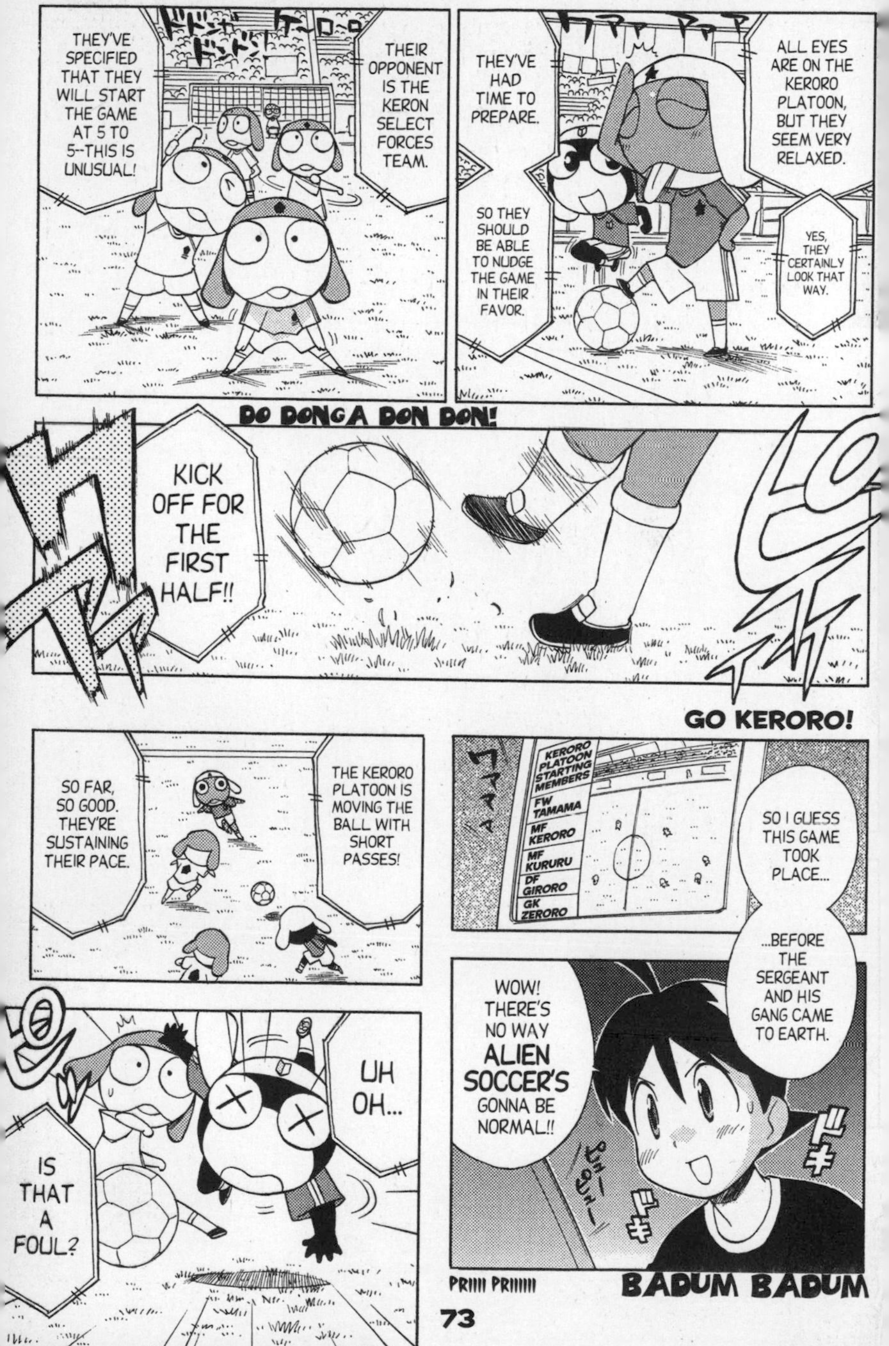

ALL EYES ARE ON THE KERORO PLATOON, BUT THEY SEEM VERY RELAXED.
THEY'VE HAD TIME TO PREPARE.
YES, THEY CERTAINLY LOOK THAT WAY.
SO THEY SHOULD BE ABLE TO NUDGE THE GAME IN THEIR FAVOR.
THEIR OPPONENT IS THE KERON SELECT FORCES TEAM.
THEY'VE SPECIFIED THAT THEY WILL START THE GAME AT 5 TO 5--THIS IS UNUSUAL!
DO DONGA DON DON!
GO KERORO!
KICK OFF FOR THE FIRST HALF!!
KERORO PLATOON STARTING MEMBERS
FW TAMAMA
MF KERORO
MF KURURU
DF GIRORO
GK ZERORO
SO I GUESS THIS GAME TOOK PLACE...
THE KERORO PLATOON IS MOVING THE BALL WITH SHORT PASSES!
SO FAR, SO GOOD. THEY'RE SUSTAINING THEIR PACE.
...BEFORE THE SERGEANT AND HIS GANG CAME TO EARTH.
WOW! THERE'S NO WAY ALIEN SOCCER'S GONNA BE NORMAL!!
BADUM BADUM
UH OH...
IS THAT A FOUL?
PRIIII PRIIIIII

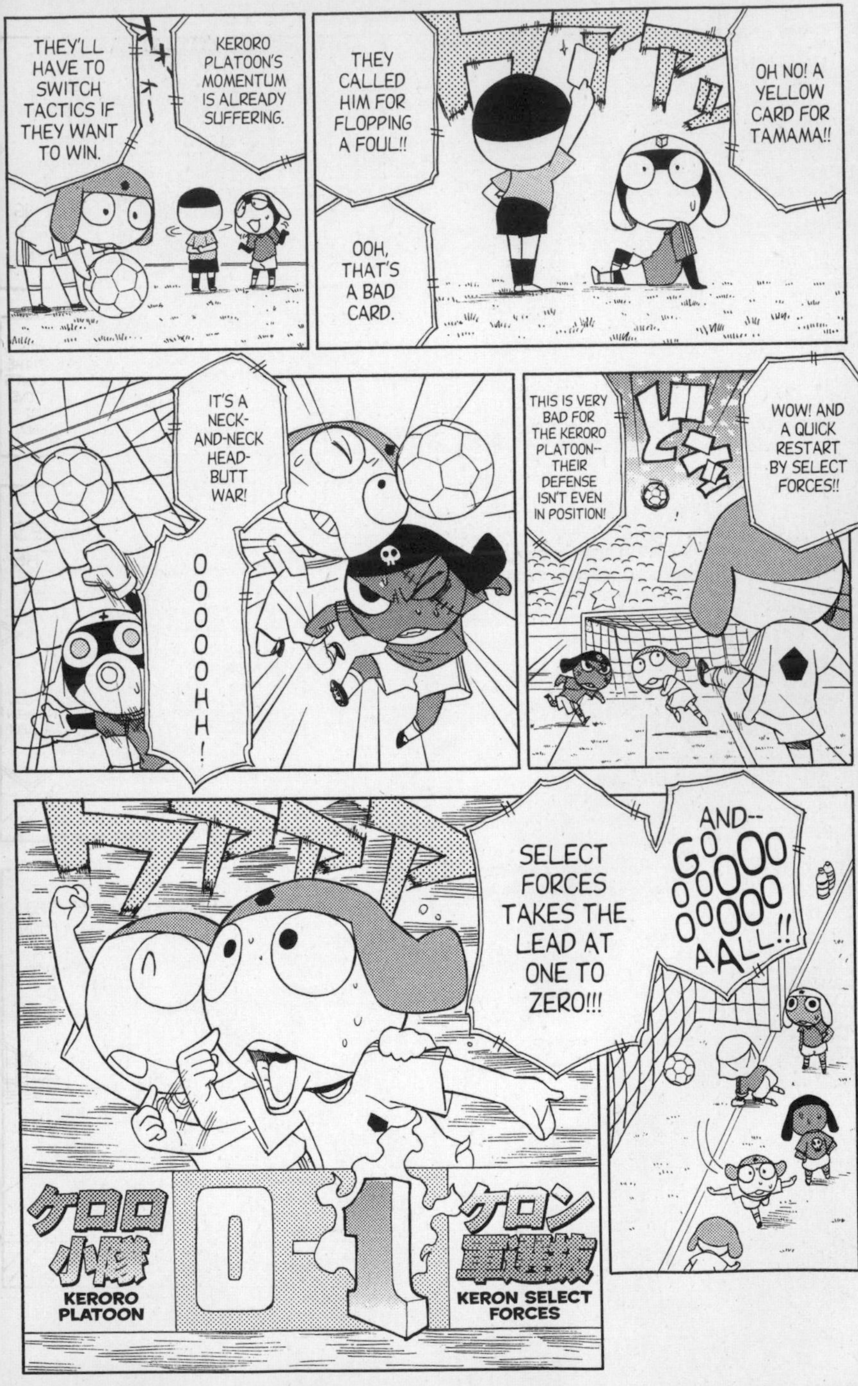
OH NO! A YELLOW CARD FOR TAMAMA!!
THEY CALLED HIM FOR FLOPPING A FOUL!!
OOH, THAT'S A BAD CARD.
KERORO PLATOON'S MOMENTUM IS ALREADY SUFFERING.
THEY'LL HAVE TO SWITCH TACTICS IF THEY WANT TO WIN.
WOW! AND A QUICK RESTART BY SELECT FORCES!!
THIS IS VERY BAD FOR THE KERORO PLATOON--THEIR DEFENSE ISN'T EVEN IN POSITION!
IT'S A NECK-AND-NECK HEAD-BUTT WAR!
OOOOOOHH!
AND-- GOOOOOOOOOOOOOOAALL!!
SELECT FORCES TAKES THE LEAD AT ONE TO ZERO!!!
ケロロ小隊
KERORO PLATOON
0-1
ケロン軍選抜
KERON SELECT FORCES

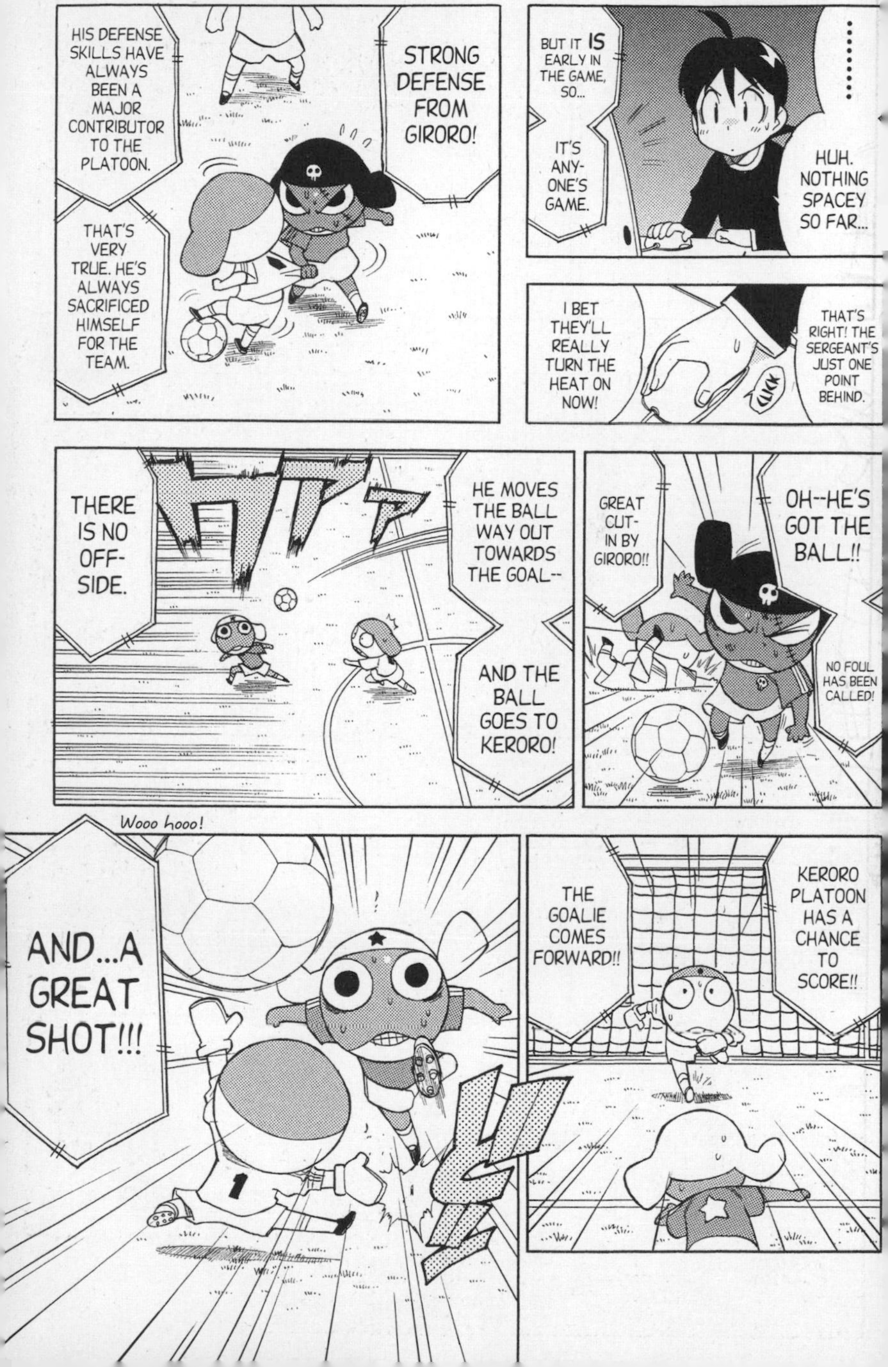

......
HUH. NOTHING SPACEY SO FAR...
BUT IT IS EARLY IN THE GAME, SO...
IT'S ANY-ONE'S GAME.
THAT'S RIGHT! THE SERGEANT'S JUST ONE POINT BEHIND.
CLICK
I BET THEY'LL REALLY TURN THE HEAT ON NOW!
STRONG DEFENSE FROM GIRORO!
HIS DEFENSE SKILLS HAVE ALWAYS BEEN A MAJOR CONTRIBUTOR TO THE PLATOON.
THAT'S VERY TRUE. HE'S ALWAYS SACRIFICED HIMSELF FOR THE TEAM.
OH--HE'S GOT THE BALL!!
GREAT CUT-IN BY GIRORO!!
NO FOUL HAS BEEN CALLED!
HE MOVES THE BALL WAY OUT TOWARDS THE GOAL--
AND THE BALL GOES TO KERORO!
THERE IS NO OFF-SIDE.
KERORO PLATOON HAS A CHANCE TO SCORE!!
THE GOALIE COMES FORWARD!!
Wooo hooo!
!
AND...A GREAT SHOT!!!

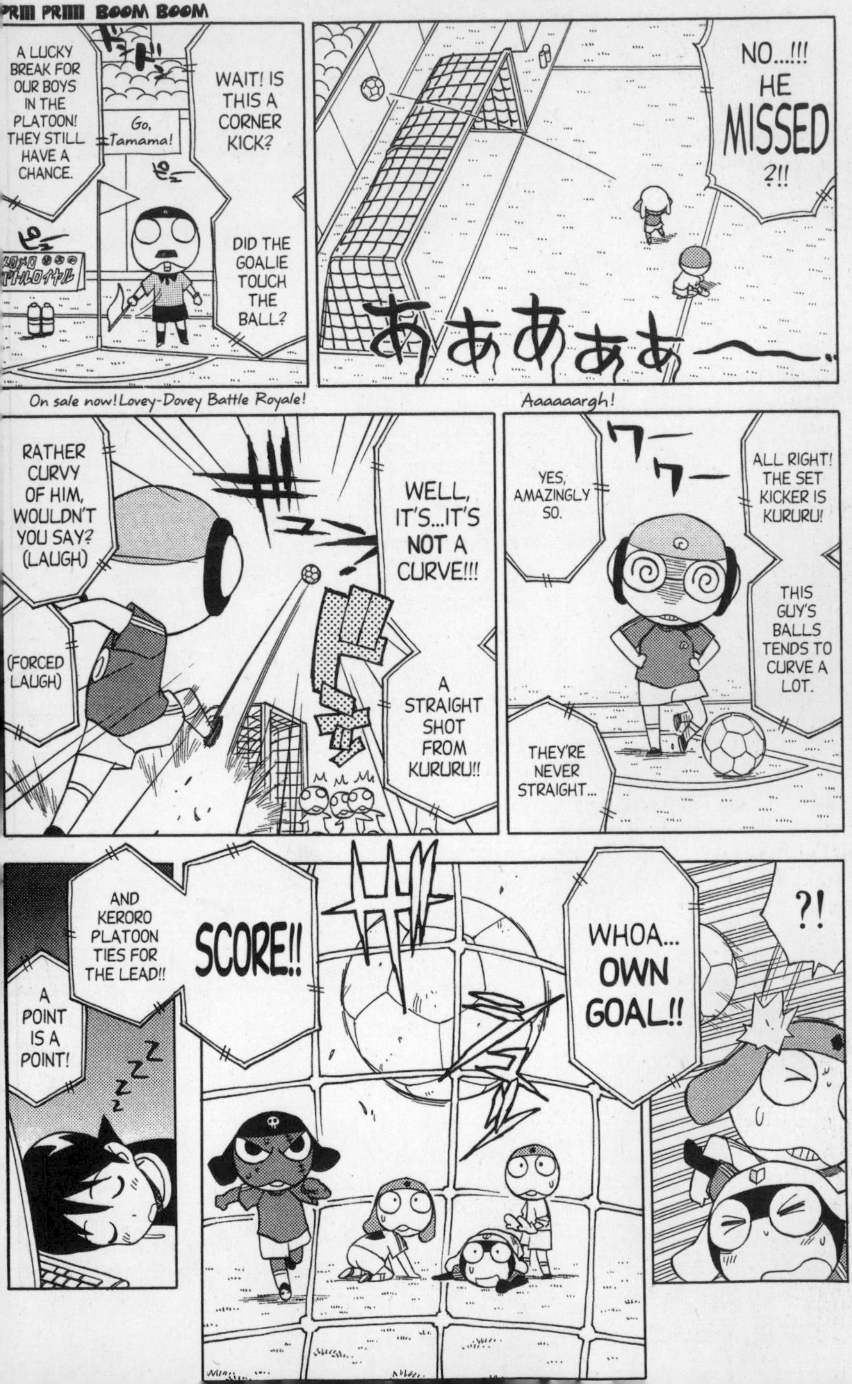
NO...!!! HE MISSED ?!!
ああああぁ～～..
Aaaaaargh!
WAIT! IS THIS A CORNER KICK?
A LUCKY BREAK FOR OUR BOYS IN THE PLATOON! THEY STILL HAVE A CHANCE.
Go, Tamama!
DID THE GOALIE TOUCH THE BALL?
On sale now! Lovey-Dovey Battle Royale!
ALL RIGHT! THE SET KICKER IS KURURU!
YES, AMAZINGLY SO.
THIS GUY'S BALLS TENDS TO CURVE A LOT.
THEY'RE NEVER STRAIGHT...
WELL, IT'S...IT'S NOT A CURVE!!!
RATHER CURVY OF HIM, WOULDN'T YOU SAY? (LAUGH)
A STRAIGHT SHOT FROM KURURU!!
(FORCED LAUGH)
?!
WHOA... OWN GOAL!!
SCORE!!
AND KERORO PLATOON TIES FOR THE LEAD!!
A POINT IS A POINT!

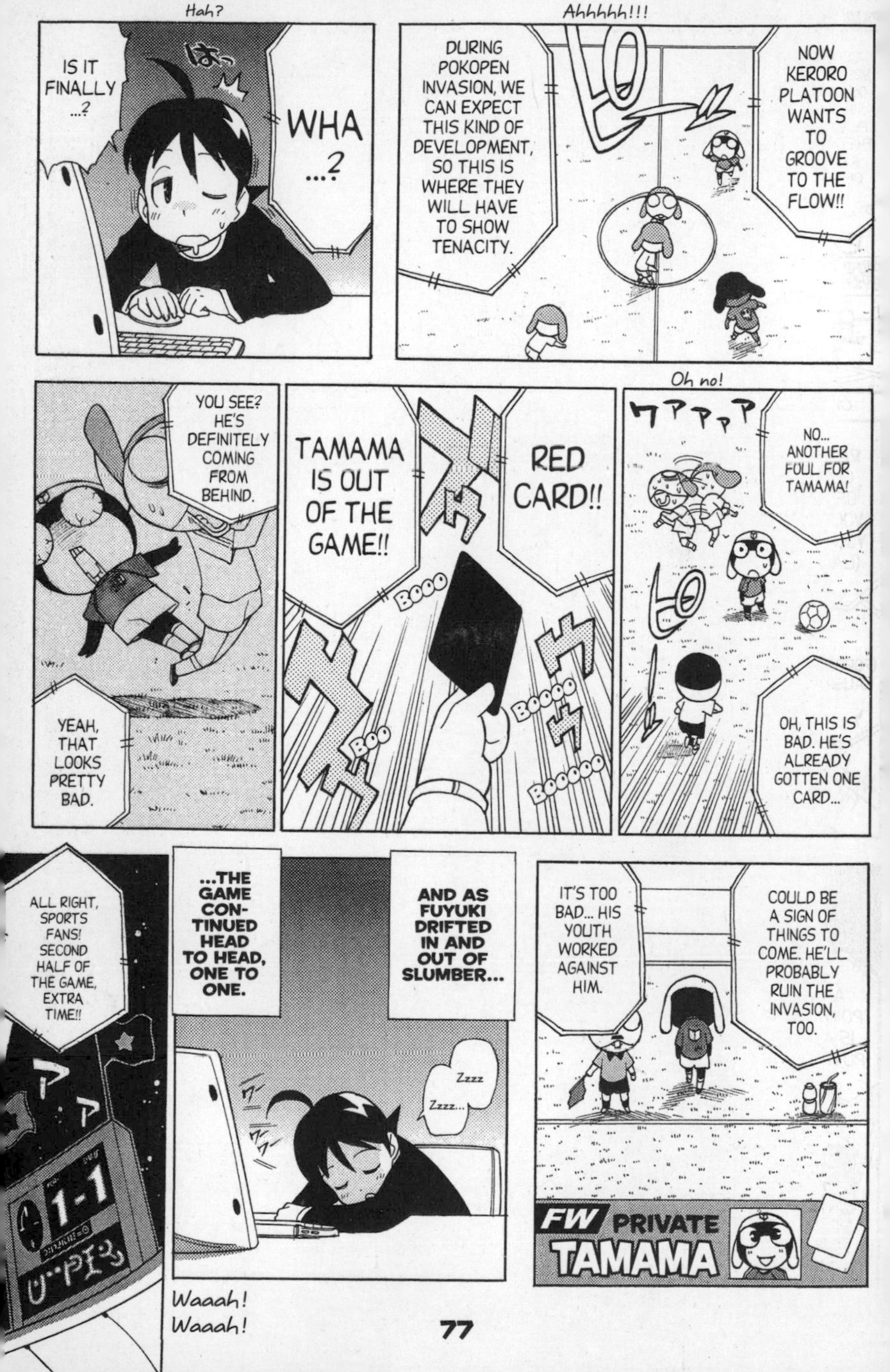

Ahhhhh!!!
NOW KERORO PLATOON WANTS TO GROOVE TO THE FLOW!!
DURING POKOPEN INVASION, WE CAN EXPECT THIS KIND OF DEVELOPMENT, SO THIS IS WHERE THEY WILL HAVE TO SHOW TENACITY.
Hah?
WHA ...?
IS IT FINALLY ...?
Oh no!
NO... ANOTHER FOUL FOR TAMAMA!
OH, THIS IS BAD. HE'S ALREADY GOTTEN ONE CARD...
RED CARD!!
TAMAMA IS OUT OF THE GAME!!
BOOO
BOOOO
BOOOOO
BOO
YOU SEE? HE'S DEFINITELY COMING FROM BEHIND.
YEAH, THAT LOOKS PRETTY BAD.
COULD BE A SIGN OF THINGS TO COME. HE'LL PROBABLY RUIN THE INVASION, TOO.
IT'S TOO BAD... HIS YOUTH WORKED AGAINST HIM.
FW PRIVATE TAMAMA
AND AS FUYUKI DRIFTED IN AND OUT OF SLUMBER...
...THE GAME CONTINUED HEAD TO HEAD, ONE TO ONE.
Zzzz
Zzzz...
Waaah!
Waaah!
ALL RIGHT, SPORTS FANS! SECOND HALF OF THE GAME, EXTRA TIME!!
1-1

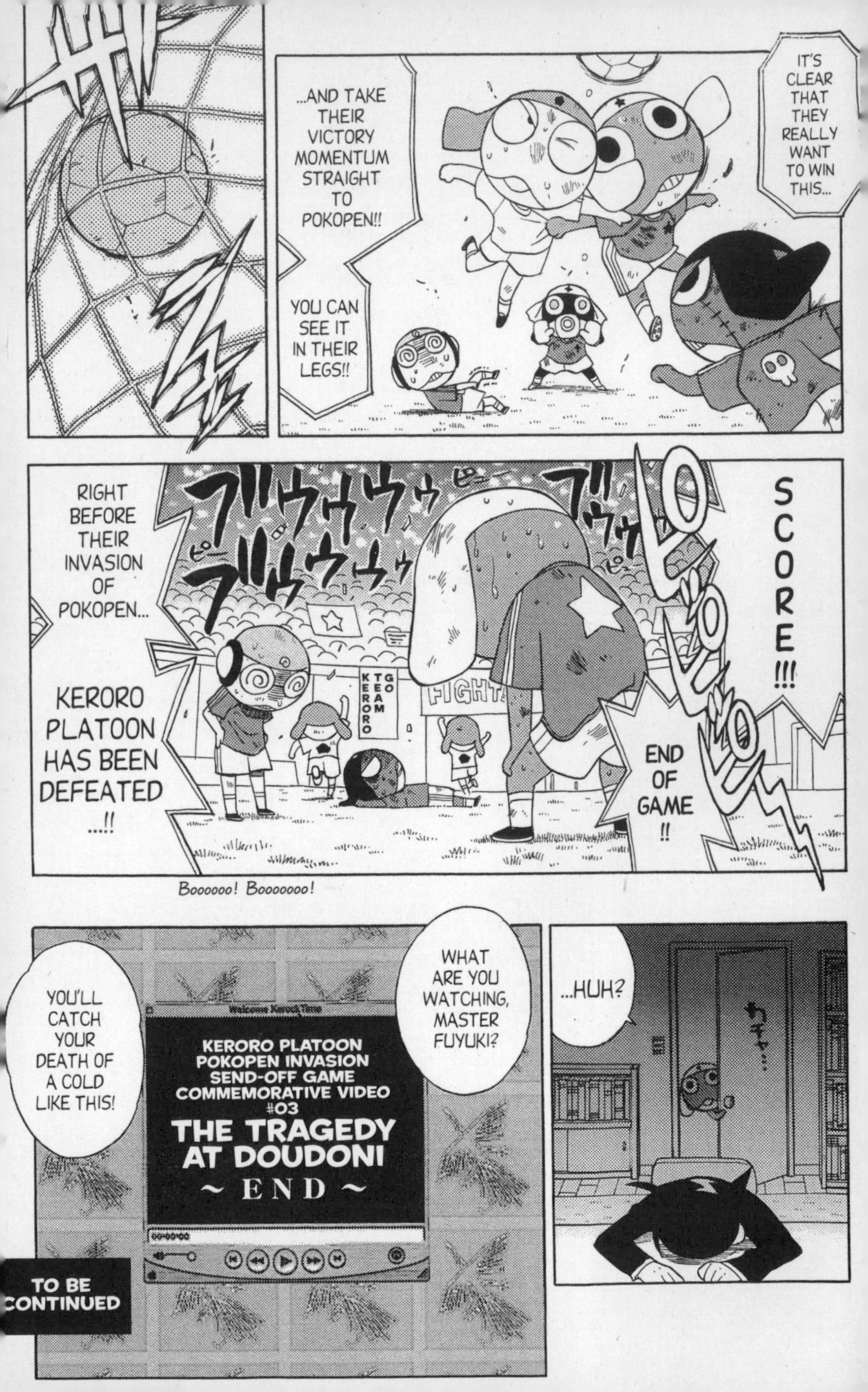
IT'S CLEAR THAT THEY REALLY WANT TO WIN THIS...
...AND TAKE THEIR VICTORY MOMENTUM STRAIGHT TO POKOPEN!!
YOU CAN SEE IT IN THEIR LEGS!!
SCORE!!!
END OF GAME !!
RIGHT BEFORE THEIR INVASION OF POKOPEN...
KERORO TEAM GO
FIGHT!
KERORO PLATOON HAS BEEN DEFEATED ...!!
Booooooo! Boooooooo!
...HUH?
WHAT ARE YOU WATCHING, MASTER FUYUKI?
YOU'LL CATCH YOUR DEATH OF A COLD LIKE THIS!
KERORO PLATOON POKOPEN INVASION SEND-OFF GAME COMMEMORATIVE VIDEO #03
THE TRAGEDY AT DOUDONI
~ END ~
TO BE CONTINUED

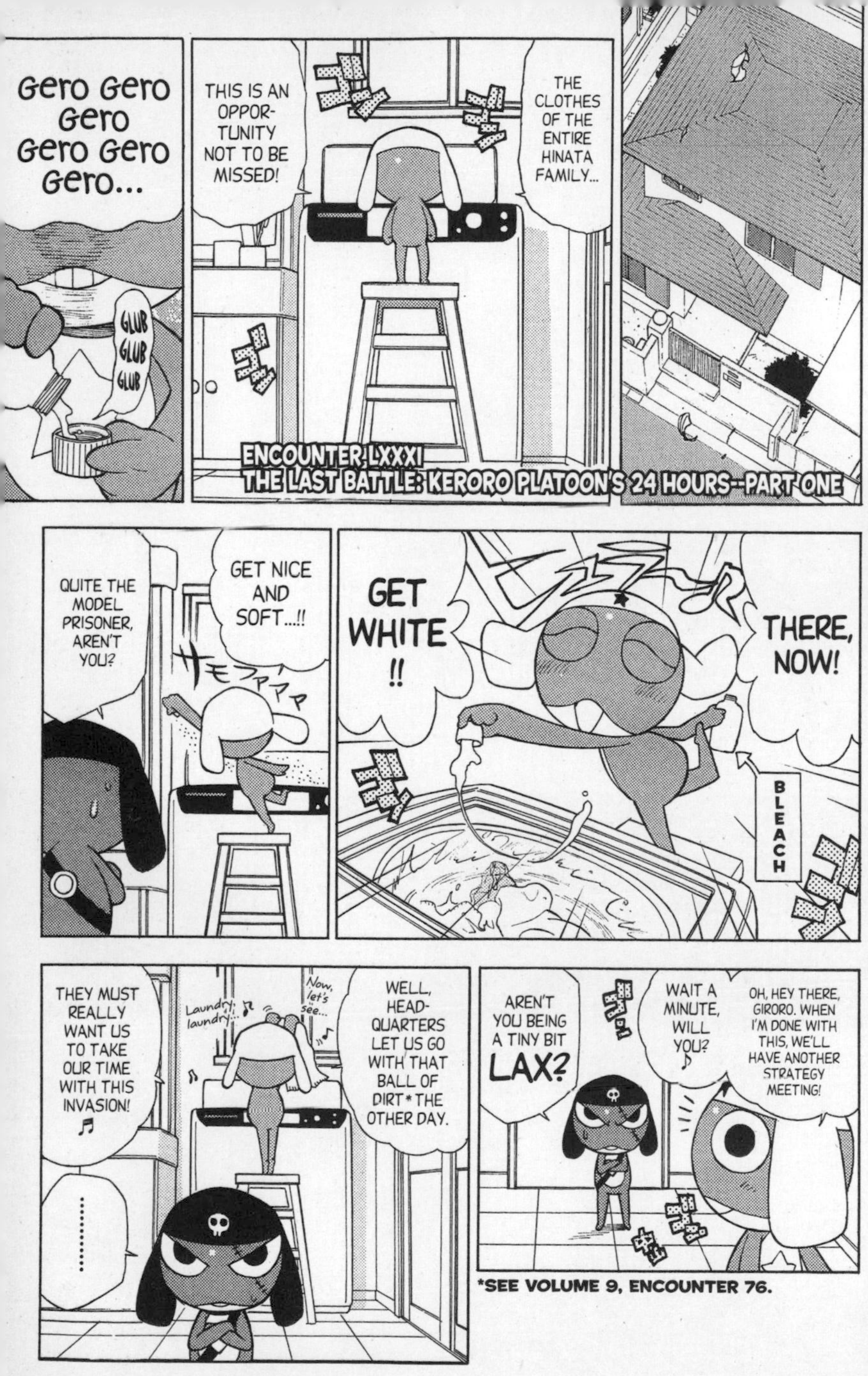

THE CLOTHES OF THE ENTIRE HINATA FAMILY...
THIS IS AN OPPORTUNITY NOT TO BE MISSED!
Gero Gero Gero Gero Gero Gero...
GLUB GLUB GLUB
ENCOUNTER LXXXI
THE LAST BATTLE: KERORO PLATOON'S 24 HOURS--PART ONE
THERE, NOW!
GET WHITE !!
BLEACH
GET NICE AND SOFT...!!
QUITE THE MODEL PRISONER, AREN'T YOU?
OH, HEY THERE, GIRORO. WHEN I'M DONE WITH THIS, WE'LL HAVE ANOTHER STRATEGY MEETING!
WAIT A MINUTE, WILL YOU? ♪
AREN'T YOU BEING A TINY BIT LAX?
WELL, HEADQUARTERS LET US GO WITH THAT BALL OF DIRT* THE OTHER DAY.
Now, let's see...
Laundry, laundry... ♪
THEY MUST REALLY WANT US TO TAKE OUR TIME WITH THIS INVASION! ♪
....

*SEE VOLUME 9, ENCOUNTER 76.

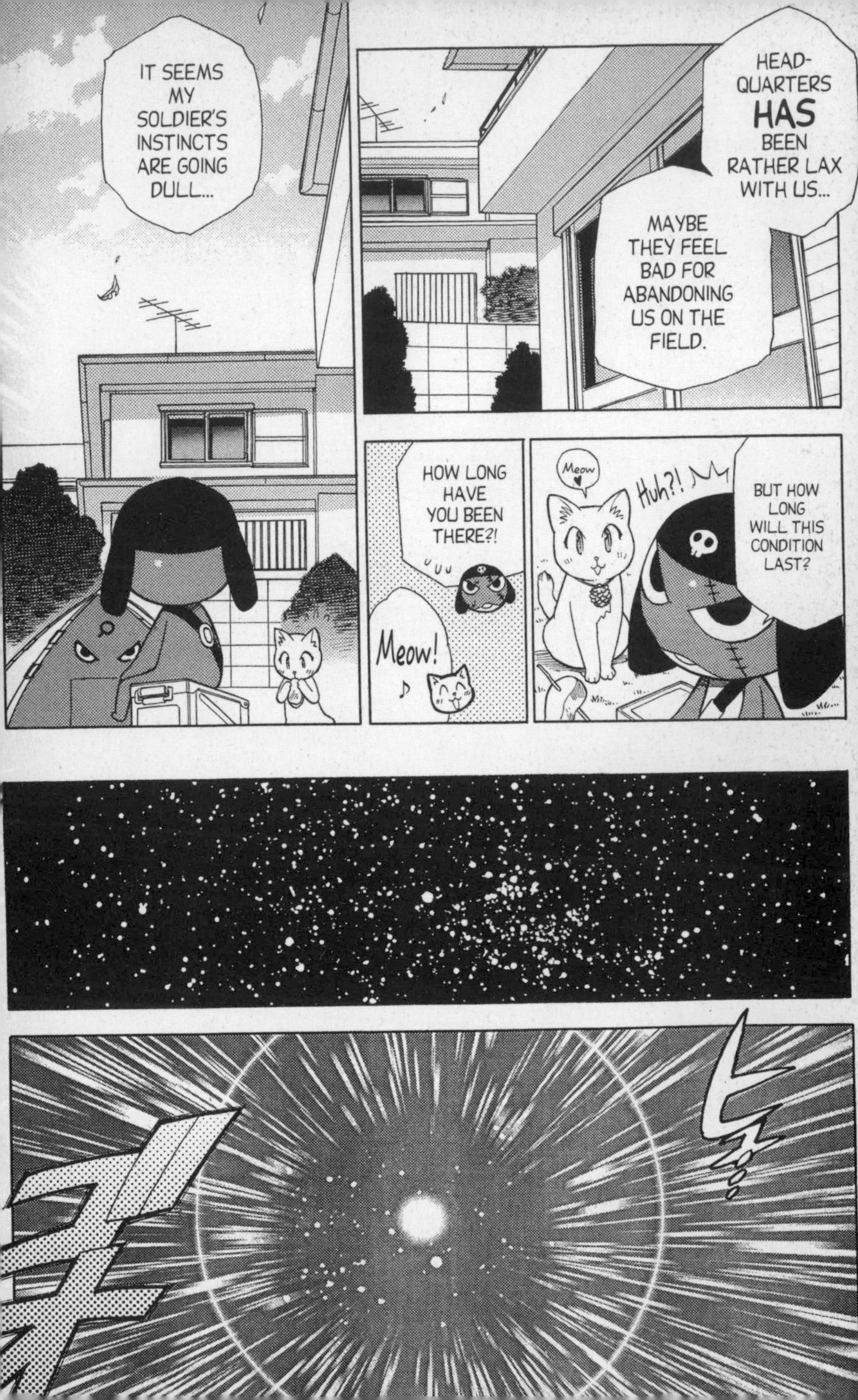
HEAD-QUARTERS **HAS** BEEN RATHER LAX WITH US...
MAYBE THEY FEEL BAD FOR ABANDONING US ON THE FIELD.
BUT HOW LONG WILL THIS CONDITION LAST?
Meow ♥
Huh?!
HOW LONG HAVE YOU BEEN THERE?!
Meow! ♪
IT SEEMS MY SOLDIER'S INSTINCTS ARE GOING DULL...

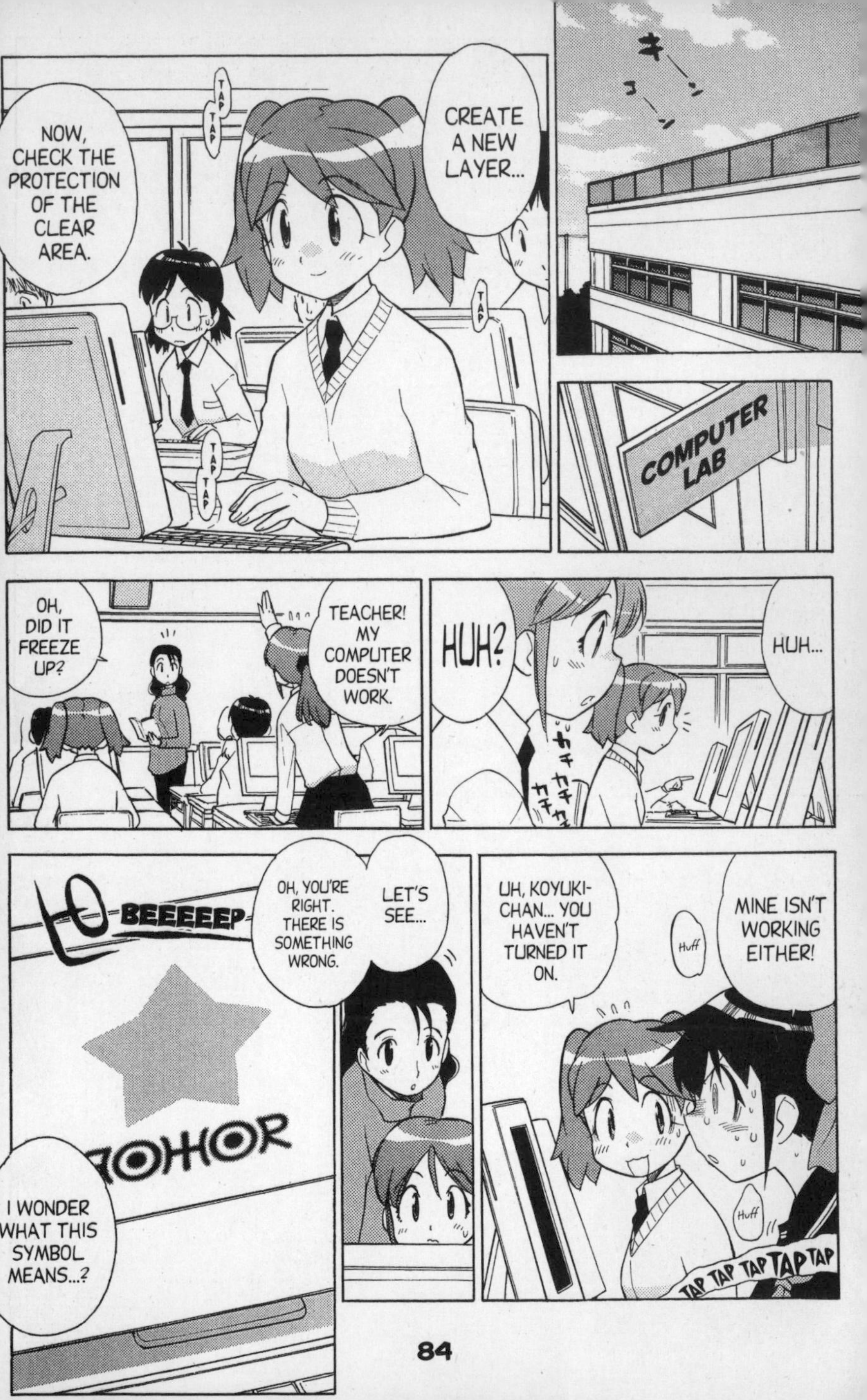

キーン コーン
COMPUTER LAB
CREATE A NEW LAYER...
TAP TAP
NOW, CHECK THE PROTECTION OF THE CLEAR AREA.
TAP
TAP TAP
HUH...
HUH?
カチ カチ カチカチ
TEACHER! MY COMPUTER DOESN'T WORK.
OH, DID IT FREEZE UP?
MINE ISN'T WORKING EITHER!
Huff
UH, KOYUKI-CHAN... YOU HAVEN'T TURNED IT ON.
Huff
TAP TAP TAP TAP TAP
LET'S SEE...
OH, YOU'RE RIGHT. THERE IS SOMETHING WRONG.
BEEEEEP
I WONDER WHAT THIS SYMBOL MEANS...?

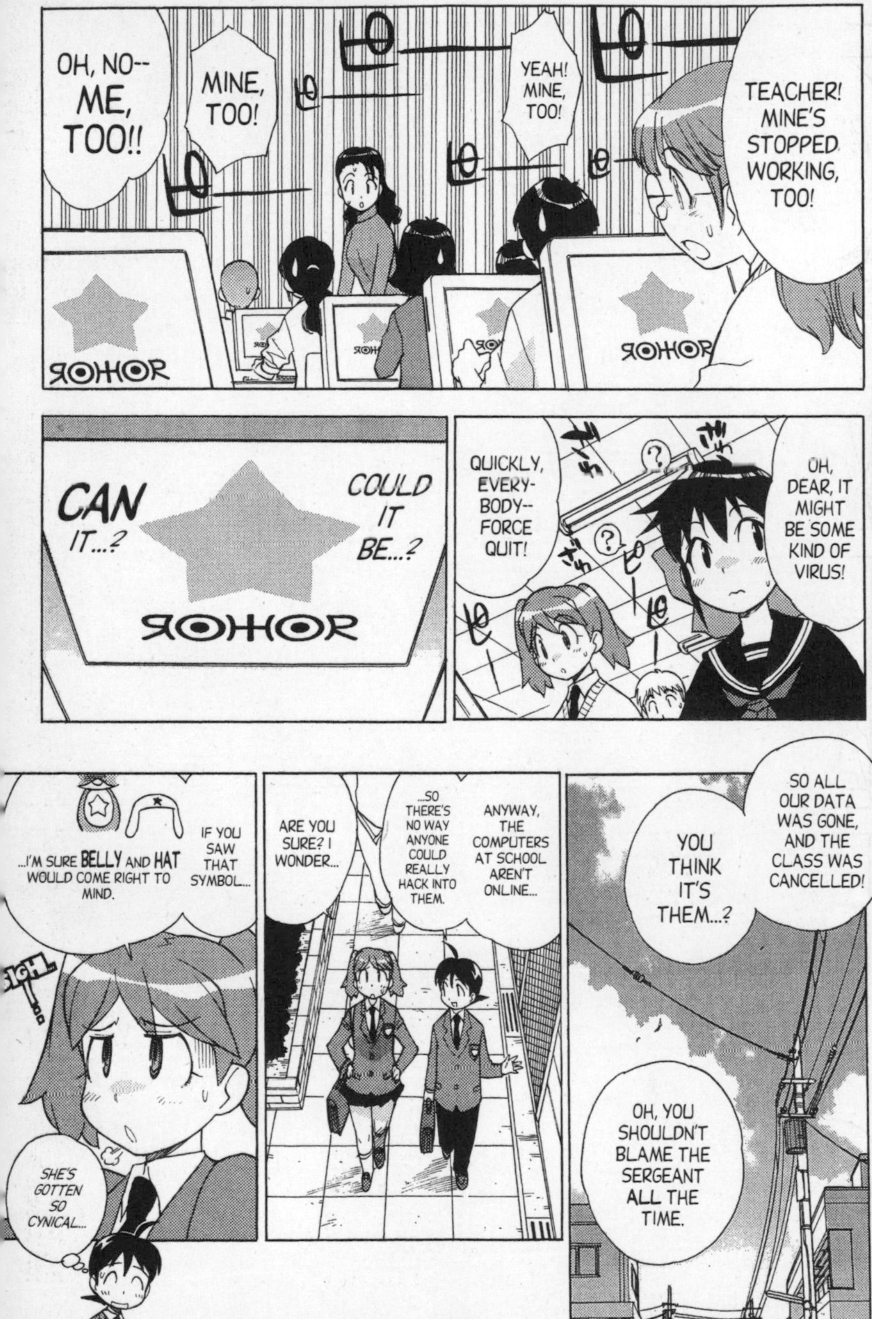
TEACHER! MINE'S STOPPED WORKING, TOO!
YEAH! MINE, TOO!
MINE, TOO!
OH, NO-- ME, TOO!!
OH, DEAR, IT MIGHT BE SOME KIND OF VIRUS!
QUICKLY, EVERY-BODY-- FORCE QUIT!
COULD IT BE...?
CAN IT...?
SO ALL OUR DATA WAS GONE, AND THE CLASS WAS CANCELLED!
YOU THINK IT'S THEM...?
OH, YOU SHOULDN'T BLAME THE SERGEANT ALL THE TIME.
ANYWAY, THE COMPUTERS AT SCHOOL AREN'T ONLINE...
...SO THERE'S NO WAY ANYONE COULD REALLY HACK INTO THEM.
ARE YOU SURE? I WONDER...
IF YOU SAW THAT SYMBOL...
...I'M SURE BELLY AND HAT WOULD COME RIGHT TO MIND.
SIGH...
SHE'S GOTTEN SO CYNICAL...

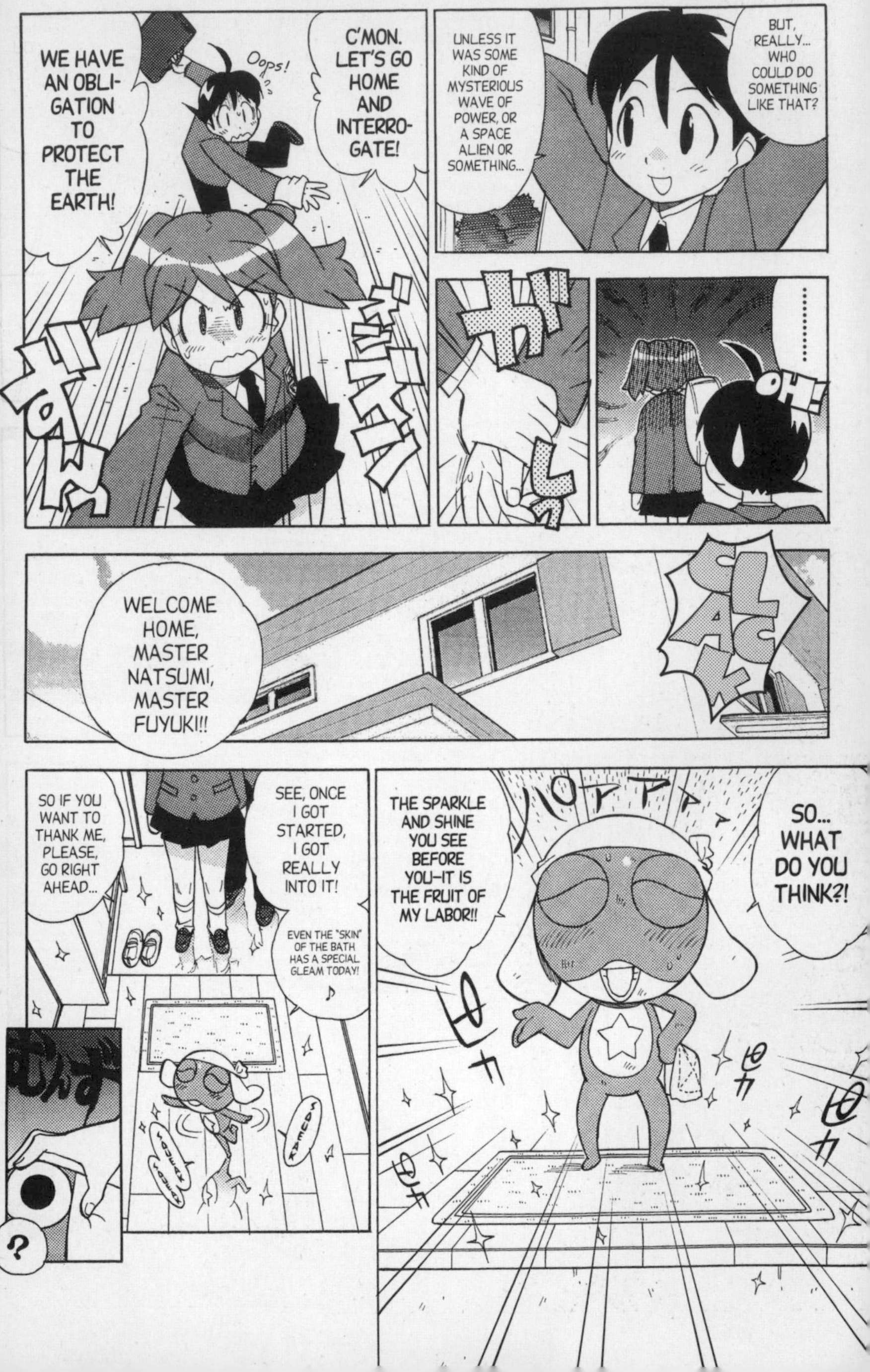
BUT, REALLY... WHO COULD DO SOMETHING LIKE THAT?
UNLESS IT WAS SOME KIND OF MYSTERIOUS WAVE OF POWER, OR A SPACE ALIEN OR SOMETHING...
......
OH!
C'MON. LET'S GO HOME AND INTERROGATE!
Oops!
WE HAVE AN OBLI-GATION TO PROTECT THE EARTH!
CLACK
WELCOME HOME, MASTER NATSUMI, MASTER FUYUKI!!
SO... WHAT DO YOU THINK?!
THE SPARKLE AND SHINE YOU SEE BEFORE YOU—IT IS THE FRUIT OF MY LABOR!!
SEE, ONCE I GOT STARTED, I GOT REALLY INTO IT!
EVEN THE "SKIN" OF THE BATH HAS A SPECIAL GLEAM TODAY! ♪
SO IF YOU WANT TO THANK ME, PLEASE, GO RIGHT AHEAD...
SQUEAK
SQUEAK SQUEAK
?

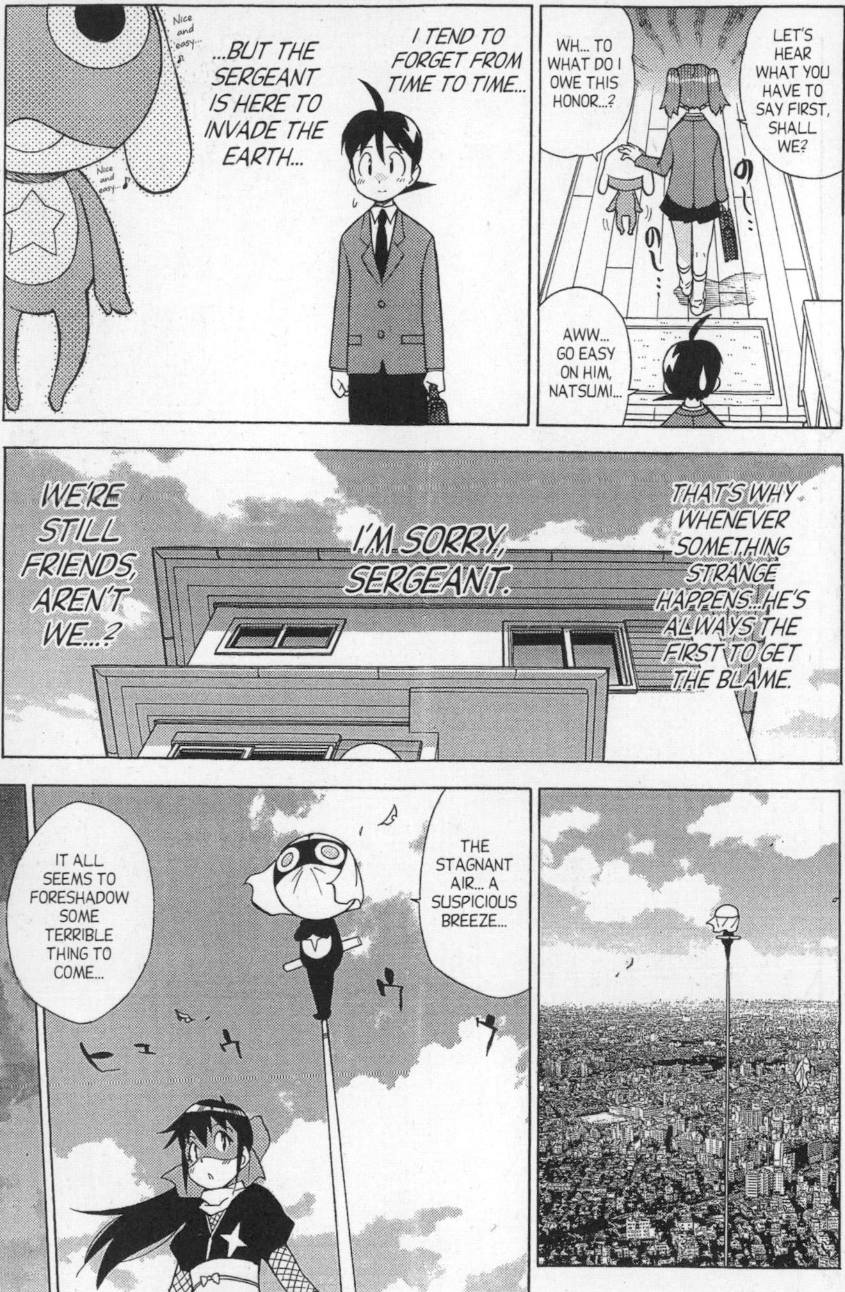
LET'S HEAR WHAT YOU HAVE TO SAY FIRST, SHALL WE?
WH... TO WHAT DO I OWE THIS HONOR...?
AWW... GO EASY ON HIM, NATSUMI...
I TEND TO FORGET FROM TIME TO TIME...
...BUT THE SERGEANT IS HERE TO INVADE THE EARTH...
Nice and easy...
Nice and easy...
THAT'S WHY WHENEVER SOMETHING STRANGE HAPPENS...HE'S ALWAYS THE FIRST TO GET THE BLAME.
I'M SORRY, SERGEANT.
WE'RE STILL FRIENDS, AREN'T WE...?
THE STAGNANT AIR... A SUSPICIOUS BREEZE...
IT ALL SEEMS TO FORESHADOW SOME TERRIBLE THING TO COME...

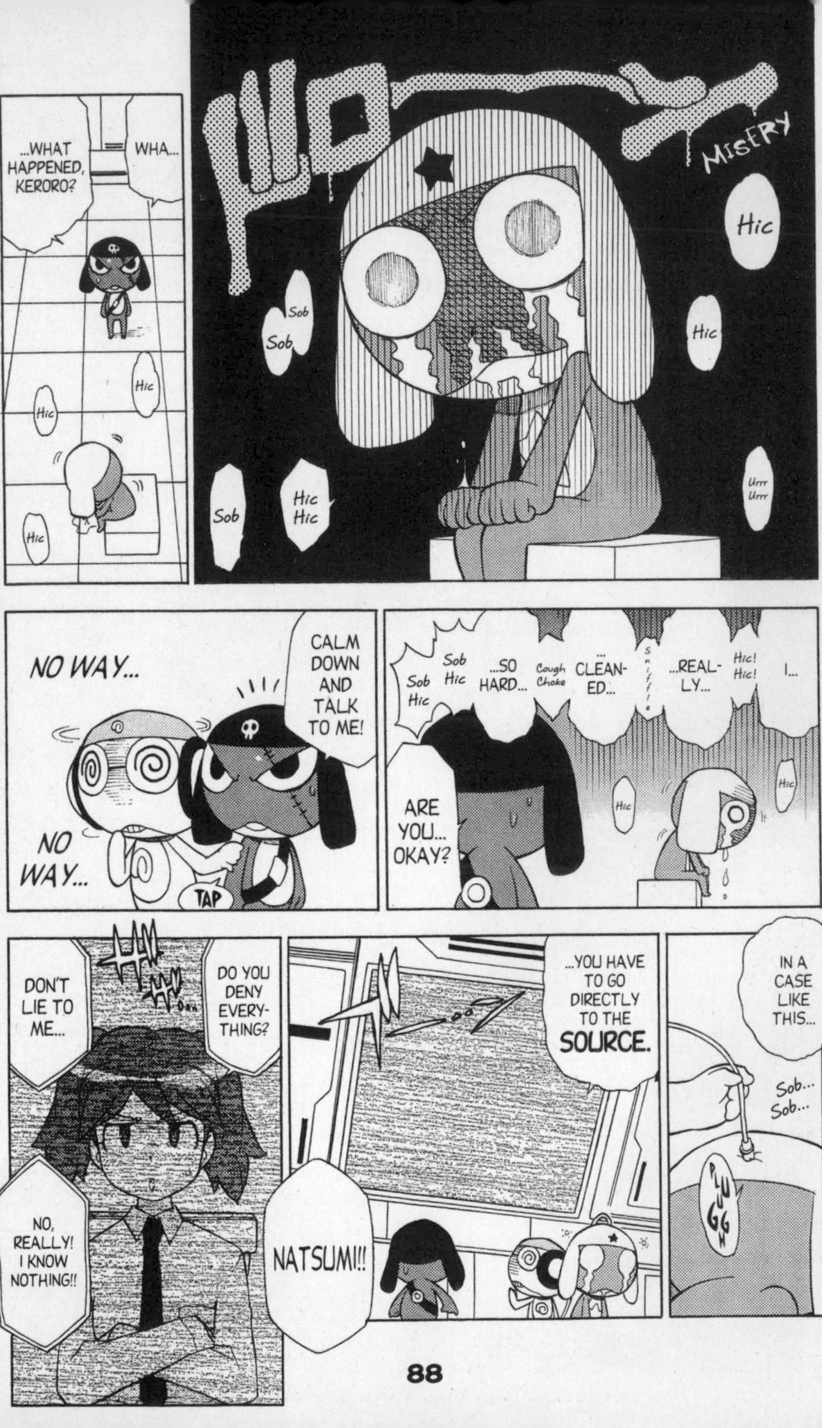
MISERY
Hic
Hic
Urrr Urrr
Sob Sob
Sob
Hic Hic
WHA...
...WHAT HAPPENED, KERORO?
Hic
Hic
Hic
I...
Hic! Hic!
...REAL-LY...
Sniffle
...CLEAN-ED...
Cough Choke
...SO HARD...
Sob Hic
Sob Hic
ARE YOU... OKAY?
Hic
Hic
CALM DOWN AND TALK TO ME!
NO WAY...
NO WAY...
TAP
IN A CASE LIKE THIS...
Sob... Sob...
PLUGGH
...YOU HAVE TO GO DIRECTLY TO THE SOURCE.
NATSUMI!!
DO YOU DENY EVERY-THING?
DON'T LIE TO ME...
NO, REALLY! I KNOW NOTHING!!

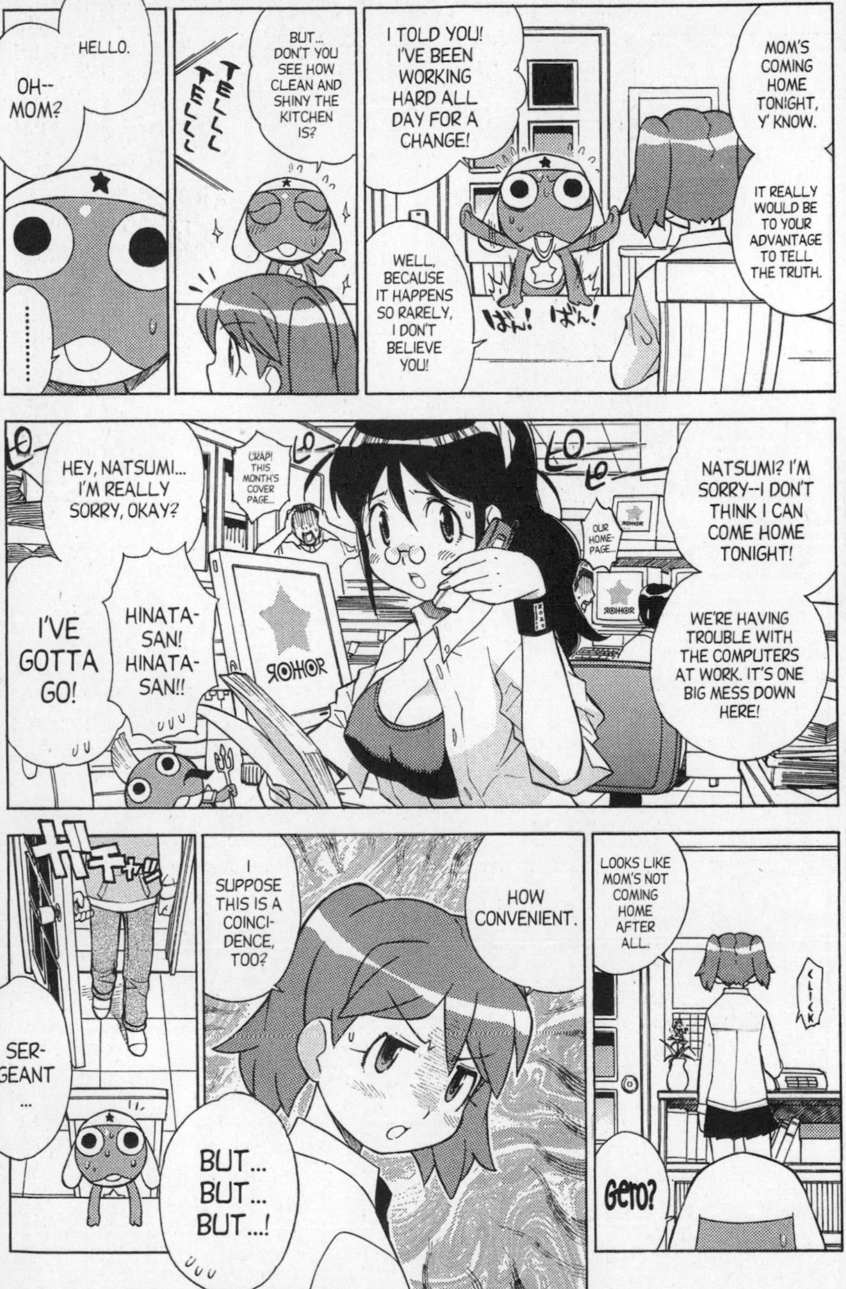
MOM'S COMING HOME TONIGHT, Y' KNOW.
IT REALLY WOULD BE TO YOUR ADVANTAGE TO TELL THE TRUTH.
I TOLD YOU! I'VE BEEN WORKING HARD ALL DAY FOR A CHANGE!
ばん! ばん!
WELL, BECAUSE IT HAPPENS SO RARELY, I DON'T BELIEVE YOU!
BUT... DON'T YOU SEE HOW CLEAN AND SHINY THE KITCHEN IS?
TELLL TELLL
HELLO.
OH-- MOM?
....
NATSUMI? I'M SORRY--I DON'T THINK I CAN COME HOME TONIGHT!
WE'RE HAVING TROUBLE WITH THE COMPUTERS AT WORK. IT'S ONE BIG MESS DOWN HERE!
OUR HOME-PAGE...
CRAP! THIS MONTH'S COVER PAGE...
HEY, NATSUMI... I'M REALLY SORRY, OKAY?
HINATA-SAN! HINATA-SAN!!
I'VE GOTTA GO!
LOOKS LIKE MOM'S NOT COMING HOME AFTER ALL.
CLICK
Gero?
HOW CONVENIENT.
I SUPPOSE THIS IS A COINCIDENCE, TOO?
BUT... BUT... BUT...!
ガチャッ
SER-GEANT...

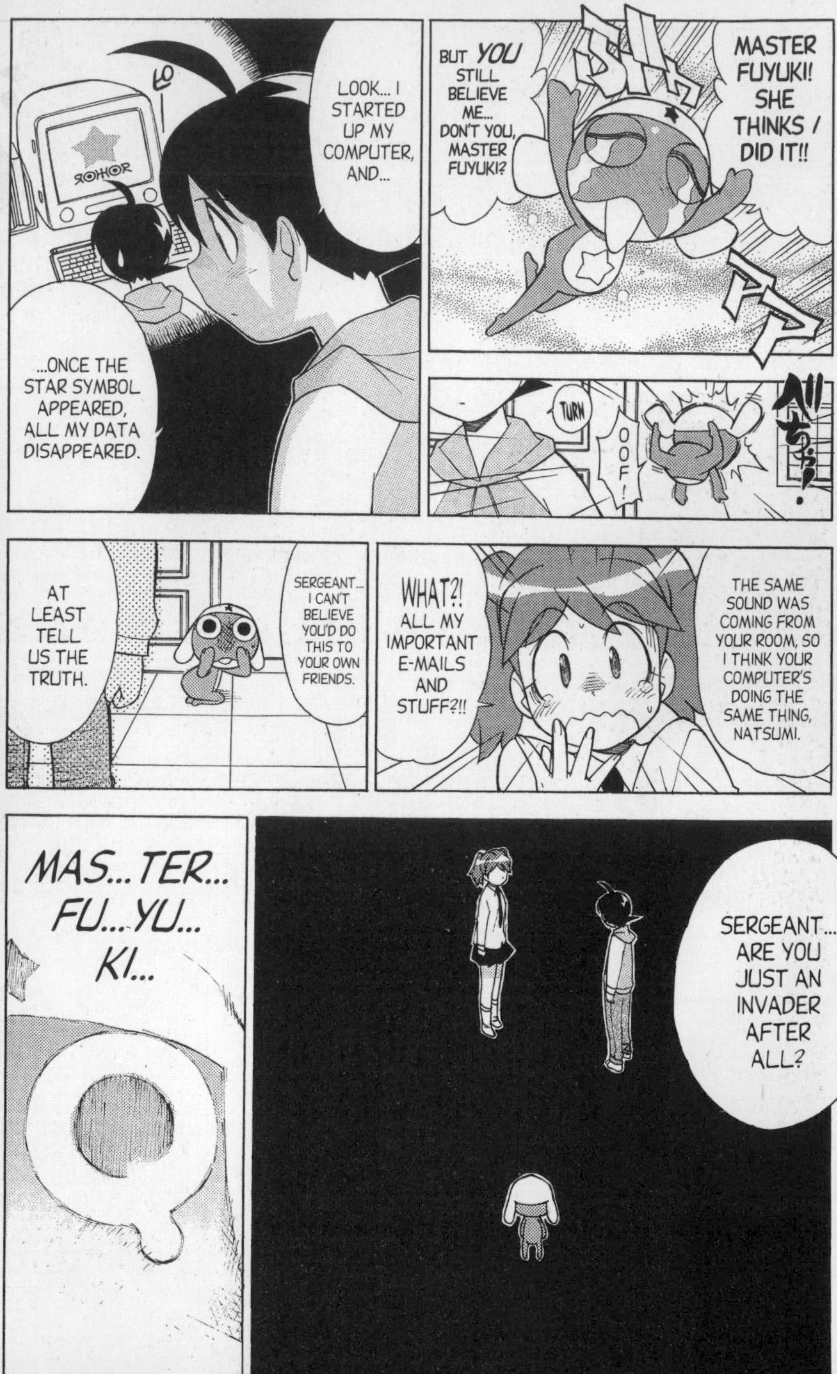
MASTER FUYUKI! SHE THINKS I DID IT!!
BUT YOU STILL BELIEVE ME... DON'T YOU, MASTER FUYUKI?
TURN
OOF!
LOOK... I STARTED UP MY COMPUTER, AND...
...ONCE THE STAR SYMBOL APPEARED, ALL MY DATA DISAPPEARED.
THE SAME SOUND WAS COMING FROM YOUR ROOM, SO I THINK YOUR COMPUTER'S DOING THE SAME THING, NATSUMI.
WHAT?! ALL MY IMPORTANT E-MAILS AND STUFF?!!
SERGEANT... I CAN'T BELIEVE YOU'D DO THIS TO YOUR OWN FRIENDS.
AT LEAST TELL US THE TRUTH.
SERGEANT... ARE YOU JUST AN INVADER AFTER ALL?
MAS...TER... FU...YU... KI...

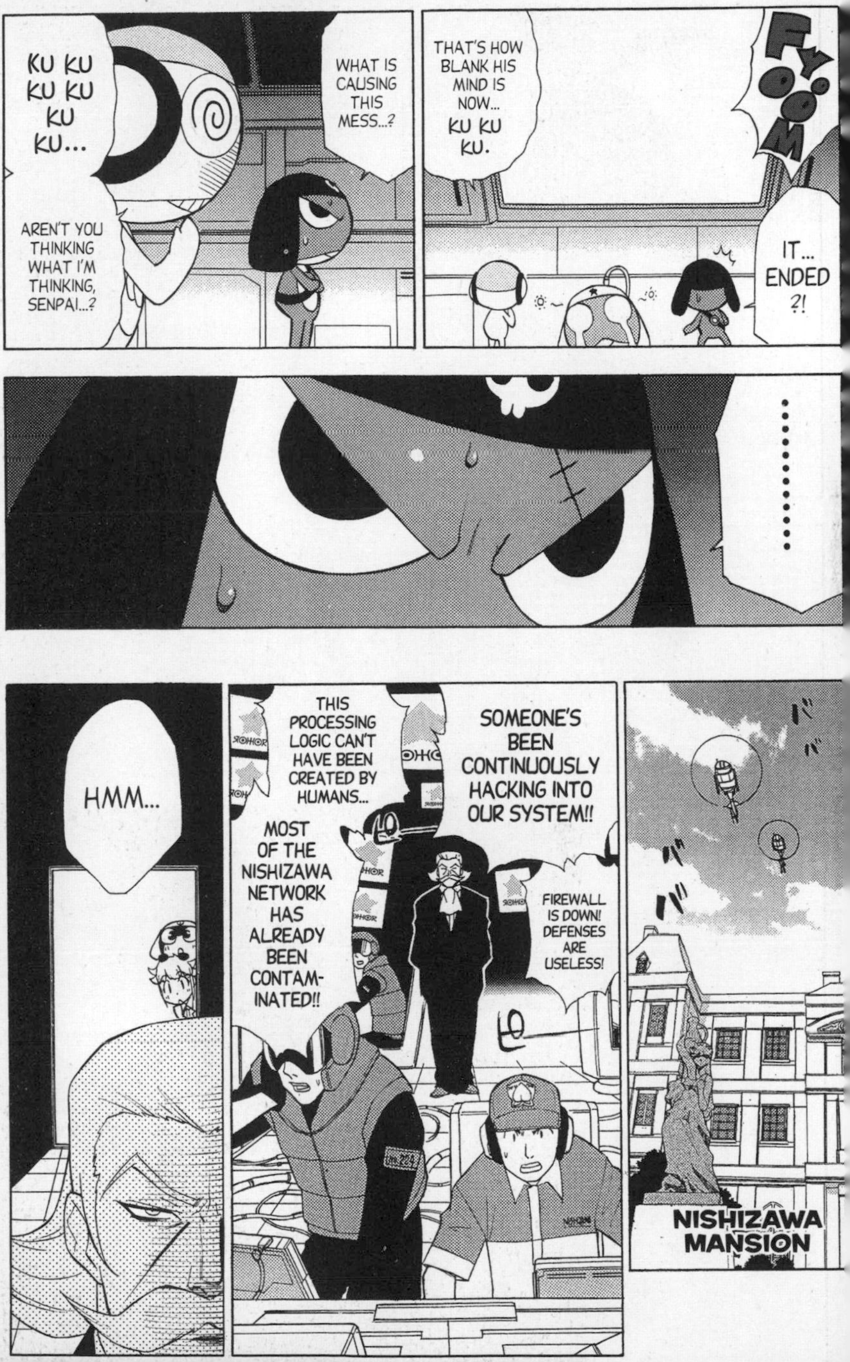
FYOOOM
IT... ENDED ?!
WHAT IS CAUSING THIS MESS...?
KU KU KU KU KU KU...
AREN'T YOU THINKING WHAT I'M THINKING, SENPAI...?
THAT'S HOW BLANK HIS MIND IS NOW... KU KU KU.
....
NISHIZAWA MANSION
SOMEONE'S BEEN CONTINUOUSLY HACKING INTO OUR SYSTEM!!
THIS PROCESSING LOGIC CAN'T HAVE BEEN CREATED BY HUMANS...
FIREWALL IS DOWN! DEFENSES ARE USELESS!
MOST OF THE NISHIZAWA NETWORK HAS ALREADY BEEN CONTAM-INATED!!
HMM...

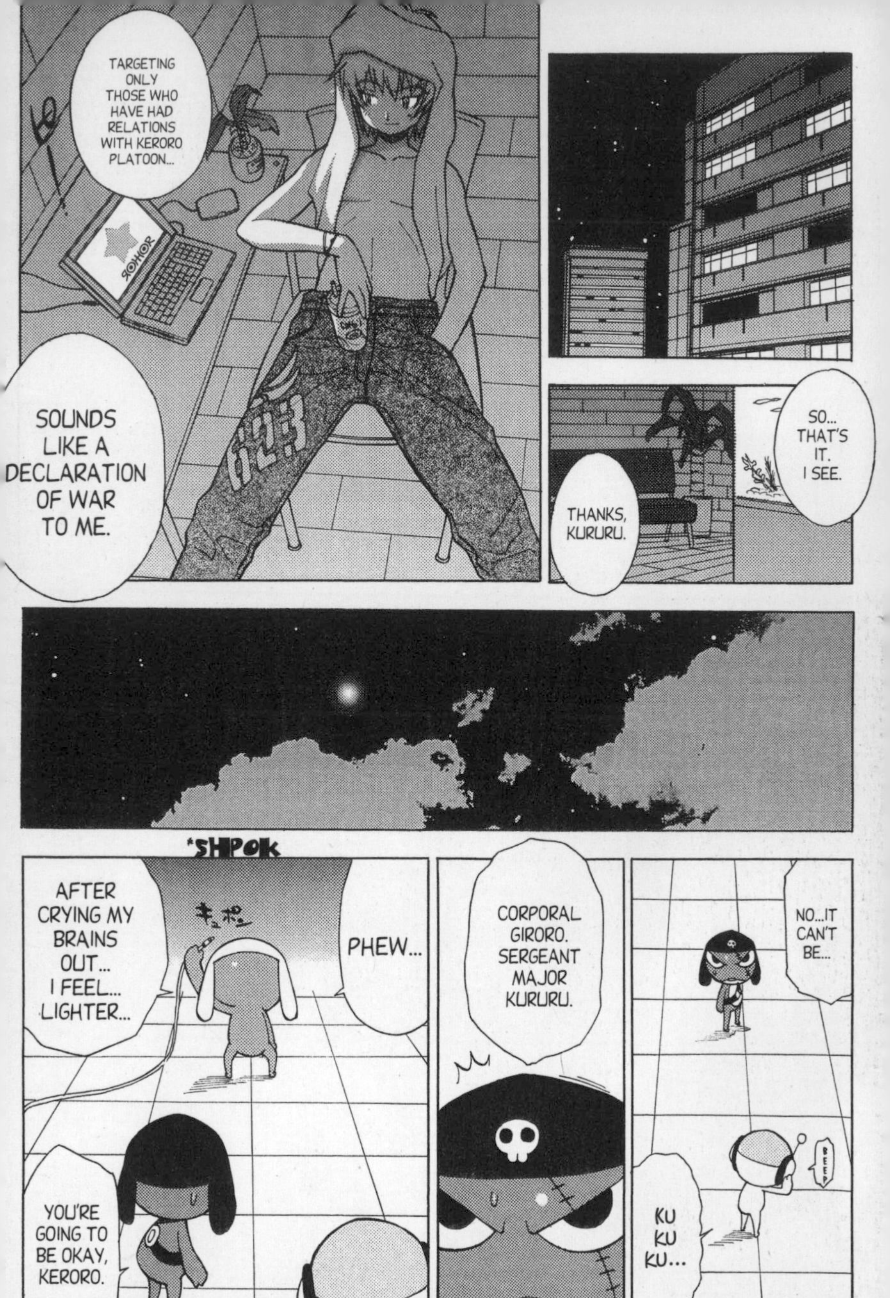
SO... THAT'S IT. I SEE.
THANKS, KURURU.
TARGETING ONLY THOSE WHO HAVE HAD RELATIONS WITH KERORO PLATOON...
SOUNDS LIKE A DECLARATION OF WAR TO ME.
NO...IT CAN'T BE...
BEEP
KU KU KU...
CORPORAL GIRORO. SERGEANT MAJOR KURURU.
*SHPOK
PHEW...
AFTER CRYING MY BRAINS OUT... I FEEL... LIGHTER...
YOU'RE GOING TO BE OKAY, KERORO.

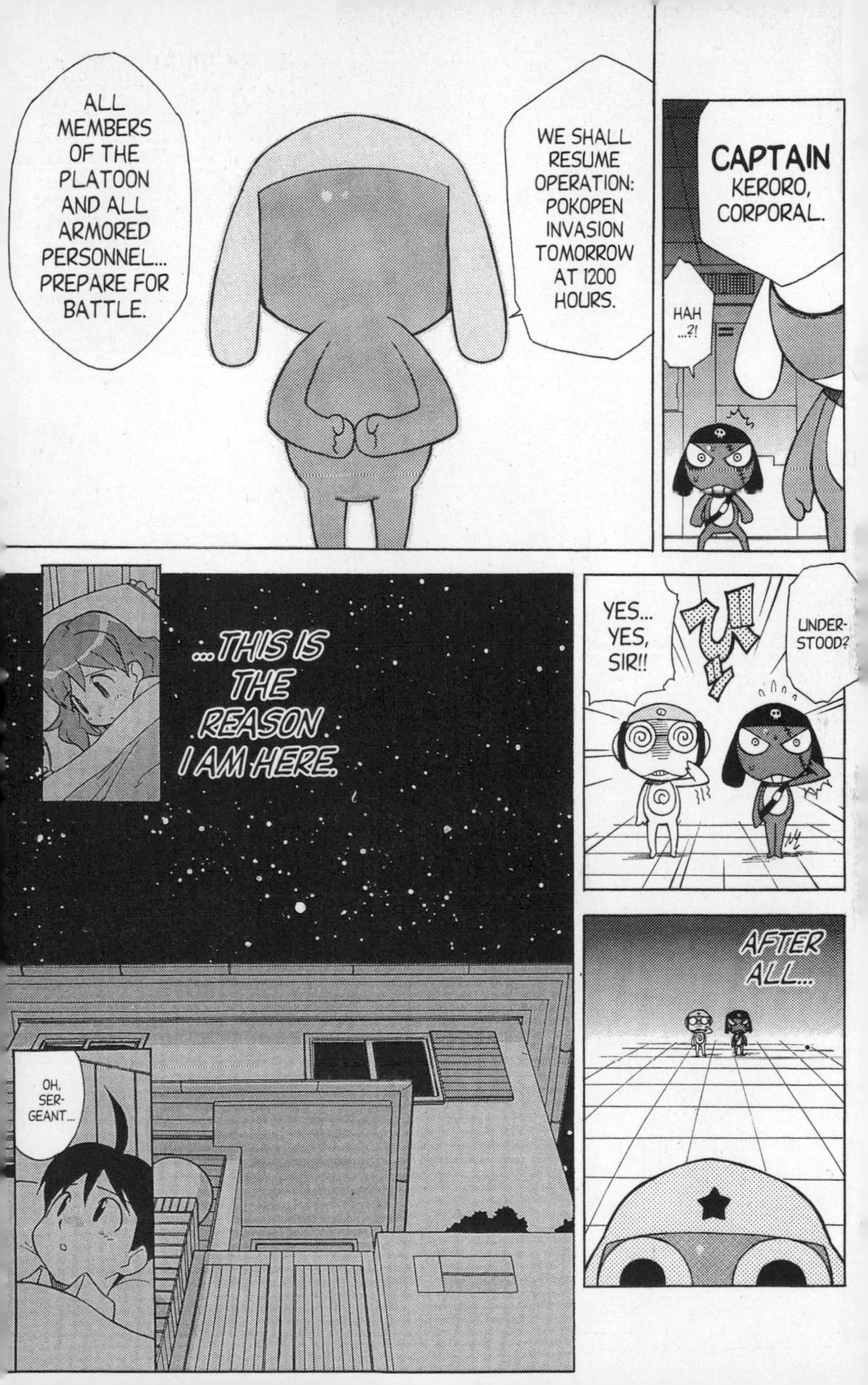
CAPTAIN KERORO, CORPORAL.
HAH ...?!
WE SHALL RESUME OPERATION: POKOPEN INVASION TOMORROW AT 1200 HOURS.
ALL MEMBERS OF THE PLATOON AND ALL ARMORED PERSONNEL... PREPARE FOR BATTLE.
UNDER-STOOD?
YES... YES, SIR!!
AFTER ALL...
...THIS IS THE REASON I AM HERE.
OH, SER-GEANT...

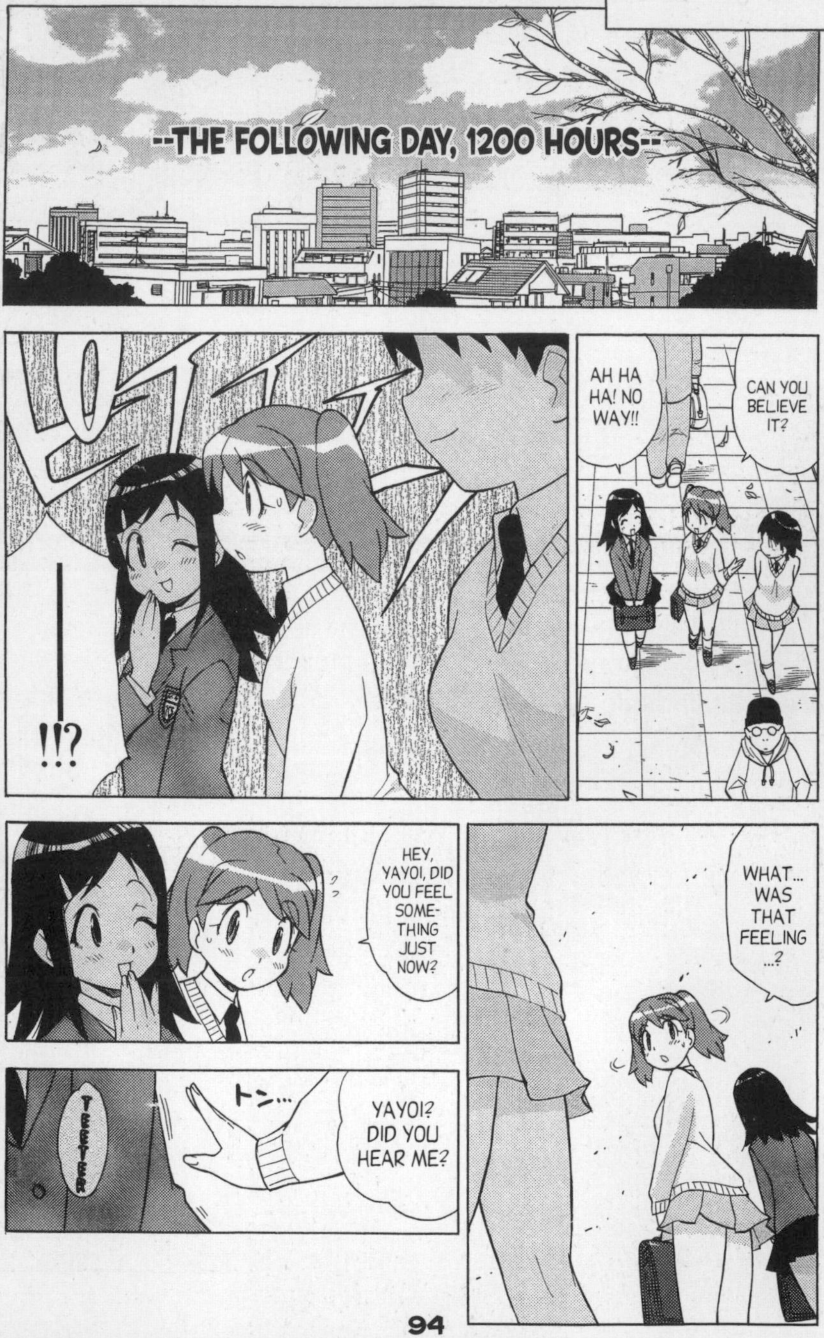
--THE FOLLOWING DAY, 1200 HOURS--
CAN YOU BELIEVE IT?
AH HA HA! NO WAY!!
!!?
WHAT... WAS THAT FEELING...?
HEY, YAYOI, DID YOU FEEL SOMETHING JUST NOW?
YAYOI? DID YOU HEAR ME?
トン...
TEETER

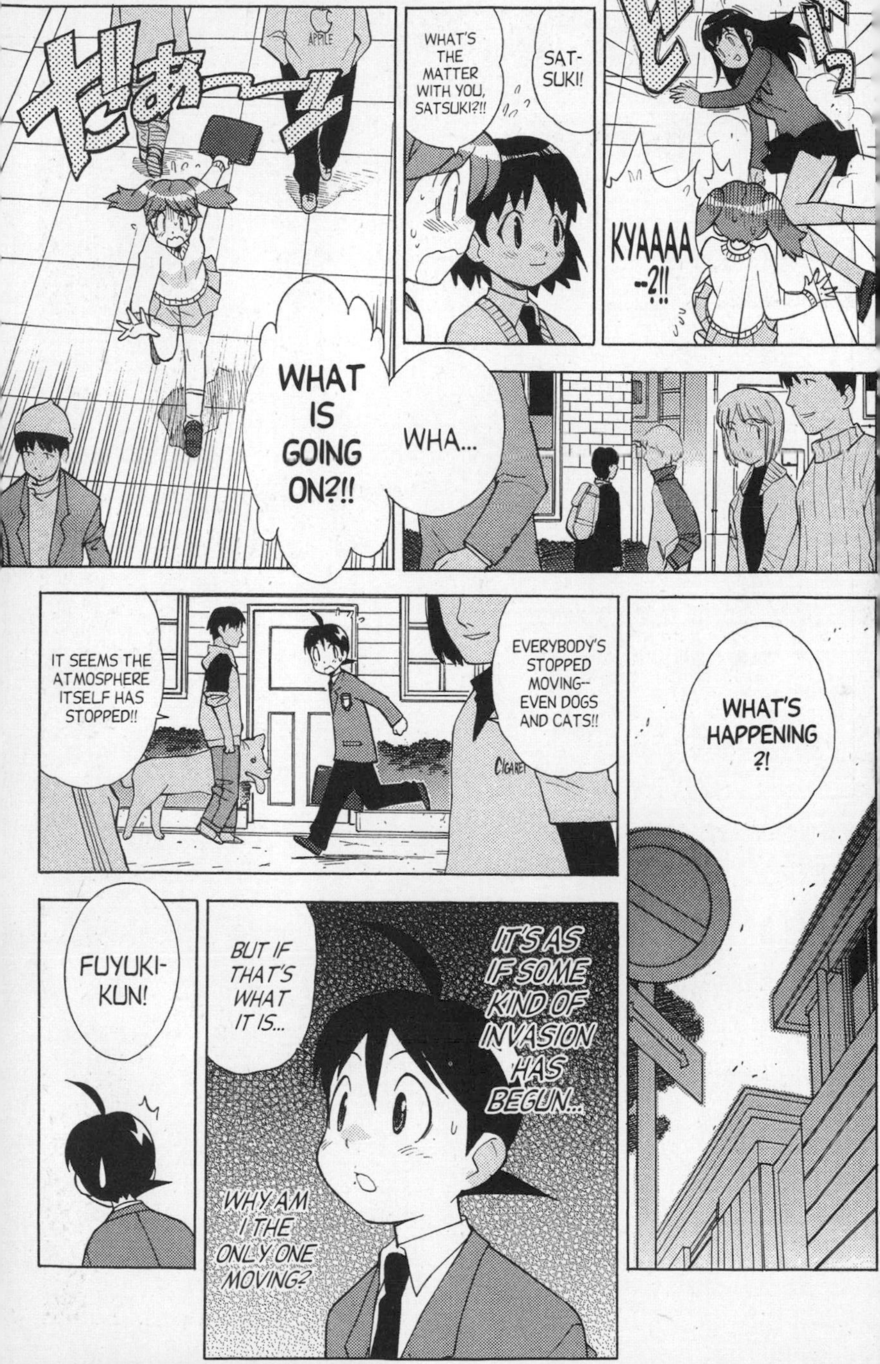
KYAAAA--?!!
SAT-SUKI!
WHAT'S THE MATTER WITH YOU, SATSUKI?!!
WHA...
WHAT IS GOING ON?!!
WHAT'S HAPPENING?!
EVERYBODY'S STOPPED MOVING-- EVEN DOGS AND CATS!!
IT SEEMS THE ATMOSPHERE ITSELF HAS STOPPED!!
BUT IF THAT'S WHAT IT IS...
IT'S AS IF SOME KIND OF INVASION HAS BEGUN...
WHY AM I THE ONLY ONE MOVING?
FUYUKI-KUN!

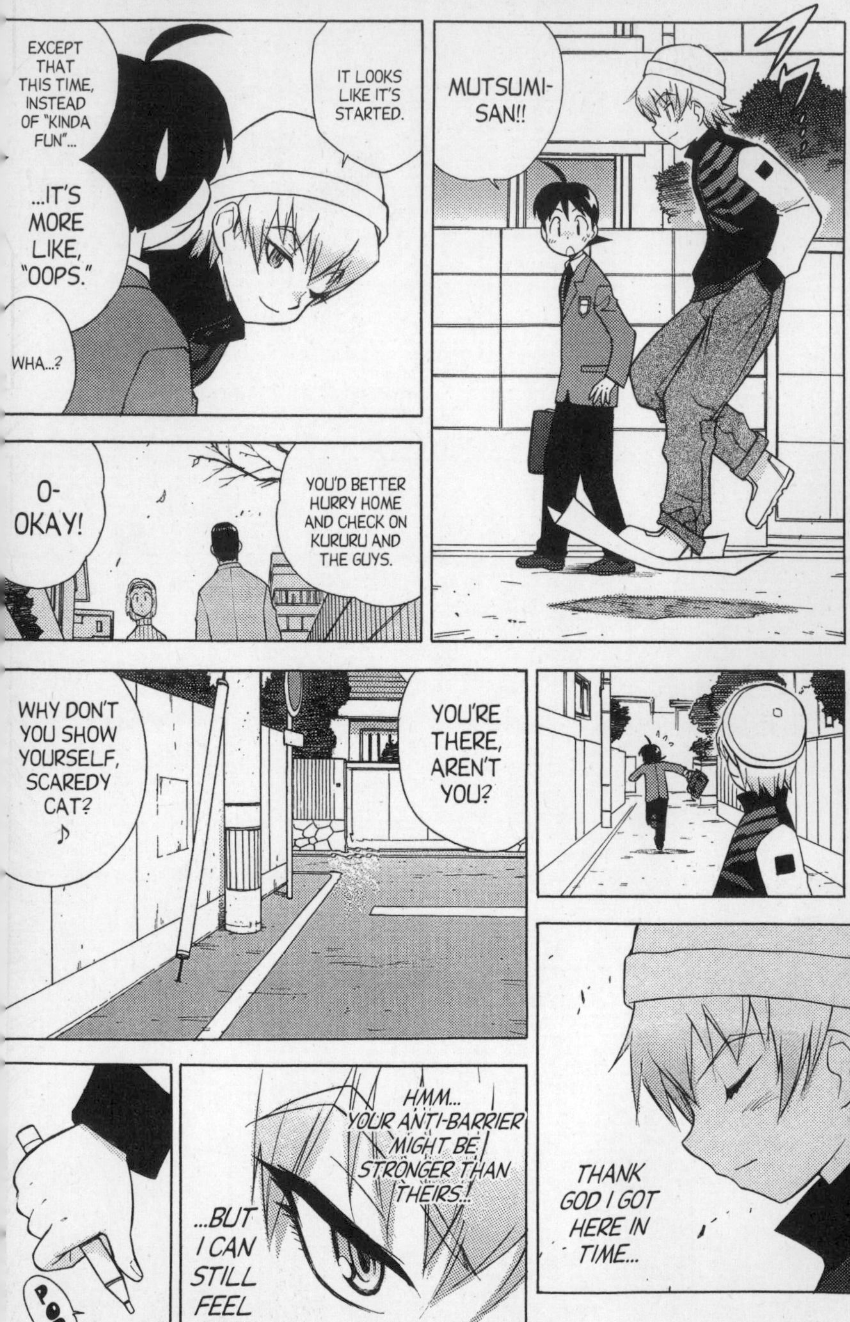
MUTSUMI-SAN!!
IT LOOKS LIKE IT'S STARTED.
EXCEPT THAT THIS TIME, INSTEAD OF "KINDA FUN"...
...IT'S MORE LIKE, "OOPS."
WHA...?
YOU'D BETTER HURRY HOME AND CHECK ON KURURU AND THE GUYS.
O-OKAY!
THANK GOD I GOT HERE IN TIME...
YOU'RE THERE, AREN'T YOU?
WHY DON'T YOU SHOW YOURSELF, SCAREDY CAT? ♪
HMM... YOUR ANTI-BARRIER MIGHT BE STRONGER THAN THEIRS...
...BUT I CAN STILL FEEL YOU.
POP

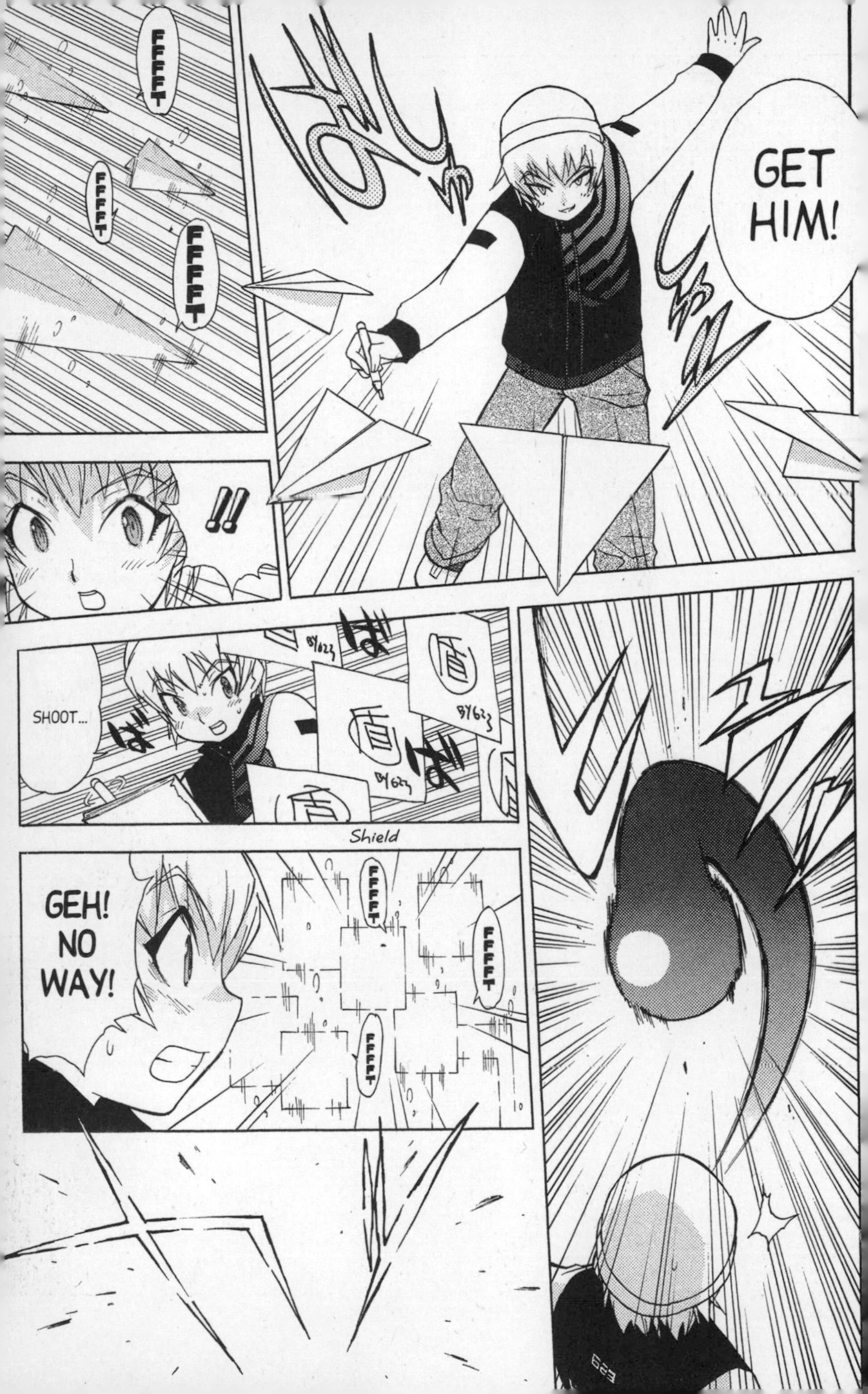
GET HIM!
FFFFT
FFFFT
FFFFT
!!
SHOOT...
Shield
GEH! NO WAY!
FFFFT
FFFFT
FFFFT

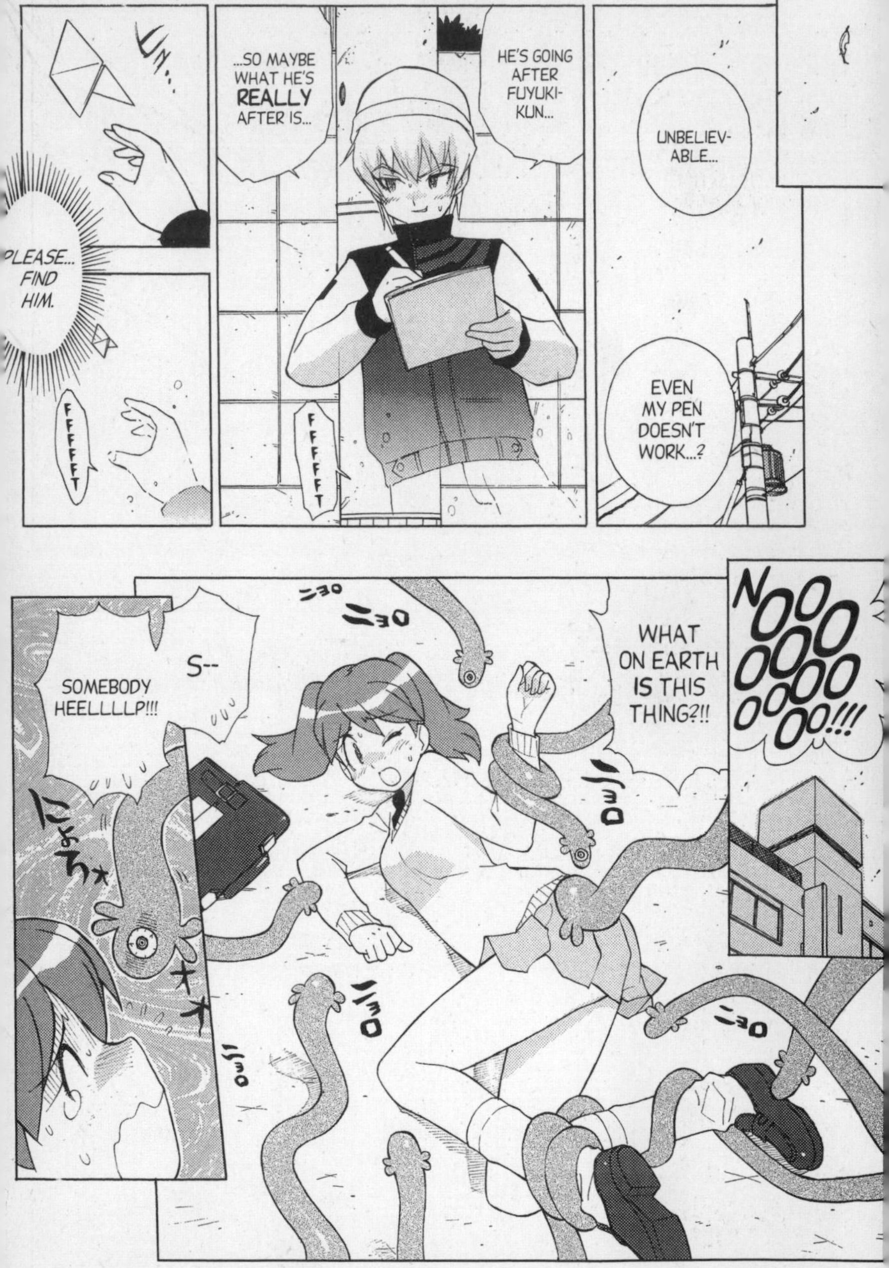
UNBELIEV-ABLE...
EVEN MY PEN DOESN'T WORK...?
HE'S GOING AFTER FUYUKI-KUN...
...SO MAYBE WHAT HE'S REALLY AFTER IS...
FFFFFFT
UN...
PLEASE... FIND HIM.
FFFFFFT
NOOOOOOOOOOOOOO!!!
WHAT ON EARTH IS THIS THING?!!
ニョロ
ニョロ
ニョロ
S--
SOMEBODY HEELLLLP!!!
ニョロ
ニョロ
ニョロ

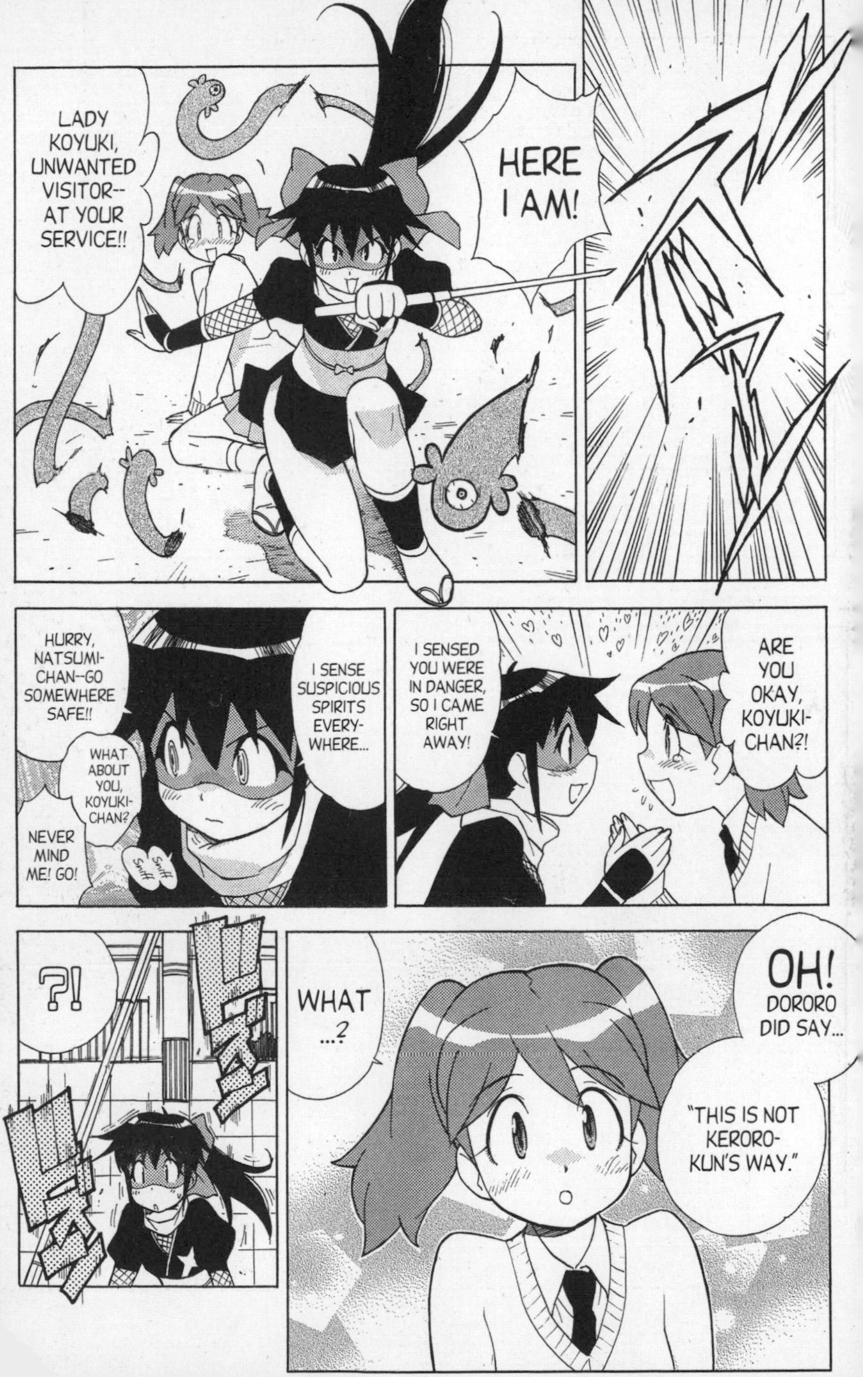
HERE I AM!
LADY KOYUKI, UNWANTED VISITOR-- AT YOUR SERVICE!!
ARE YOU OKAY, KOYUKI-CHAN?!
I SENSED YOU WERE IN DANGER, SO I CAME RIGHT AWAY!
I SENSE SUSPICIOUS SPIRITS EVERY-WHERE...
HURRY, NATSUMI-CHAN--GO SOMEWHERE SAFE!!
WHAT ABOUT YOU, KOYUKI-CHAN?
Sniff Sniff
NEVER MIND ME! GO!
OH! DORORO DID SAY...
WHAT ...?
"THIS IS NOT KERORO-KUN'S WAY."
?!

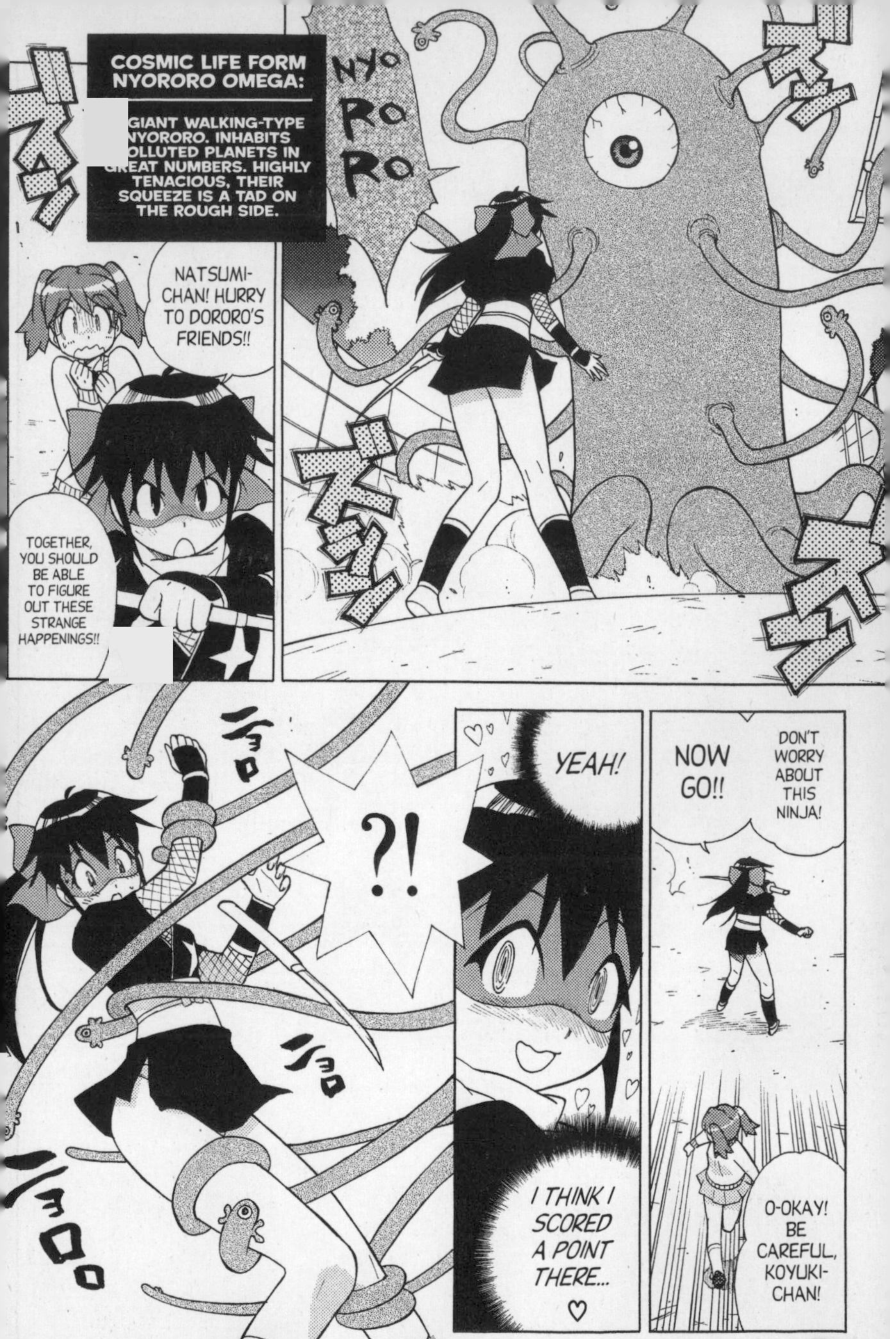

NYO RO RO
COSMIC LIFE FORM NYORORO OMEGA:
GIANT WALKING-TYPE NYORORO. INHABITS POLLUTED PLANETS IN GREAT NUMBERS. HIGHLY TENACIOUS, THEIR SQUEEZE IS A TAD ON THE ROUGH SIDE.
NATSUMI-CHAN! HURRY TO DORORO'S FRIENDS!!
TOGETHER, YOU SHOULD BE ABLE TO FIGURE OUT THESE STRANGE HAPPENINGS!!
DON'T WORRY ABOUT THIS NINJA!
NOW GO!!
O-OKAY! BE CAREFUL, KOYUKI-CHAN!
YEAH!
I THINK I SCORED A POINT THERE... ♡
?!

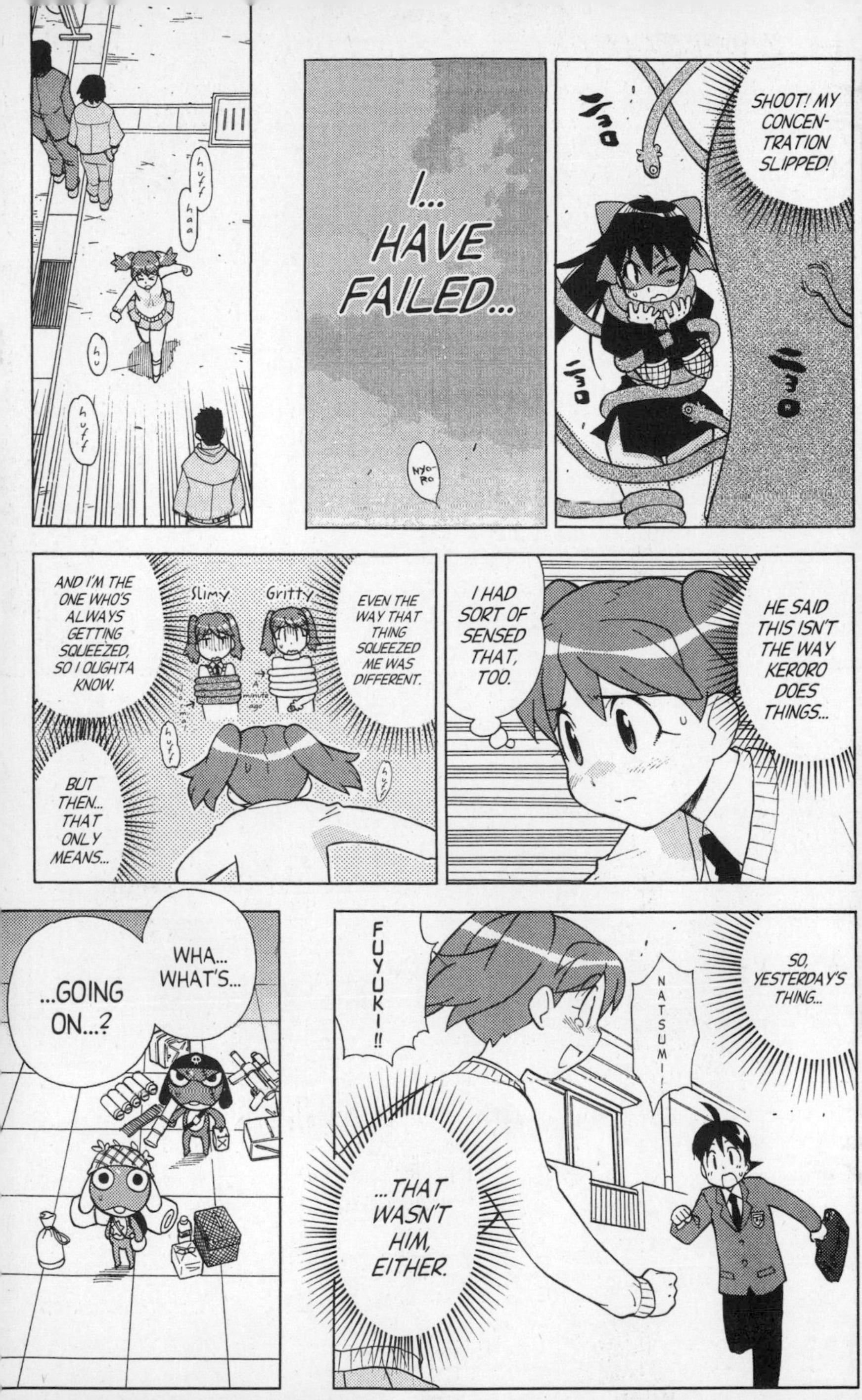

SHOOT! MY CONCEN-TRATION SLIPPED!
ニョロ
ニョロ
ニョロ
I... HAVE FAILED...
NYO-RO
huff haa
hu
huff
HE SAID THIS ISN'T THE WAY KERORO DOES THINGS...
I HAD SORT OF SENSED THAT, TOO.
EVEN THE WAY THAT THING SQUEEZED ME WAS DIFFERENT.
Gritty
Slimy
A minute ago
AND I'M THE ONE WHO'S ALWAYS GETTING SQUEEZED, SO I OUGHTA KNOW.
huff
huff
BUT THEN... THAT ONLY MEANS...
SO, YESTERDAY'S THING...
NATSUMI!
FUYUKI!!
...THAT WASN'T HIM, EITHER.
WHA... WHAT'S...
...GOING ON...?

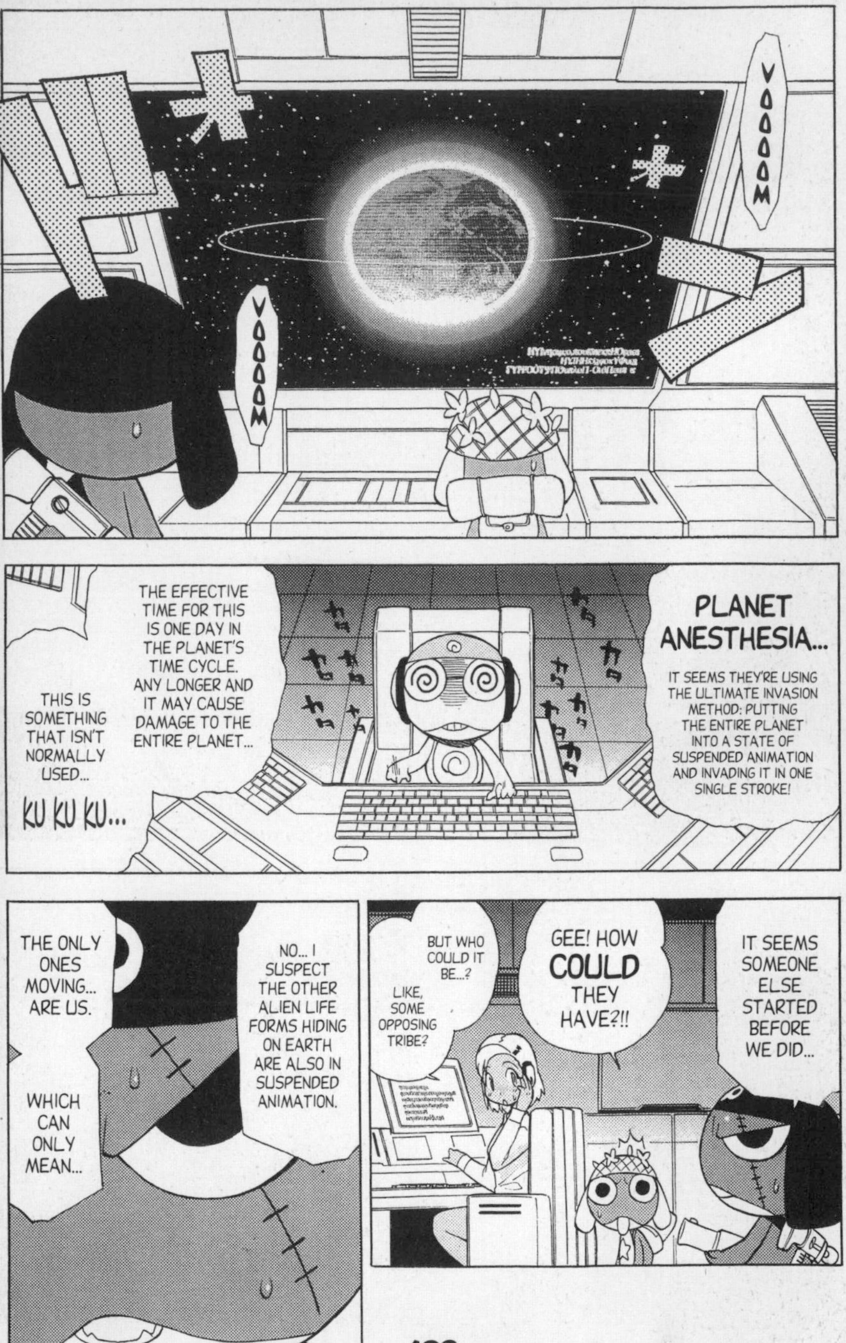
VOOOOM
VOOOOM
PLANET ANESTHESIA...
IT SEEMS THEY'RE USING THE ULTIMATE INVASION METHOD: PUTTING THE ENTIRE PLANET INTO A STATE OF SUSPENDED ANIMATION AND INVADING IT IN ONE SINGLE STROKE!
THE EFFECTIVE TIME FOR THIS IS ONE DAY IN THE PLANET'S TIME CYCLE. ANY LONGER AND IT MAY CAUSE DAMAGE TO THE ENTIRE PLANET...
THIS IS SOMETHING THAT ISN'T NORMALLY USED...
KU KU KU...
IT SEEMS SOMEONE ELSE STARTED BEFORE WE DID...
GEE! HOW COULD THEY HAVE?!!
BUT WHO COULD IT BE...?
LIKE, SOME OPPOSING TRIBE?
NO... I SUSPECT THE OTHER ALIEN LIFE FORMS HIDING ON EARTH ARE ALSO IN SUSPENDED ANIMATION.
THE ONLY ONES MOVING... ARE US.
WHICH CAN ONLY MEAN...

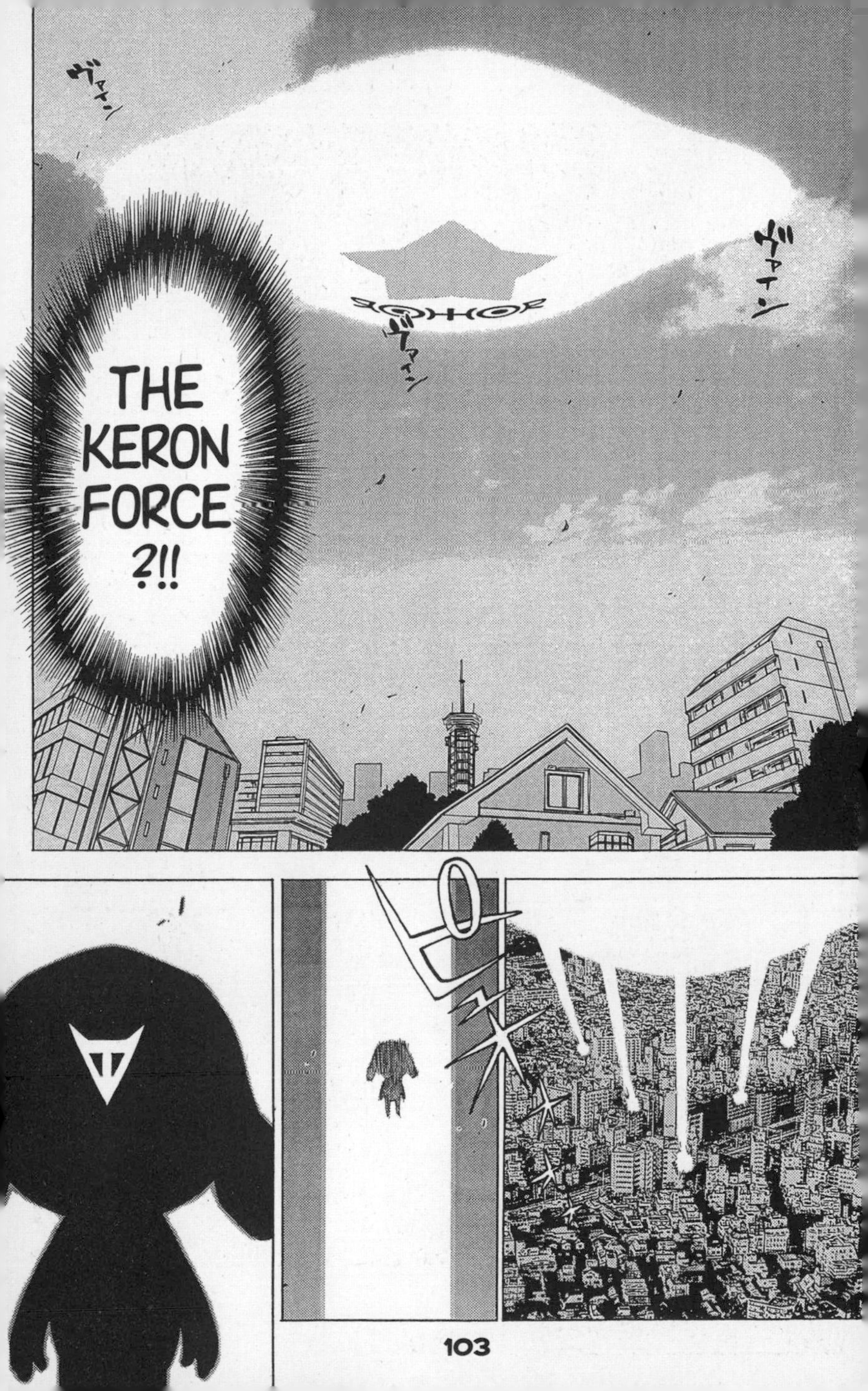
THE KERON FORCE ?!!

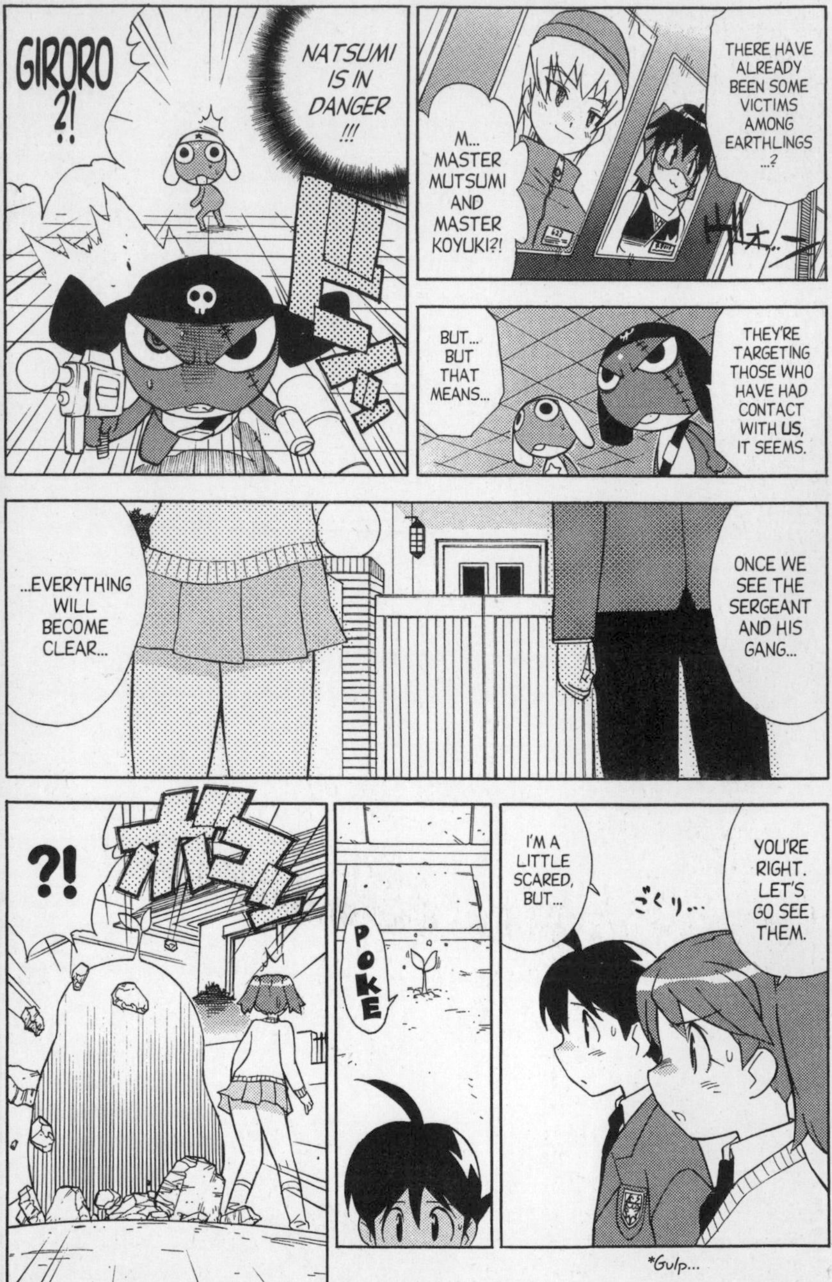
THERE HAVE ALREADY BEEN SOME VICTIMS AMONG EARTHLINGS ...?
M... MASTER MUTSUMI AND MASTER KOYUKI?!
THEY'RE TARGETING THOSE WHO HAVE HAD CONTACT WITH US, IT SEEMS.
BUT... BUT THAT MEANS...
NATSUMI IS IN DANGER !!!
GIRORO ?!
ONCE WE SEE THE SERGEANT AND HIS GANG...
...EVERYTHING WILL BECOME CLEAR...
YOU'RE RIGHT. LET'S GO SEE THEM.
ごくり...
I'M A LITTLE SCARED, BUT...
POKE
?!

*Gulp...

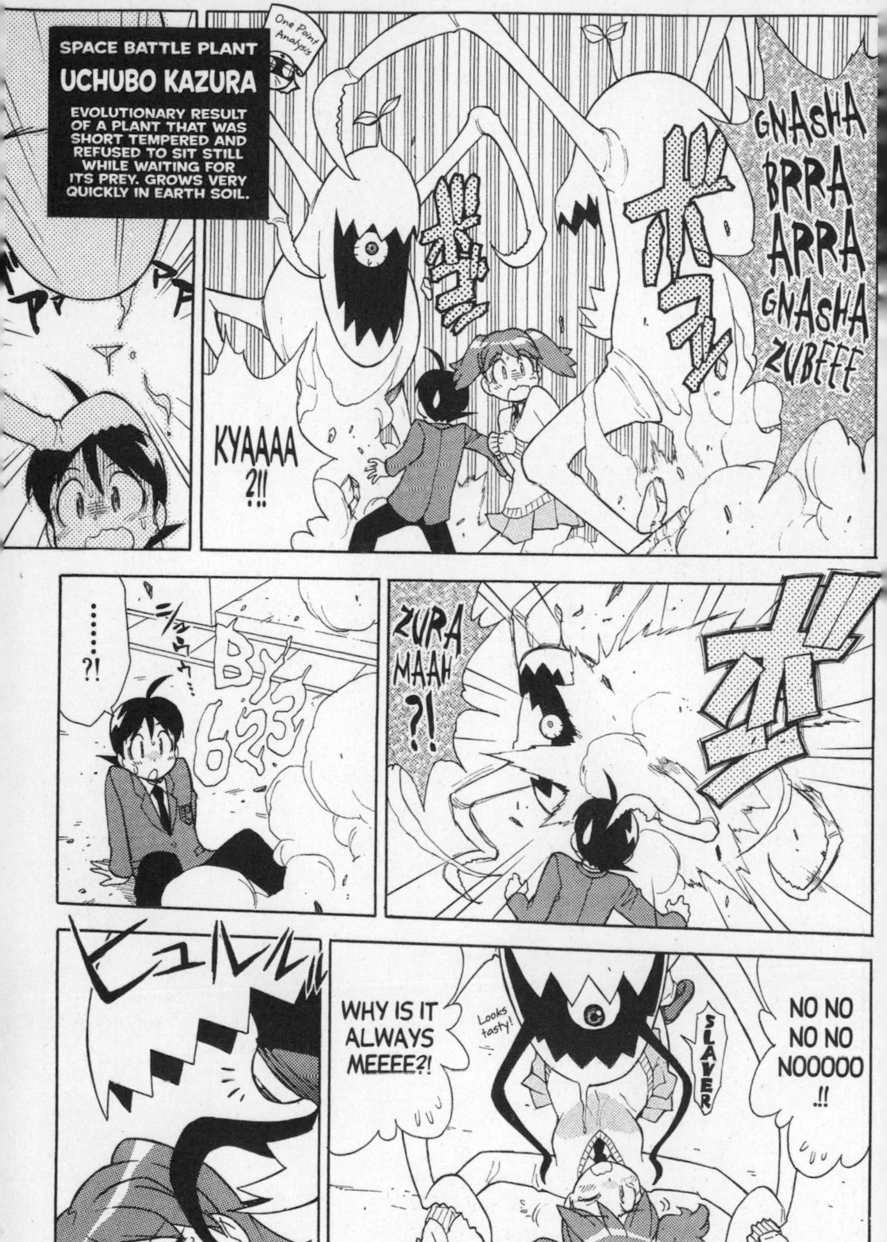
GNASHA BRRA ARRA GNASHA ZUBEEE
One Point Analysis
SPACE BATTLE PLANT
UCHUBO KAZURA
EVOLUTIONARY RESULT OF A PLANT THAT WAS SHORT TEMPERED AND REFUSED TO SIT STILL WHILE WAITING FOR ITS PREY. GROWS VERY QUICKLY IN EARTH SOIL.
KYAAAA ?!!
ZURA MAAH ?!
.....?!
NO NO NO NO NOOOOO !!
SLAVER
Looks tasty!
WHY IS IT ALWAYS MEEEE?!

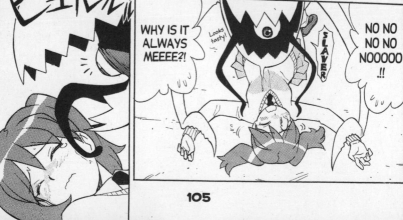

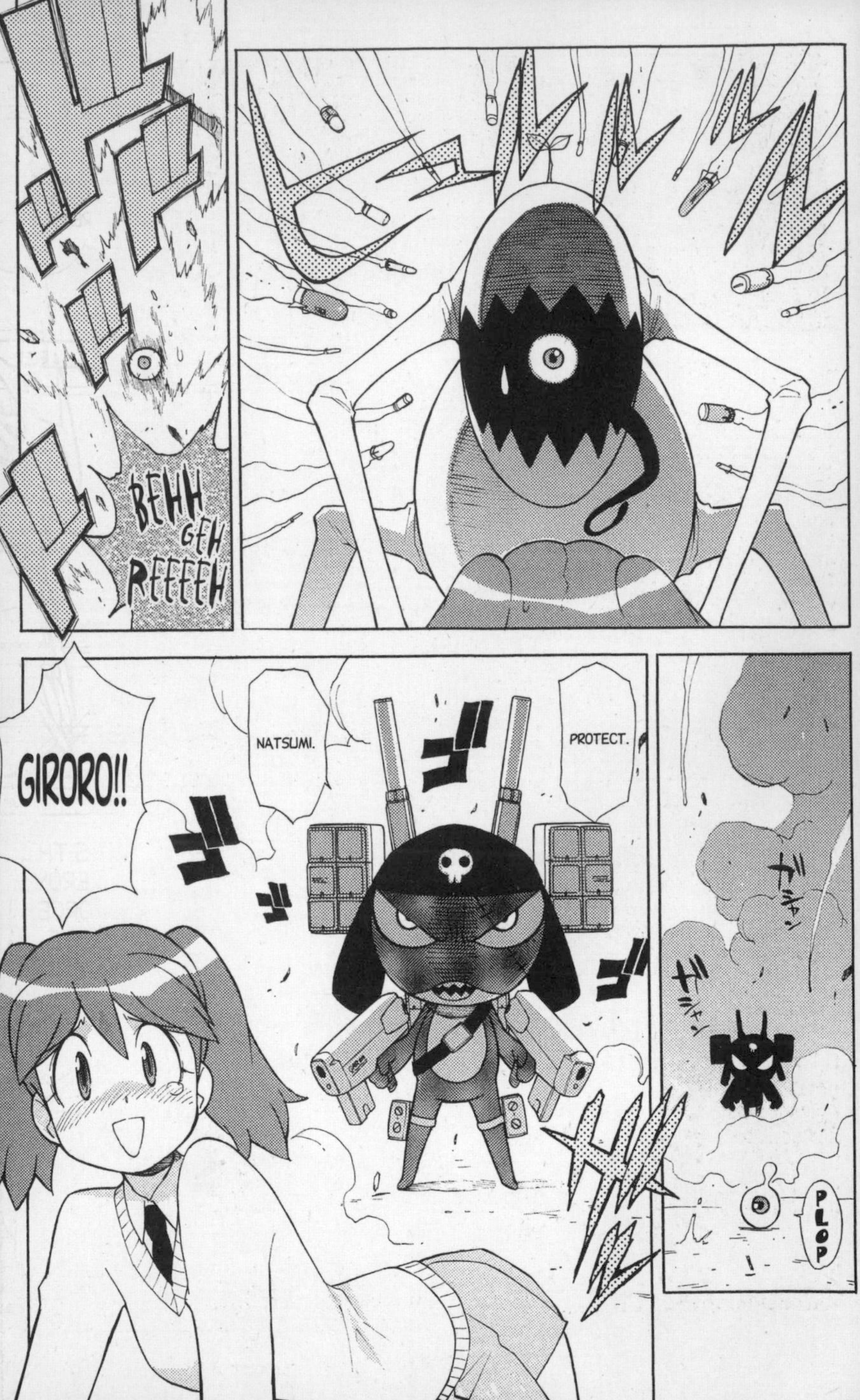
BEHH GEH REEEEH
PLOP
PROTECT.
NATSUMI.
GIRORO!!

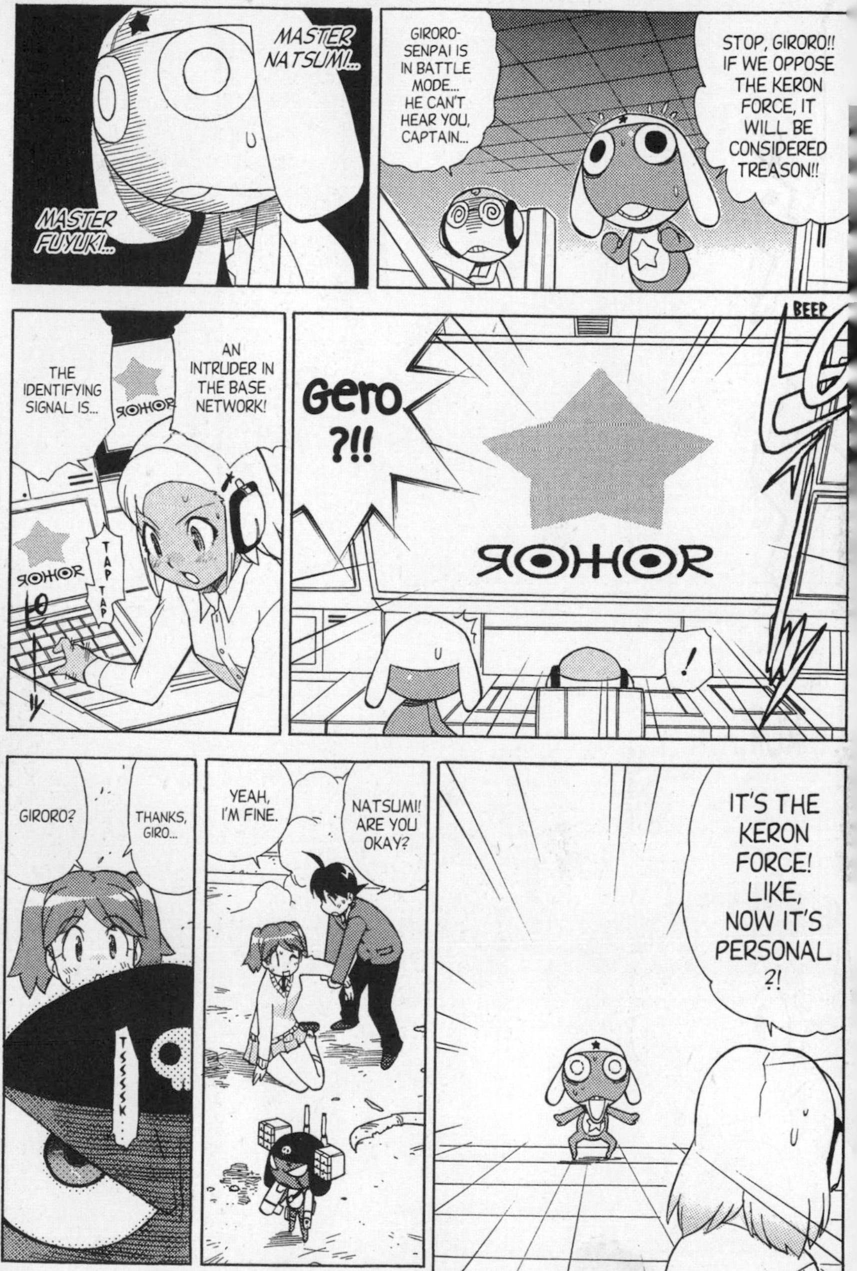
STOP, GIRORO!! IF WE OPPOSE THE KERON FORCE, IT WILL BE CONSIDERED TREASON!!
GIRORO-SENPAI IS IN BATTLE MODE... HE CAN'T HEAR YOU, CAPTAIN...
MASTER NATSUMI...
MASTER FUYUKI...
BEEP
Gero ?!!
!
AN INTRUDER IN THE BASE NETWORK!
THE IDENTIFYING SIGNAL IS...
TAP TAP
IT'S THE KERON FORCE! LIKE, NOW IT'S PERSONAL ?!
NATSUMI! ARE YOU OKAY?
YEAH, I'M FINE.
THANKS, GIRO...
GIRORO?
TSSSK...

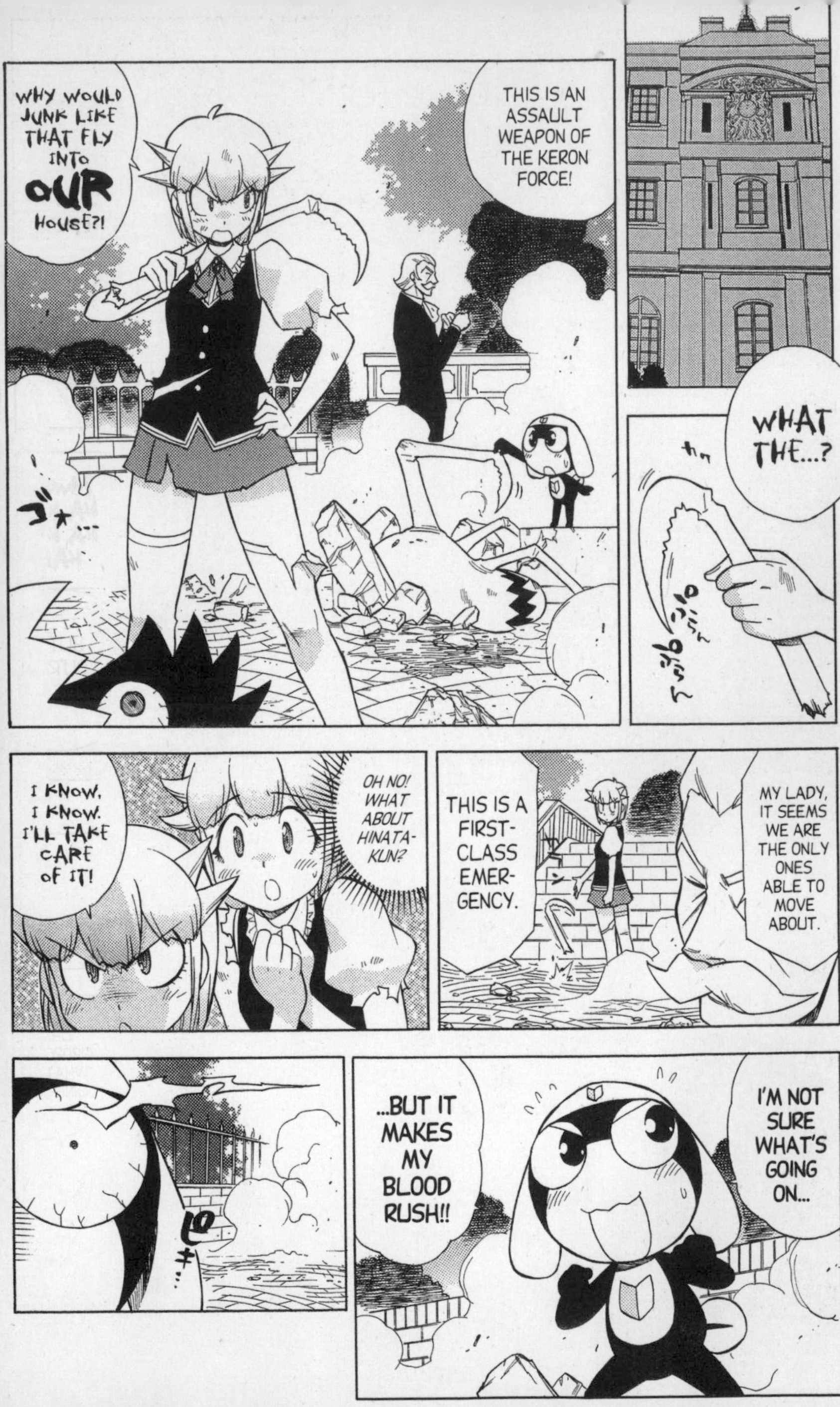
WHAT THE...?
THIS IS AN ASSAULT WEAPON OF THE KERON FORCE!
WHY WOULD JUNK LIKE THAT FLY INTO OUR HOUSE?!
MY LADY, IT SEEMS WE ARE THE ONLY ONES ABLE TO MOVE ABOUT.
THIS IS A FIRST-CLASS EMERGENCY.
OH NO! WHAT ABOUT HINATA-KUN?
I KNOW, I KNOW. I'LL TAKE CARE OF IT!
I'M NOT SURE WHAT'S GOING ON...
...BUT IT MAKES MY BLOOD RUSH!!

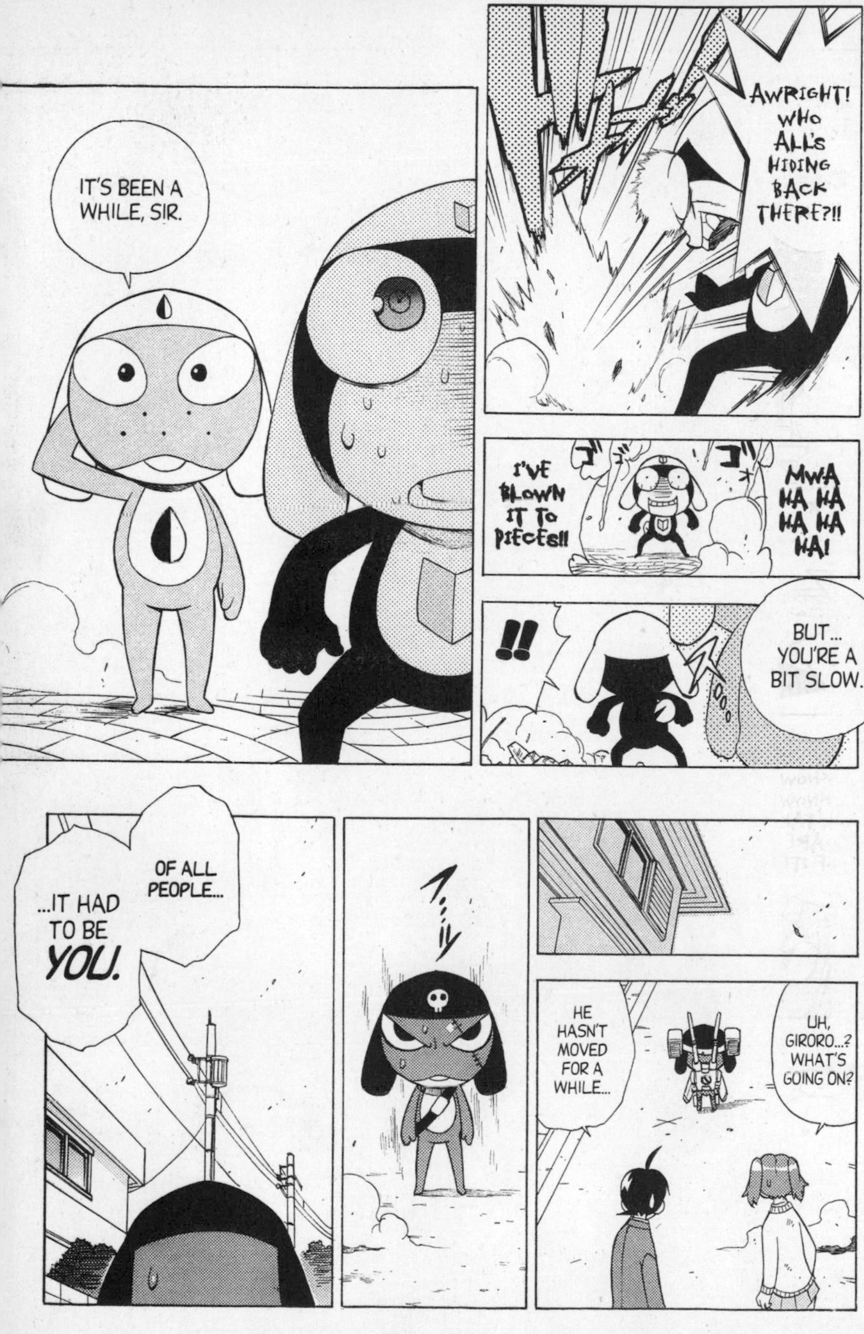
AWRIGHT! WHO ALL'S HIDING BACK THERE?!!
MWA HA HA HA HA HA!
I'VE BLOWN IT TO PIECES!!
!!
BUT... YOU'RE A BIT SLOW.
IT'S BEEN A WHILE, SIR.
UH, GIRORO...? WHAT'S GOING ON?
HE HASN'T MOVED FOR A WHILE...
OF ALL PEOPLE...
...IT HAD TO BE *YOU.*

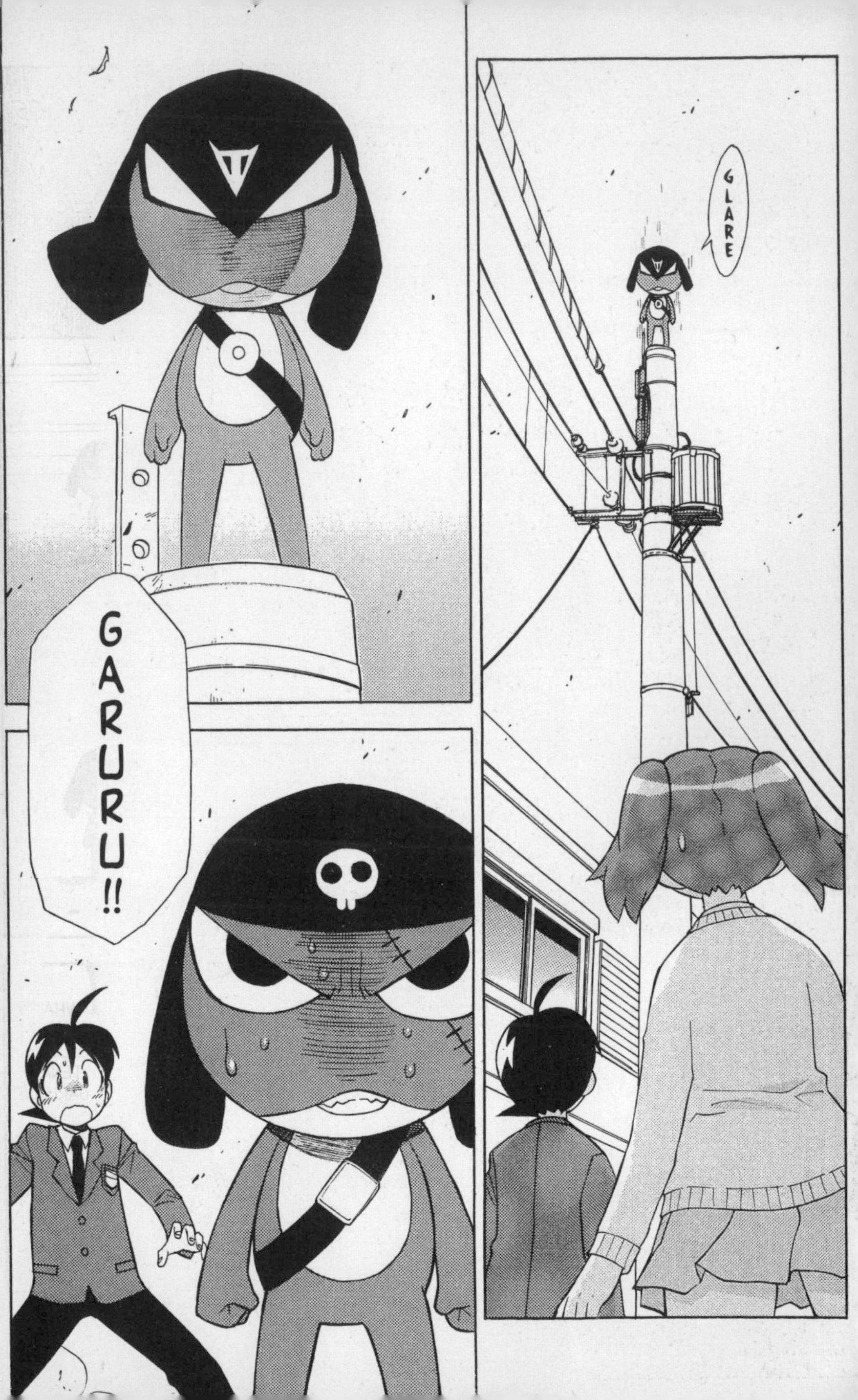
GLARE
GARURU!!

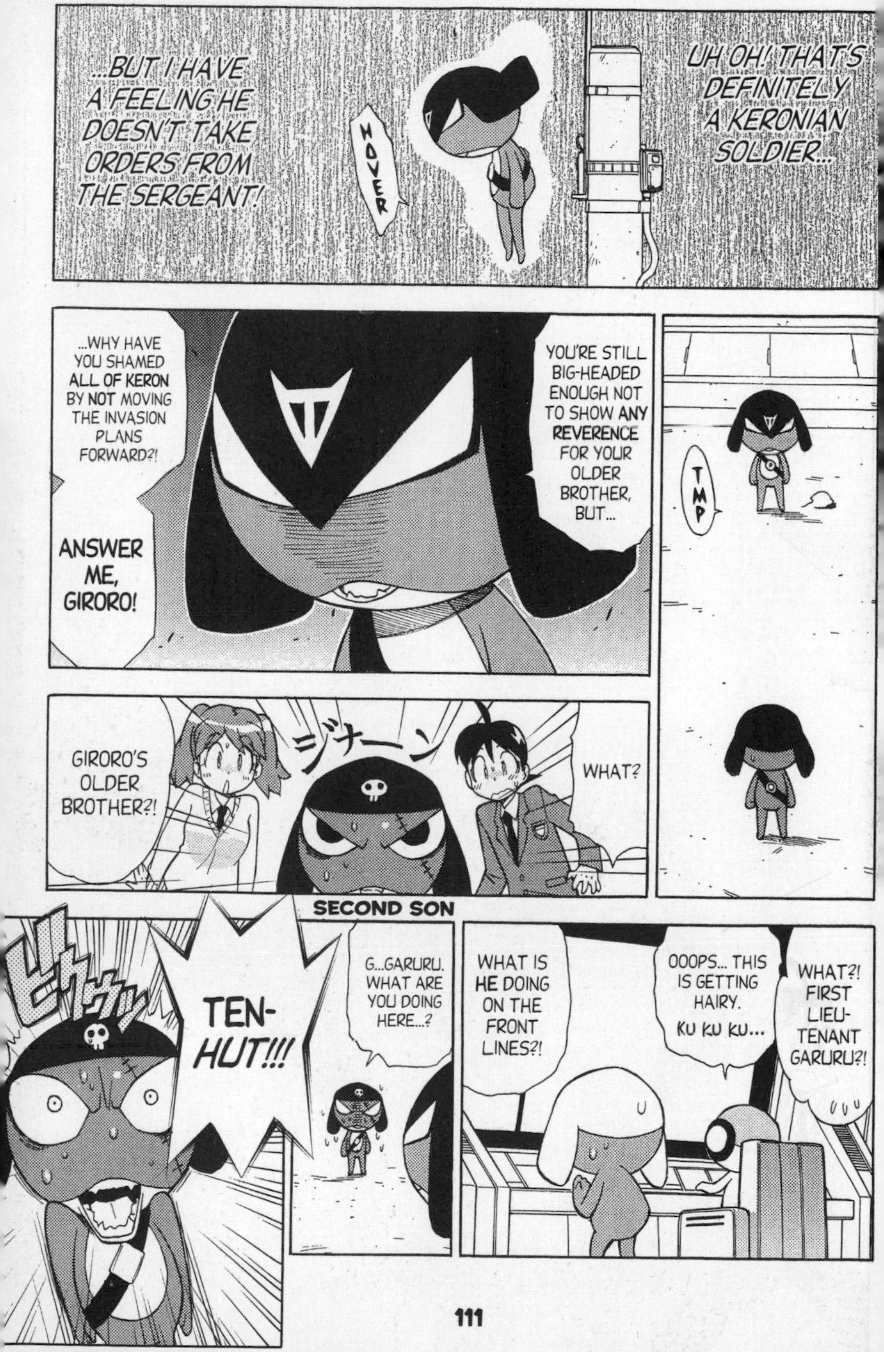
UH OH! THAT'S DEFINITELY A KERONIAN SOLDIER...
HOVER
...BUT I HAVE A FEELING HE DOESN'T TAKE ORDERS FROM THE SERGEANT!
TMP
YOU'RE STILL BIG-HEADED ENOUGH NOT TO SHOW ANY REVERENCE FOR YOUR OLDER BROTHER, BUT...
...WHY HAVE YOU SHAMED ALL OF KERON BY NOT MOVING THE INVASION PLANS FORWARD?!
ANSWER ME, GIRORO!
WHAT?
GIRORO'S OLDER BROTHER?!
SECOND SON
WHAT?! FIRST LIEU- TENANT GARURU?!
OOOPS... THIS IS GETTING HAIRY. KU KU KU...
WHAT IS HE DOING ON THE FRONT LINES?!
G...GARURU. WHAT ARE YOU DOING HERE...?
TEN- HUT!!!

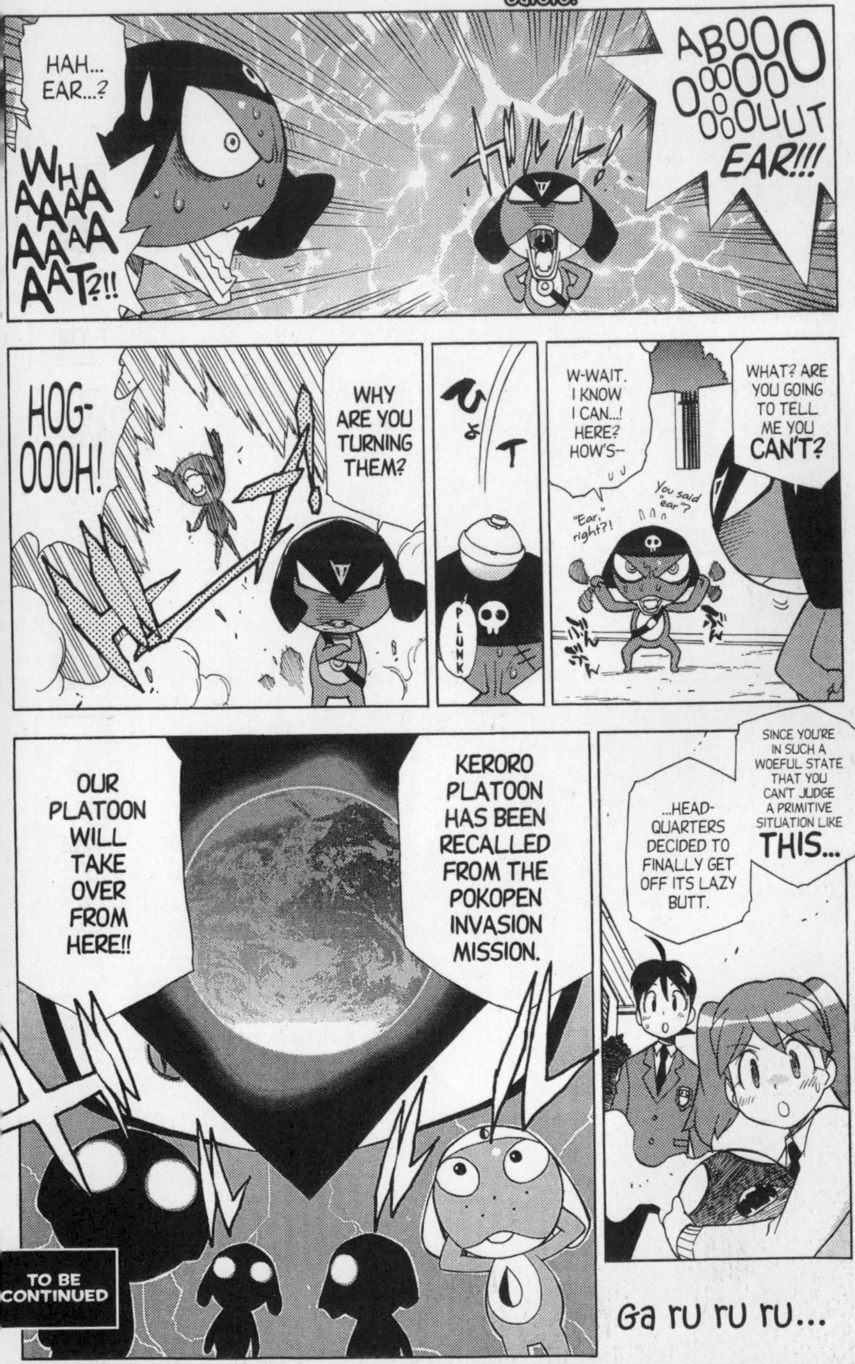
ABOOOOOOOOOOOOOOOUUT EAR!!!
HAH... EAR...?
WHAAAAAAAAAAAT?!!
WHAT? ARE YOU GOING TO TELL ME YOU CAN'T?
W-WAIT. I KNOW I CAN...! HERE? HOW'S--
You said "ear"?
"Ear," right?!
PLUNK
WHY ARE YOU TURNING THEM?
HOG-OOOH!
SINCE YOU'RE IN SUCH A WOEFUL STATE THAT YOU CAN'T JUDGE A PRIMITIVE SITUATION LIKE THIS...
...HEAD-QUARTERS DECIDED TO FINALLY GET OFF ITS LAZY BUTT.
Ga ru ru ru...
KERORO PLATOON HAS BEEN RECALLED FROM THE POKOPEN INVASION MISSION.
OUR PLATOON WILL TAKE OVER FROM HERE!!
TO BE CONTINUED

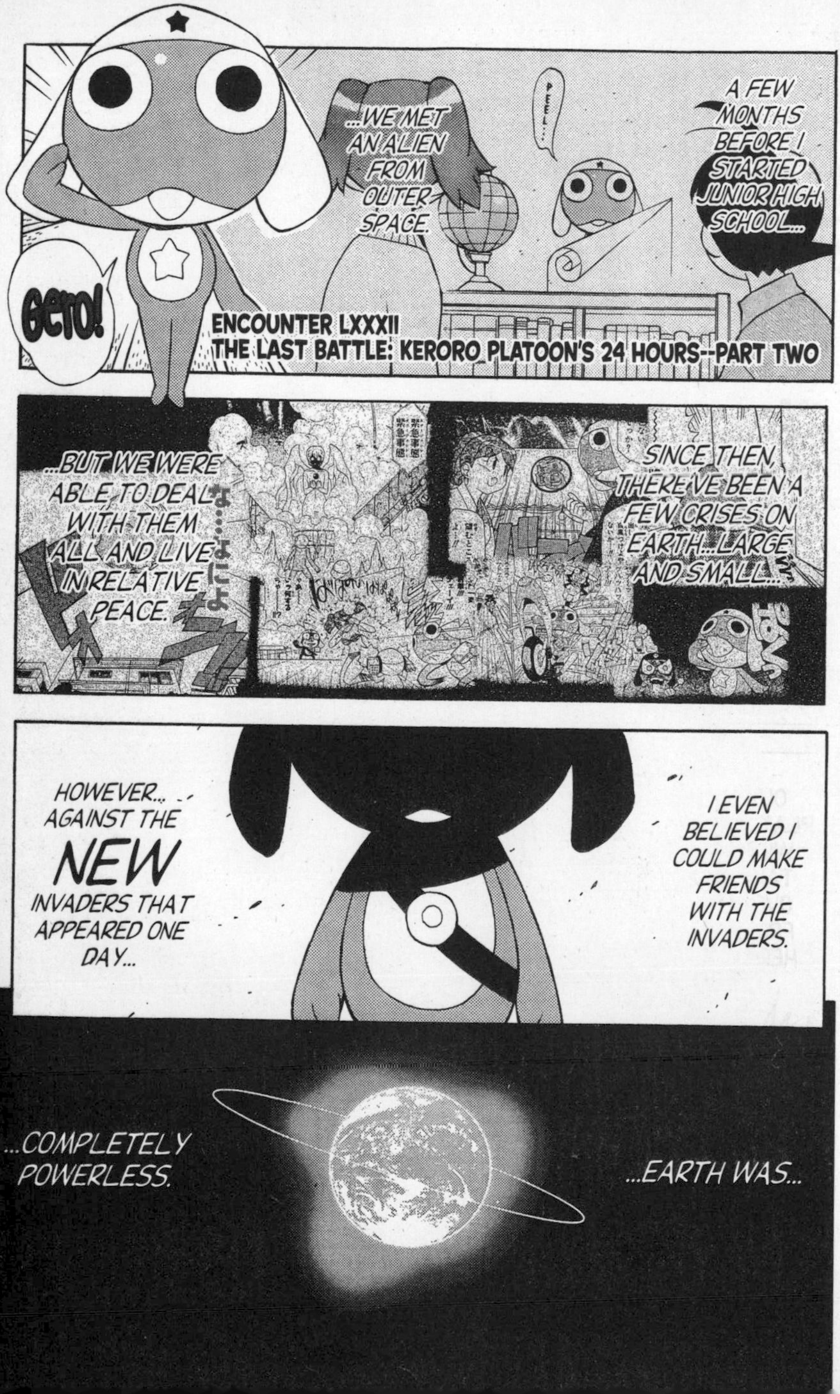
A FEW MONTHS BEFORE I STARTED JUNIOR HIGH SCHOOL...
PEEL...
...WE MET AN ALIEN FROM OUTER SPACE.
GERO!
ENCOUNTER LXXXII
THE LAST BATTLE: KERORO PLATOON'S 24 HOURS--PART TWO
SINCE THEN, THERE'VE BEEN A FEW CRISES ON EARTH...LARGE AND SMALL...
...BUT WE WERE ABLE TO DEAL WITH THEM ALL AND LIVE IN RELATIVE PEACE.
I EVEN BELIEVED I COULD MAKE FRIENDS WITH THE INVADERS.
HOWEVER... AGAINST THE NEW INVADERS THAT APPEARED ONE DAY...
...EARTH WAS...
...COMPLETELY POWERLESS.

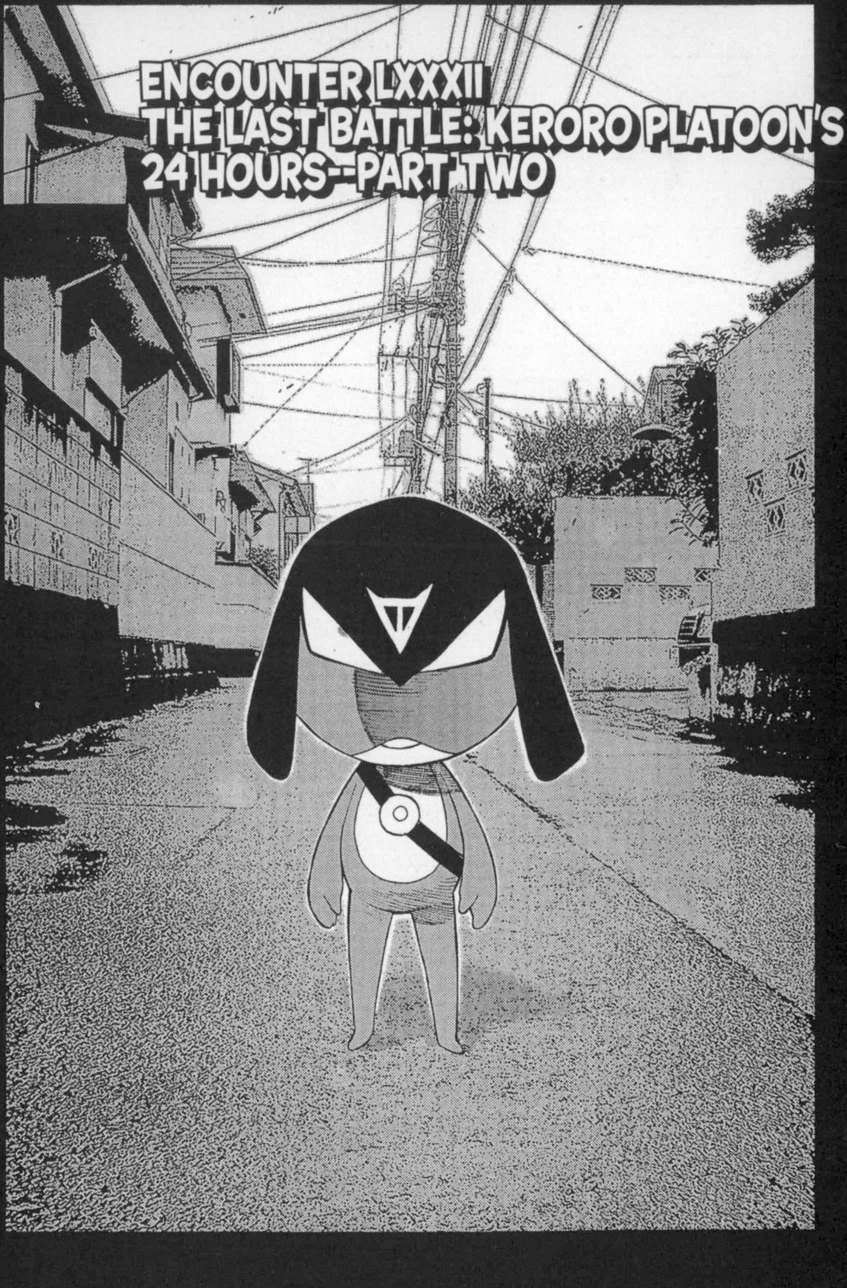
ENCOUNTER LXXXII
THE LAST BATTLE: KERORO PLATOON'S
24 HOURS--PART TWO

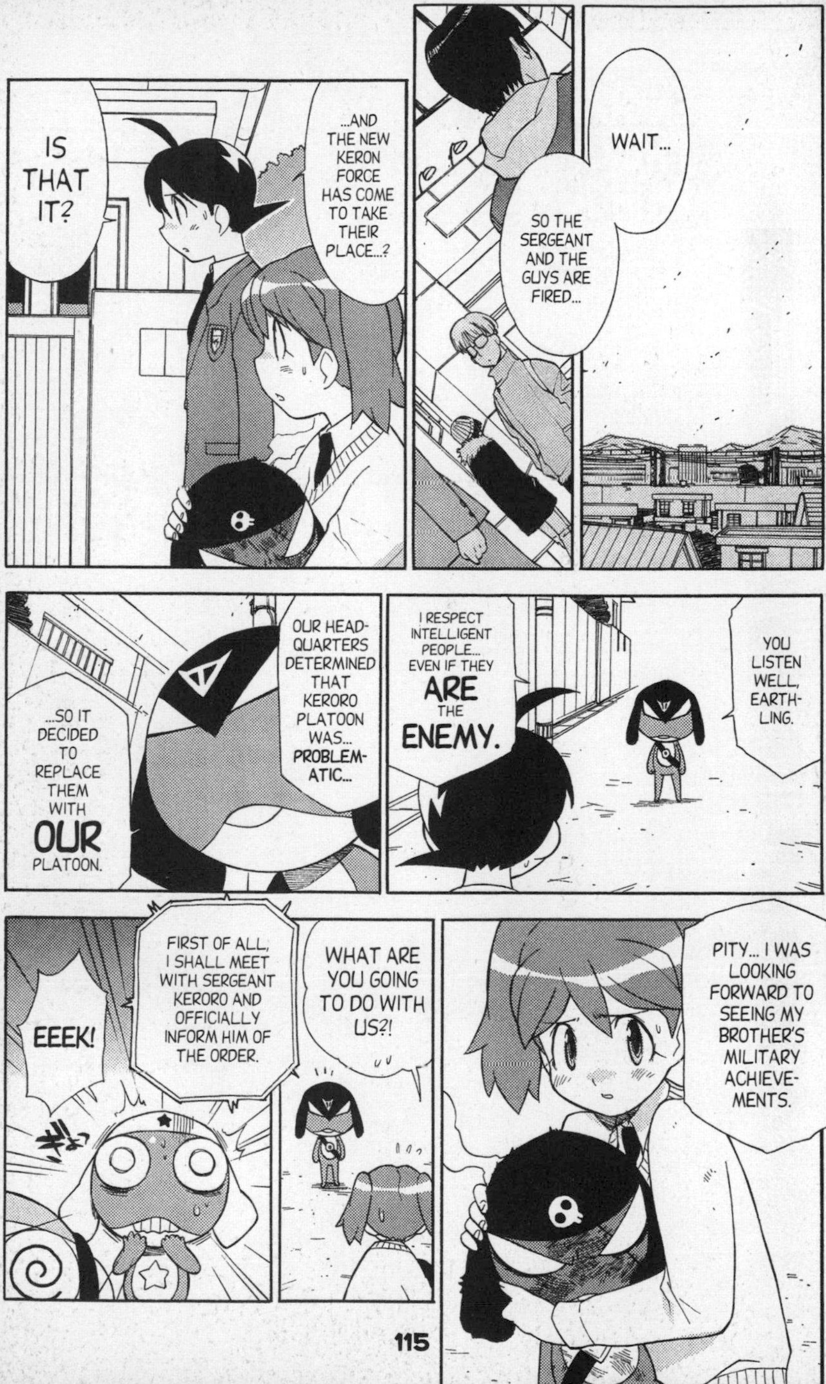
WAIT...
SO THE SERGEANT AND THE GUYS ARE FIRED...
...AND THE NEW KERON FORCE HAS COME TO TAKE THEIR PLACE...?
IS THAT IT?
YOU LISTEN WELL, EARTHLING.
I RESPECT INTELLIGENT PEOPLE... EVEN IF THEY ARE THE ENEMY.
OUR HEAD-QUARTERS DETERMINED THAT KERORO PLATOON WAS... PROBLEM-ATIC...
...SO IT DECIDED TO REPLACE THEM WITH OUR PLATOON.
PITY... I WAS LOOKING FORWARD TO SEEING MY BROTHER'S MILITARY ACHIEVE-MENTS.
WHAT ARE YOU GOING TO DO WITH US?!
FIRST OF ALL, I SHALL MEET WITH SERGEANT KERORO AND OFFICIALLY INFORM HIM OF THE ORDER.
EEEK!

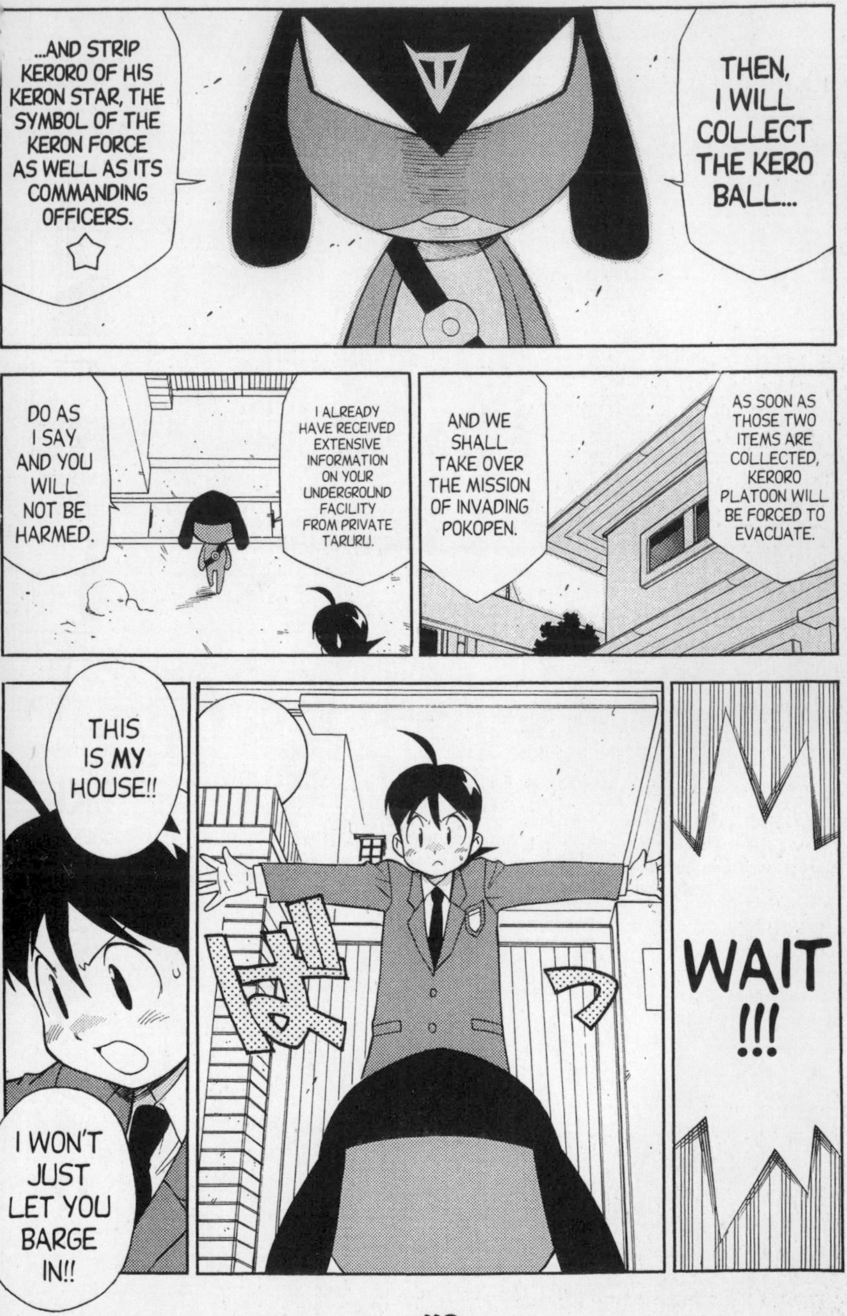
THEN, I WILL COLLECT THE KERO BALL...
...AND STRIP KERORO OF HIS KERON STAR, THE SYMBOL OF THE KERON FORCE AS WELL AS ITS COMMANDING OFFICERS. ☆
AS SOON AS THOSE TWO ITEMS ARE COLLECTED, KERORO PLATOON WILL BE FORCED TO EVACUATE.
AND WE SHALL TAKE OVER THE MISSION OF INVADING POKOPEN.
I ALREADY HAVE RECEIVED EXTENSIVE INFORMATION ON YOUR UNDERGROUND FACILITY FROM PRIVATE TARURU.
DO AS I SAY AND YOU WILL NOT BE HARMED.
WAIT !!!
ばっ
THIS IS MY HOUSE!!
I WON'T JUST LET YOU BARGE IN!!

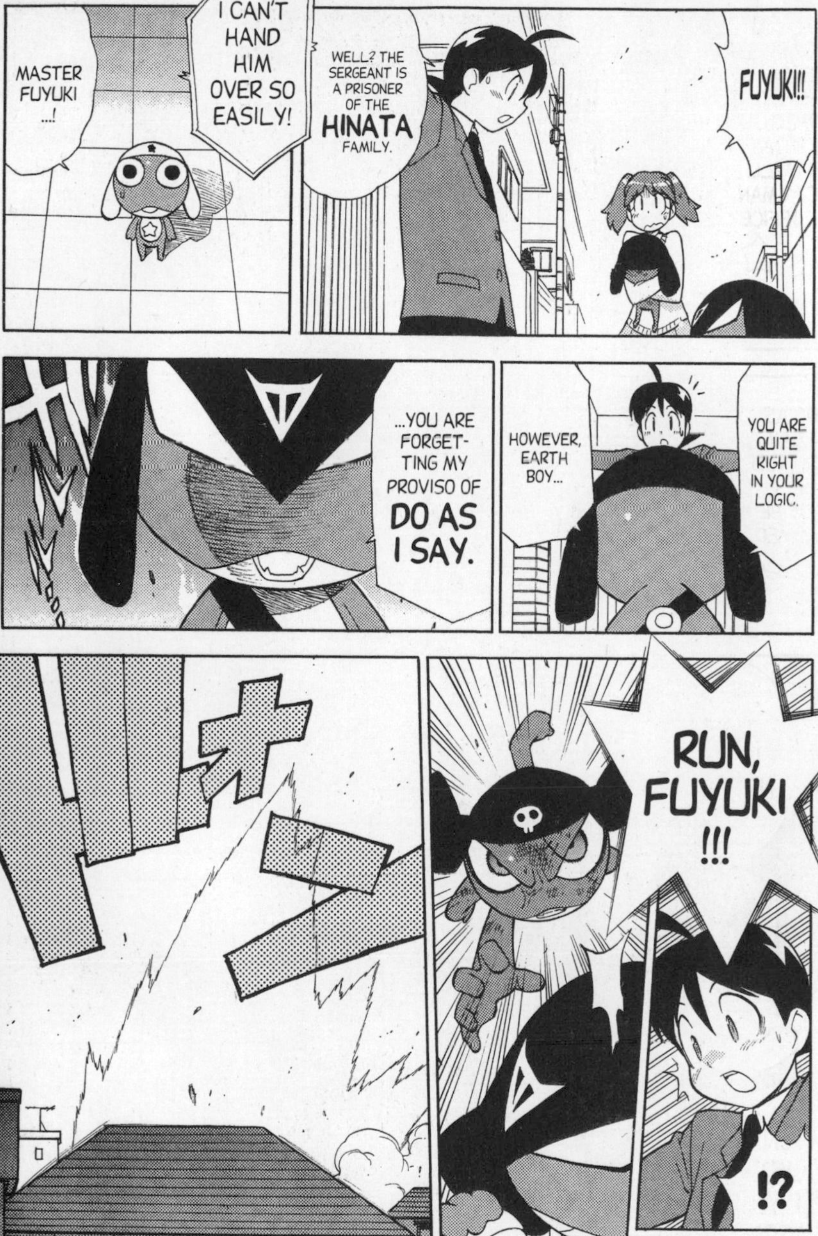
FUYUKI!!
WELL? THE SERGEANT IS A PRISONER OF THE HINATA FAMILY.
I CAN'T HAND HIM OVER SO EASILY!
MASTER FUYUKI ...!
YOU ARE QUITE KIGHT IN YOUR LOGIC.
HOWEVER, EARTH BOY...
...YOU ARE FORGET-TING MY PROVISO OF DO AS I SAY.
RUN, FUYUKI !!!
!?

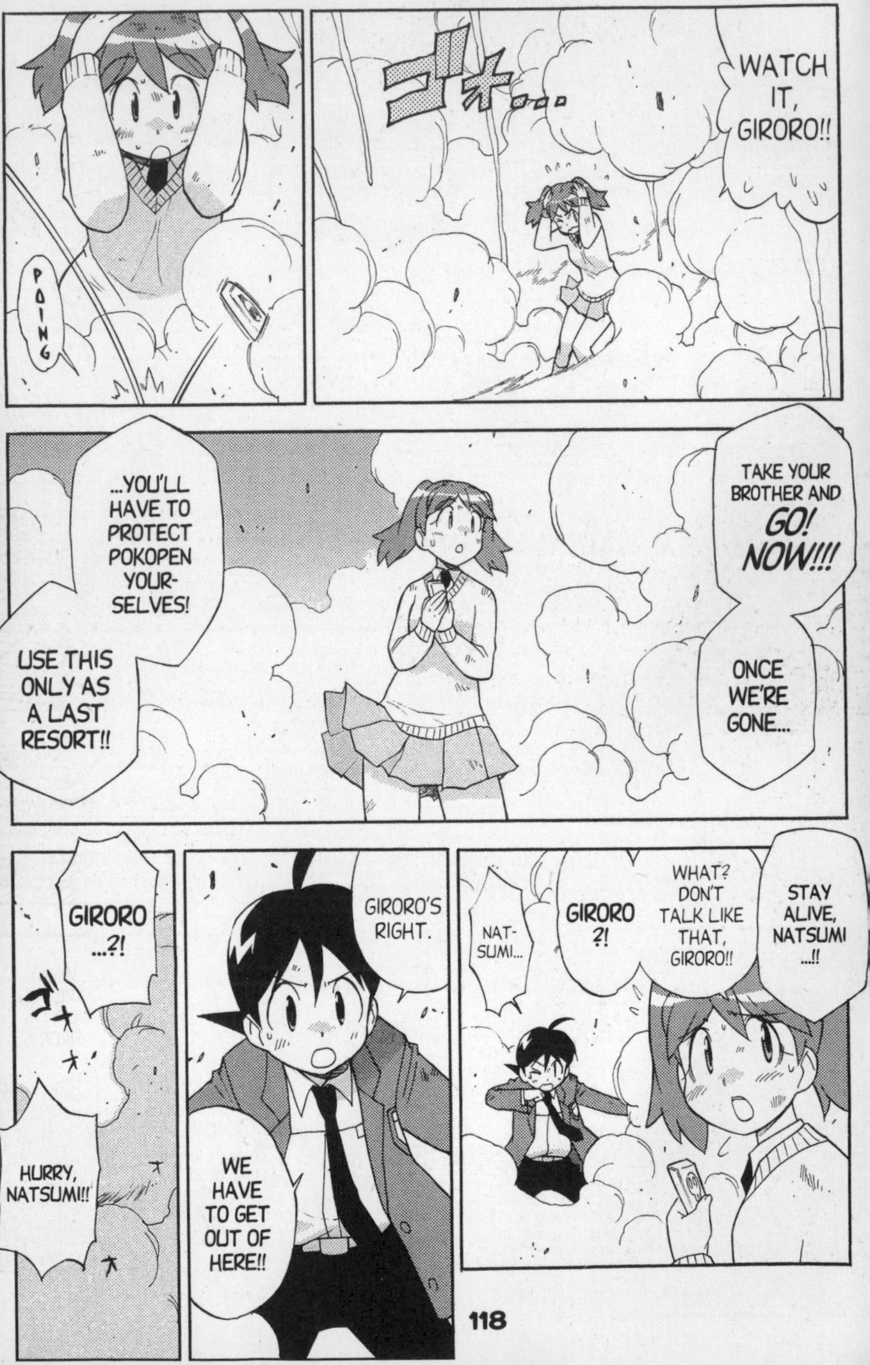
ゴオ…
WATCH IT, GIRORO!!
POING
TAKE YOUR BROTHER AND GO! NOW!!!
ONCE WE'RE GONE...
...YOU'LL HAVE TO PROTECT POKOPEN YOUR-SELVES!
USE THIS ONLY AS A LAST RESORT!!
STAY ALIVE, NATSUMI ...!!
WHAT? DON'T TALK LIKE THAT, GIRORO!!
GIRORO ?!
NAT-SUMI...
GIRORO'S RIGHT.
WE HAVE TO GET OUT OF HERE!!
GIRORO ...?!
ゴオオ
HURRY, NATSUMI!!

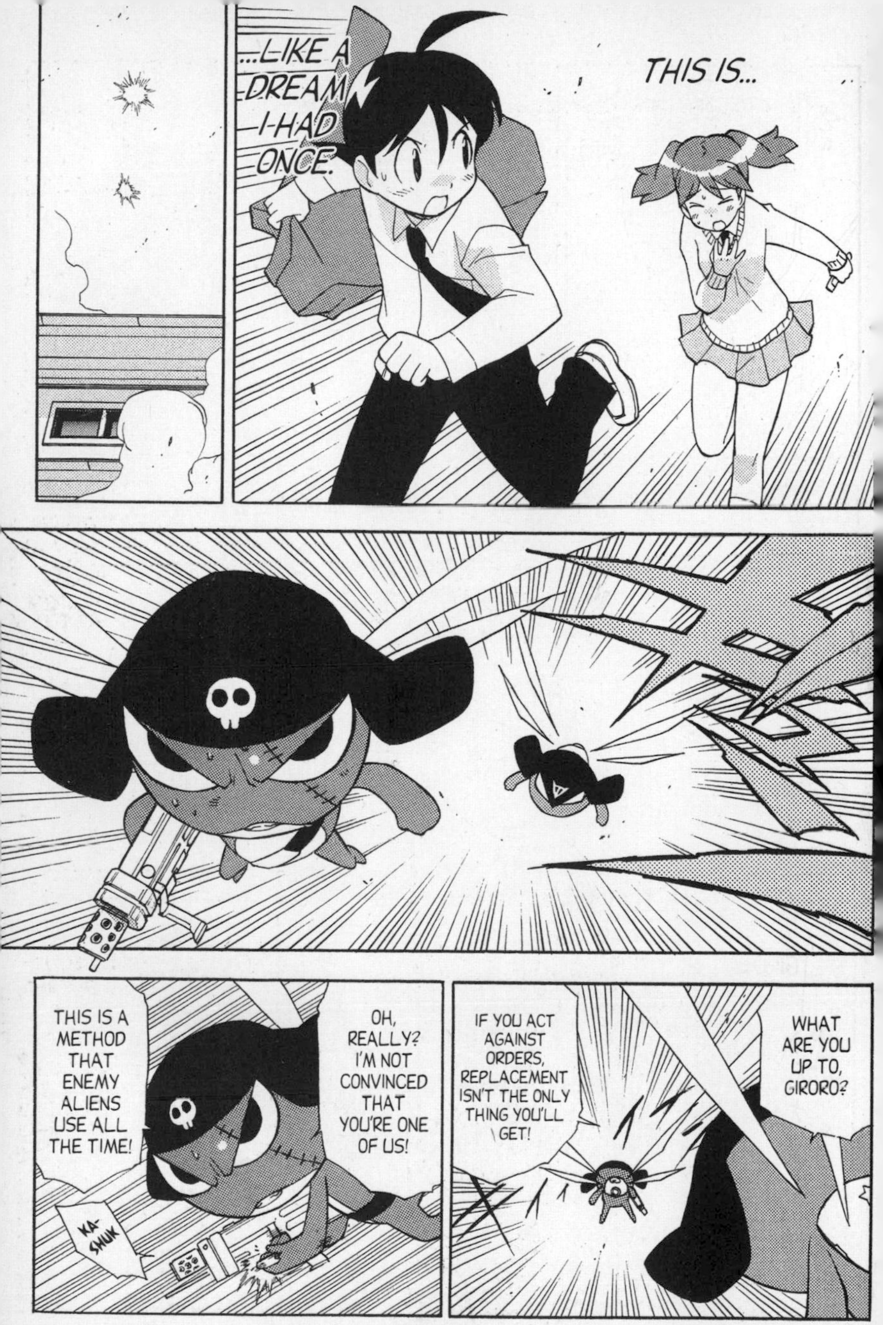
THIS IS...
...LIKE A DREAM I HAD ONCE.
WHAT ARE YOU UP TO, GIRORO?
IF YOU ACT AGAINST ORDERS, REPLACEMENT ISN'T THE ONLY THING YOU'LL GET!
OH, REALLY? I'M NOT CONVINCED THAT YOU'RE ONE OF US!
THIS IS A METHOD THAT ENEMY ALIENS USE ALL THE TIME!
KA-SHUK

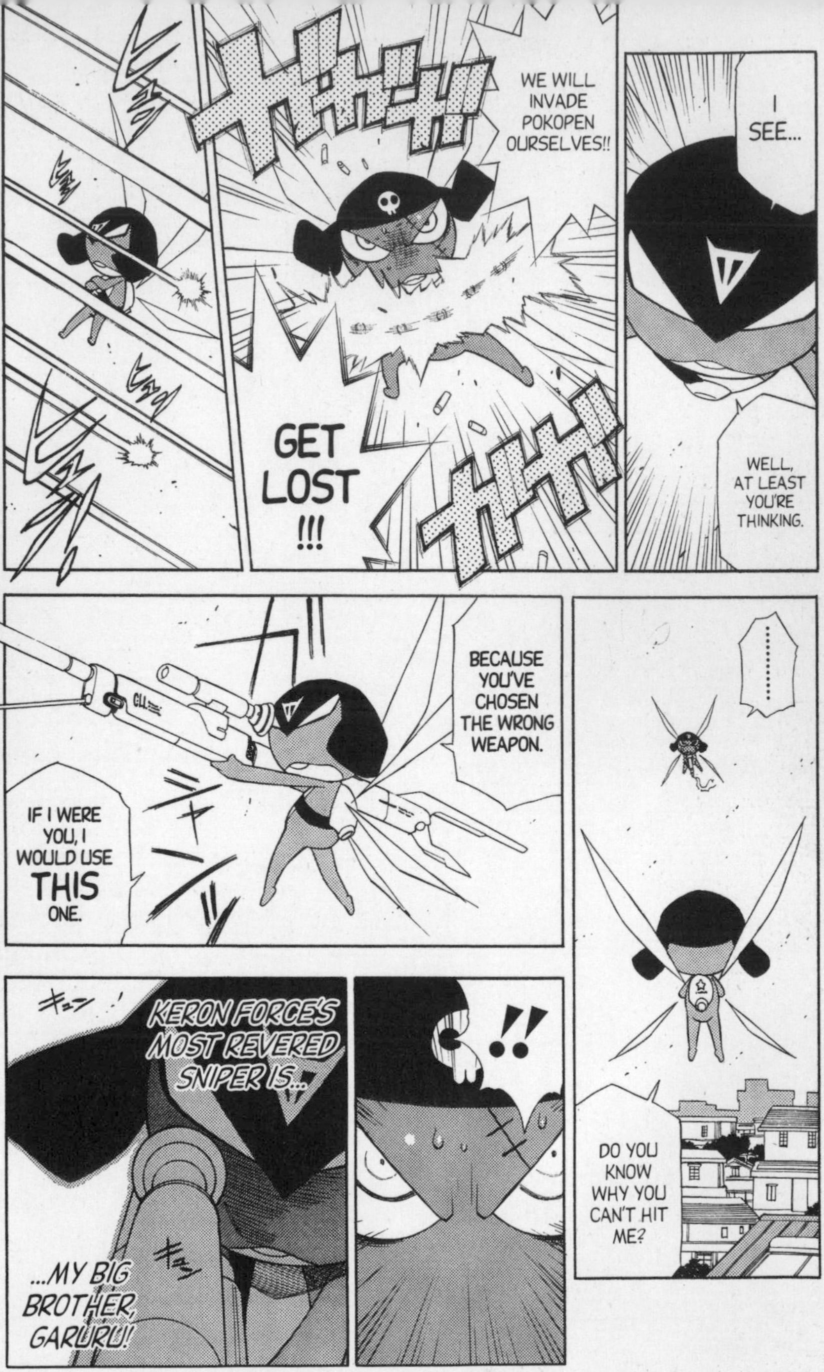
I SEE...
WELL, AT LEAST YOU'RE THINKING.
WE WILL INVADE POKOPEN OURSELVES!!
GET LOST !!!
......
DO YOU KNOW WHY YOU CAN'T HIT ME?
BECAUSE YOU'VE CHOSEN THE WRONG WEAPON.
IF I WERE YOU, I WOULD USE THIS ONE.
!!
KERON FORCE'S MOST REVERED SNIPER IS...
...MY BIG BROTHER, GARURU!

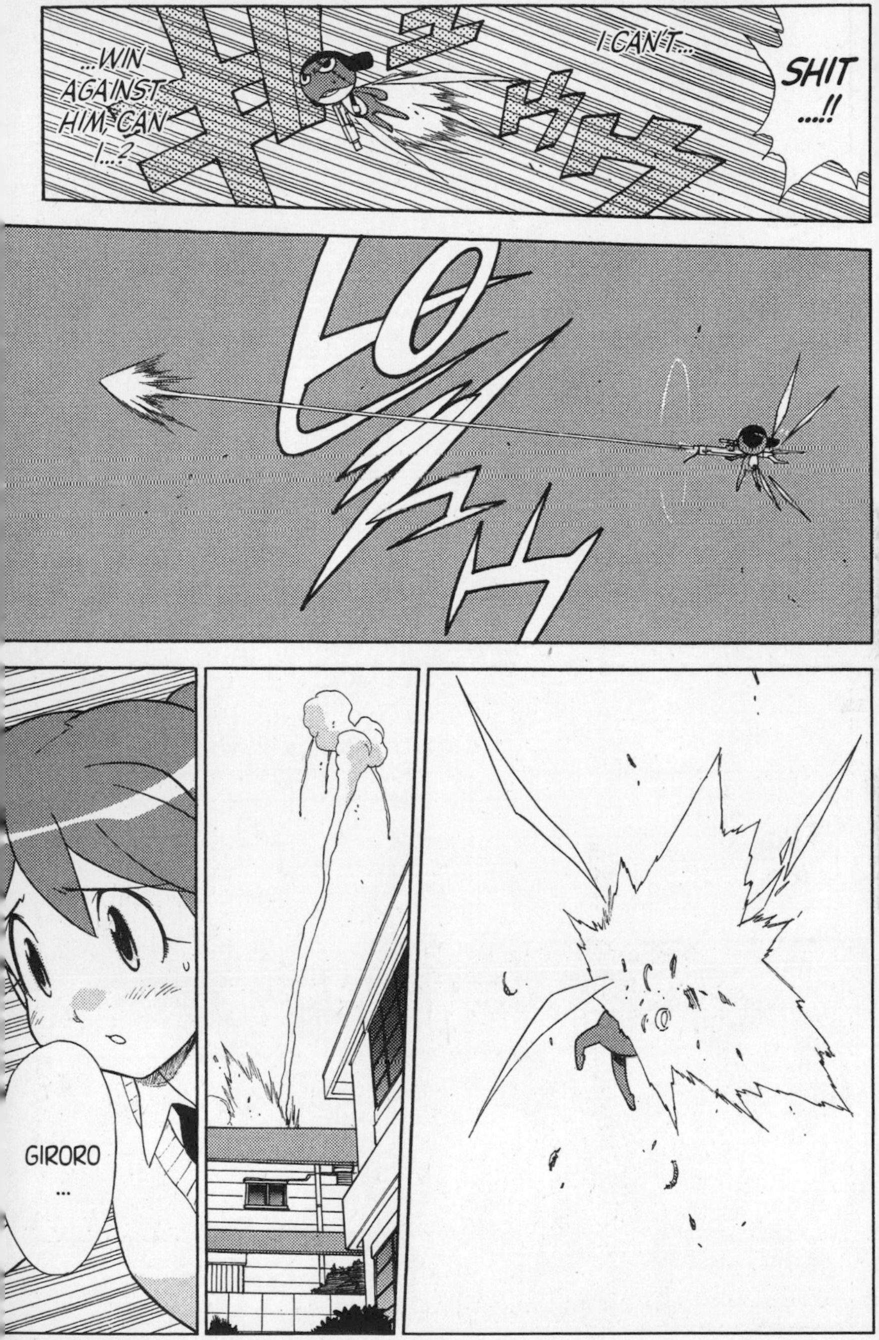
SHIT ...!!
I CAN'T...
...WIN AGAINST HIM, CAN I...?
GIRORO ...

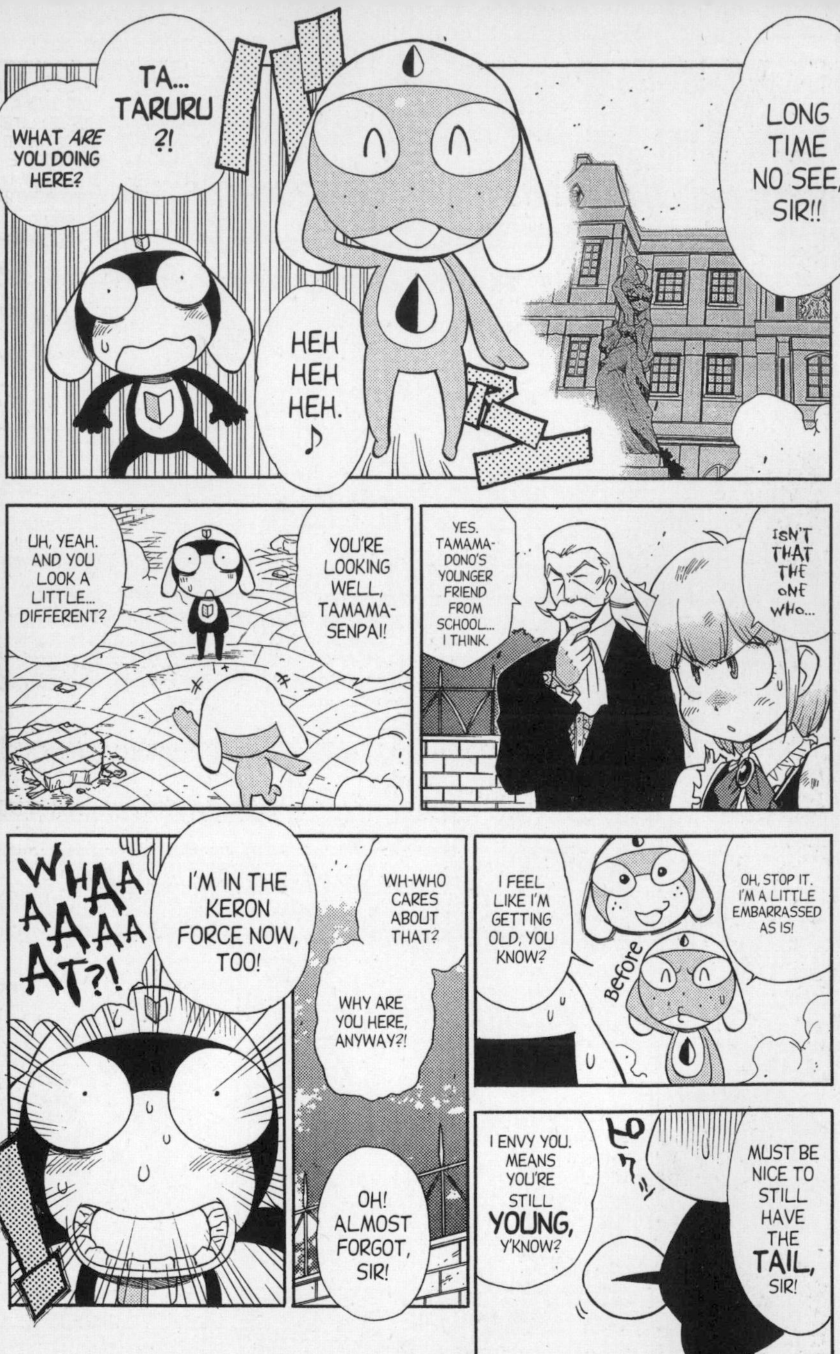
LONG TIME NO SEE, SIR!!
TA... TARURU?!
WHAT ARE YOU DOING HERE?
HEH HEH HEH. ♪
ISN'T THAT THE ONE WHO...
YES. TAMAMA-DONO'S YOUNGER FRIEND FROM SCHOOL... I THINK.
YOU'RE LOOKING WELL, TAMAMA-SENPAI!
UH, YEAH. AND YOU LOOK A LITTLE... DIFFERENT?
OH, STOP IT. I'M A LITTLE EMBARRASSED AS IS!
I FEEL LIKE I'M GETTING OLD, YOU KNOW?
Before
MUST BE NICE TO STILL HAVE THE TAIL, SIR!
I ENVY YOU. MEANS YOU'RE STILL YOUNG, Y'KNOW?
WH-WHO CARES ABOUT THAT?
WHY ARE YOU HERE, ANYWAY?!
OH! ALMOST FORGOT, SIR!
I'M IN THE KERON FORCE NOW, TOO!
WHAAAAAAAAT?!

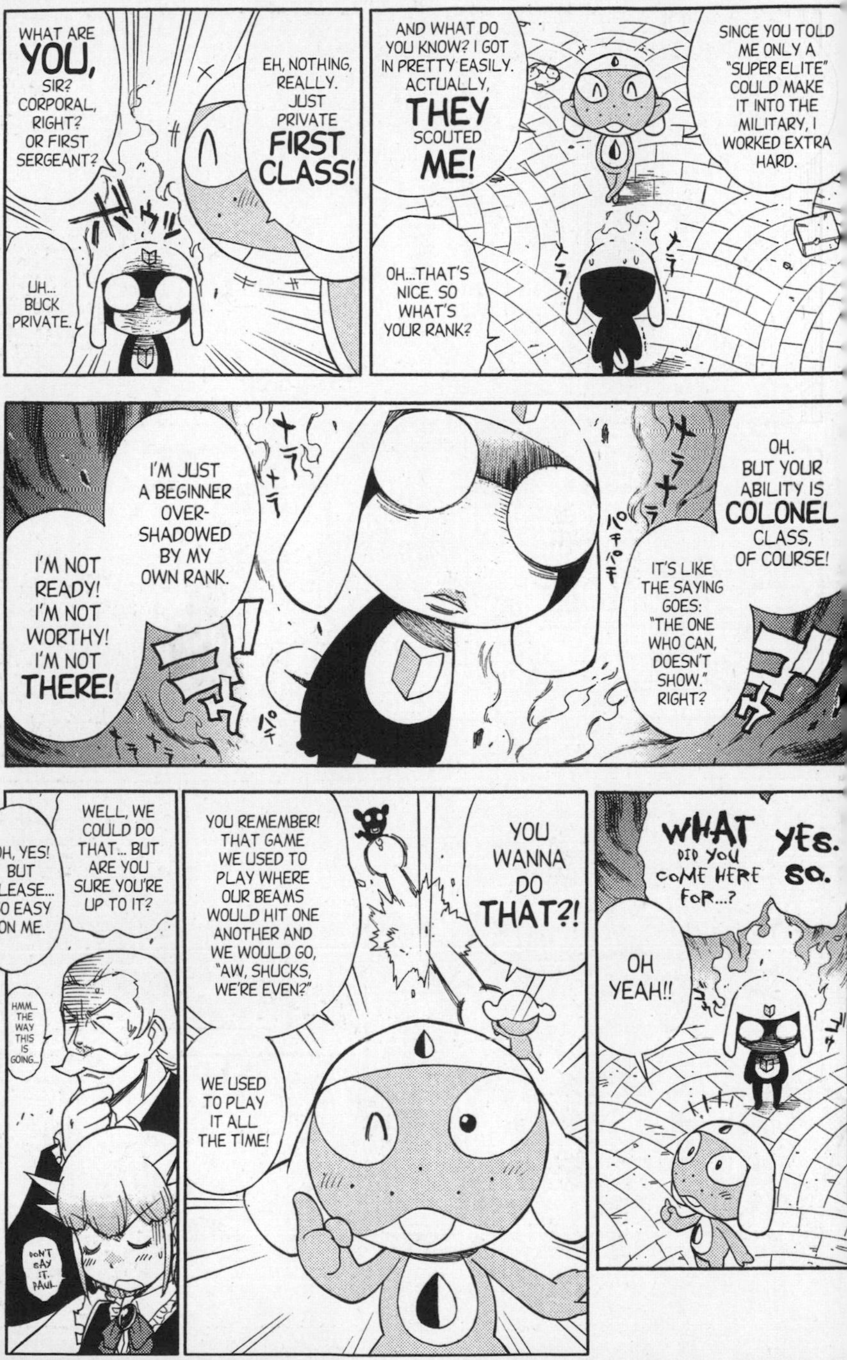
SINCE YOU TOLD ME ONLY A "SUPER ELITE" COULD MAKE IT INTO THE MILITARY, I WORKED EXTRA HARD.
AND WHAT DO YOU KNOW? I GOT IN PRETTY EASILY. ACTUALLY, THEY SCOUTED ME!
OH...THAT'S NICE. SO WHAT'S YOUR RANK?
EH, NOTHING, REALLY. JUST PRIVATE FIRST CLASS!
WHAT ARE YOU, SIR? CORPORAL, RIGHT? OR FIRST SERGEANT?
UH... BUCK PRIVATE.
OH. BUT YOUR ABILITY IS COLONEL CLASS, OF COURSE!
IT'S LIKE THE SAYING GOES: "THE ONE WHO CAN, DOESN'T SHOW." RIGHT?
I'M JUST A BEGINNER OVER-SHADOWED BY MY OWN RANK.
I'M NOT READY! I'M NOT WORTHY! I'M NOT THERE!
YES. SO.
WHAT DID YOU COME HERE FOR...?
OH YEAH!!
YOU WANNA DO THAT?!
YOU REMEMBER! THAT GAME WE USED TO PLAY WHERE OUR BEAMS WOULD HIT ONE ANOTHER AND WE WOULD GO, "AW, SHUCKS, WE'RE EVEN?"
WE USED TO PLAY IT ALL THE TIME!
WELL, WE COULD DO THAT... BUT ARE YOU SURE YOU'RE UP TO IT?
OH, YES! BUT PLEASE... GO EASY ON ME.
HMM... THE WAY THIS IS GOING...
DON'T SAY IT, PAUL.

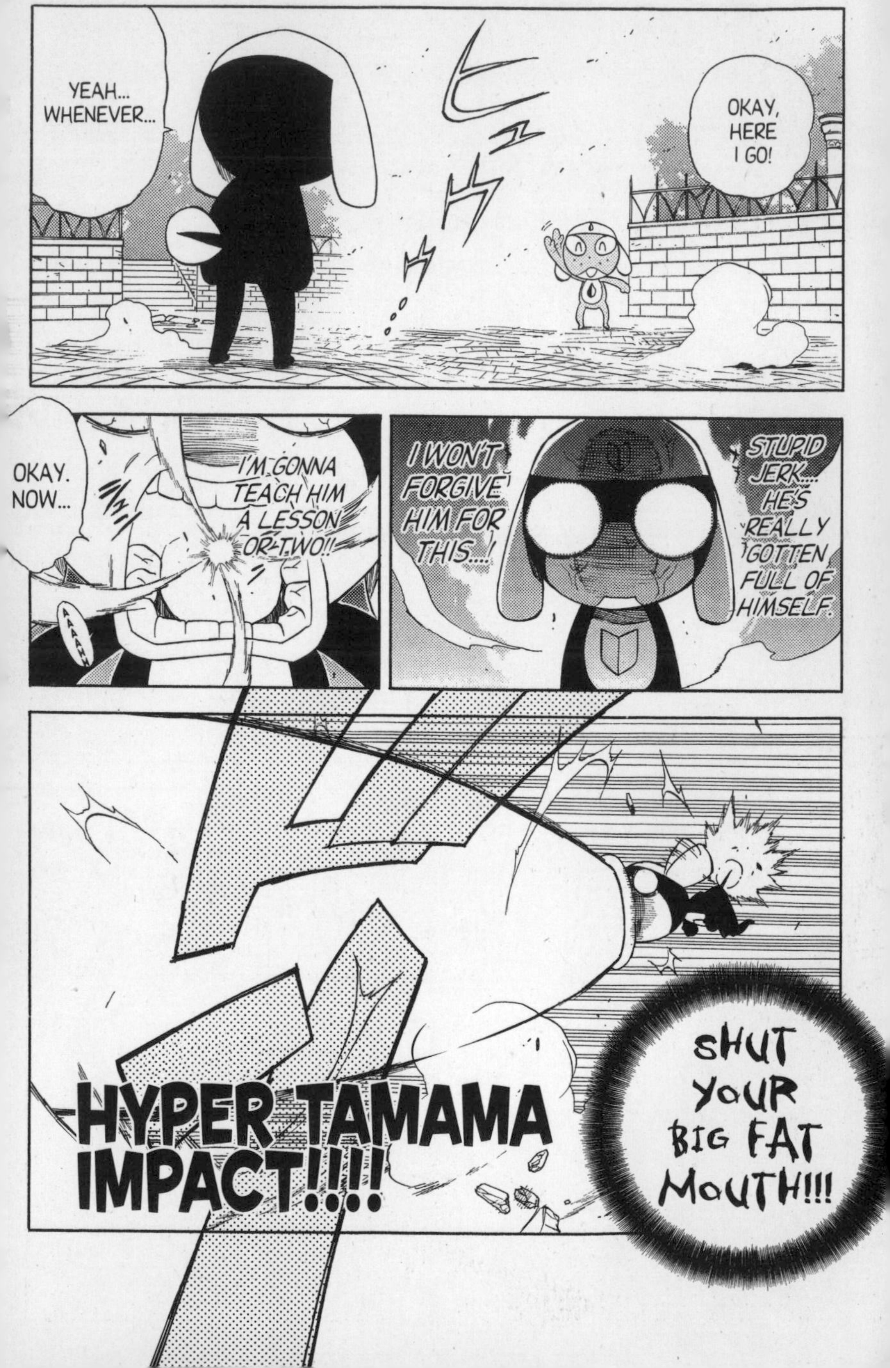
OKAY, HERE I GO!
YEAH... WHENEVER...
STUPID JERK... HE'S REALLY GOTTEN FULL OF HIMSELF.
I WON'T FORGIVE HIM FOR THIS...!
I'M GONNA TEACH HIM A LESSON OR TWO!!
OKAY. NOW...
AAAAH
SHUT YOUR BIG FAT MOUTH!!!
HYPER TAMAMA IMPACT!!!!

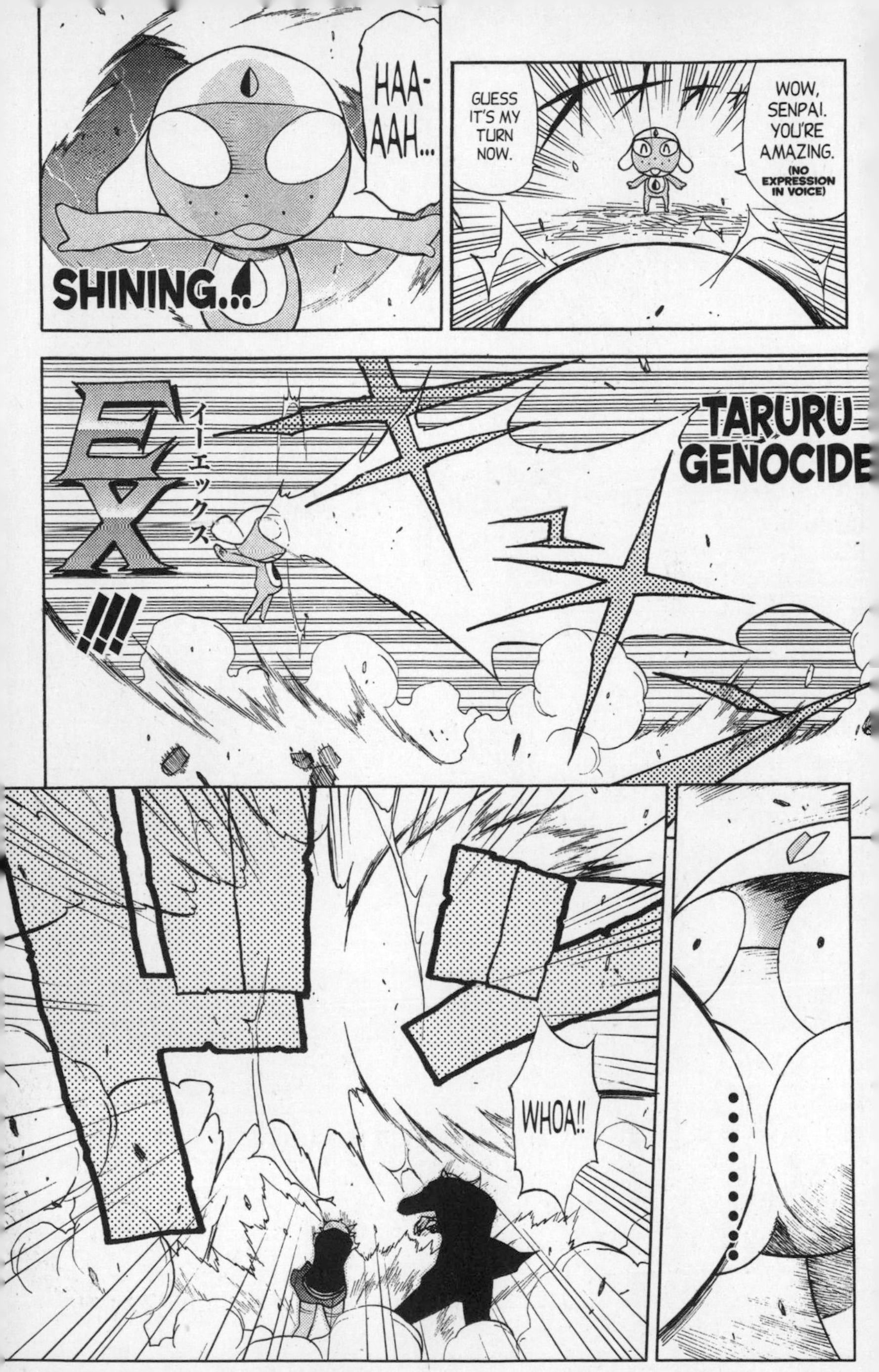
WOW, SENPAI. YOU'RE AMAZING.
(NO EXPRESSION IN VOICE)
GUESS IT'S MY TURN NOW.
HAA-AAH...
SHINING..!
TARURU GENOCIDE
EX
イーエックス
!!!
....
WHOA!!

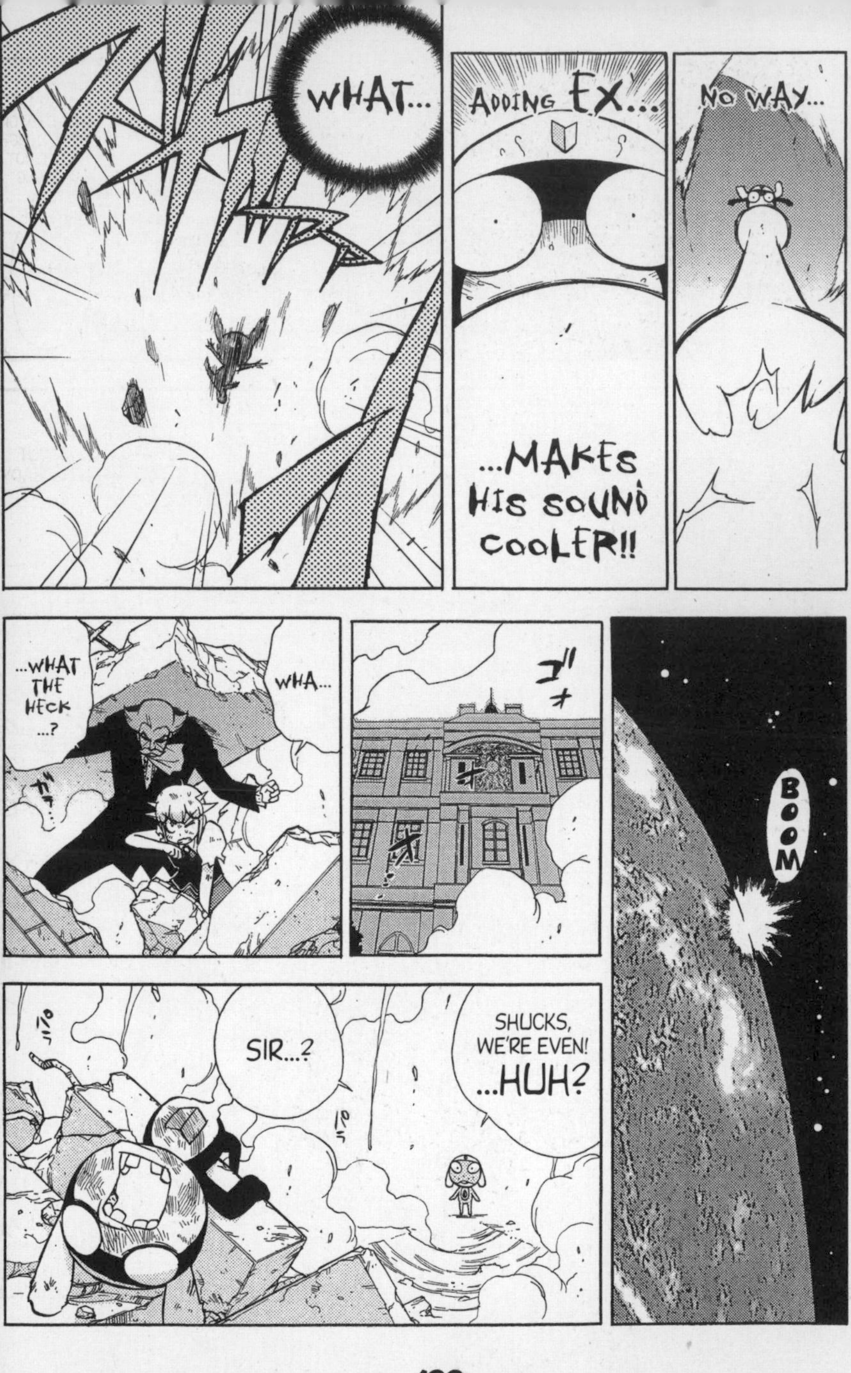
NO WAY...
ADDING EX...
...MAKES HIS SOUND COOLER!!
WHAT...
BOOM
ゴォ
WHA...
...WHAT THE HECK ...?
SHUCKS, WE'RE EVEN!
...HUH?
SIR...?

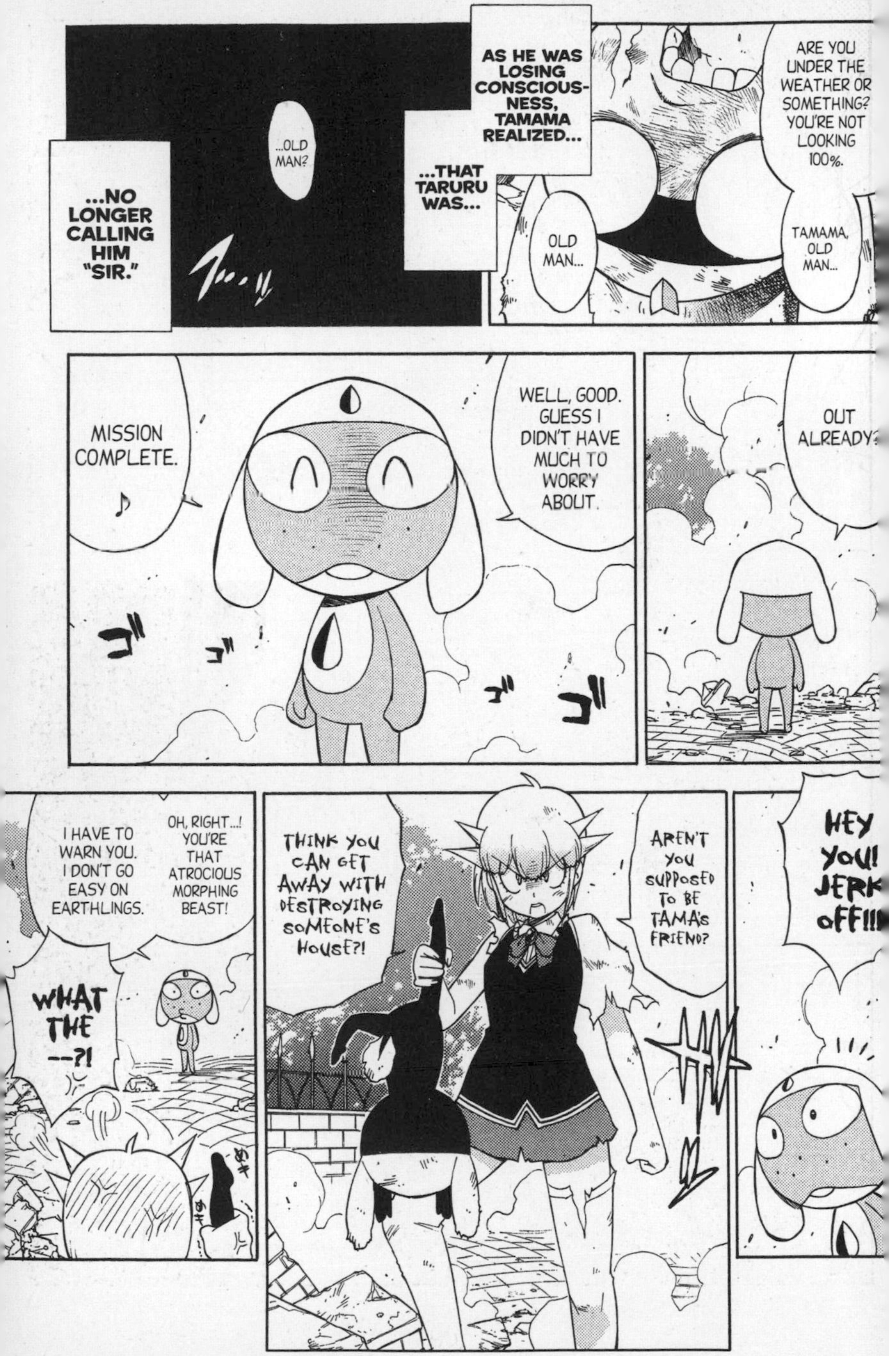
ARE YOU UNDER THE WEATHER OR SOMETHING? YOU'RE NOT LOOKING 100%.
TAMAMA, OLD MAN...
OLD MAN...
AS HE WAS LOSING CONSCIOUS-NESS, TAMAMA REALIZED...
...THAT TARURU WAS...
...OLD MAN?
...NO LONGER CALLING HIM "SIR."
OUT ALREADY?
WELL, GOOD. GUESS I DIDN'T HAVE MUCH TO WORRY ABOUT.
MISSION COMPLETE. ♪
HEY YOU! JERK OFF!!!
AREN'T YOU SUPPOSED TO BE TAMA'S FRIEND?
THINK YOU CAN GET AWAY WITH DESTROYING SOMEONE'S HOUSE?!
OH, RIGHT...! YOU'RE THAT ATROCIOUS MORPHING BEAST!
I HAVE TO WARN YOU. I DON'T GO EASY ON EARTHLINGS.
WHAT THE --?!

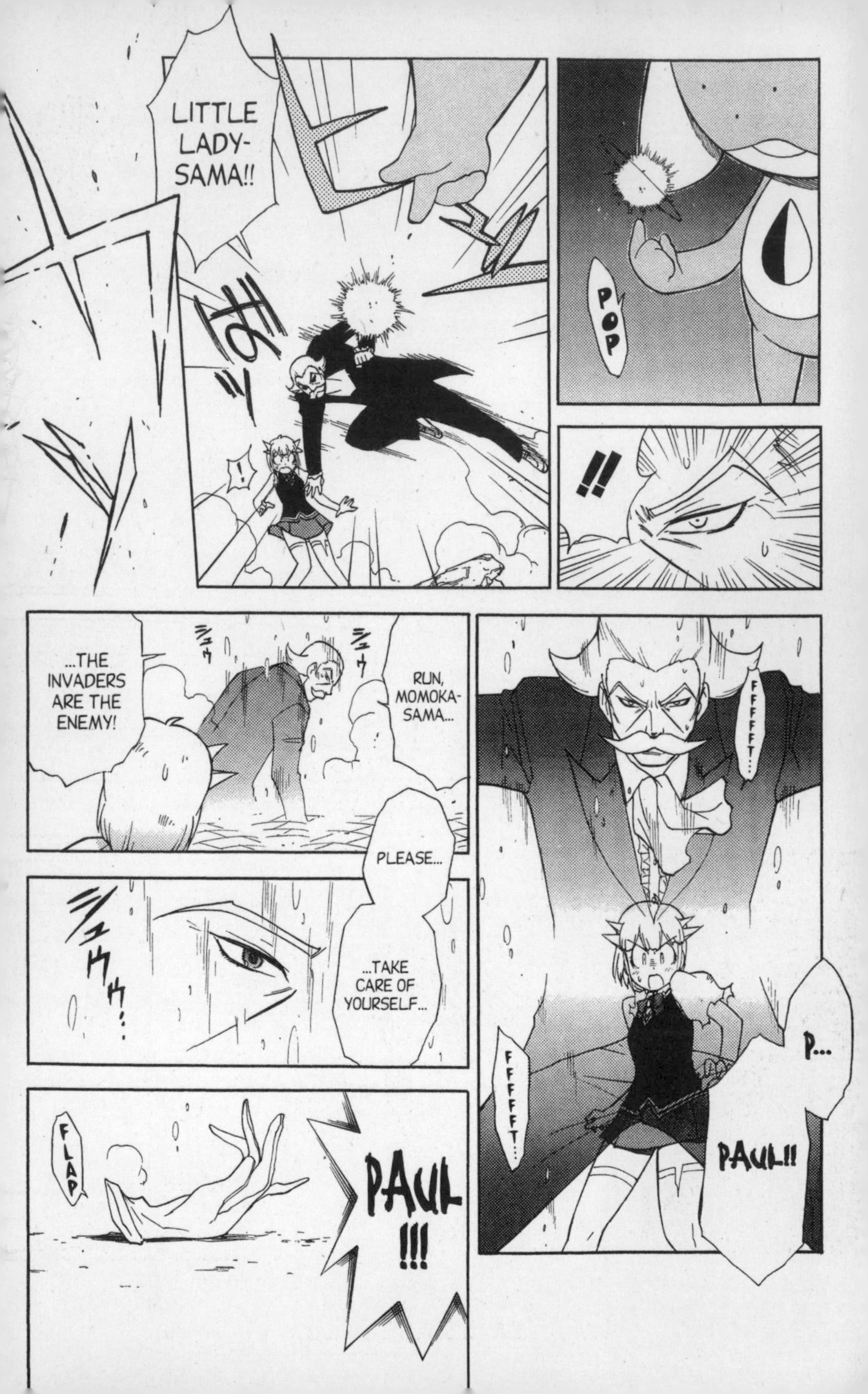
POP
!!
LITTLE LADY-SAMA!!
FFFFFT...
P...
PAUL!!
FFFFFT...
RUN, MOMOKA-SAMA...
...THE INVADERS ARE THE ENEMY!
PLEASE...
...TAKE CARE OF YOURSELF...
FLAP
PAUL!!!

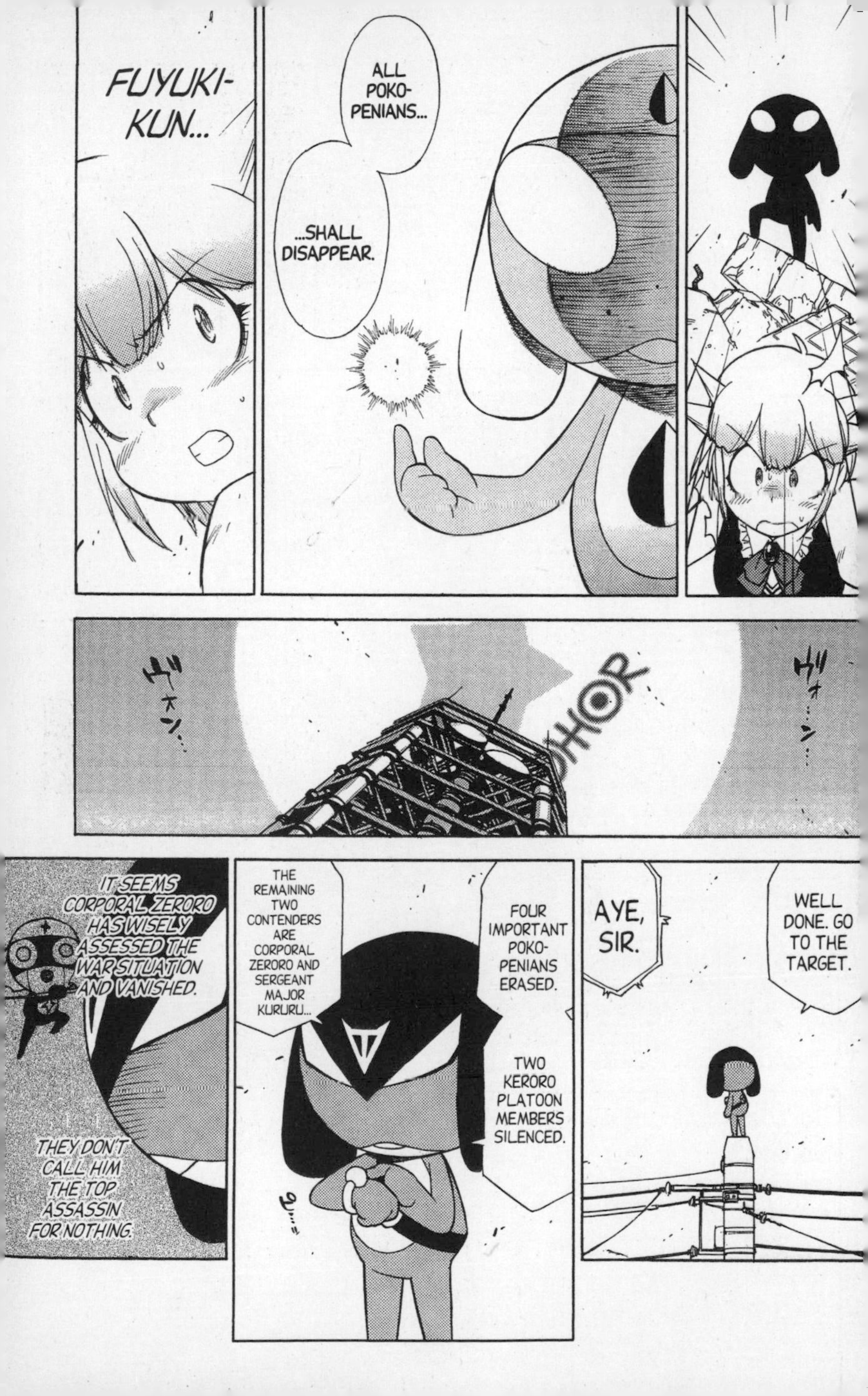
ALL POKO-PENIANS...
...SHALL DISAPPEAR.
FUYUKI-KUN...
WELL DONE. GO TO THE TARGET.
AYE, SIR.
FOUR IMPORTANT POKO-PENIANS ERASED.
TWO KERORO PLATOON MEMBERS SILENCED.
THE REMAINING TWO CONTENDERS ARE CORPORAL ZERORO AND SERGEANT MAJOR KURURU...
IT SEEMS CORPORAL ZERORO HAS WISELY ASSESSED THE WAR SITUATION AND VANISHED.
THEY DON'T CALL HIM THE TOP ASSASSIN FOR NOTHING.

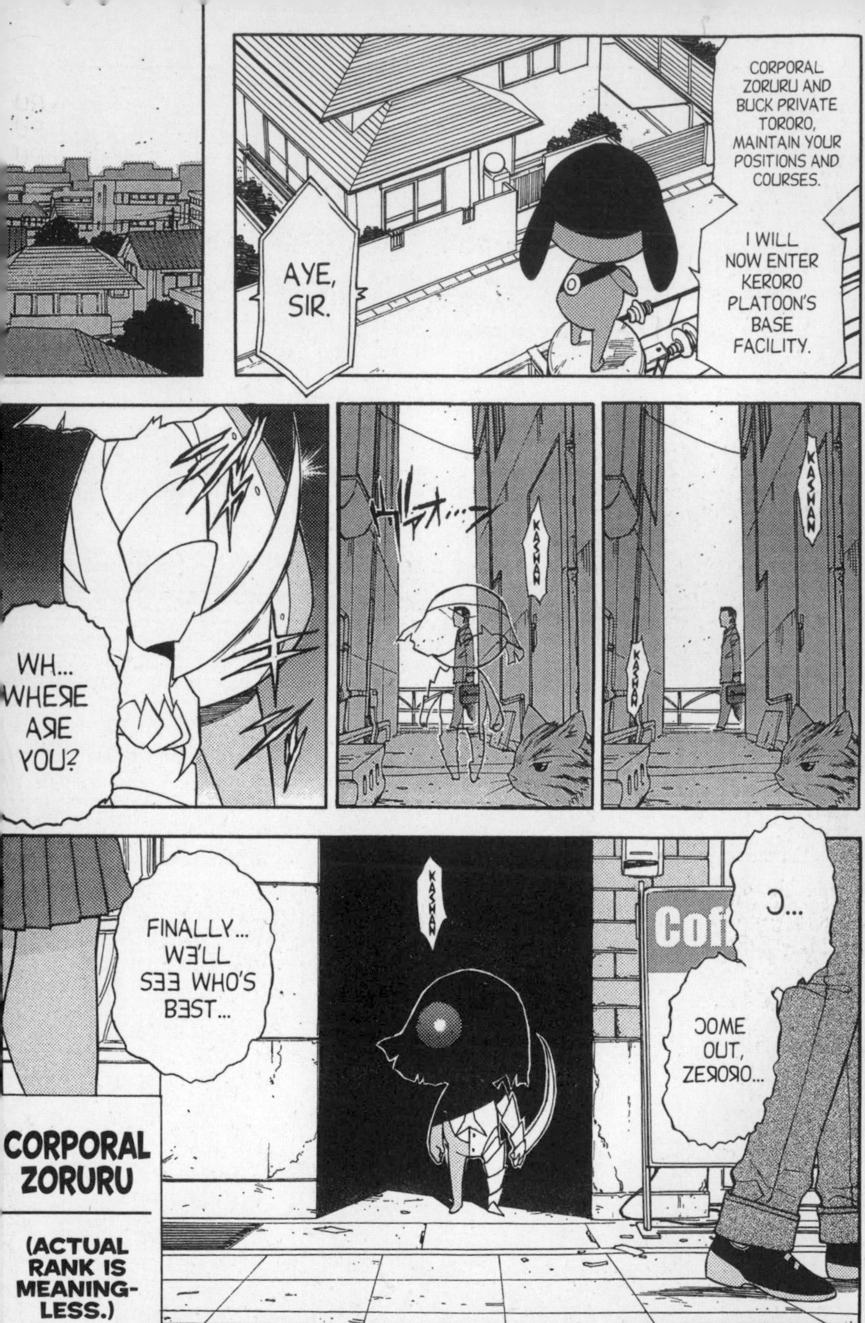
CORPORAL ZORURU AND BUCK PRIVATE TORORO, MAINTAIN YOUR POSITIONS AND COURSES.
I WILL NOW ENTER KERORO PLATOON'S BASE FACILITY.
AYE, SIR.
KASHAN
KASHAN
KASHAN
WH... WHERE ARE YOU?
C...
COME OUT, ZERORO...
KASHAN
FINALLY... WE'LL SEE WHO'S BEST...
CORPORAL ZORURU
(ACTUAL RANK IS MEANING-LESS.)

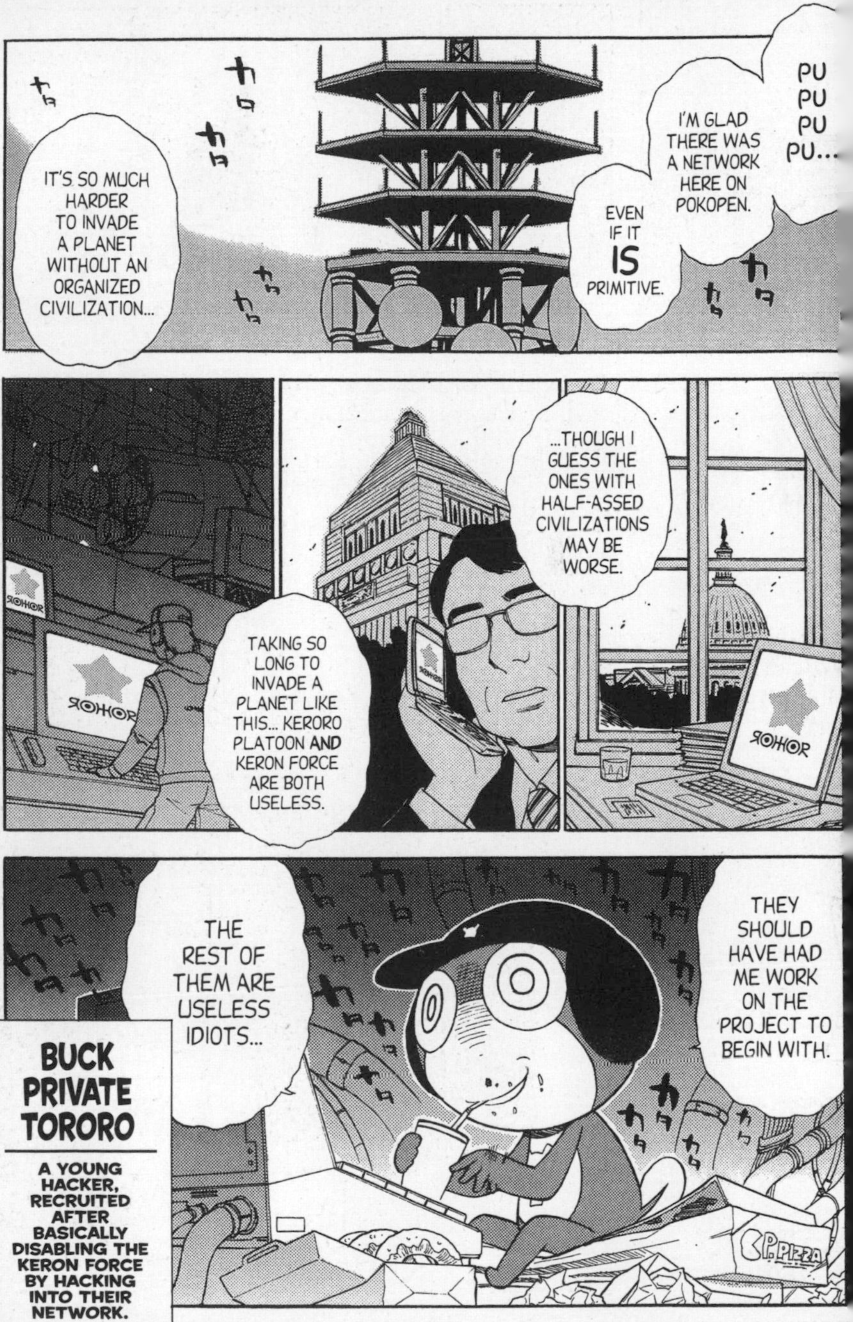

PU PU PU PU...
I'M GLAD THERE WAS A NETWORK HERE ON POKOPEN.
EVEN IF IT IS PRIMITIVE.
IT'S SO MUCH HARDER TO INVADE A PLANET WITHOUT AN ORGANIZED CIVILIZATION...
...THOUGH I GUESS THE ONES WITH HALF-ASSED CIVILIZATIONS MAY BE WORSE.
TAKING SO LONG TO INVADE A PLANET LIKE THIS... KERORO PLATOON AND KERON FORCE ARE BOTH USELESS.
THEY SHOULD HAVE HAD ME WORK ON THE PROJECT TO BEGIN WITH.
THE REST OF THEM ARE USELESS IDIOTS...
BUCK PRIVATE TORORO
A YOUNG HACKER, RECRUITED AFTER BASICALLY DISABLING THE KERON FORCE BY HACKING INTO THEIR NETWORK.

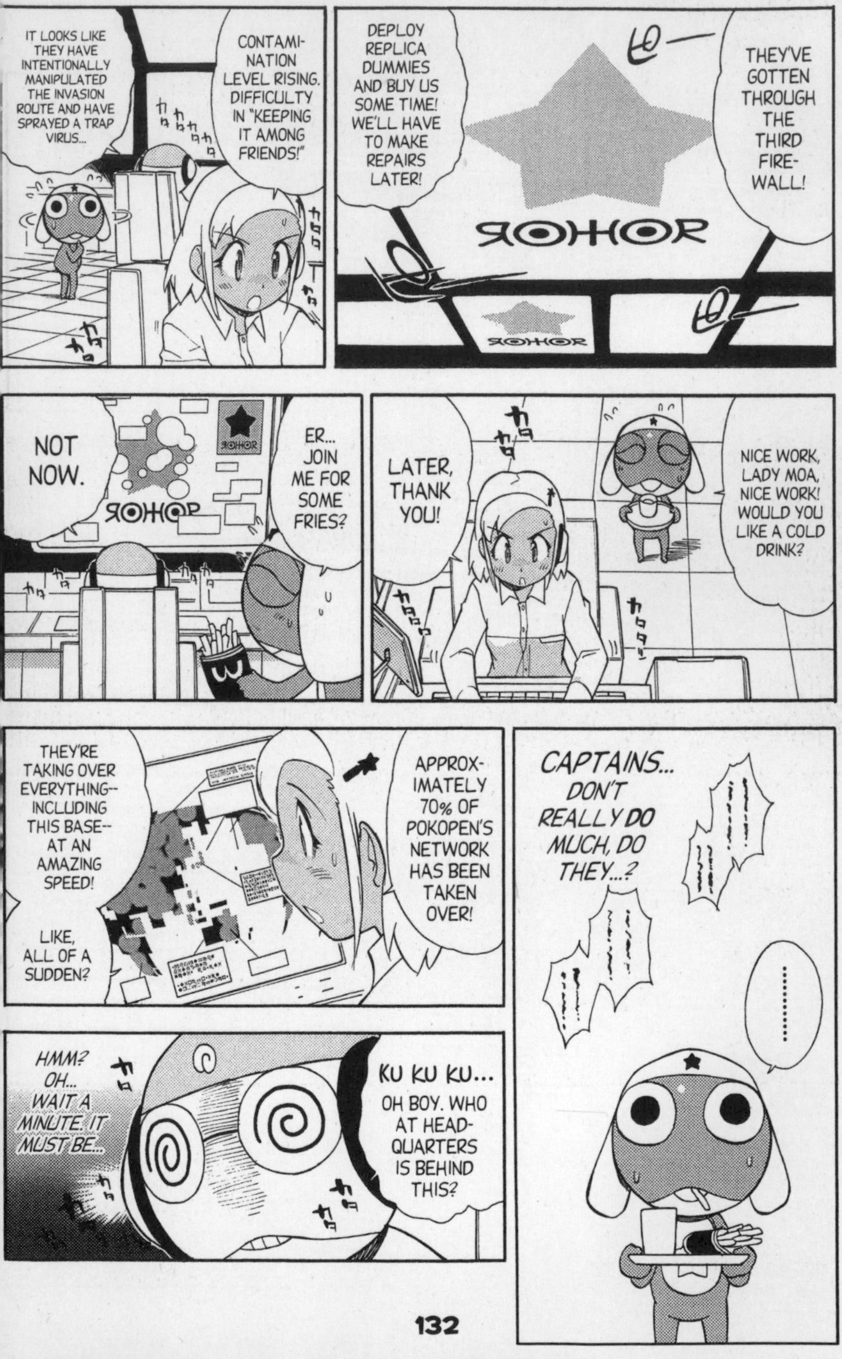
THEY'VE GOTTEN THROUGH THE THIRD FIRE-WALL!
DEPLOY REPLICA DUMMIES AND BUY US SOME TIME! WE'LL HAVE TO MAKE REPAIRS LATER!
ROHOR
CONTAMI-NATION LEVEL RISING. DIFFICULTY IN "KEEPING IT AMONG FRIENDS!"
IT LOOKS LIKE THEY HAVE INTENTIONALLY MANIPULATED THE INVASION ROUTE AND HAVE SPRAYED A TRAP VIRUS...
NICE WORK, LADY MOA, NICE WORK! WOULD YOU LIKE A COLD DRINK?
LATER, THANK YOU!
ER... JOIN ME FOR SOME FRIES?
NOT NOW.
ROHOR
CAPTAINS... DON'T REALLY DO MUCH, DO THEY...?
....
APPROX-IMATELY 70% OF POKOPEN'S NETWORK HAS BEEN TAKEN OVER!
THEY'RE TAKING OVER EVERYTHING-- INCLUDING THIS BASE-- AT AN AMAZING SPEED!
LIKE, ALL OF A SUDDEN?
KU KU KU... OH BOY. WHO AT HEAD-QUARTERS IS BEHIND THIS?
HMM? OH... WAIT A MINUTE. IT MUST BE...

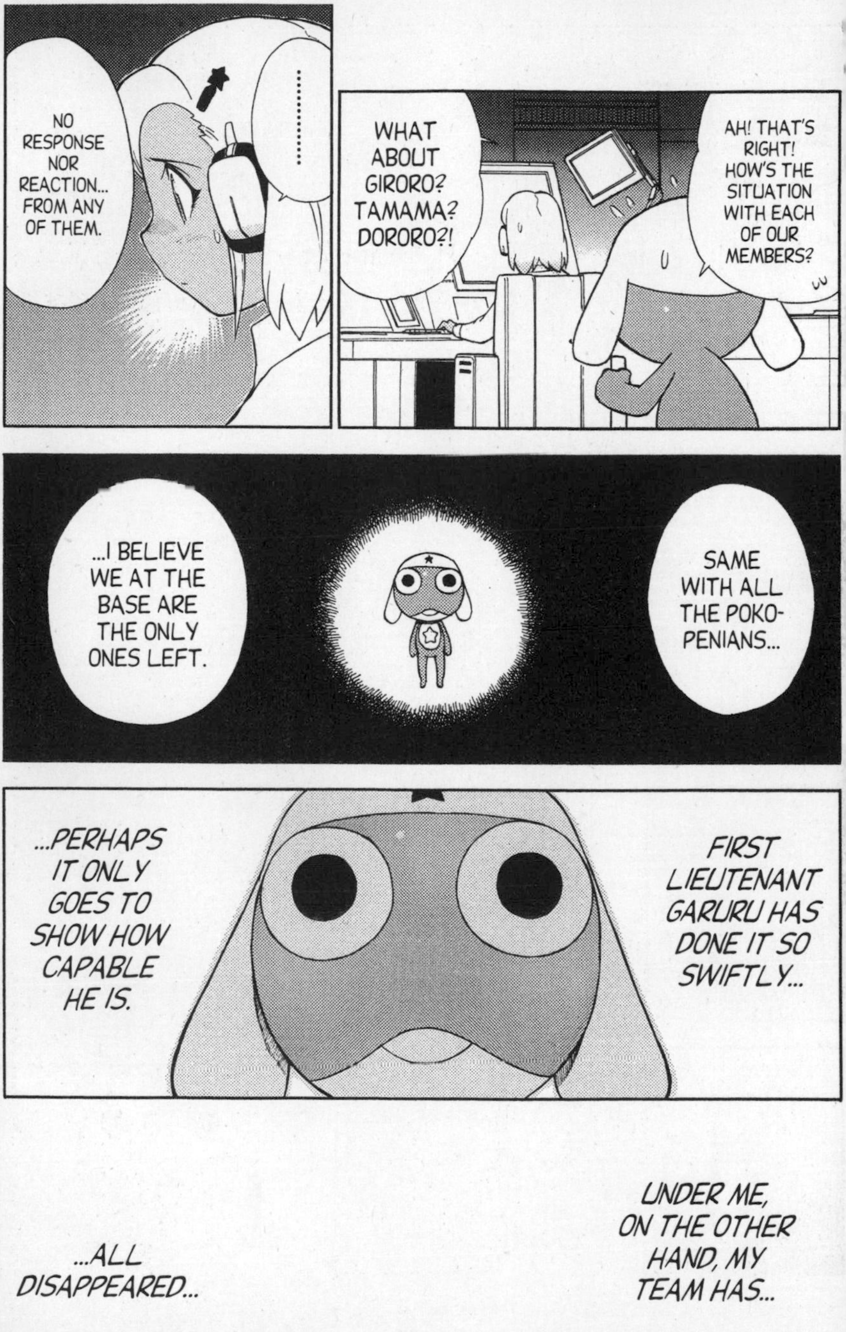
AH! THAT'S RIGHT! HOW'S THE SITUATION WITH EACH OF OUR MEMBERS?
WHAT ABOUT GIRORO? TAMAMA? DORORO?!
......
NO RESPONSE NOR REACTION... FROM ANY OF THEM.
SAME WITH ALL THE POKO-PENIANS...
...I BELIEVE WE AT THE BASE ARE THE ONLY ONES LEFT.
FIRST LIEUTENANT GARURU HAS DONE IT SO SWIFTLY...
...PERHAPS IT ONLY GOES TO SHOW HOW CAPABLE HE IS.
UNDER ME, ON THE OTHER HAND, MY TEAM HAS...
...ALL DISAPPEARED...

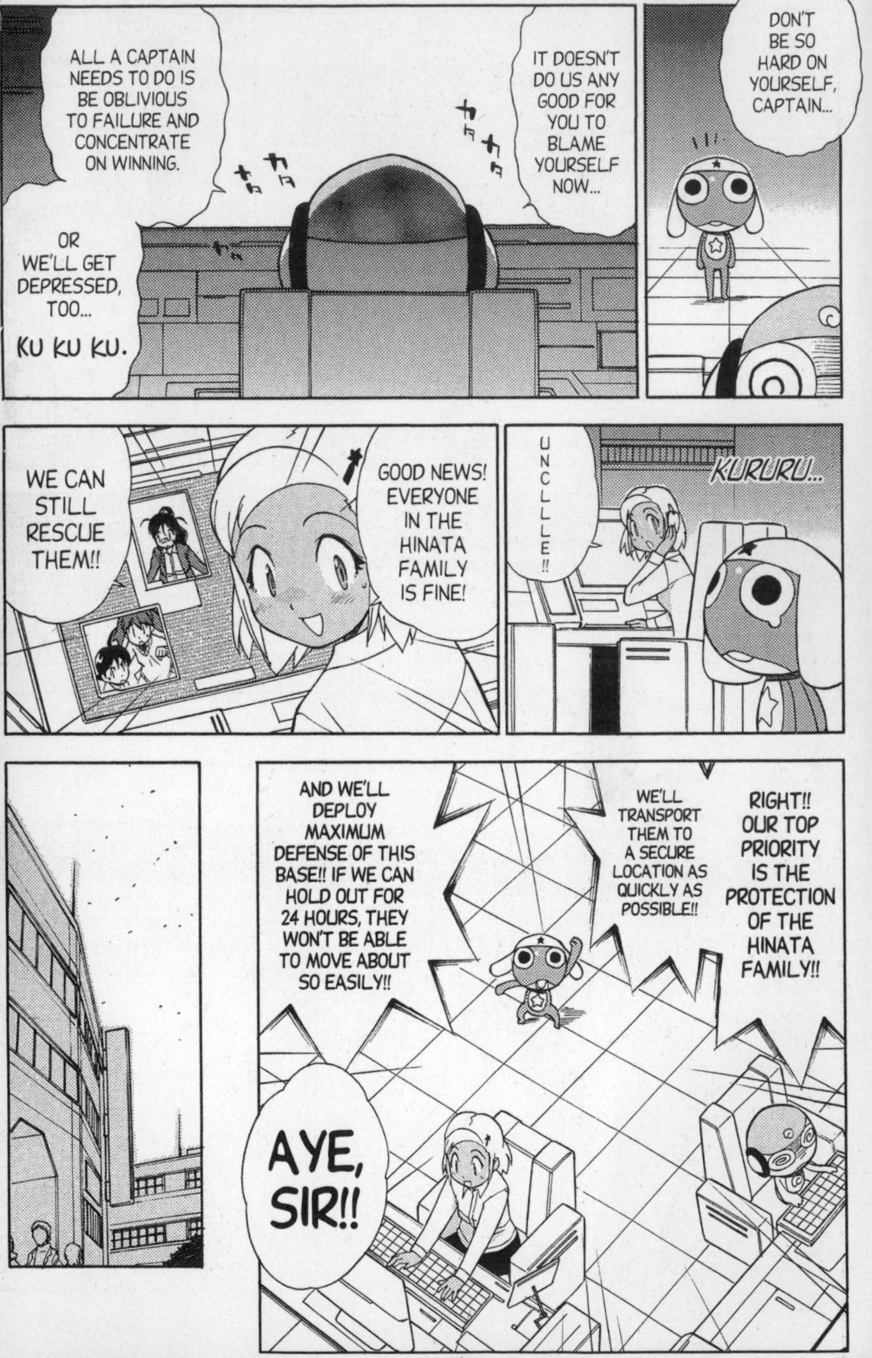
DON'T BE SO HARD ON YOURSELF, CAPTAIN...
IT DOESN'T DO US ANY GOOD FOR YOU TO BLAME YOURSELF NOW...
ALL A CAPTAIN NEEDS TO DO IS BE OBLIVIOUS TO FAILURE AND CONCENTRATE ON WINNING.
OR WE'LL GET DEPRESSED, TOO...
KU KU KU.
KURURU...
UNCLLLE!!
GOOD NEWS! EVERYONE IN THE HINATA FAMILY IS FINE!
WE CAN STILL RESCUE THEM!!
RIGHT!! OUR TOP PRIORITY IS THE PROTECTION OF THE HINATA FAMILY!!
WE'LL TRANSPORT THEM TO A SECURE LOCATION AS QUICKLY AS POSSIBLE!!
AND WE'LL DEPLOY MAXIMUM DEFENSE OF THIS BASE!! IF WE CAN HOLD OUT FOR 24 HOURS, THEY WON'T BE ABLE TO MOVE ABOUT SO EASILY!!
AYE, SIR!!

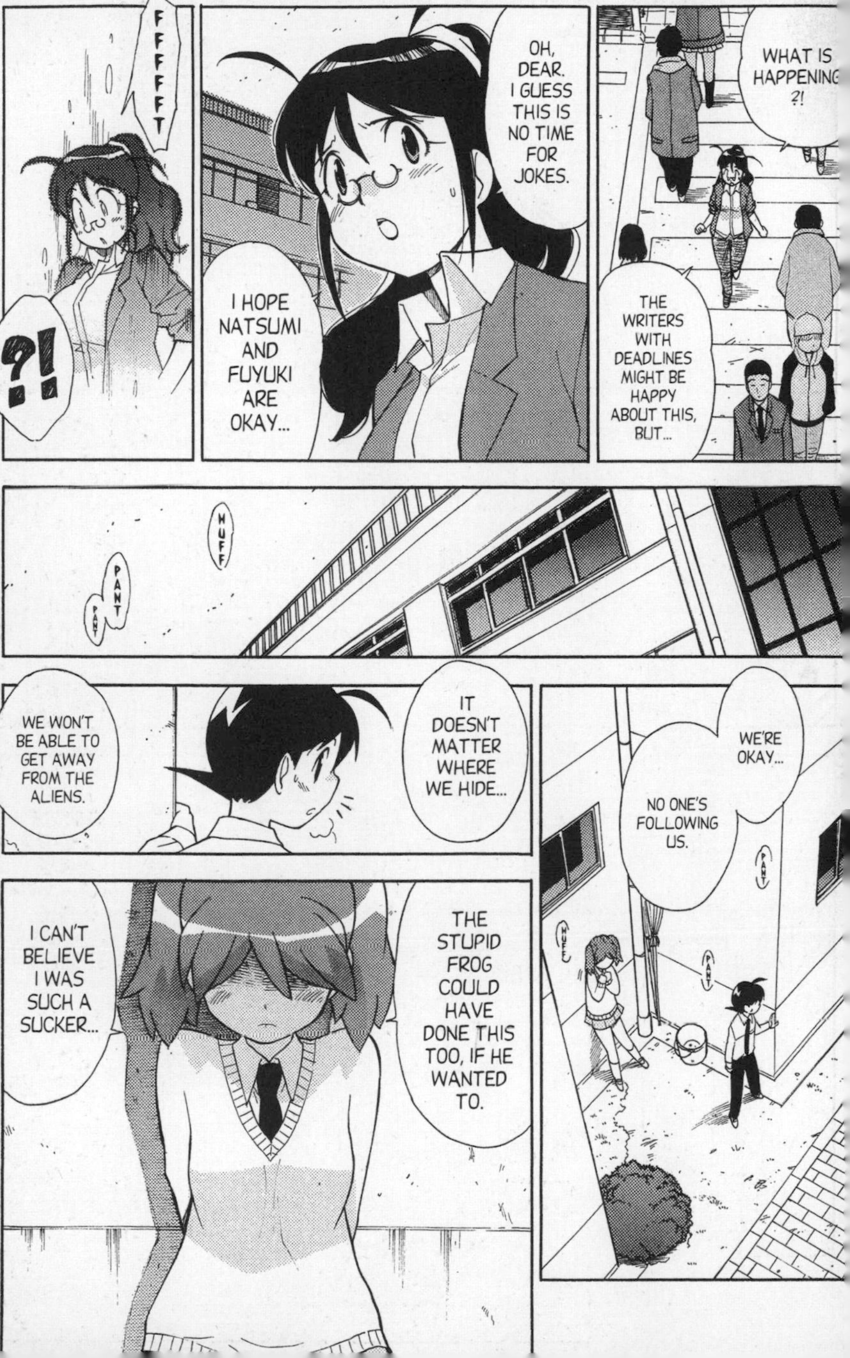
WHAT IS HAPPENING?!
THE WRITERS WITH DEADLINES MIGHT BE HAPPY ABOUT THIS, BUT...
OH, DEAR. I GUESS THIS IS NO TIME FOR JOKES.
I HOPE NATSUMI AND FUYUKI ARE OKAY...
FFFFFT
?!
HUFF
PANT
PANT
WE'RE OKAY...
NO ONE'S FOLLOWING US.
PANT
HUFF
PANT
IT DOESN'T MATTER WHERE WE HIDE...
WE WON'T BE ABLE TO GET AWAY FROM THE ALIENS.
THE STUPID FROG COULD HAVE DONE THIS TOO, IF HE WANTED TO.
I CAN'T BELIEVE I WAS SUCH A SUCKER...

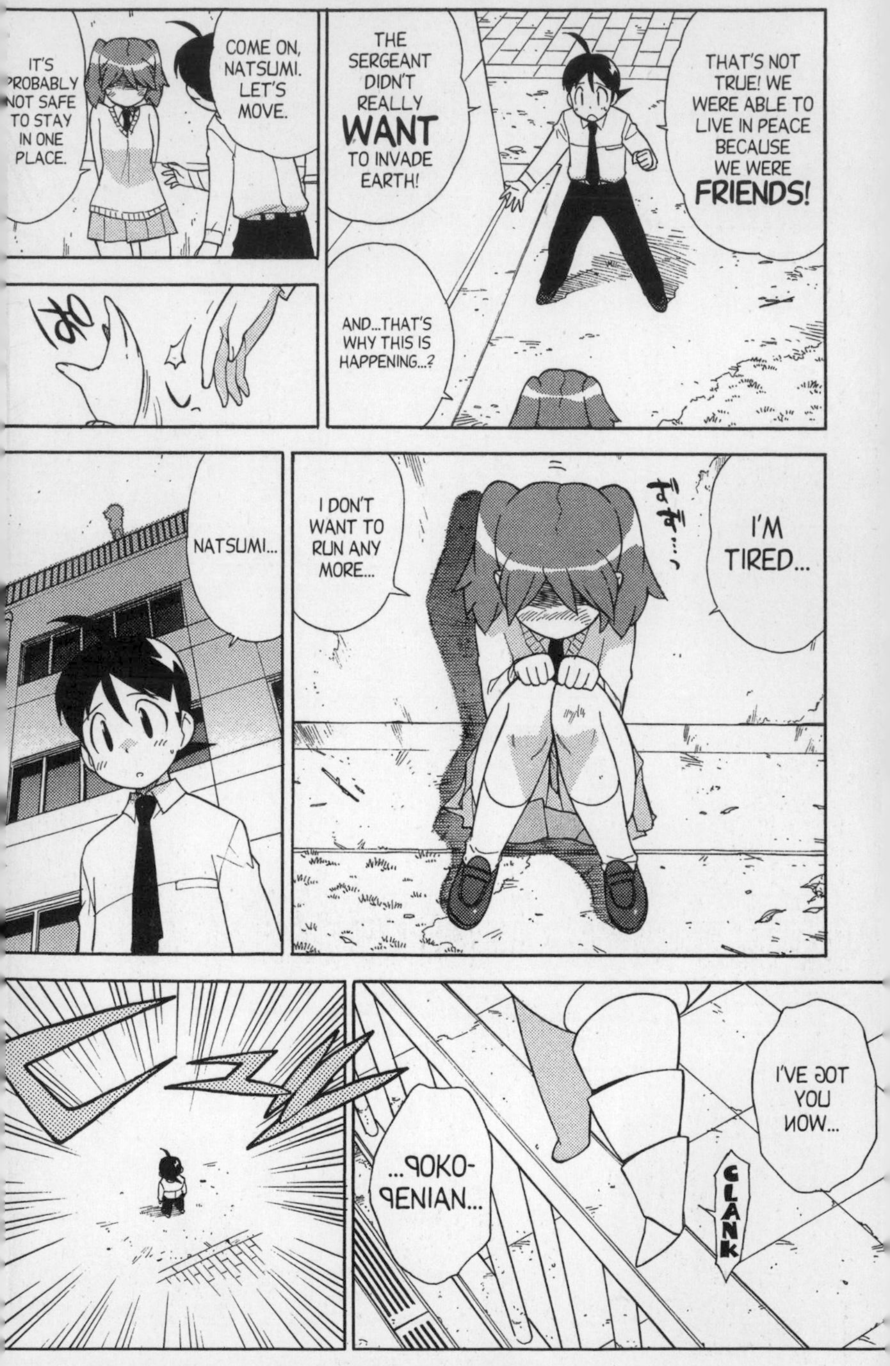
THAT'S NOT TRUE! WE WERE ABLE TO LIVE IN PEACE BECAUSE WE WERE **FRIENDS!**
THE SERGEANT DIDN'T REALLY **WANT** TO INVADE EARTH!
AND...THAT'S WHY THIS IS HAPPENING...?
COME ON, NATSUMI. LET'S MOVE.
IT'S PROBABLY NOT SAFE TO STAY IN ONE PLACE.
I'M TIRED...
ずず…
I DON'T WANT TO RUN ANY MORE...
NATSUMI...
I'VE GOT YOU NOW...
CLANK
...POKO-PENIAN...

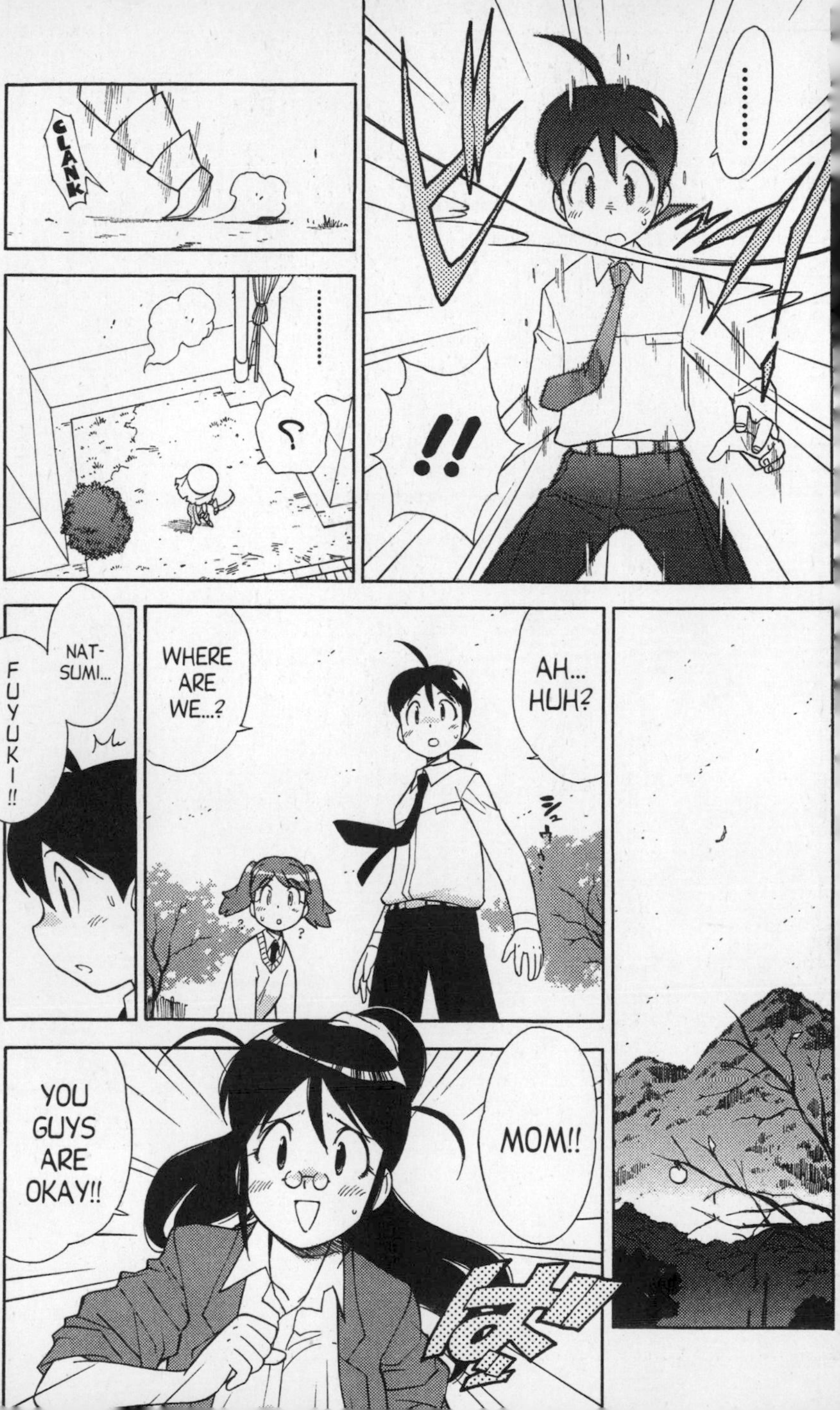
......
!!
CLANK
......
?
AH... HUH?
WHERE ARE WE...?
NAT-SUMI...
FUYUKI!!
MOM!!
YOU GUYS ARE OKAY!!

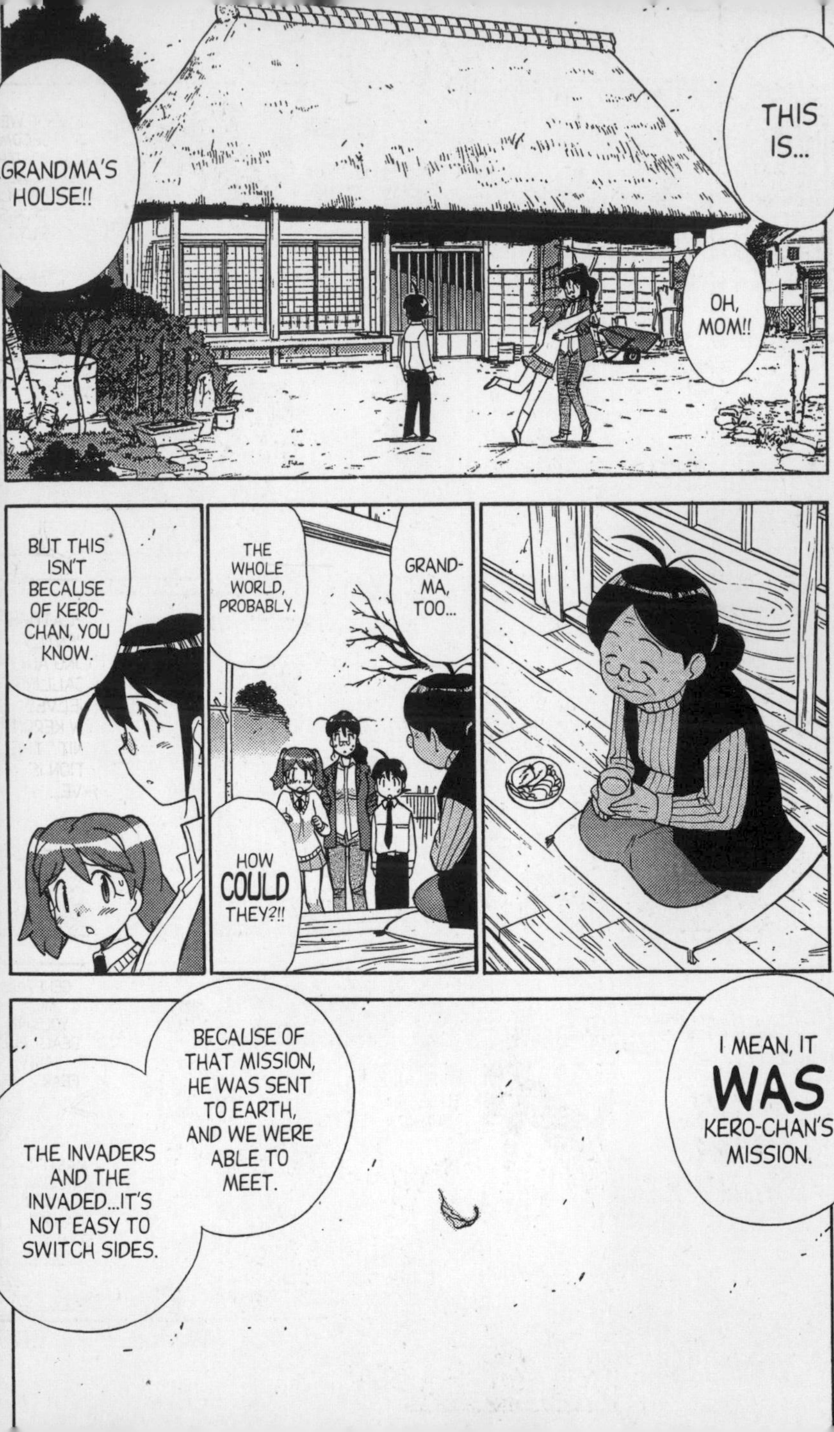
THIS IS...
..GRANDMA'S HOUSE!!
OH, MOM!!
GRAND-MA, TOO...
THE WHOLE WORLD, PROBABLY.
HOW COULD THEY?!!
BUT THIS ISN'T BECAUSE OF KERO-CHAN, YOU KNOW.
I MEAN, IT WAS KERO-CHAN'S MISSION.
BECAUSE OF THAT MISSION, HE WAS SENT TO EARTH, AND WE WERE ABLE TO MEET.
THE INVADERS AND THE INVADED...IT'S NOT EASY TO SWITCH SIDES.

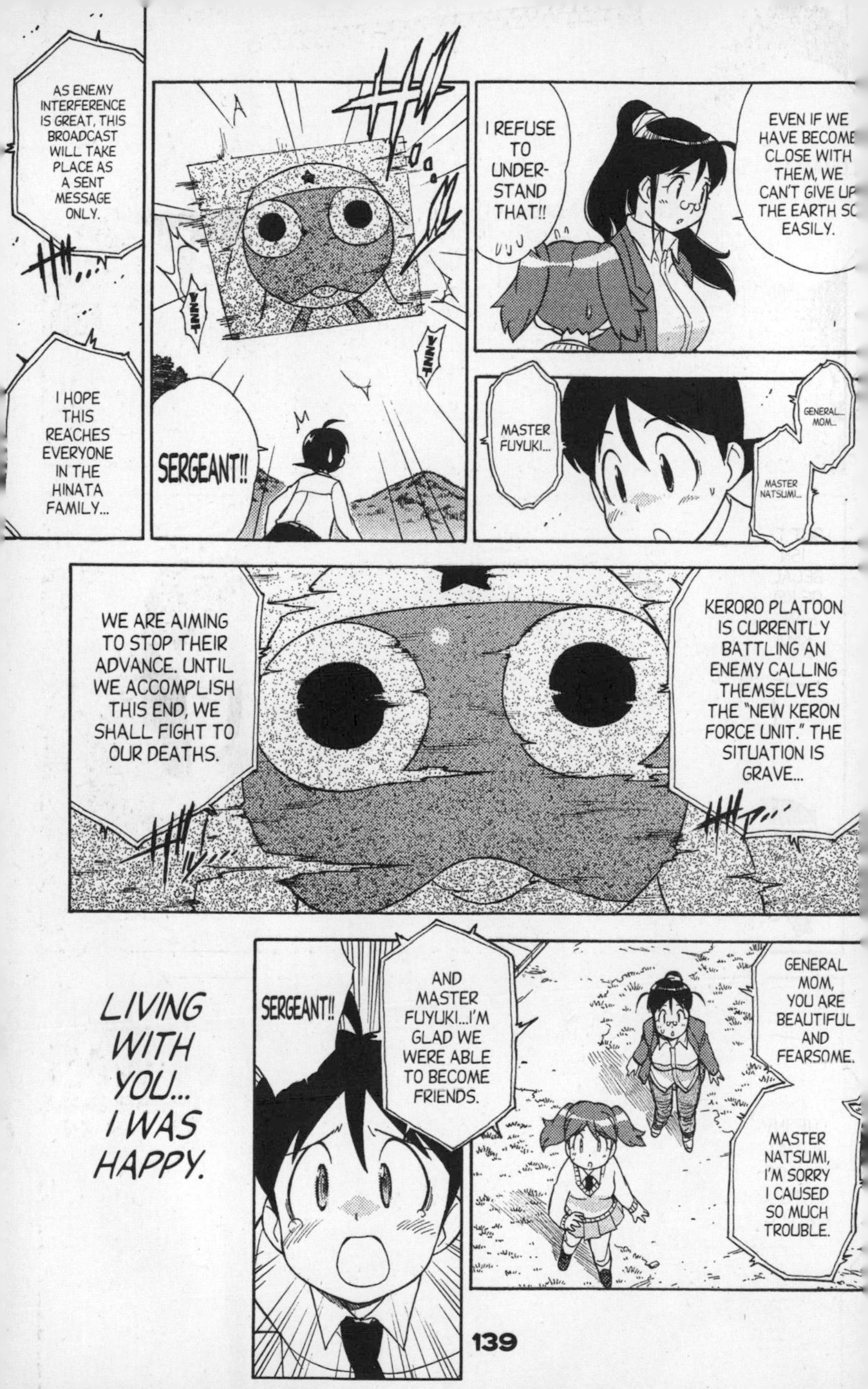
EVEN IF WE HAVE BECOME CLOSE WITH THEM, WE CAN'T GIVE UP THE EARTH SO EASILY.
I REFUSE TO UNDER-STAND THAT!!
GENERAL... MOM...
MASTER NATSUMI...
MASTER FUYUKI...
ZZZT
ZZZT
SERGEANT!!
AS ENEMY INTERFERENCE IS GREAT, THIS BROADCAST WILL TAKE PLACE AS A SENT MESSAGE ONLY.
I HOPE THIS REACHES EVERYONE IN THE HINATA FAMILY...
KERORO PLATOON IS CURRENTLY BATTLING AN ENEMY CALLING THEMSELVES THE "NEW KERON FORCE UNIT." THE SITUATION IS GRAVE...
WE ARE AIMING TO STOP THEIR ADVANCE. UNTIL WE ACCOMPLISH THIS END, WE SHALL FIGHT TO OUR DEATHS.
GENERAL MOM, YOU ARE BEAUTIFUL AND FEARSOME.
MASTER NATSUMI, I'M SORRY I CAUSED SO MUCH TROUBLE.
AND MASTER FUYUKI...I'M GLAD WE WERE ABLE TO BECOME FRIENDS.
SERGEANT!!
LIVING WITH YOU... I WAS HAPPY.

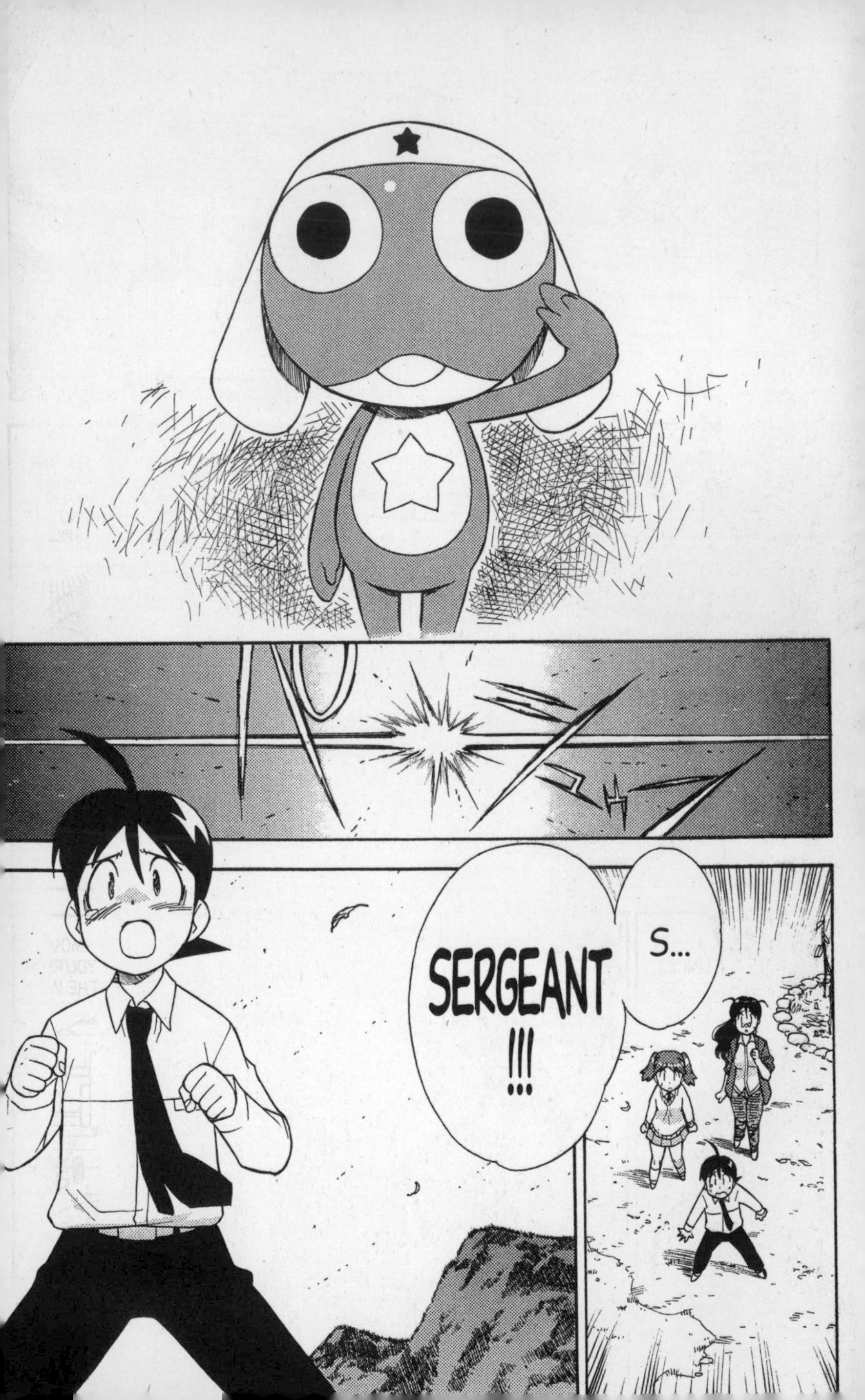
S...
SERGEANT !!!

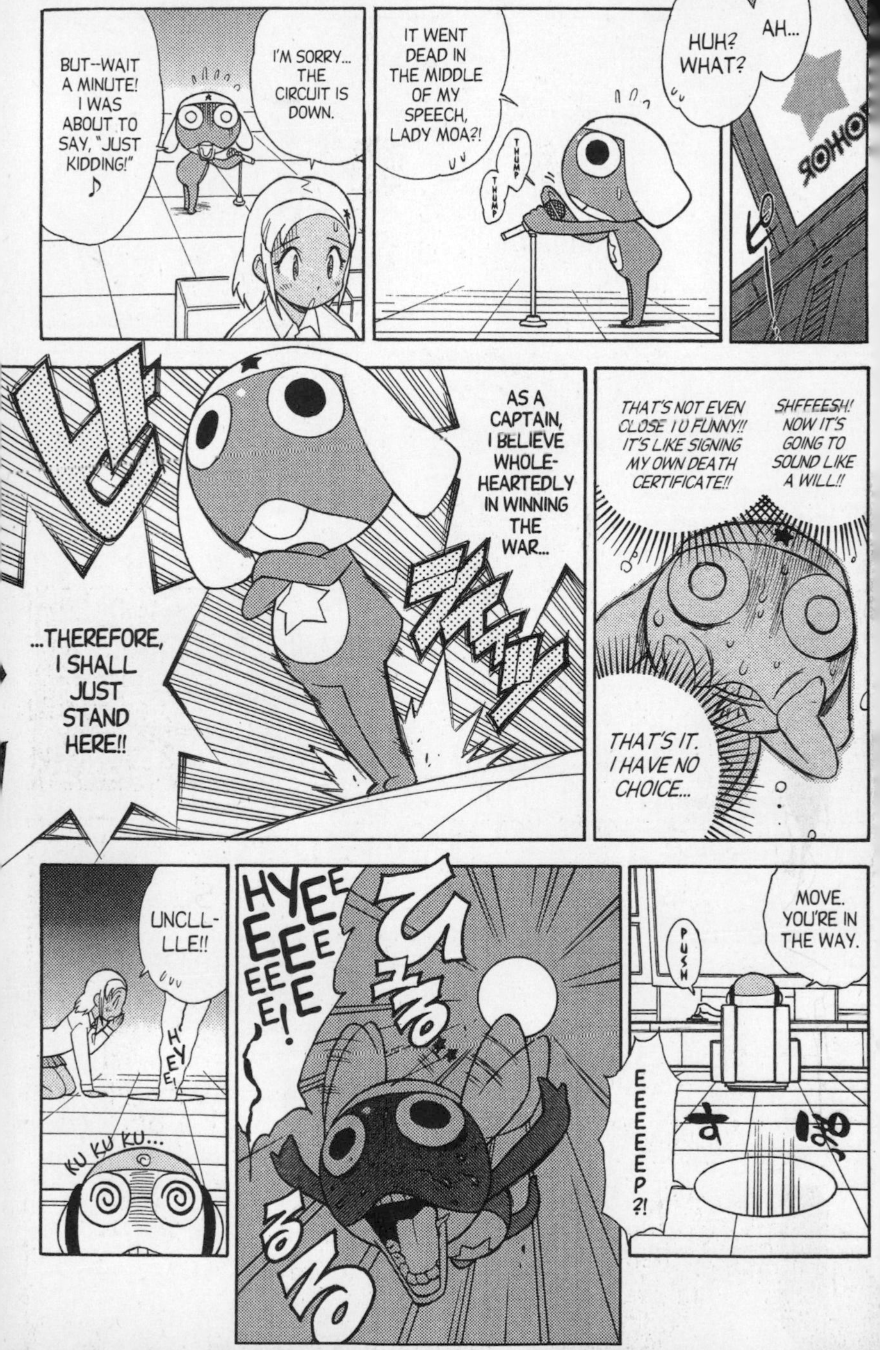
AH...
HUH? WHAT?
IT WENT DEAD IN THE MIDDLE OF MY SPEECH, LADY MOA?!
THUMP
THUMP
I'M SORRY... THE CIRCUIT IS DOWN.
BUT--WAIT A MINUTE! I WAS ABOUT TO SAY, "JUST KIDDING!" ♪
SHFFEESH! NOW IT'S GOING TO SOUND LIKE A WILL!!
THAT'S NOT EVEN CLOSE TO FUNNY!! IT'S LIKE SIGNING MY OWN DEATH CERTIFICATE!!
THAT'S IT. I HAVE NO CHOICE...
AS A CAPTAIN, I BELIEVE WHOLE-HEARTEDLY IN WINNING THE WAR...
...THEREFORE, I SHALL JUST STAND HERE!!
MOVE. YOU'RE IN THE WAY.
PUSH
EEEEEEP?!
HYEEEEEEEEE!
UNCLLLE!!
HEYE
KU KU KU...

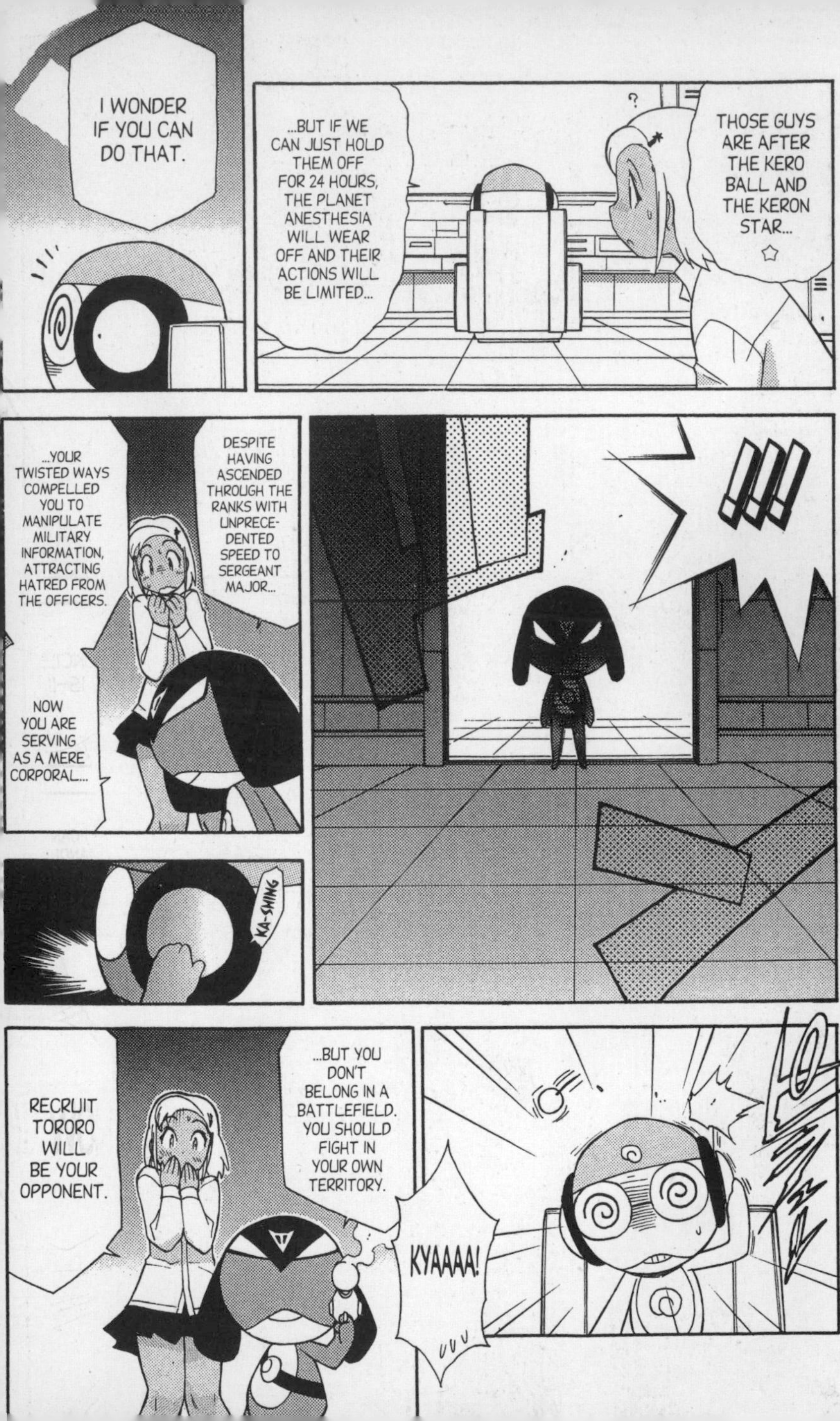
THOSE GUYS ARE AFTER THE KERO BALL AND THE KERON STAR...
...BUT IF WE CAN JUST HOLD THEM OFF FOR 24 HOURS, THE PLANET ANESTHESIA WILL WEAR OFF AND THEIR ACTIONS WILL BE LIMITED...
I WONDER IF YOU CAN DO THAT.
!!!
DESPITE HAVING ASCENDED THROUGH THE RANKS WITH UNPRECE-DENTED SPEED TO SERGEANT MAJOR...
...YOUR TWISTED WAYS COMPELLED YOU TO MANIPULATE MILITARY INFORMATION, ATTRACTING HATRED FROM THE OFFICERS.
NOW YOU ARE SERVING AS A MERE CORPORAL...
KA-SHING
KYAAAA!
...BUT YOU DON'T BELONG IN A BATTLEFIELD. YOU SHOULD FIGHT IN YOUR OWN TERRITORY.
RECRUIT TORORO WILL BE YOUR OPPONENT.

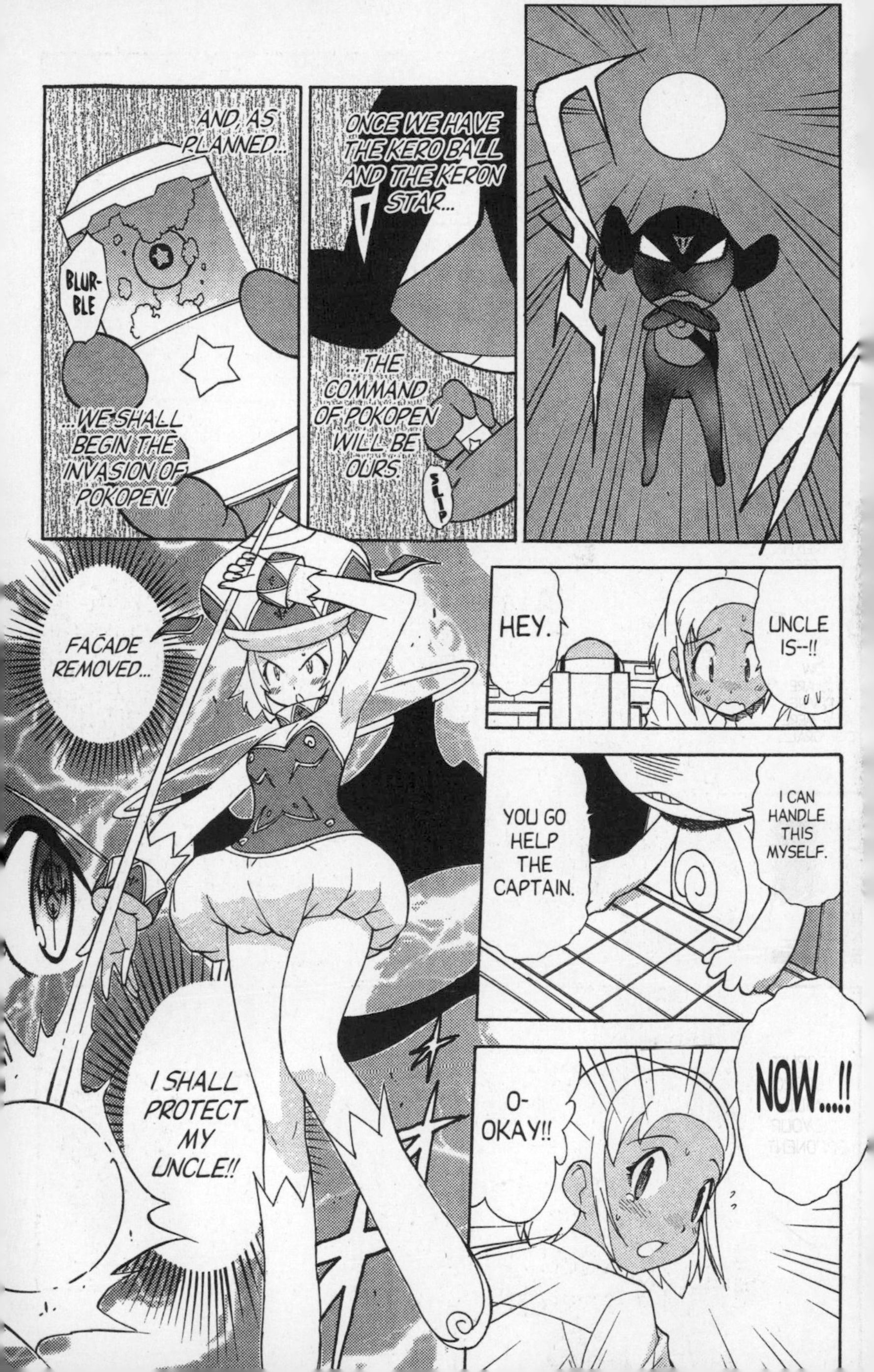
ONCE WE HAVE THE KERO BALL AND THE KERON STAR...
...THE COMMAND OF POKOPEN WILL BE OURS.
SLIP
AND, AS PLANNED...
BLUR-BLE
...WE SHALL BEGIN THE INVASION OF POKOPEN!
UNCLE IS--!!
HEY.
I CAN HANDLE THIS MYSELF.
YOU GO HELP THE CAPTAIN.
NOW...!!
O-OKAY!!
FAÇADE REMOVED...
I SHALL PROTECT MY UNCLE!!

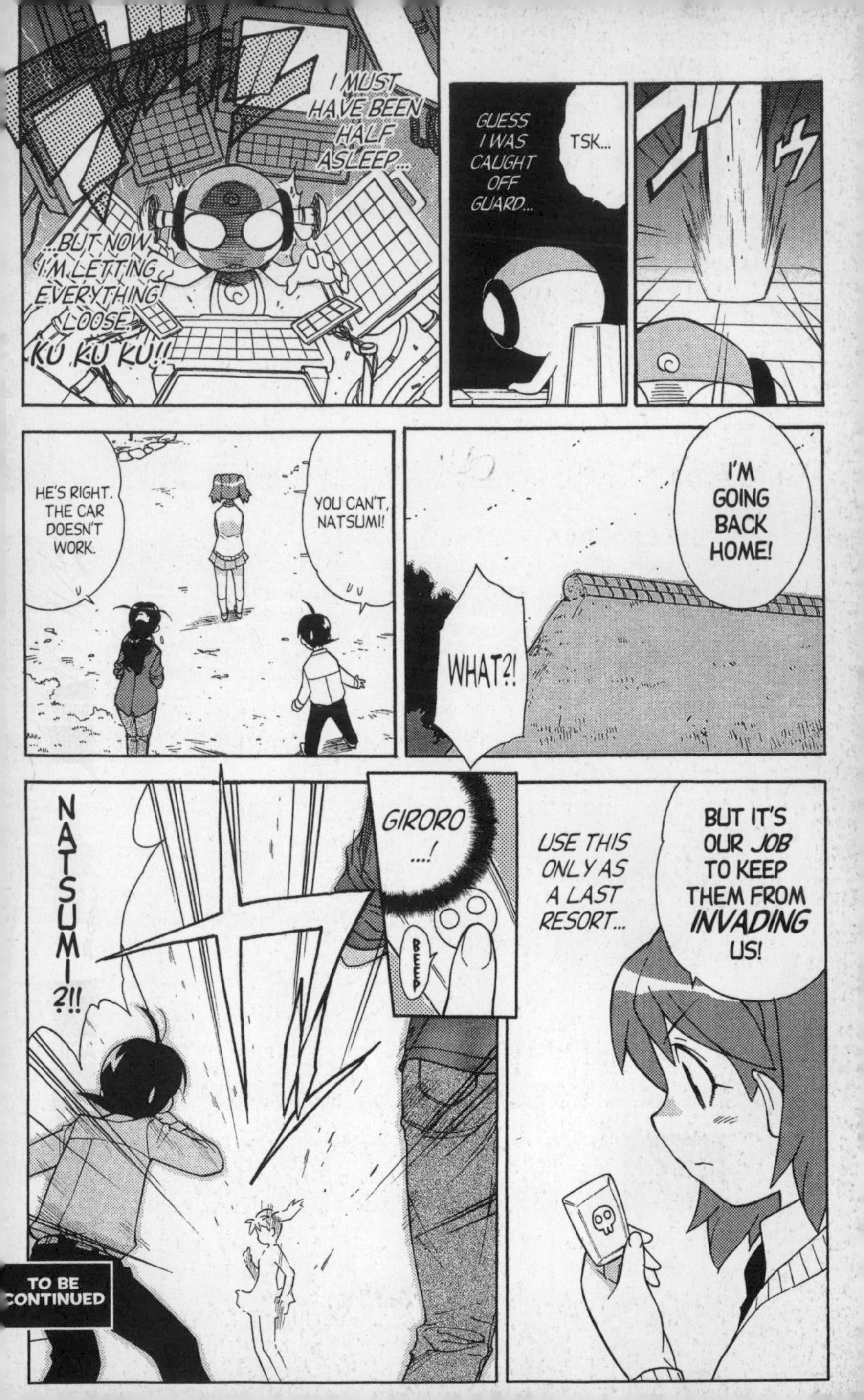
TSK...
GUESS I WAS CAUGHT OFF GUARD...
I MUST HAVE BEEN HALF ASLEEP...
...BUT NOW I'M LETTING EVERYTHING LOOSE.
KU KU KU!!
I'M GOING BACK HOME!
WHAT?!
YOU CAN'T, NATSUMI!
HE'S RIGHT. THE CAR DOESN'T WORK.
BUT IT'S OUR *JOB* TO KEEP THEM FROM *INVADING* US!
USE THIS ONLY AS A LAST RESORT...
GIRORO ...!
BEEP
NATSUMI?!!
TO BE CONTINUED

ENCOUNTER LXXXII
THE LAST BATTLE: KERORO PLATOON'S 24 HOURS--PART THREE

PROGRESS REPORT

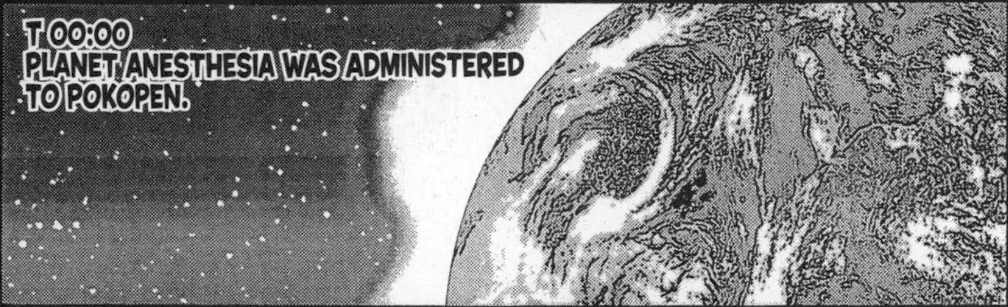

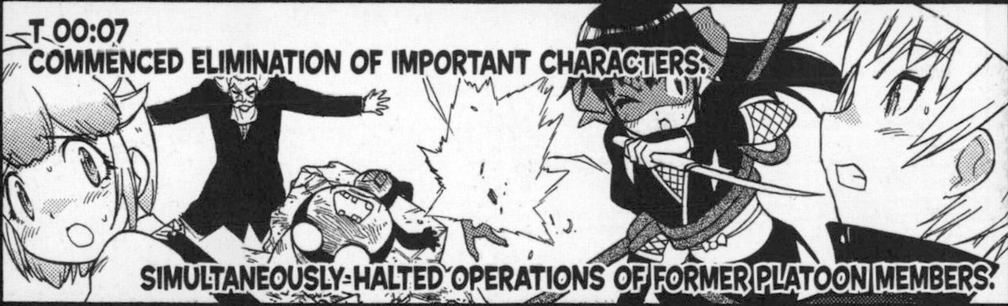

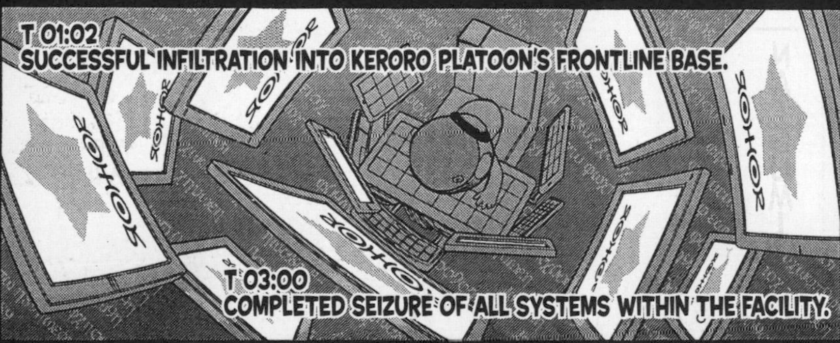

CURRENTLY OUR MISSION IS PROCEEDING QUITE WELL.

--FIRST LIEUTENANT GARURU--

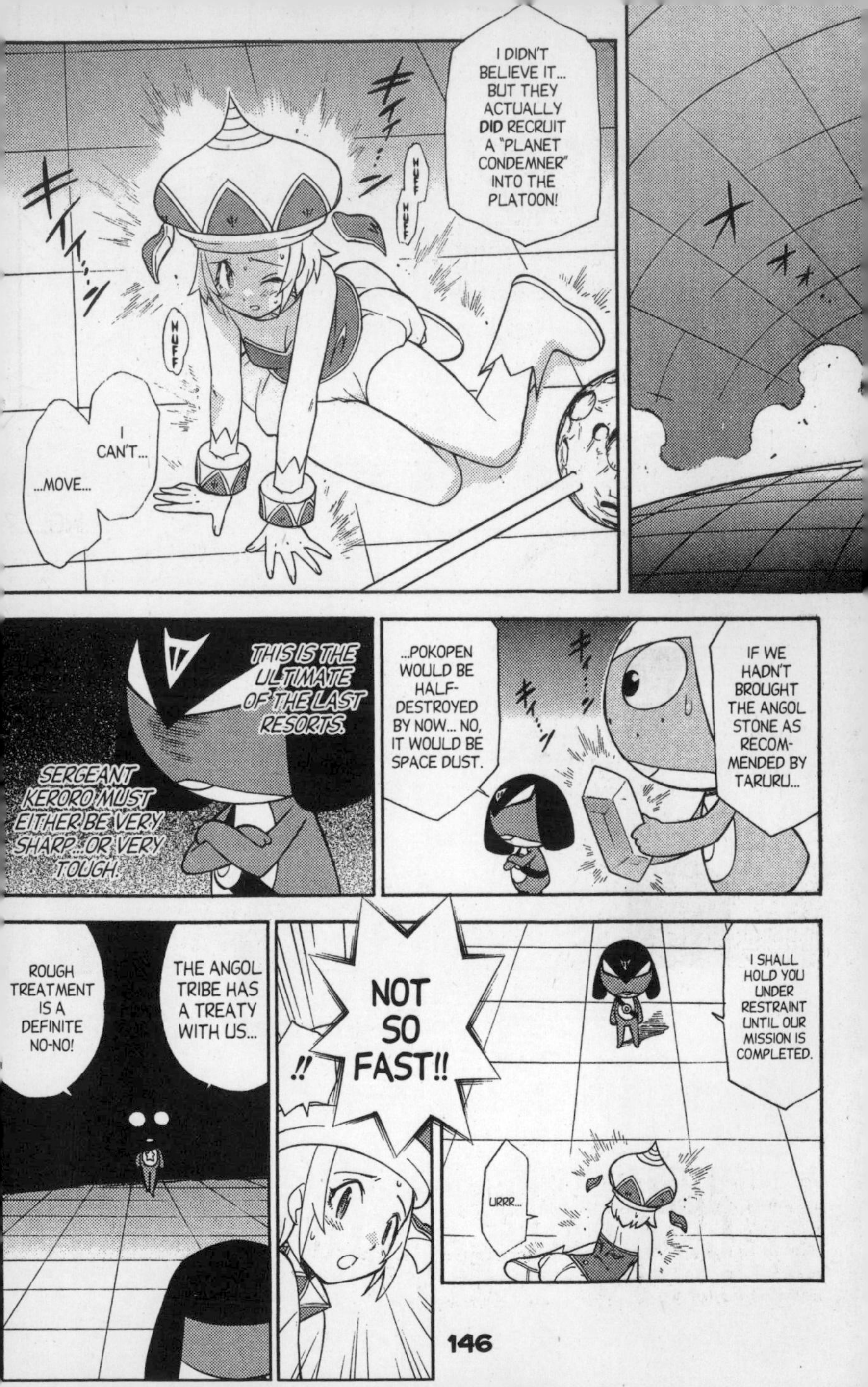
HUFF HUFF
I DIDN'T BELIEVE IT... BUT THEY ACTUALLY **DID** RECRUIT A "PLANET CONDEMNER" INTO THE PLATOON!
HUFF
I CAN'T... ...MOVE...
IF WE HADN'T BROUGHT THE ANGOL STONE AS RECOMMENDED BY TARURU...
...POKOPEN WOULD BE HALF-DESTROYED BY NOW... NO, IT WOULD BE SPACE DUST.
THIS IS THE ULTIMATE OF THE LAST RESORTS.
SERGEANT KERORO MUST EITHER BE VERY SHARP...OR VERY TOUGH.
I SHALL HOLD YOU UNDER RESTRAINT UNTIL OUR MISSION IS COMPLETED.
NOT SO FAST!!
!!
URRR...
THE ANGOL TRIBE HAS A TREATY WITH US...
ROUGH TREATMENT IS A DEFINITE NO-NO!

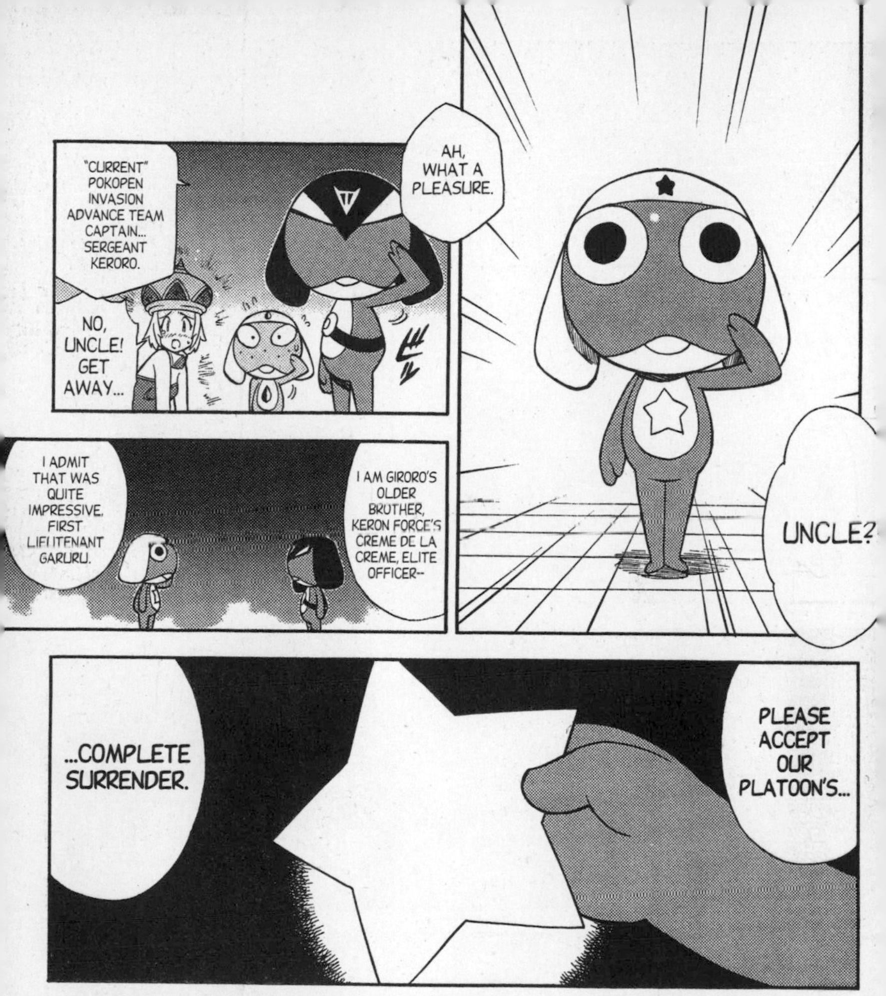
AH, WHAT A PLEASURE.
UNCLE?
"CURRENT" POKOPEN INVASION ADVANCE TEAM CAPTAIN... SERGEANT KERORO.
NO, UNCLE! GET AWAY...
I AM GIRORO'S OLDER BROTHER, KERON FORCE'S CREME DE LA CREME, ELITE OFFICER--
I ADMIT THAT WAS QUITE IMPRESSIVE, FIRST LIEUTENANT GARURU.
PLEASE ACCEPT OUR PLATOON'S...
...COMPLETE SURRENDER.

ENCOUNTER LXXXIII
THE LAST BATTLE: KERORO PLATOON'S 24 HOURS--PART THREE

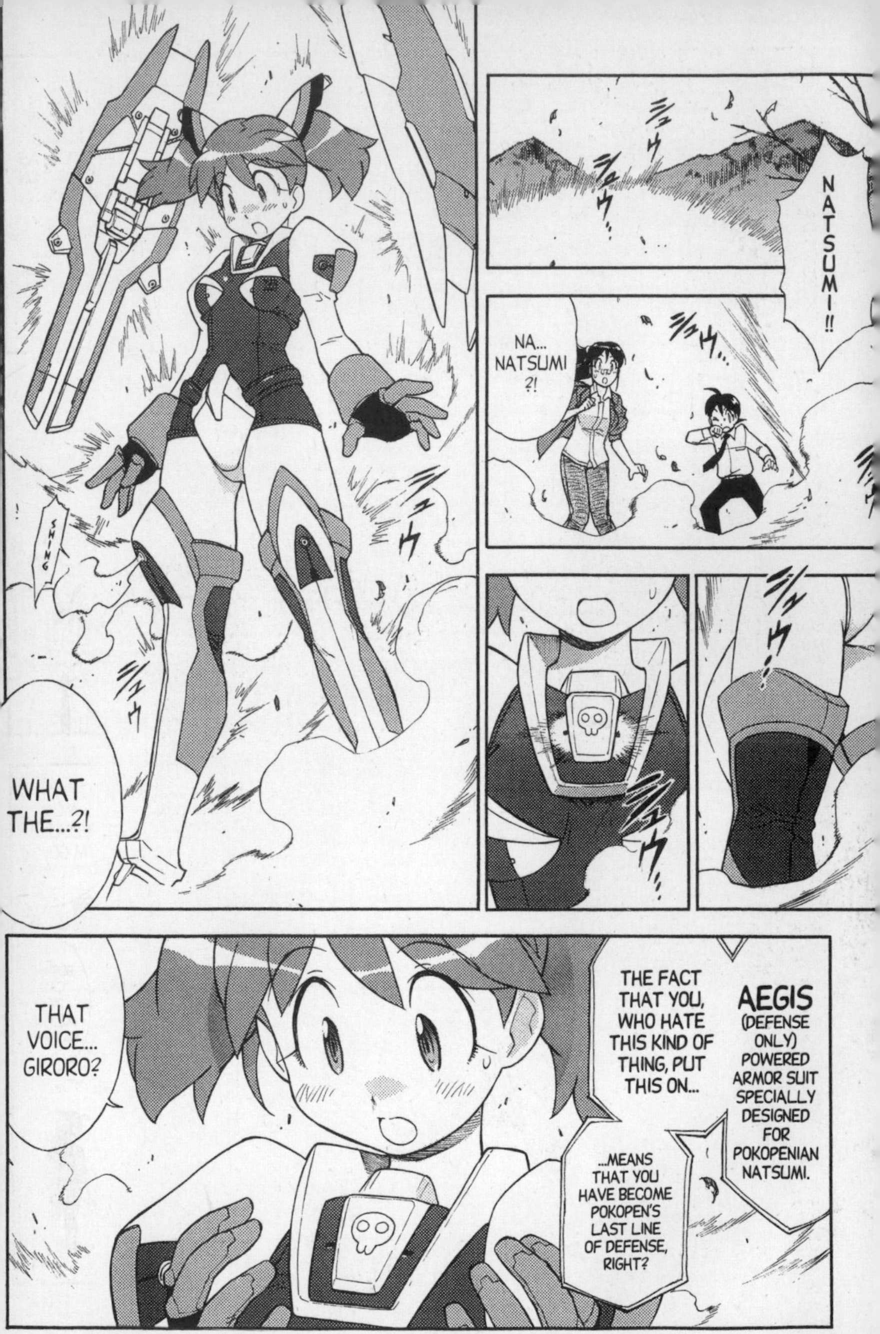
NATSUMI!!
NA... NATSUMI ?!
SHING
WHAT THE...?!
AEGIS (DEFENSE ONLY) POWERED ARMOR SUIT SPECIALLY DESIGNED FOR POKOPENIAN NATSUMI.
THE FACT THAT YOU, WHO HATE THIS KIND OF THING, PUT THIS ON...
...MEANS THAT YOU HAVE BECOME POKOPEN'S LAST LINE OF DEFENSE, RIGHT?
THAT VOICE... GIRORO?

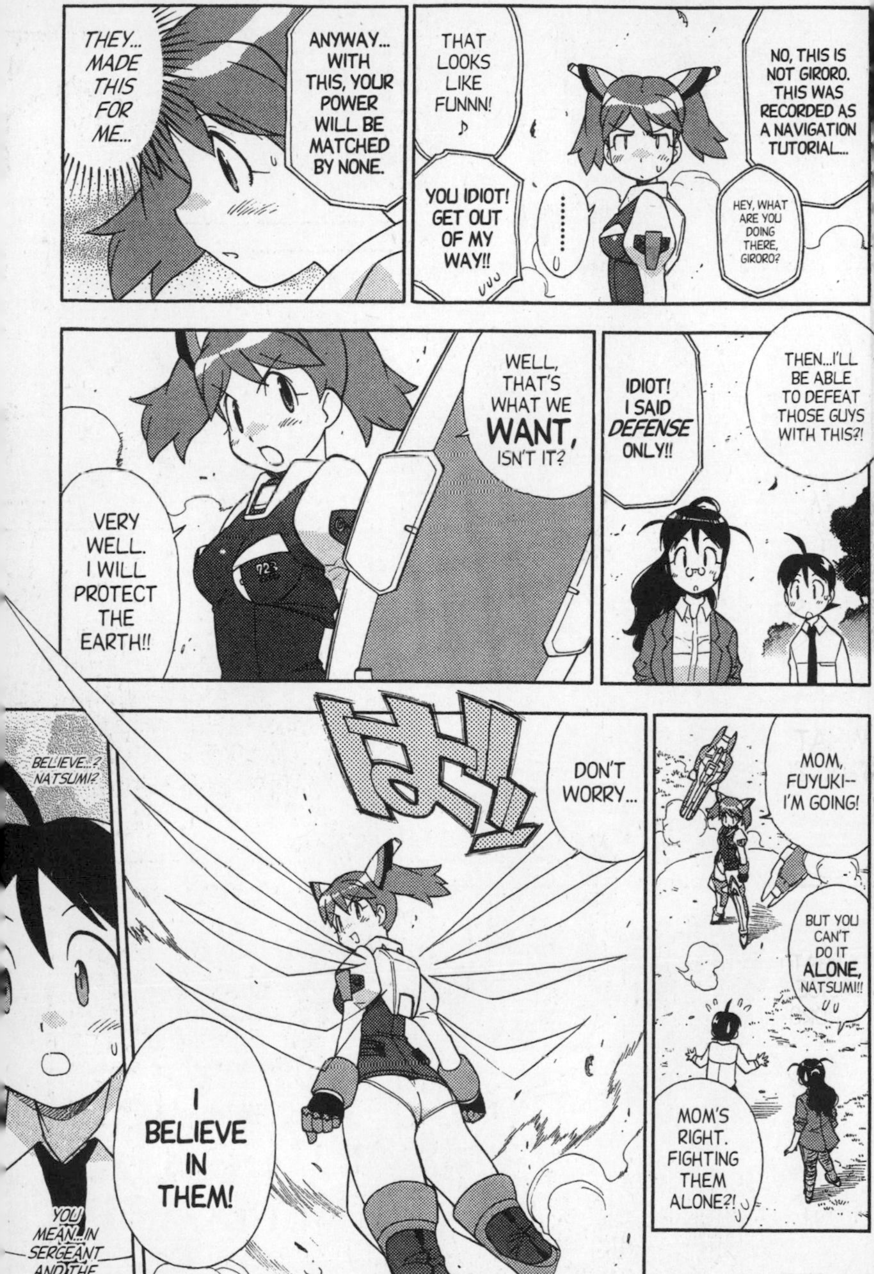
NO, THIS IS NOT GIRORO. THIS WAS RECORDED AS A NAVIGATION TUTORIAL...
HEY, WHAT ARE YOU DOING THERE, GIRORO?
......
THAT LOOKS LIKE FUNNN! ♪
YOU IDIOT! GET OUT OF MY WAY!!
ANYWAY... WITH THIS, YOUR POWER WILL BE MATCHED BY NONE.
THEY... MADE THIS FOR ME...
THEN...I'LL BE ABLE TO DEFEAT THOSE GUYS WITH THIS?!
IDIOT! I SAID DEFENSE ONLY!!
WELL, THAT'S WHAT WE WANT, ISN'T IT?
VERY WELL. I WILL PROTECT THE EARTH!!
MOM, FUYUKI-- I'M GOING!
BUT YOU CAN'T DO IT ALONE, NATSUMI!!
MOM'S RIGHT. FIGHTING THEM ALONE?!
DON'T WORRY...
I BELIEVE IN THEM!
BELIEVE...? NATSUMI?
YOU MEAN...IN SERGEANT AND THE GUYS...?

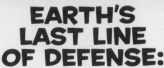

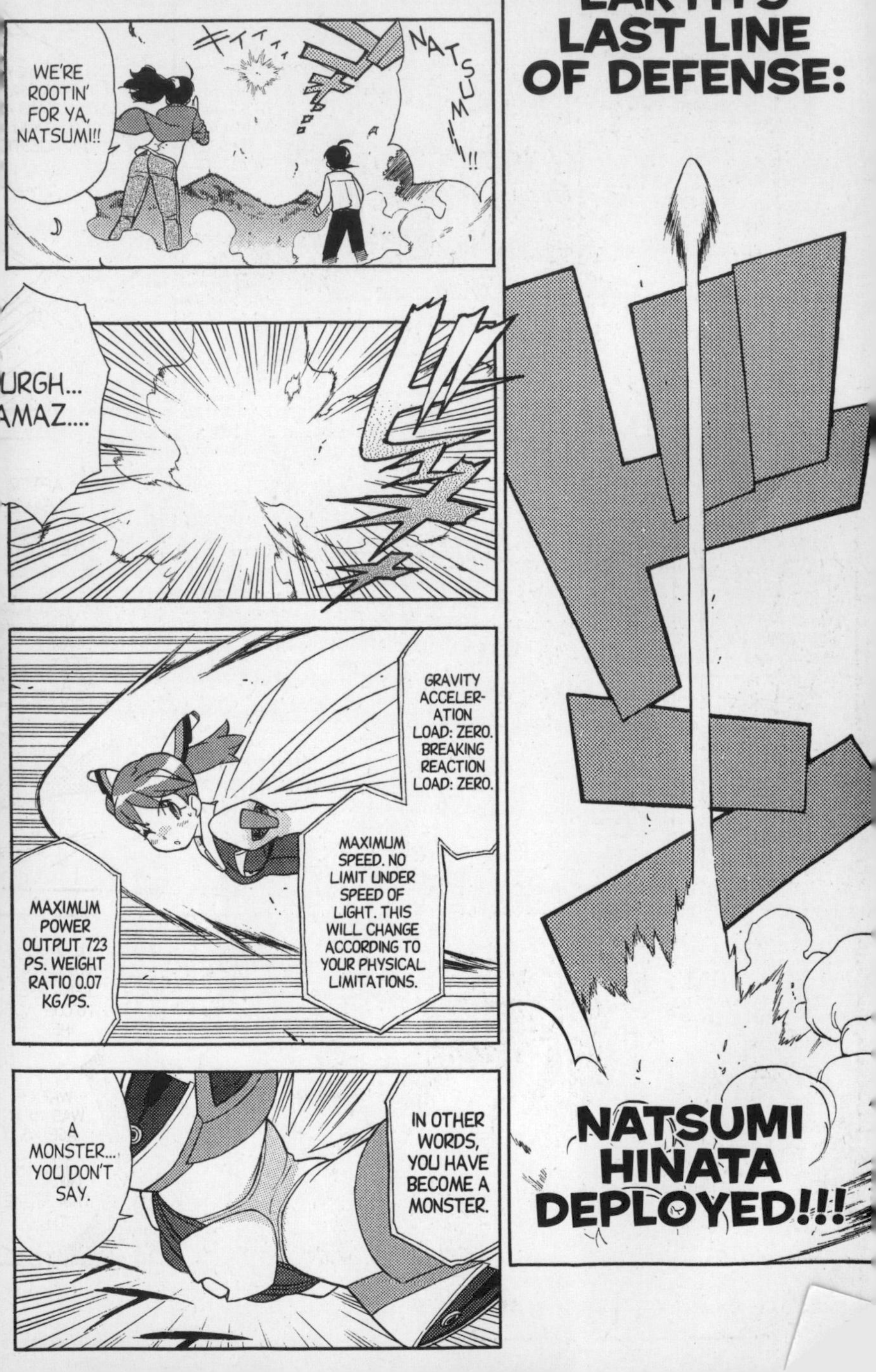
EARTH'S LAST LINE OF DEFENSE:
NATSUMI HINATA DEPLOYED!!!
NATSUMI!!
WE'RE ROOTIN' FOR YA, NATSUMI!!
URGH... AMAZ....
GRAVITY ACCELER-ATION LOAD: ZERO. BREAKING REACTION LOAD: ZERO.
MAXIMUM SPEED. NO LIMIT UNDER SPEED OF LIGHT. THIS WILL CHANGE ACCORDING TO YOUR PHYSICAL LIMITATIONS.
MAXIMUM POWER OUTPUT 723 PS. WEIGHT RATIO 0.07 KG/PS.
IN OTHER WORDS, YOU HAVE BECOME A MONSTER.
A MONSTER... YOU DON'T SAY.

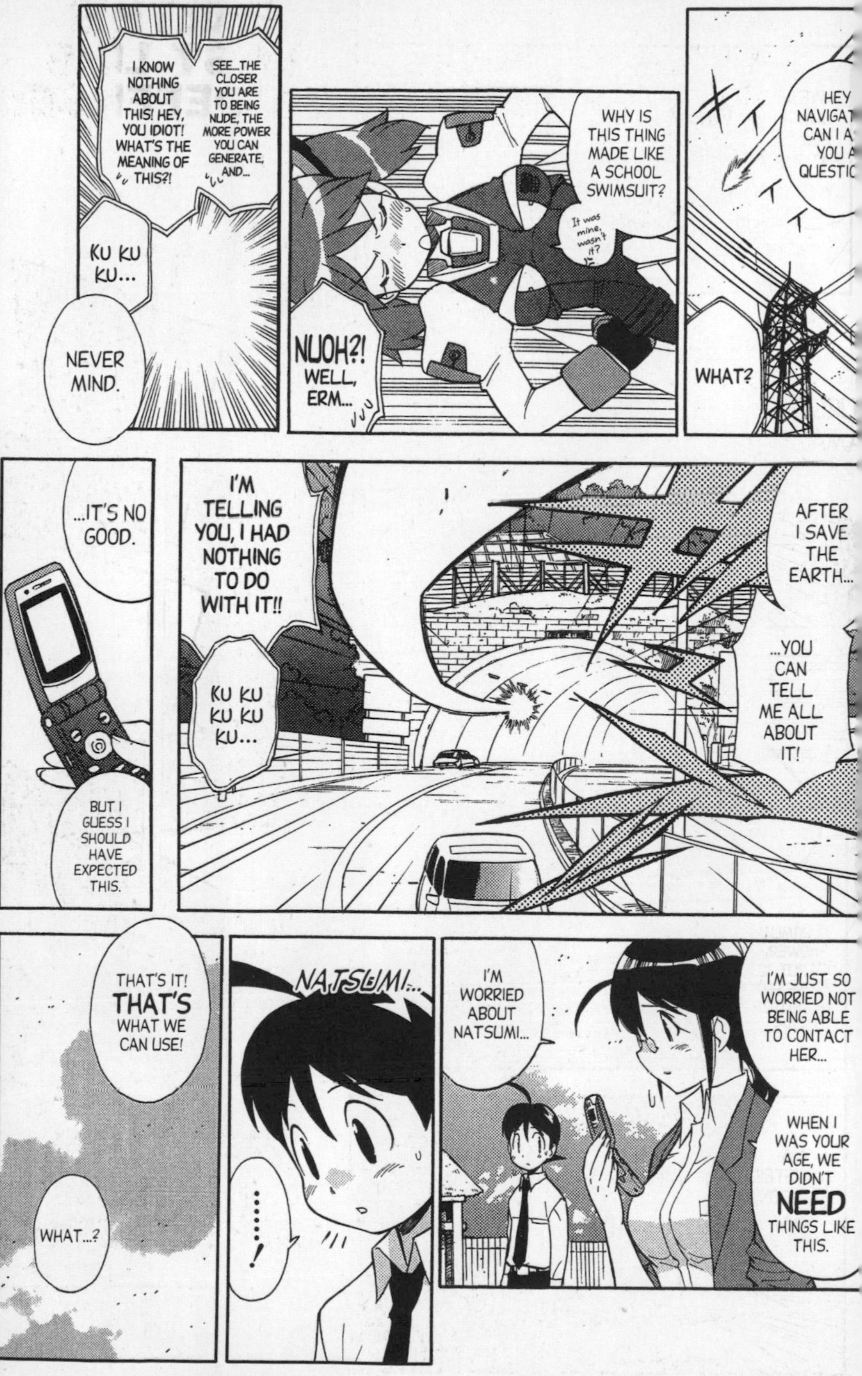
HEY NAVIGAT CAN I A YOU A QUESTIC
WHAT?
WHY IS THIS THING MADE LIKE A SCHOOL SWIMSUIT?
It was mine, wasn't it?
NUOH?! WELL, ERM...
SEE...THE CLOSER YOU ARE TO BEING NUDE, THE MORE POWER YOU CAN GENERATE, AND...
I KNOW NOTHING ABOUT THIS! HEY, YOU IDIOT! WHAT'S THE MEANING OF THIS?!
KU KU KU...
NEVER MIND.
AFTER I SAVE THE EARTH...
...YOU CAN TELL ME ALL ABOUT IT!
I'M TELLING YOU, I HAD NOTHING TO DO WITH IT!!
KU KU KU KU KU...
...IT'S NO GOOD.
BUT I GUESS I SHOULD HAVE EXPECTED THIS.
I'M JUST SO WORRIED NOT BEING ABLE TO CONTACT HER...
WHEN I WAS YOUR AGE, WE DIDN'T NEED THINGS LIKE THIS.
I'M WORRIED ABOUT NATSUMI...
NATSUMI...
......!
THAT'S IT! THAT'S WHAT WE CAN USE!
WHAT...?

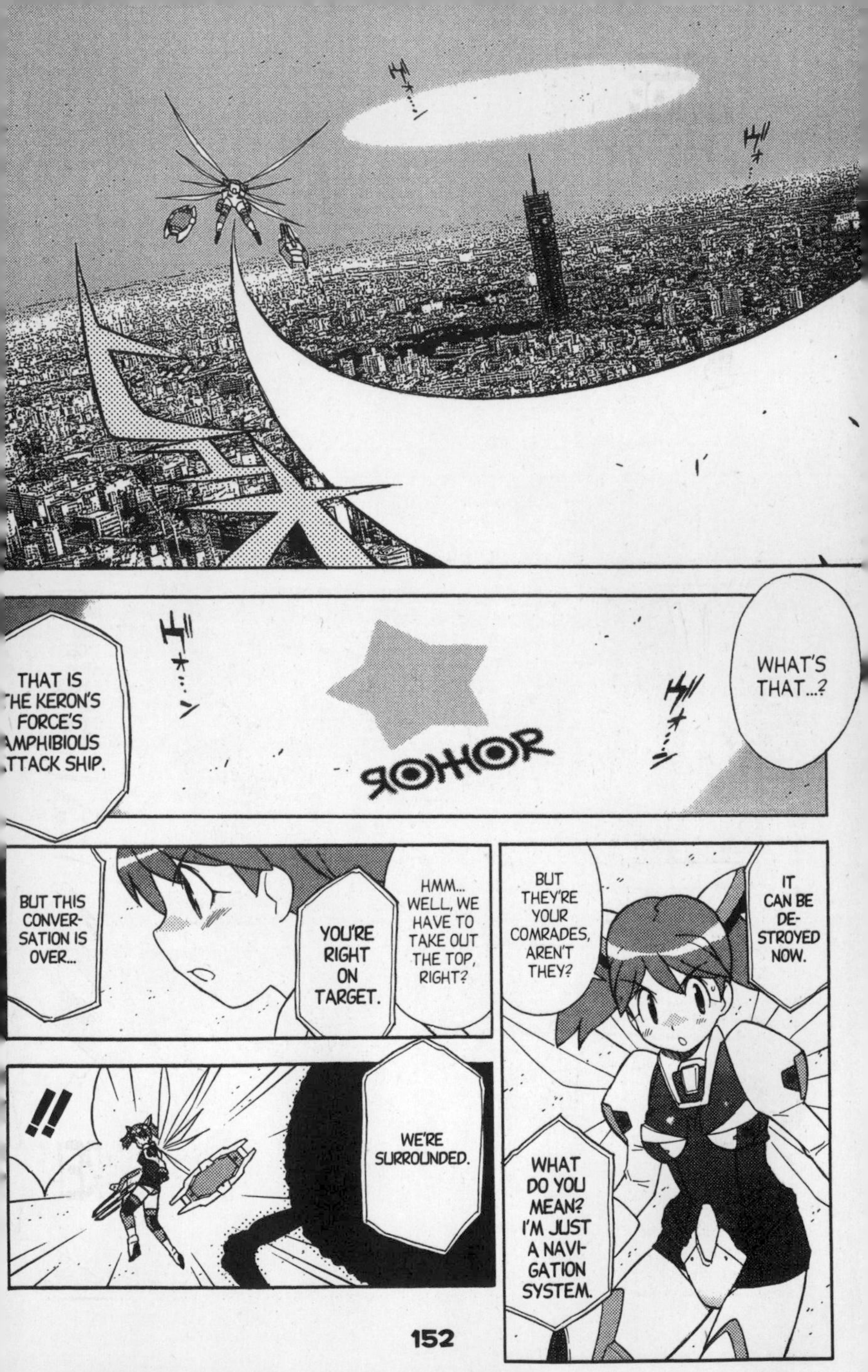
WHAT'S THAT...?
THAT IS THE KERON'S FORCE'S MPHIBIOUS TTACK SHIP.
IT CAN BE DE-STROYED NOW.
BUT THEY'RE YOUR COMRADES, AREN'T THEY?
WHAT DO YOU MEAN? I'M JUST A NAVI-GATION SYSTEM.
HMM... WELL, WE HAVE TO TAKE OUT THE TOP, RIGHT?
YOU'RE RIGHT ON TARGET.
BUT THIS CONVER-SATION IS OVER...
WE'RE SURROUNDED.
!!

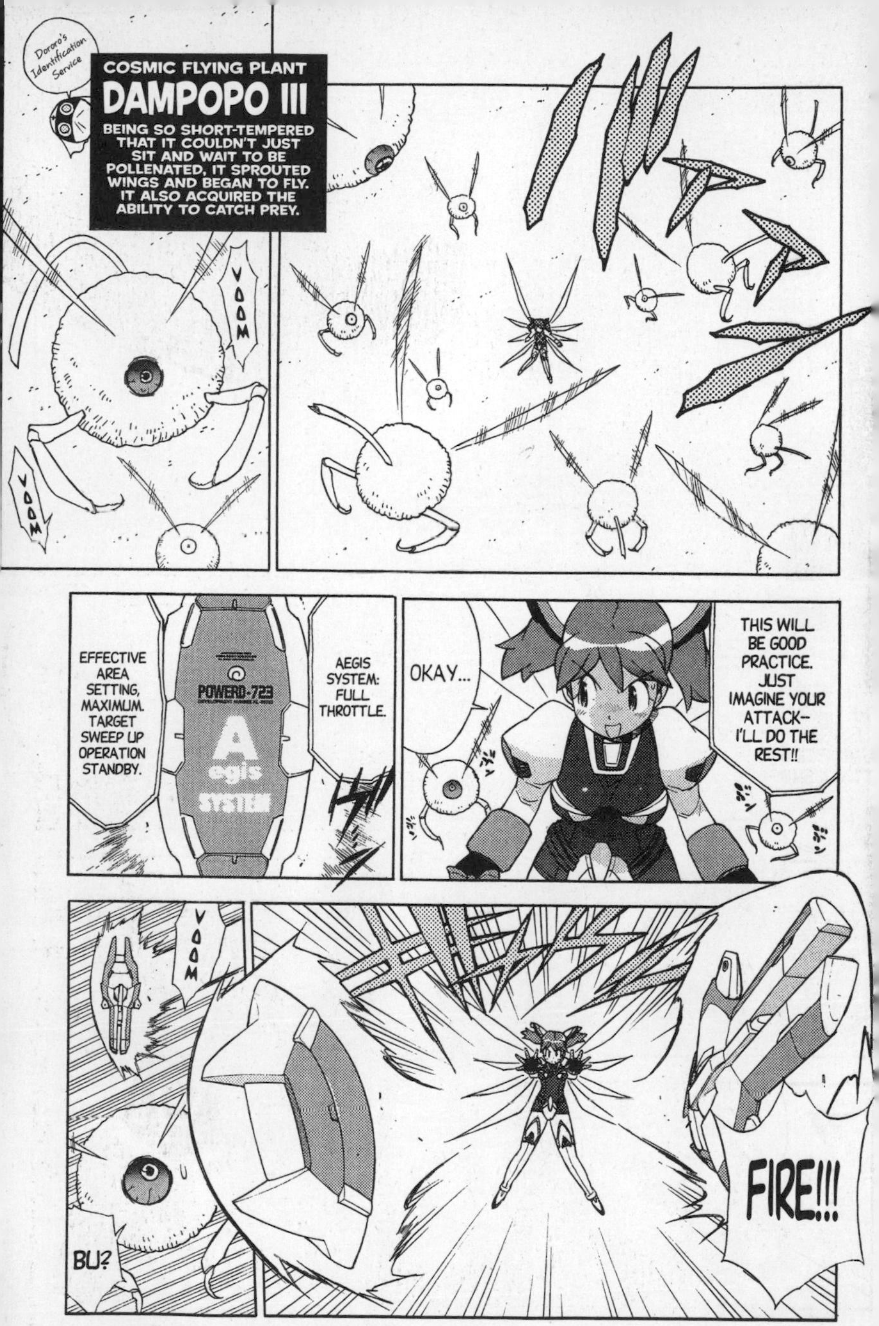

Dororo's Identification Service
COSMIC FLYING PLANT
DAMPOPO III
BEING SO SHORT-TEMPERED THAT IT COULDN'T JUST SIT AND WAIT TO BE POLLENATED, IT SPROUTED WINGS AND BEGAN TO FLY. IT ALSO ACQUIRED THE ABILITY TO CATCH PREY.
VOOM
VOOM
THIS WILL BE GOOD PRACTICE. JUST IMAGINE YOUR ATTACK-- I'LL DO THE REST!!
OKAY...
AEGIS SYSTEM: FULL THROTTLE.
POWERD-723
A egis SYSTEM
EFFECTIVE AREA SETTING, MAXIMUM. TARGET SWEEP UP OPERATION STANDBY.
FIRE!!!
VOOM
BU?

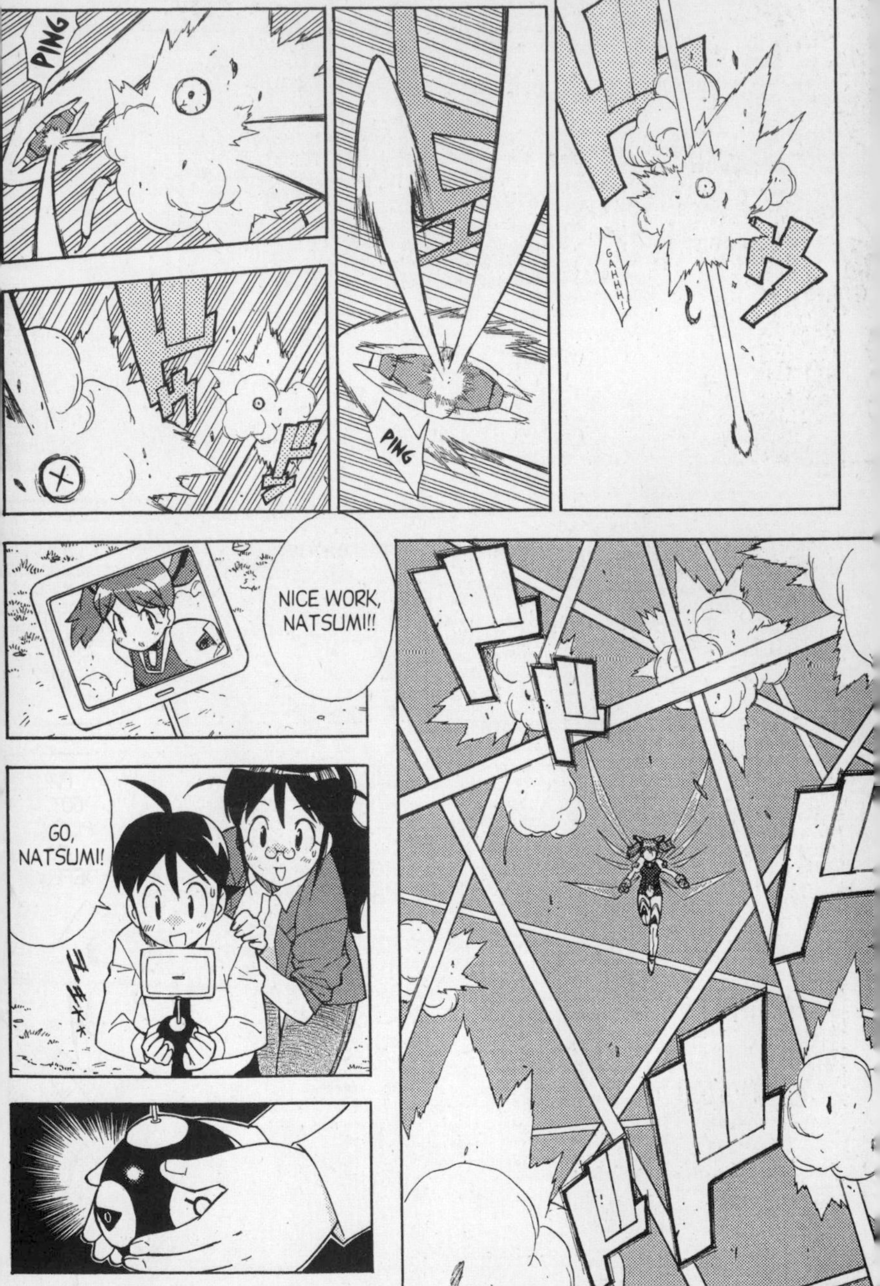
GAHHH!
PING
PING
NICE WORK, NATSUMI!!
GO, NATSUMI!

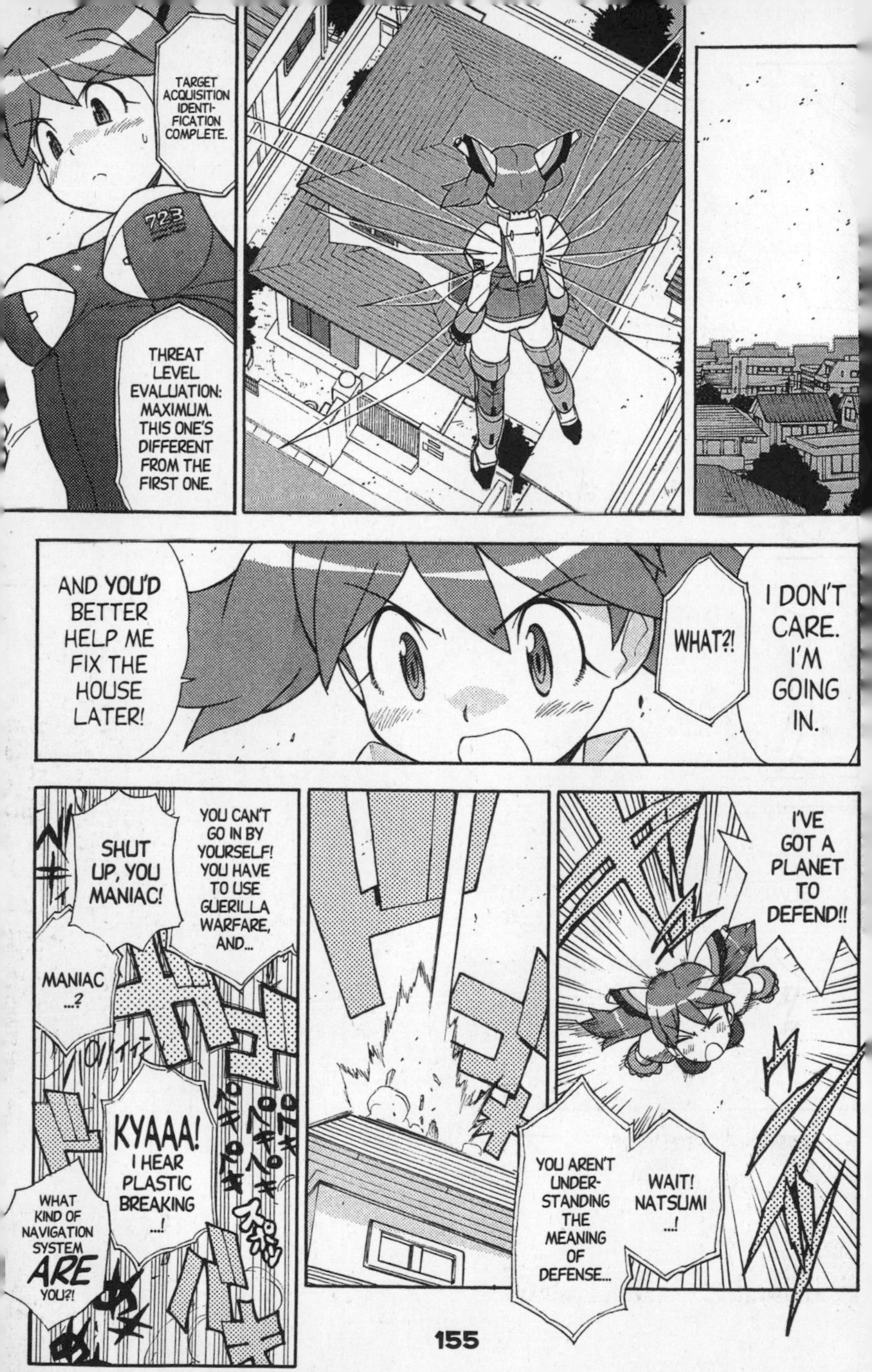
TARGET ACQUISITION IDENTI-FICATION COMPLETE.
THREAT LEVEL EVALUATION: MAXIMUM. THIS ONE'S DIFFERENT FROM THE FIRST ONE.
I DON'T CARE. I'M GOING IN.
WHAT?!
AND YOU'D BETTER HELP ME FIX THE HOUSE LATER!
I'VE GOT A PLANET TO DEFEND!!
WAIT! NATSUMI ...!
YOU AREN'T UNDER-STANDING THE MEANING OF DEFENSE...
YOU CAN'T GO IN BY YOURSELF! YOU HAVE TO USE GUERILLA WARFARE, AND...
SHUT UP, YOU MANIAC!
MANIAC ...?
KYAAA! I HEAR PLASTIC BREAKING ...!
WHAT KIND OF NAVIGATION SYSTEM ARE YOU?!

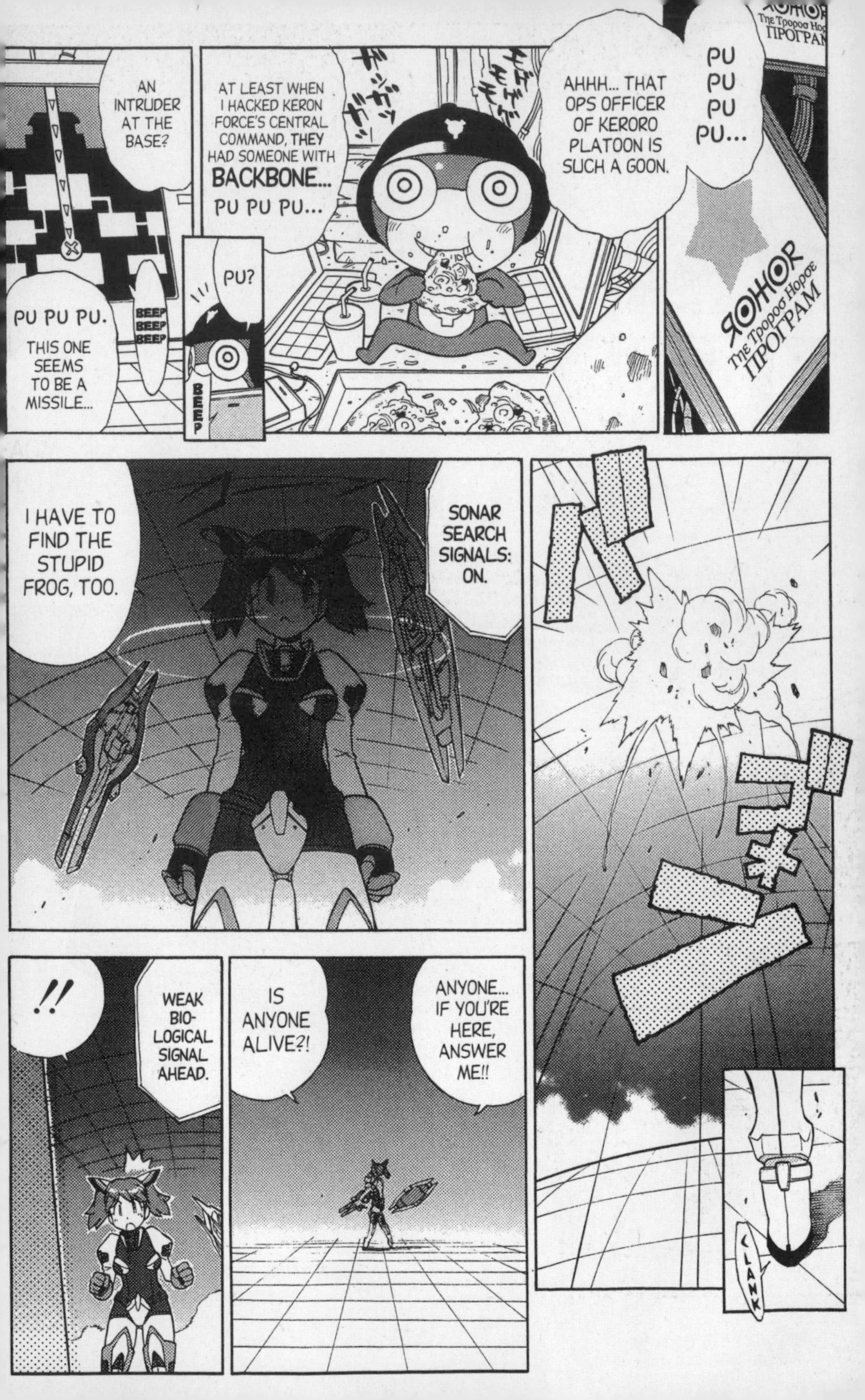
PU PU PU PU...
AHHH... THAT OPS OFFICER OF KERORO PLATOON IS SUCH A GOON.
AT LEAST WHEN I HACKED KERON FORCE'S CENTRAL COMMAND, THEY HAD SOMEONE WITH BACKBONE... PU PU PU...
AN INTRUDER AT THE BASE?
PU?
BEEP BEEP BEEP
BEEP
PU PU PU. THIS ONE SEEMS TO BE A MISSILE...
CLANK
SONAR SEARCH SIGNALS: ON.
I HAVE TO FIND THE STUPID FROG, TOO.
ANYONE... IF YOU'RE HERE, ANSWER ME!!
IS ANYONE ALIVE?!
WEAK BIO-LOGICAL SIGNAL AHEAD.
!!

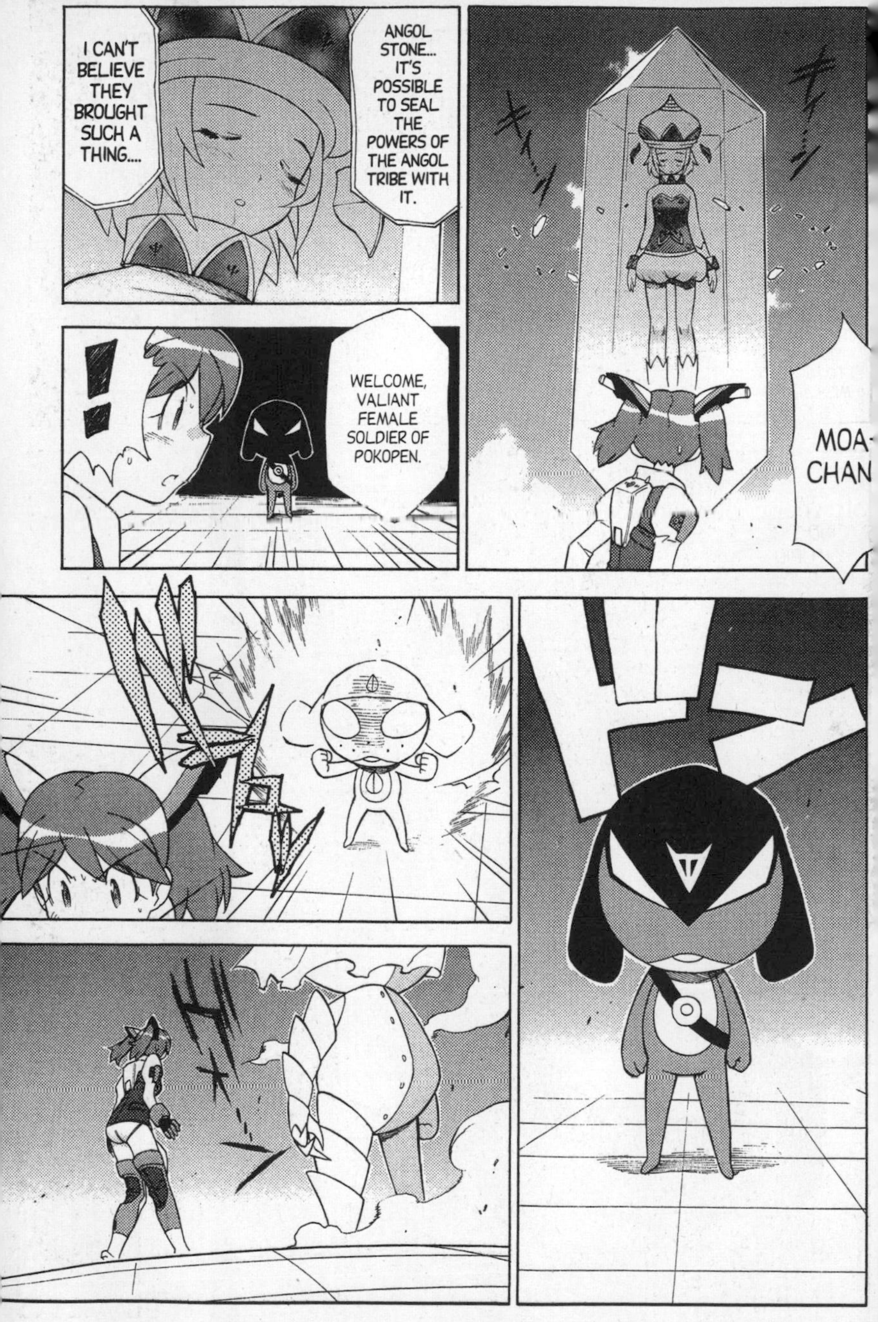
MOA-CHAN
ANGOL STONE... IT'S POSSIBLE TO SEAL THE POWERS OF THE ANGOL TRIBE WITH IT.
I CAN'T BELIEVE THEY BROUGHT SUCH A THING....
WELCOME, VALIANT FEMALE SOLDIER OF POKOPEN.

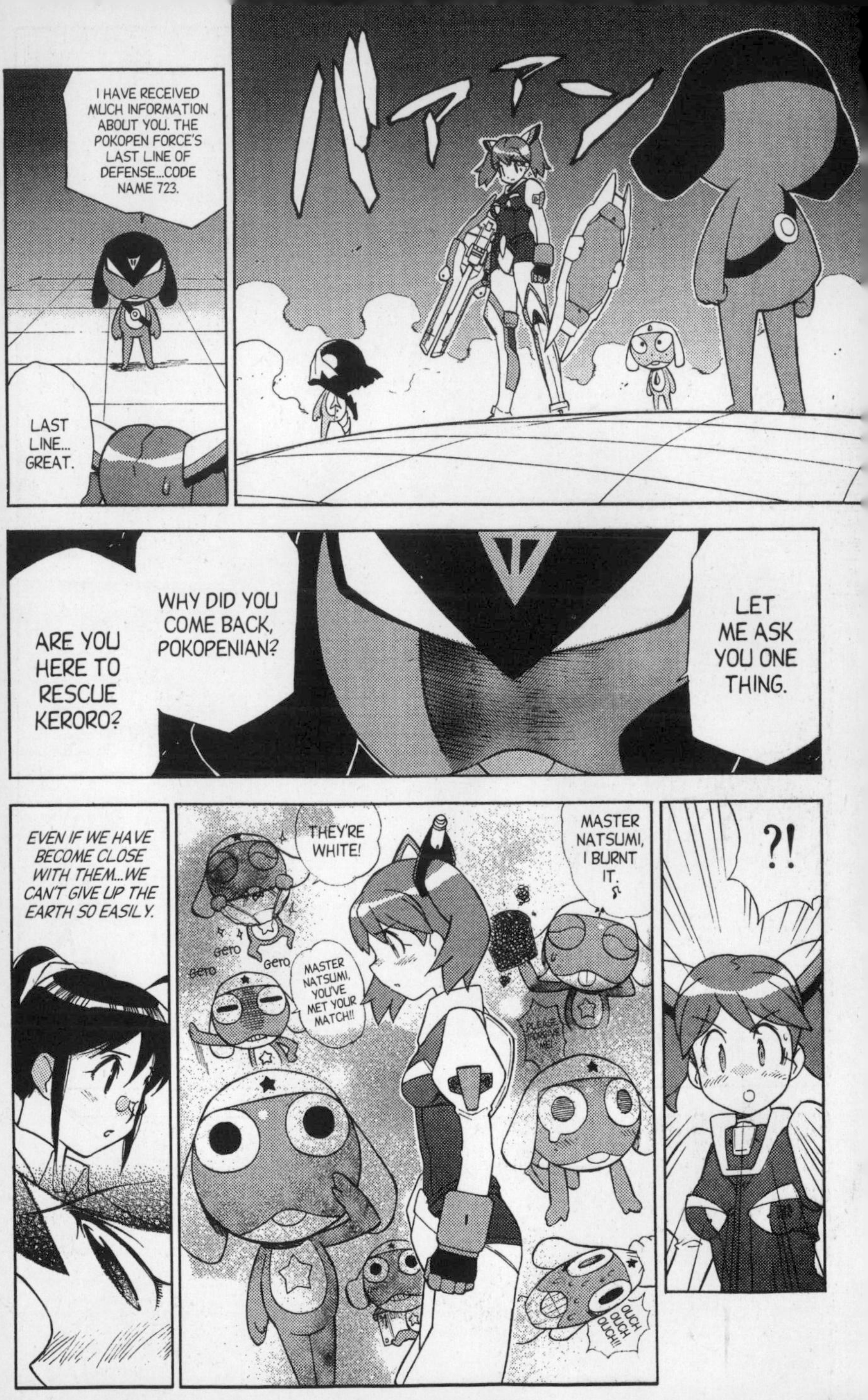
I HAVE RECEIVED MUCH INFORMATION ABOUT YOU. THE POKOPEN FORCE'S LAST LINE OF DEFENSE...CODE NAME 723.
LAST LINE... GREAT.
LET ME ASK YOU ONE THING.
WHY DID YOU COME BACK, POKOPENIAN?
ARE YOU HERE TO RESCUE KERORO?
?!
MASTER NATSUMI, I BURNT IT.
THEY'RE WHITE!
PLEASE FORGIVE ME!
MASTER NATSUMI, YOU'VE MET YOUR MATCH!!
GETO
GETO
GETO
OUCH OUCH OUCH!!
EVEN IF WE HAVE BECOME CLOSE WITH THEM...WE CAN'T GIVE UP THE EARTH SO EASILY.

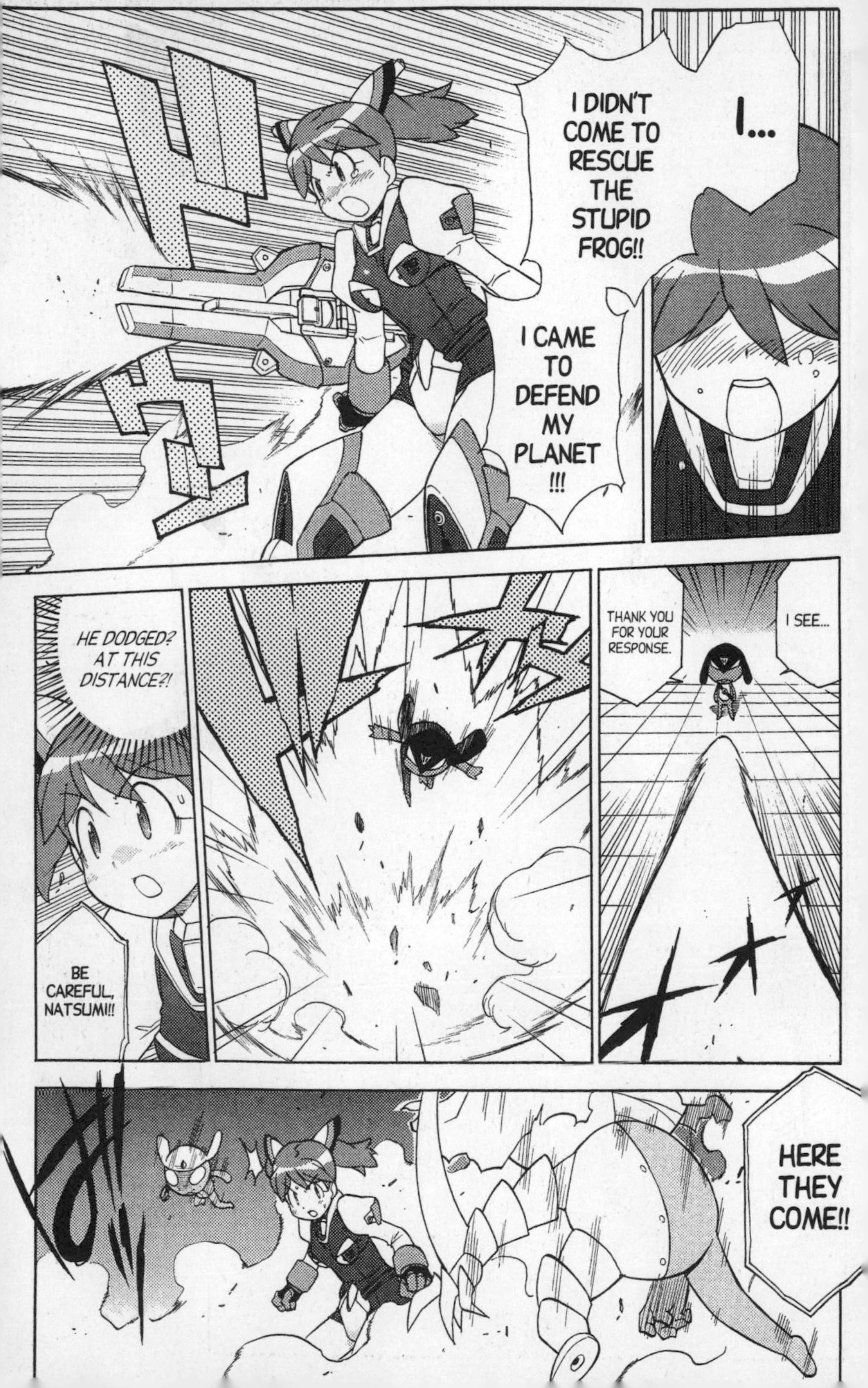
I...
I DIDN'T COME TO RESCUE THE STUPID FROG!!
I CAME TO DEFEND MY PLANET!!!
I SEE...
THANK YOU FOR YOUR RESPONSE.
HE DODGED? AT THIS DISTANCE?!
BE CAREFUL, NATSUMI!!
HERE THEY COME!!

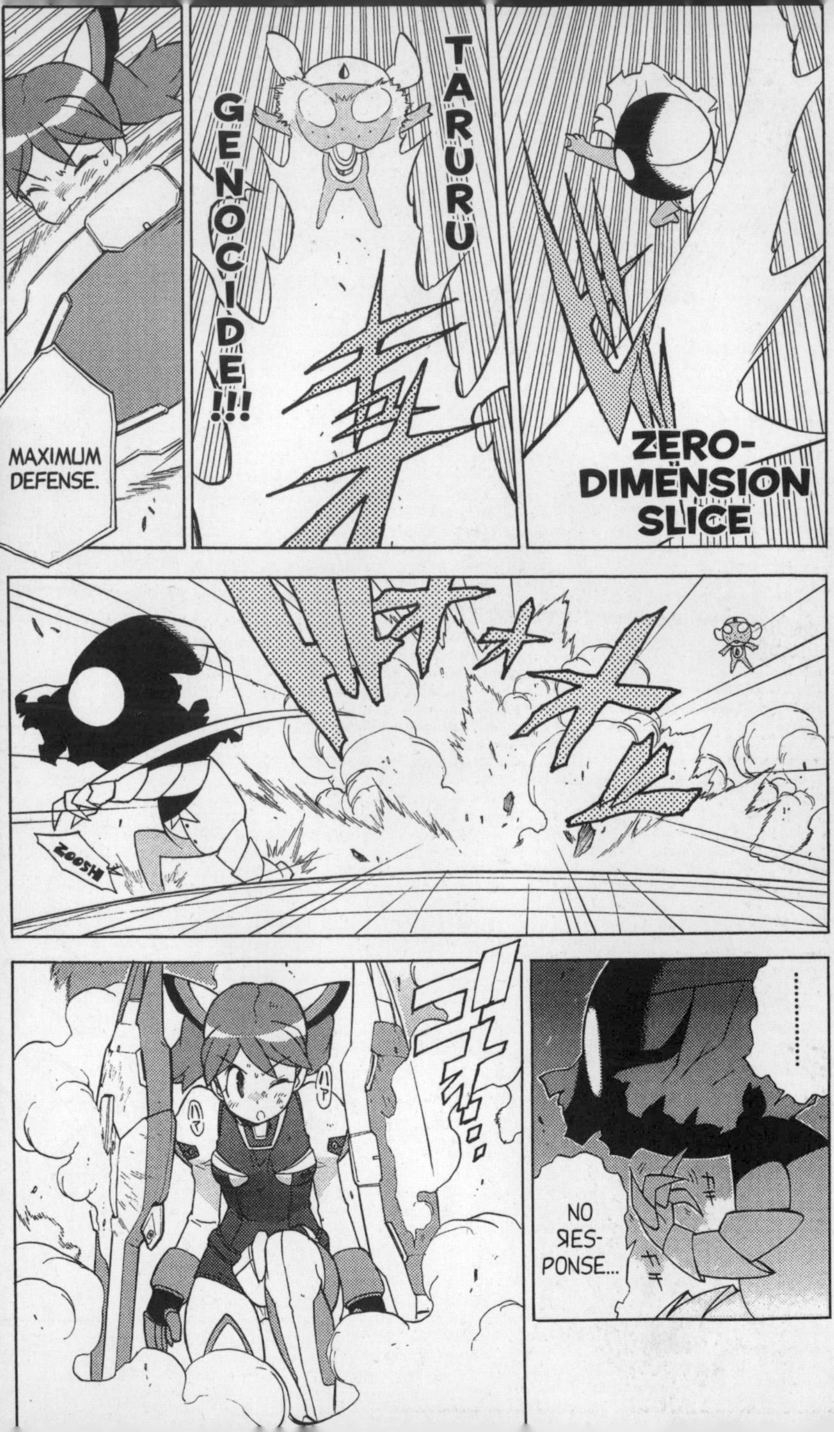
ZERO-DIMENSION SLICE
TARURU GENOCIDE!!!
MAXIMUM DEFENSE.
ZOOSH
......
NO ЯES-PONSE...

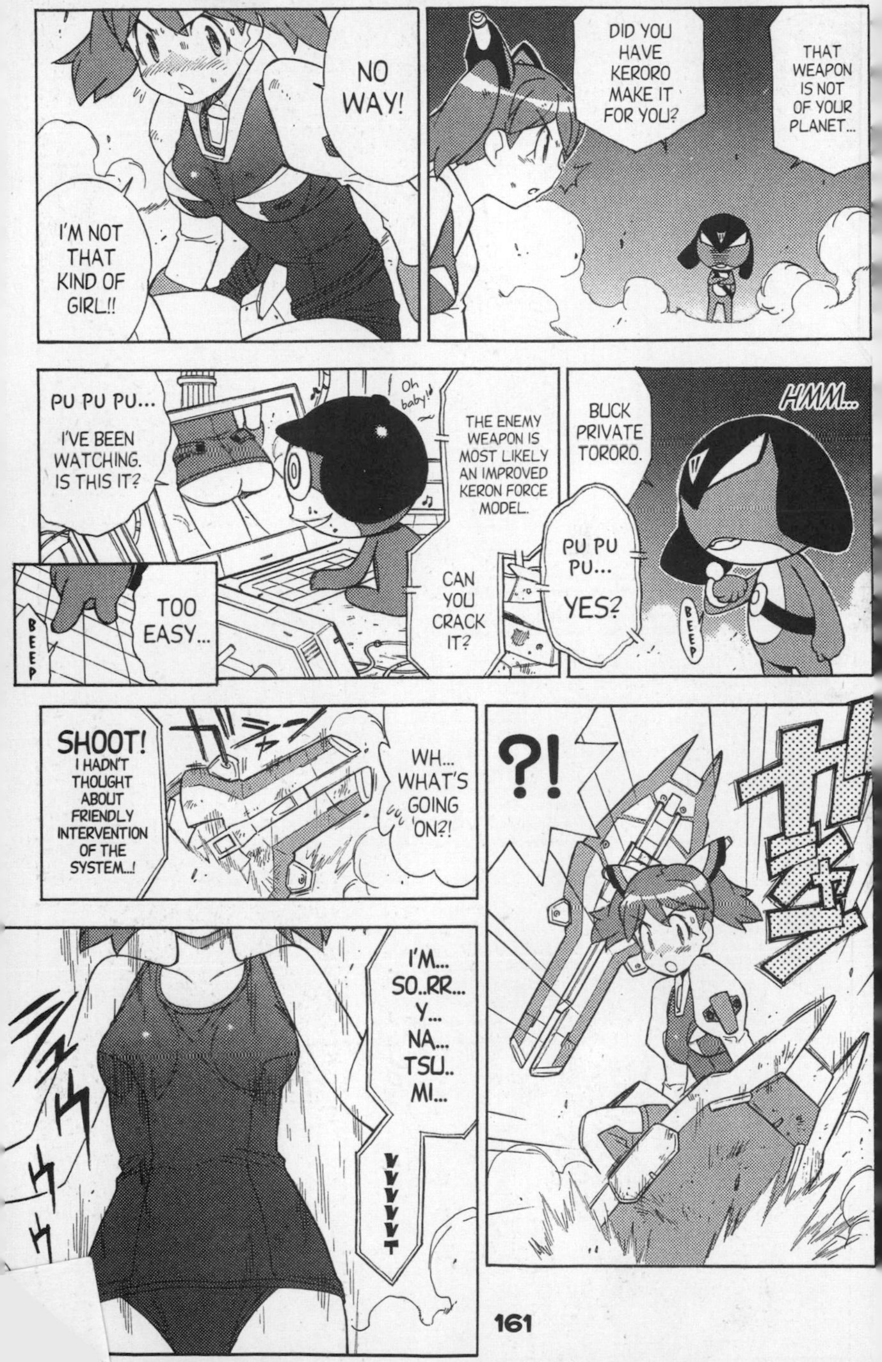
THAT WEAPON IS NOT OF YOUR PLANET...
DID YOU HAVE KERORO MAKE IT FOR YOU?
NO WAY!
I'M NOT THAT KIND OF GIRL!!
HMM...
BUCK PRIVATE TORORO.
PU PU PU... YES?
BEEP
THE ENEMY WEAPON IS MOST LIKELY AN IMPROVED KERON FORCE MODEL.
CAN YOU CRACK IT?
Oh baby!
PU PU PU...
I'VE BEEN WATCHING. IS THIS IT?
TOO EASY...
BEEP
?!
WH... WHAT'S GOING ON?!
SHOOT! I HADN'T THOUGHT ABOUT FRIENDLY INTERVENTION OF THE SYSTEM...!
I'M... SO..RR... Y... NA... TSU.. MI...
VVVVVVT

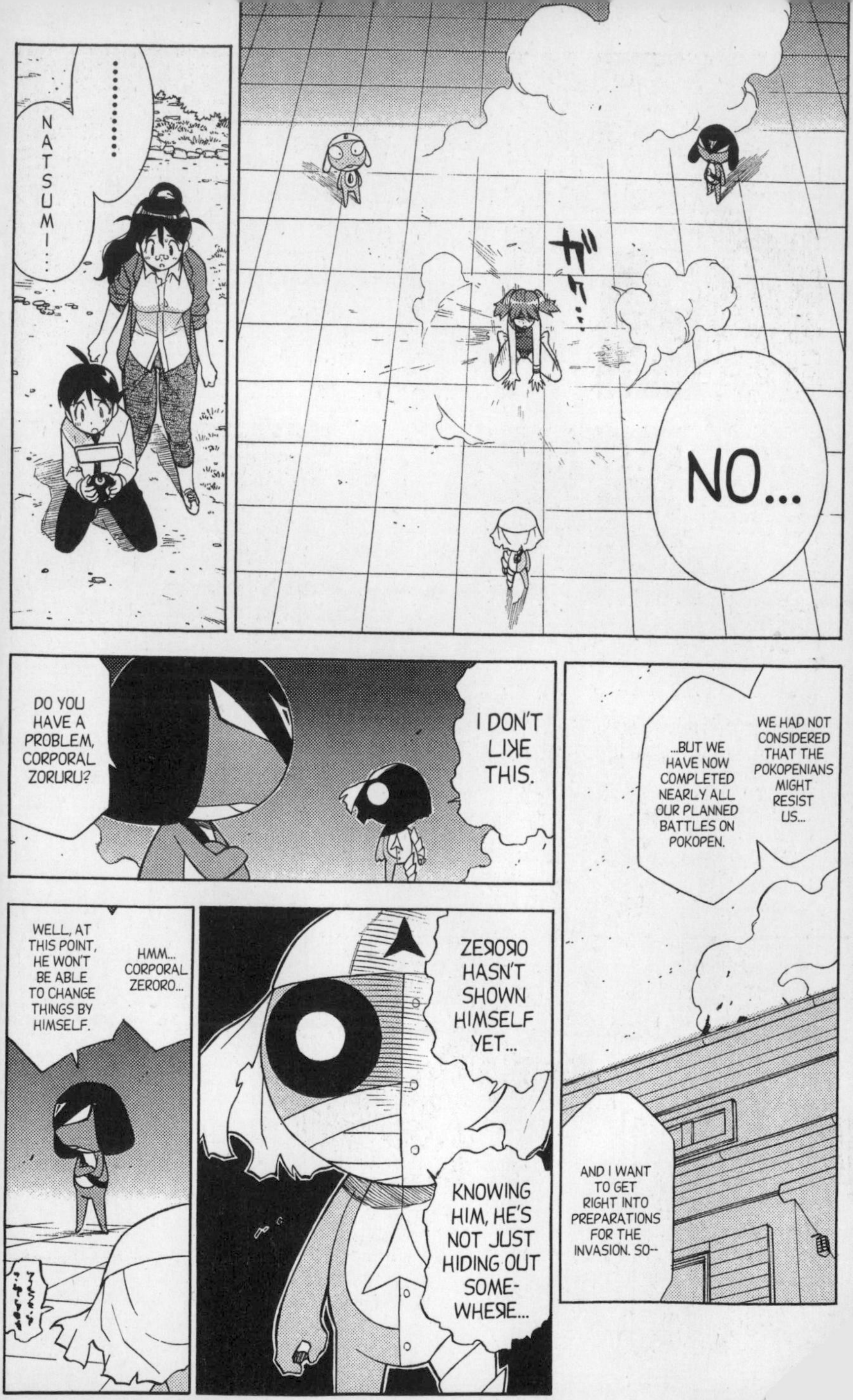

ガク…
NO...
......
NATSUMI...
WE HAD NOT CONSIDERED THAT THE POKOPENIANS MIGHT RESIST US...
...BUT WE HAVE NOW COMPLETED NEARLY ALL OUR PLANNED BATTLES ON POKOPEN.
AND I WANT TO GET RIGHT INTO PREPARATIONS FOR THE INVASION. SO--
I DON'T LIKE THIS.
DO YOU HAVE A PROBLEM, CORPORAL ZORURU?
ZERORO HASN'T SHOWN HIMSELF YET...
KNOWING HIM, HE'S NOT JUST HIDING OUT SOMEWHERE...
HMM... CORPORAL ZERORO...
WELL, AT THIS POINT, HE WON'T BE ABLE TO CHANGE THINGS BY HIMSELF.

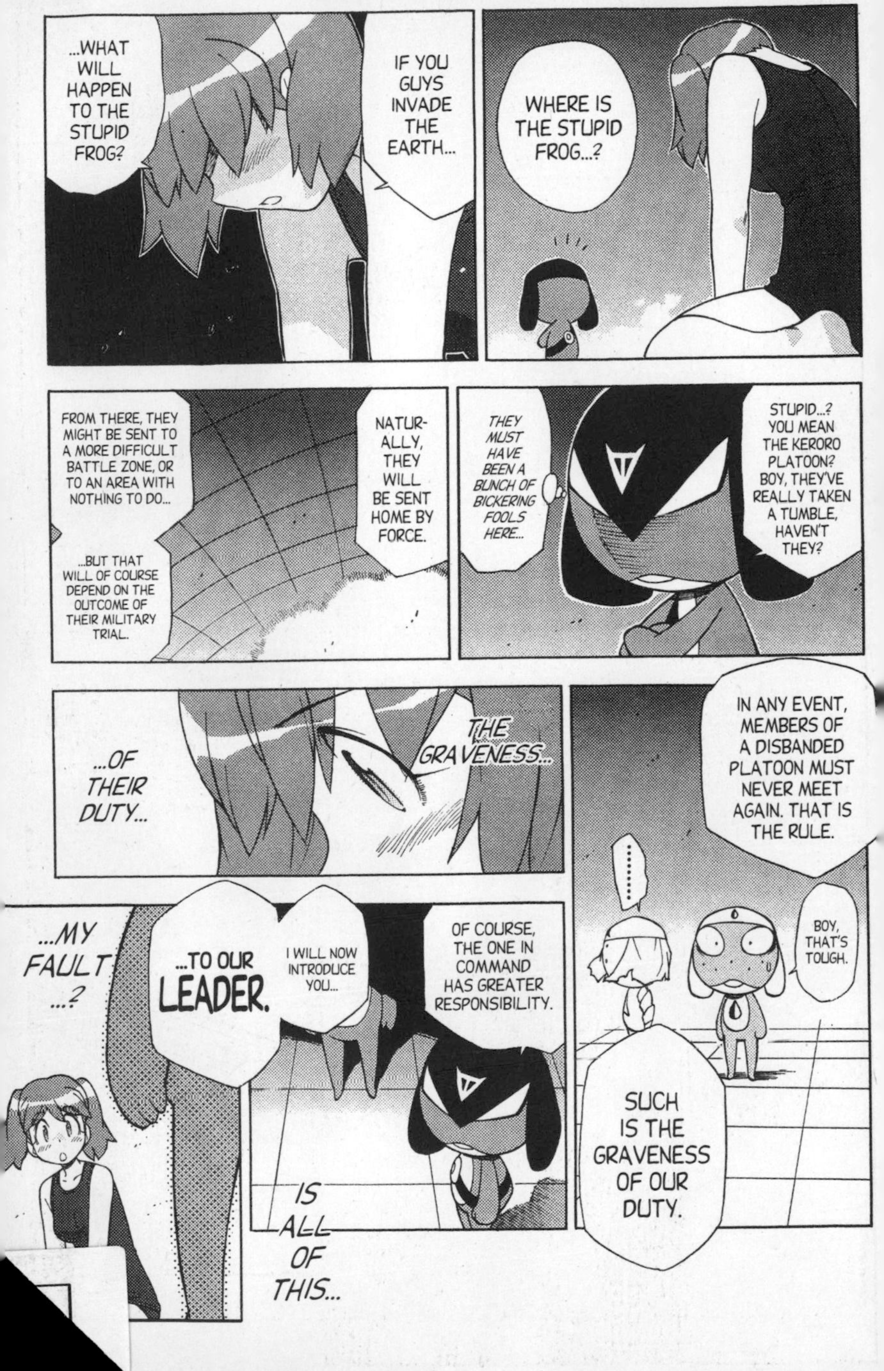
WHERE IS THE STUPID FROG...?
IF YOU GUYS INVADE THE EARTH...
...WHAT WILL HAPPEN TO THE STUPID FROG?
STUPID...? YOU MEAN THE KERORO PLATOON? BOY, THEY'VE REALLY TAKEN A TUMBLE, HAVEN'T THEY?
THEY MUST HAVE BEEN A BUNCH OF BICKERING FOOLS HERE...
NATUR-ALLY, THEY WILL BE SENT HOME BY FORCE.
FROM THERE, THEY MIGHT BE SENT TO A MORE DIFFICULT BATTLE ZONE, OR TO AN AREA WITH NOTHING TO DO...
...BUT THAT WILL OF COURSE DEPEND ON THE OUTCOME OF THEIR MILITARY TRIAL.
IN ANY EVENT, MEMBERS OF A DISBANDED PLATOON MUST NEVER MEET AGAIN. THAT IS THE RULE.
BOY, THAT'S TOUGH.
......
SUCH IS THE GRAVENESS OF OUR DUTY.
THE GRAVENESS...
...OF THEIR DUTY...
OF COURSE, THE ONE IN COMMAND HAS GREATER RESPONSIBILITY.
I WILL NOW INTRODUCE YOU...
...TO OUR LEADER.
IS ALL OF THIS...
...MY FAULT ...?

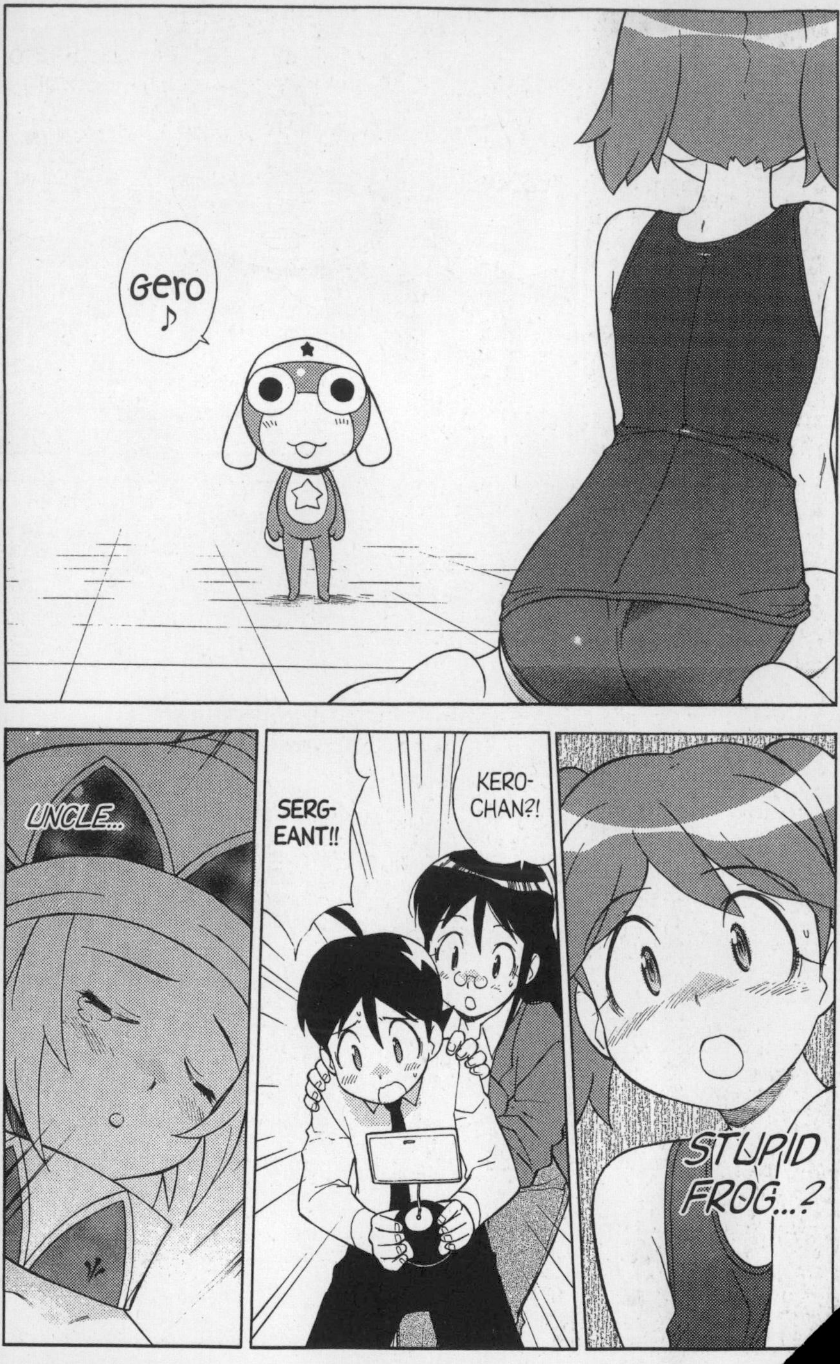
Gero ♪
STUPID FROG...?
KERO-CHAN?!
SERG-EANT!!
UNCLE...

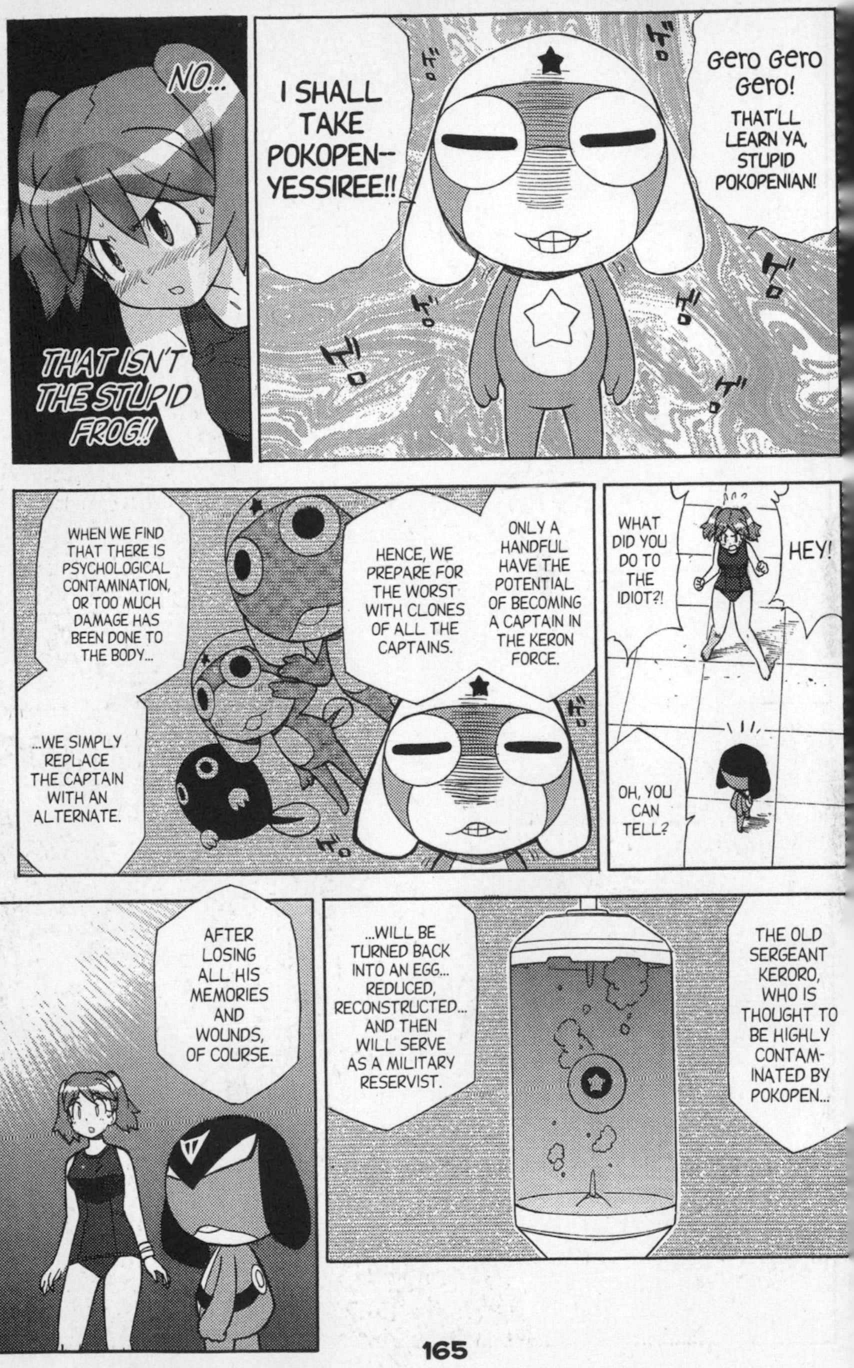
Gero Gero Gero!
THAT'LL LEARN YA, STUPID POKOPENIAN!
I SHALL TAKE POKOPEN-- YESSIREE!!
NO...
THAT ISN'T THE STUPID FROG!!
HEY!
WHAT DID YOU DO TO THE IDIOT?!
OH, YOU CAN TELL?
ONLY A HANDFUL HAVE THE POTENTIAL OF BECOMING A CAPTAIN IN THE KERON FORCE.
HENCE, WE PREPARE FOR THE WORST WITH CLONES OF ALL THE CAPTAINS.
WHEN WE FIND THAT THERE IS PSYCHOLOGICAL CONTAMINATION, OR TOO MUCH DAMAGE HAS BEEN DONE TO THE BODY...
...WE SIMPLY REPLACE THE CAPTAIN WITH AN ALTERNATE.
THE OLD SERGEANT KERORO, WHO IS THOUGHT TO BE HIGHLY CONTAM-INATED BY POKOPEN...
...WILL BE TURNED BACK INTO AN EGG... REDUCED, RECONSTRUCTED... AND THEN WILL SERVE AS A MILITARY RESERVIST.
AFTER LOSING ALL HIS MEMORIES AND WOUNDS, OF COURSE.

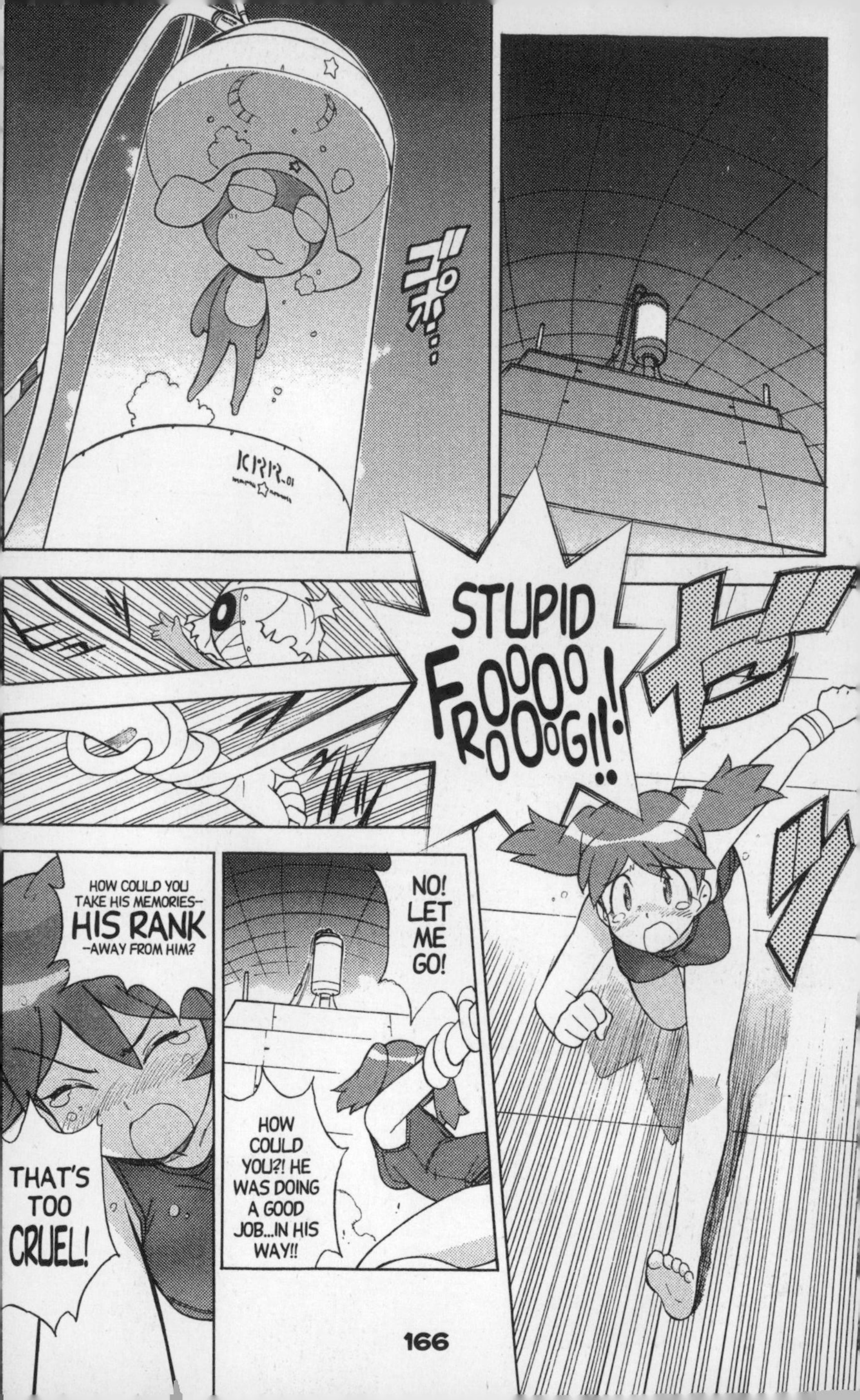
STUPID FROOOOROOOOG!!
NO! LET ME GO!
HOW COULD YOU?! HE WAS DOING A GOOD JOB...IN HIS WAY!!
HOW COULD YOU TAKE HIS MEMORIES--HIS RANK--AWAY FROM HIM?
THAT'S TOO CRUEL!

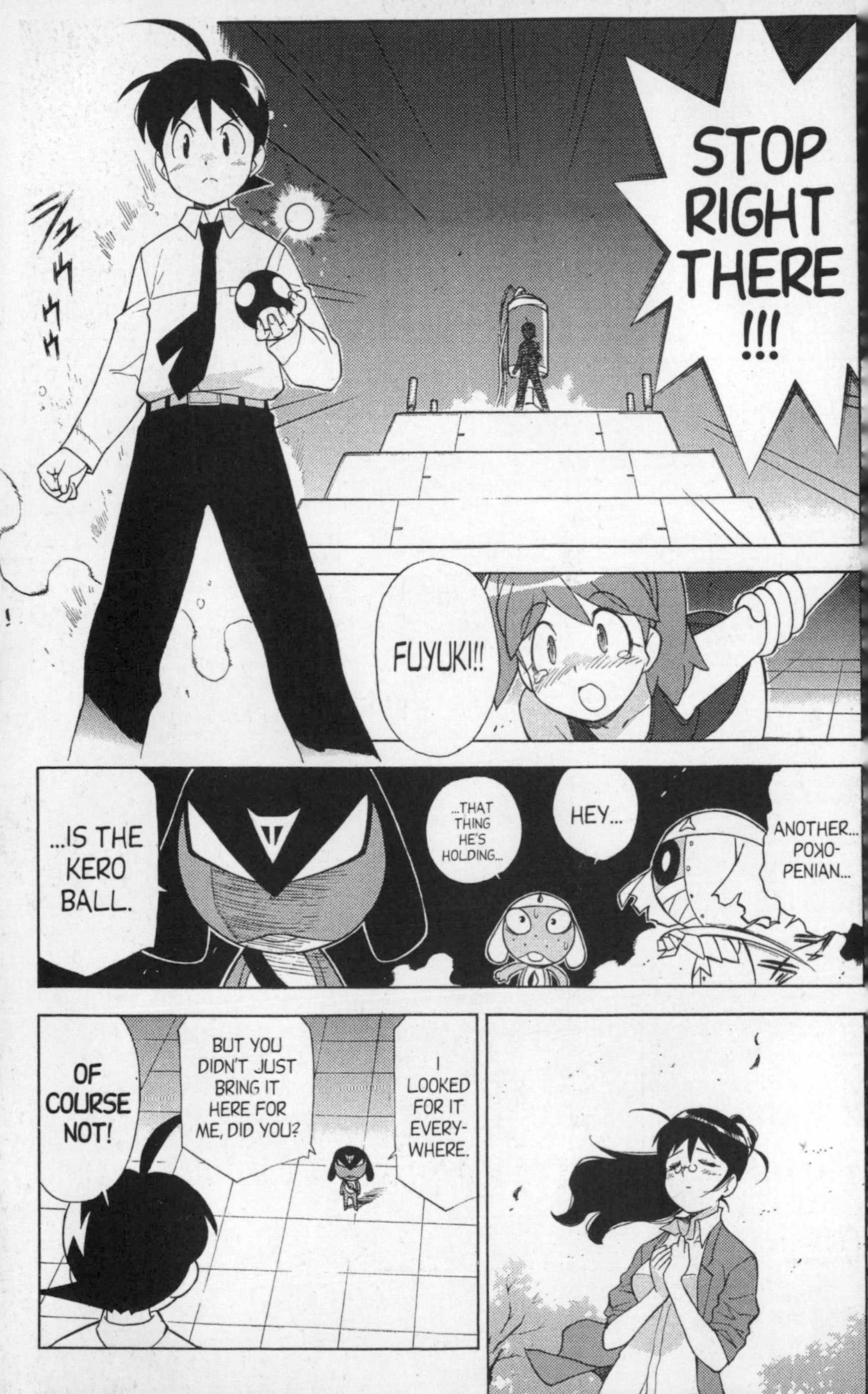
STOP RIGHT THERE!!!
FUYUKI!!!
ANOTHER... POKO-PENIAN...
HEY...
...THAT THING HE'S HOLDING...
...IS THE KERO BALL.
I LOOKED FOR IT EVERYWHERE.
BUT YOU DIDN'T JUST BRING IT HERE FOR ME, DID YOU?
OF COURSE NOT!

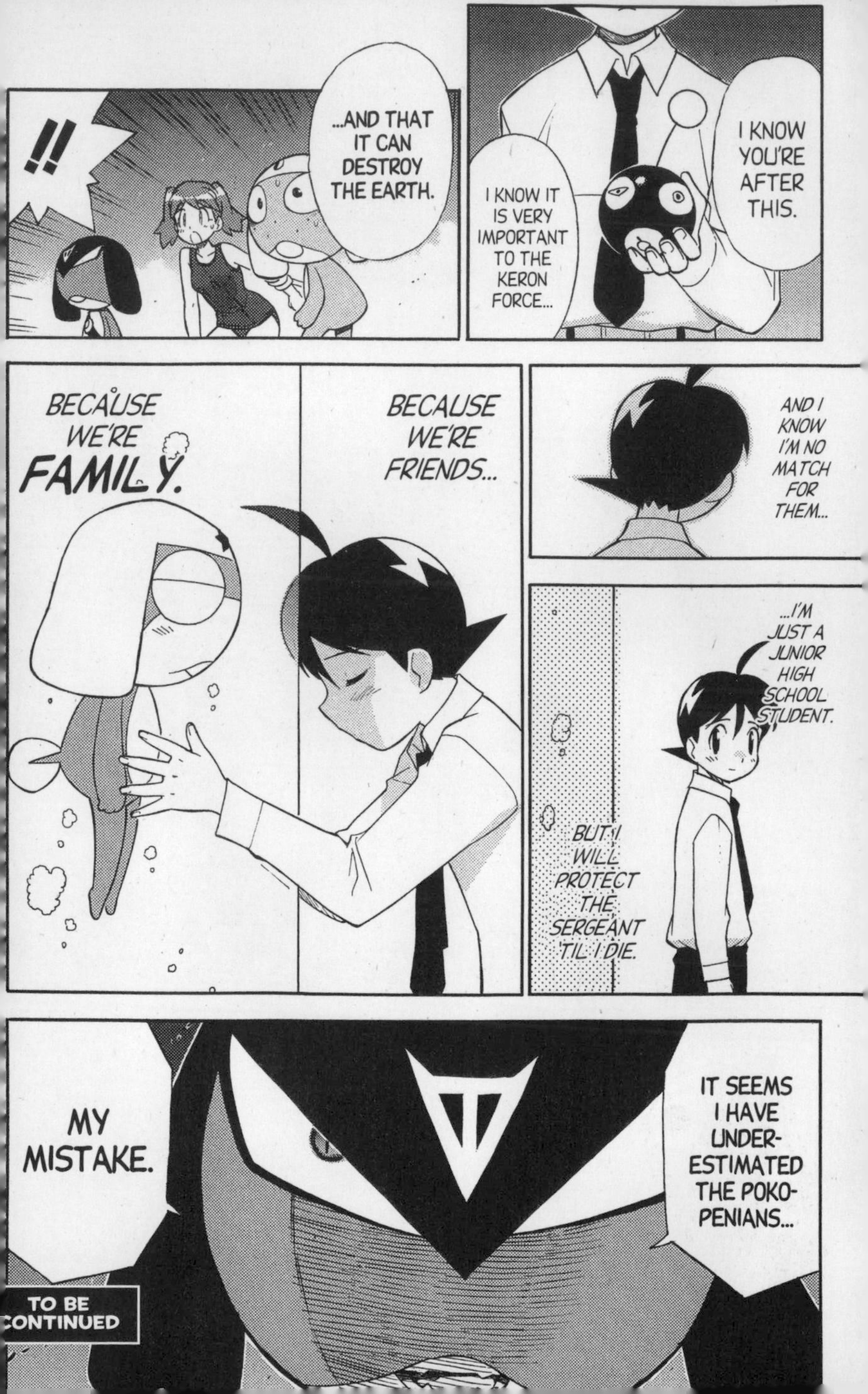
I KNOW YOU'RE AFTER THIS.
I KNOW IT IS VERY IMPORTANT TO THE KERON FORCE...
...AND THAT IT CAN DESTROY THE EARTH.
!!
AND I KNOW I'M NO MATCH FOR THEM...
...I'M JUST A JUNIOR HIGH SCHOOL STUDENT.
BUT I WILL PROTECT THE SERGEANT 'TIL I DIE.
BECAUSE WE'RE FRIENDS...
BECAUSE WE'RE FAMILY.
IT SEEMS I HAVE UNDER-ESTIMATED THE POKO-PENIANS...
MY MISTAKE.
TO BE CONTINUED

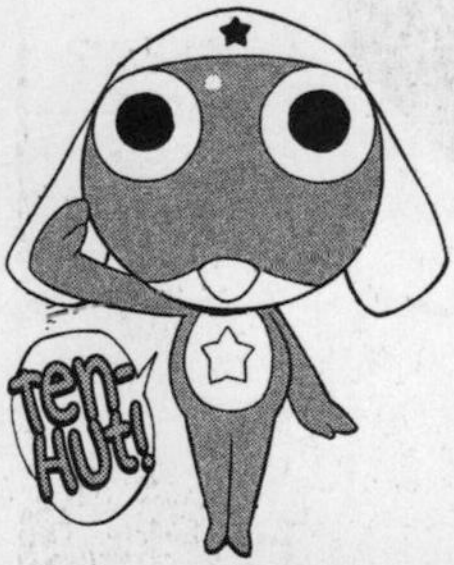
Ten-Hut!

ケロロ小隊 極秘 FILE

KERON FORCE AND POKOPEN'S MOST POWERFUL COLLABORATION
POWER NATSUMI: THE AUTHORITATIVE GUIDE!

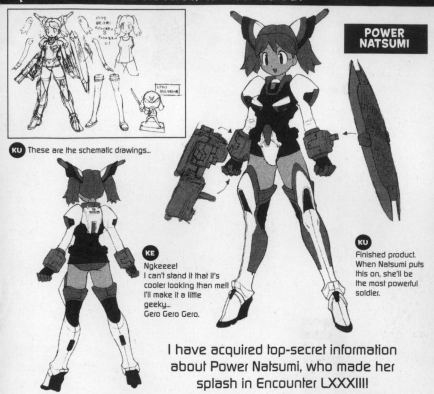

KERORO PLATOON **TOP SECRET** FILE

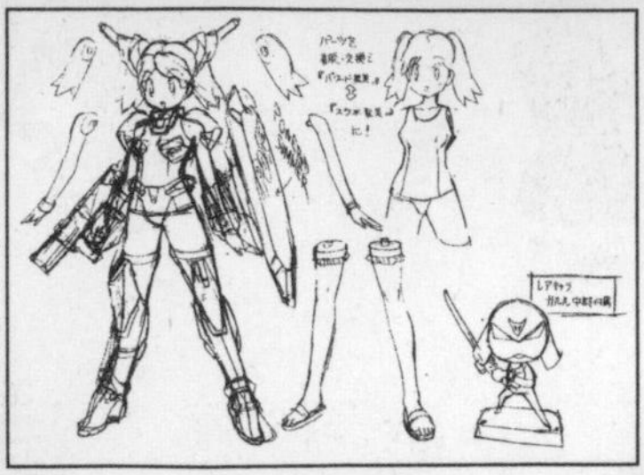

KU These are the schematic drawings...

POWER NATSUMI

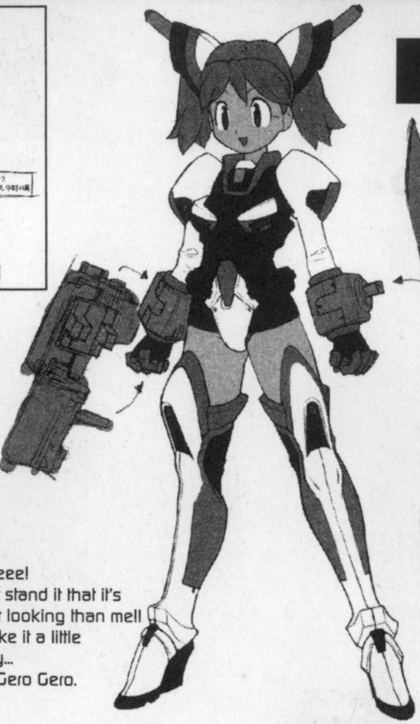

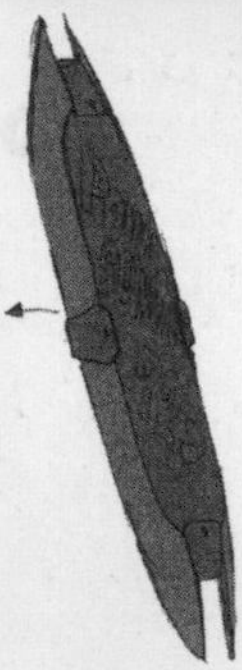

KU Finished product. When Natsumi puts this on, she'll be the most powerful soldier.

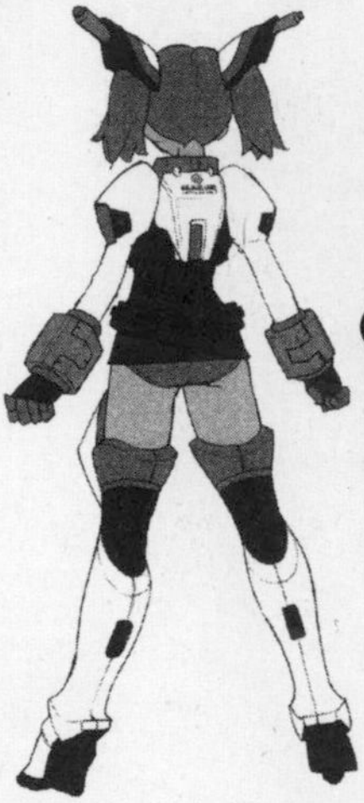

KE Ngkeeee! I can't stand it that it's cooler looking than me!! I'll make it a little geeky... Gero Gero Gero.

I have acquired top-secret information about Power Natsumi, who made her splash in Encounter LXXXIII!

This weapon was in development by Keroro and the guys ever since they noticed Natsumi's potential fighting power. They finished the project long before Garuru and his team arrived, but didn't know how they could get Natsumi to put it on without being kicked in the behind, so the suit was stashed in the closet for the interim.

Kururu was the one who developed its compatibility with school swimsuits; Keroro came up with the rifle and shield bit; Giroro suggested nonchalantly that it should emphasize defense power, thinking about Natsumi's safety. Tamama's idea was to make it the "Super-Duper Strongest!" "It was finished before I even knew about it," was Dororo's take on the matter. So as you can see, Power Natsumi was perfected with input from each member of the platoon. Of course, Natsumi never gave permission, so who knows what might happen to the guys later! But the best part is that Power Natsumi will appear in the anime version of Sgt. Keroro. See Power Natsumi's action in Story 38 (to be included in DVD Volume 10)--and get your paparazzi gear ready!

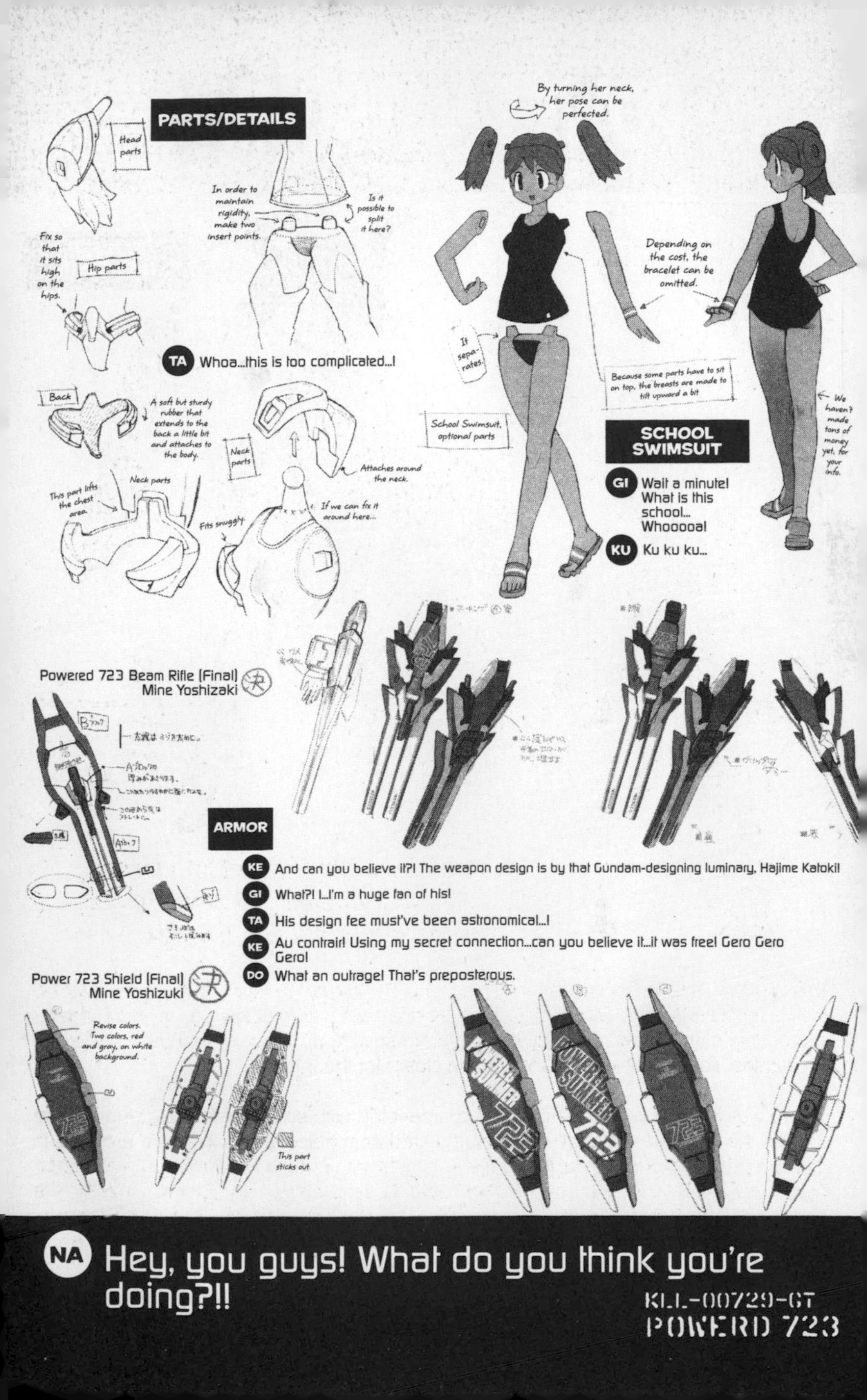
PARTS/DETAILS
Head parts
In order to maintain rigidity, make two insert points.
Is it possible to split it here?
Fix so that it sits high on the hips.
Hip parts
TA Whoa...this is too complicated...!
Back
A soft but sturdy rubber that extends to the back a little bit and attaches to the body.
Neck parts
Attaches around the neck.
Neck parts
This part lifts the chest area.
Fits snuggly.
If we can fix it around here...
By turning her neck, her pose can be perfected.
Depending on the cost, the bracelet can be omitted.
It separates.
Because some parts have to sit on top, the breasts are made to tilt upward a bit
School Swimsuit, optional parts
We haven't made tons of money yet, for your info.
SCHOOL SWIMSUIT
GI Wait a minute! What is this school... Whoooa!
KU Ku ku ku...
Powered 723 Beam Rifle (Final) Mine Yoshizaki
ARMOR
KE And can you believe it?! The weapon design is by that Gundam-designing luminary, Hajime Katoki!
GI What?! I...I'm a huge fan of his!
TA His design fee must've been astronomical...!
KE Au contrair! Using my secret connection...can you believe it...it was free! Gero Gero Gero!
DO What an outrage! That's preposterous.
Power 723 Shield (Final) Mine Yoshizuki
Revise colors. Two colors, red and gray, on white background.
This part sticks out
POWERED SUMMER 723
NA Hey, you guys! What do you think you're doing?!!
KLL-00729-GT
POWERD 723

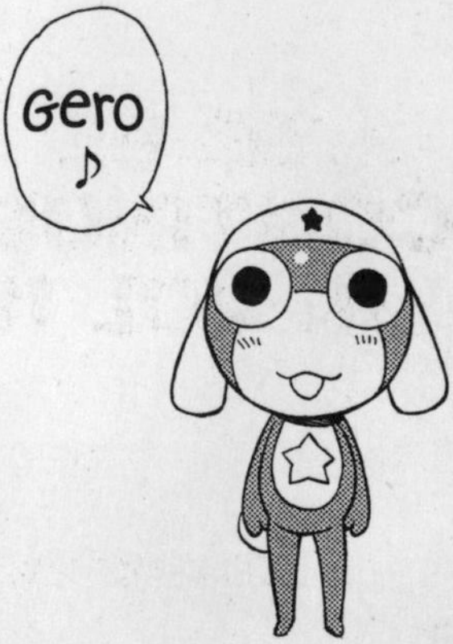
Gero ♪

JAPAN STAFF

CREATOR
MINE YOSHIZAKI

BACKGROUNDS
OYSTER

FINISHES
GOMOKU AKATSUKI
ROBIN TOKYO
TOMMI NARIHARA
634 (ROMEO)

TO BE
CONTINUED
IN VOL 11

KOYUKI-CHAN

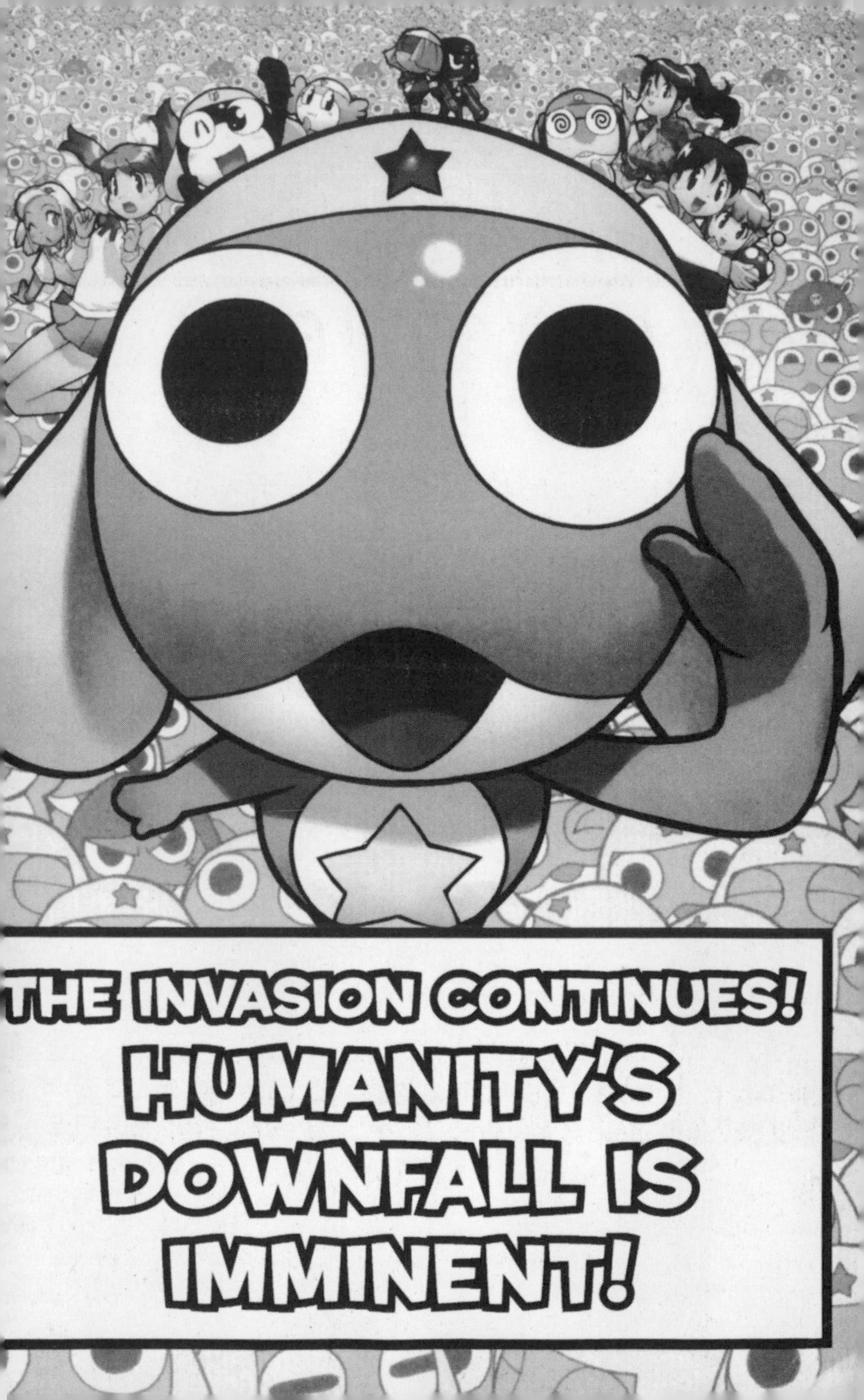
THE INVASION CONTINUES!
HUMANITY'S DOWNFALL IS IMMINENT!

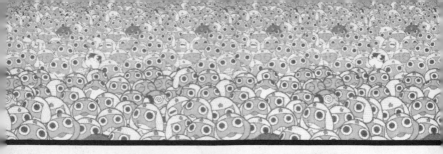

GERO! GERO! GERO!

GREETINGS, POKOPENIANS! HAVE YOU MISSED ANY EXCITING DETAILS SURROUNDING YOUR EVENTUAL SUBJUGATION? FEAR NOT. VOLUMES 1 THROUGH 9 OF SGT. FROG WILL BRIEF YOU. AND READING ABOUT ALL OF MY FAILED PLOTS AND SCHEMES WILL ONLY LULL YOU INTO A FALSE SENSE OF SECURITY!

SGT FROG
KERORO GUNSO

TOKYOPOP PRESENTS
MANGA 漫画™
THE NEW SIZZLING HOT
MANGA
MAGAZINE
ZELDA AND FRIEND FROM
WAR ON FLESH
©2005 Justin Boring, Greg Hildebrandt and TOKYOPOP
SIGN UP FOR FREE WWW.TOKYOPOP.COM

TOKYOPOP SHOP

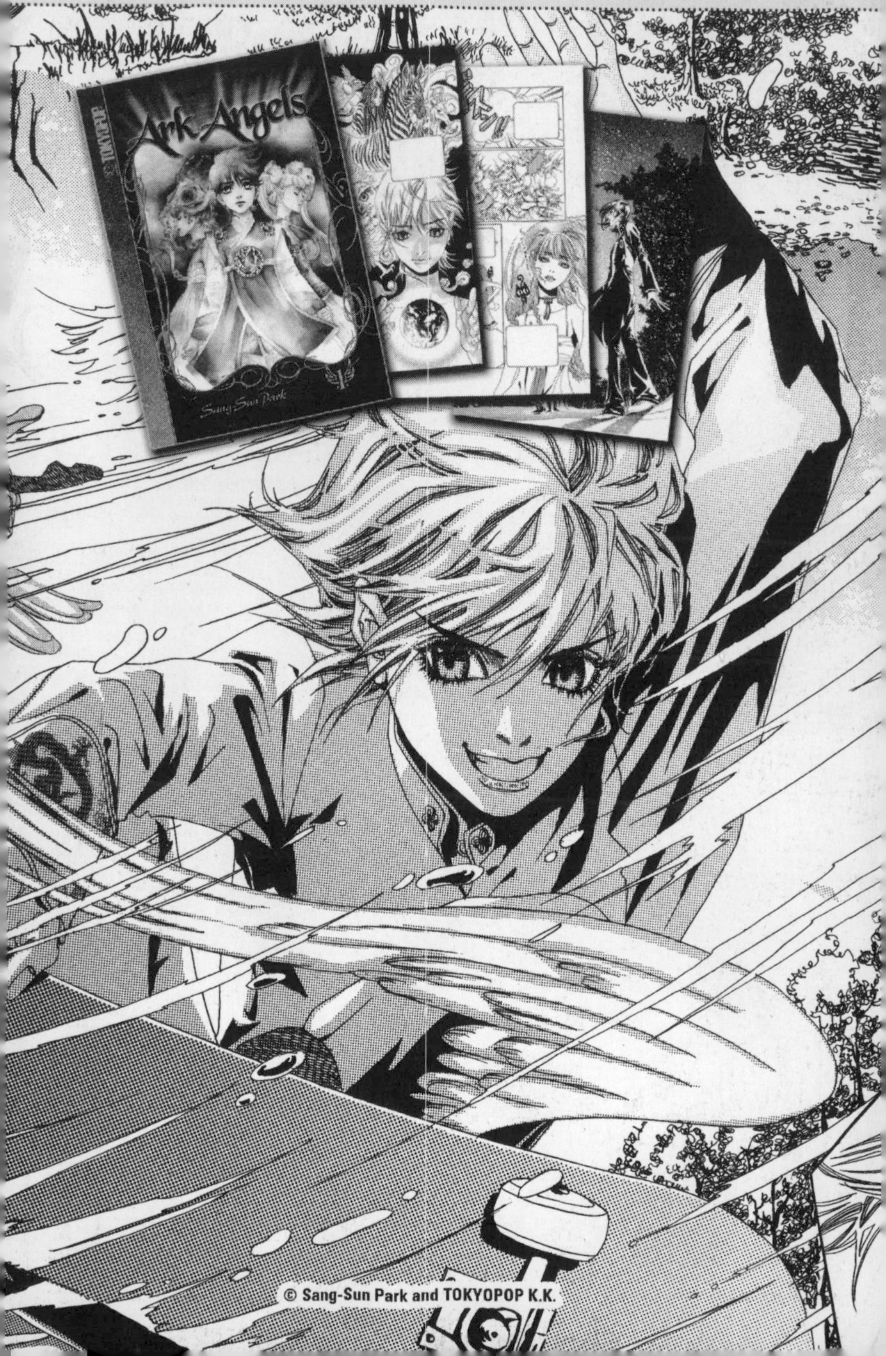
Ark Angels
TOKYOPOP
Sang-Sun Park

SPOTLIGHT TOKYOPOP MANGA SUPPLEMENT

THE DREAMING

BY QUEENIE CHAN

TOKYOPOP
the dreaming
1
Queenie Chan
THE DORMS ARE ON THE SECOND FLOOR.
THIS WAY!
LIGHTS OUT AT TEN - BUT YOU CAN READ IN BED.
IS YOUR ROOM NUMBER!
SO...
...AND WHAT'S BEHIND THAT DOOR ANYWAY?!
!
WHAT THE--

T TEEN AGE 13+

ALL OF THEM VANISHED...WITHOUT A TRACE.

When twin sisters Amber and Jeanie enroll in an Australian boarding school, they soon uncover a dark, unexplained secret: Students have been known to walk off into the surrounding bushlands, where they have vanished completely! Few know how the girls disappeared...fewer yet know why. Amber and Jeanie soon realize that the key to unlocking a secret that has been hidden for years may lie in the world of their dreams!

SUSPENSE-HORROR SHOJO FROM THE CREATOR OF THE HIT WEB MANGA *BLOCK G.*

FOR MORE INFORMATION VISIT: WWW.TOKYOPOP.COM/THEDREAMING

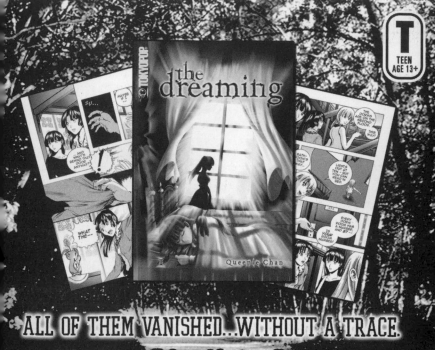

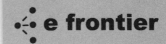

EDITORS' PICKS

TOKYOPOP MANGA SUPPLEMENT

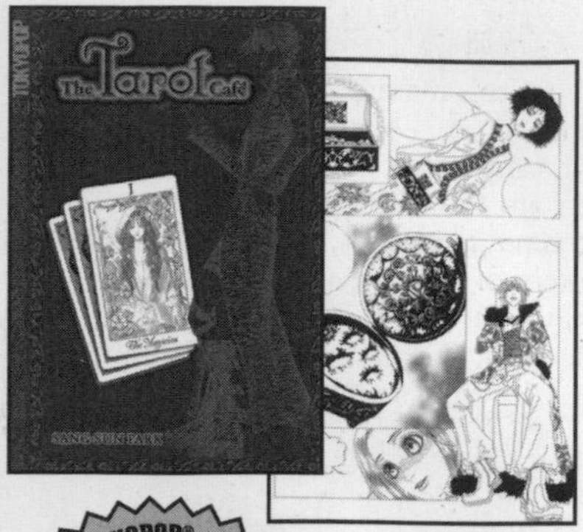
TOKYOPOP
The Tarot Café
SANG-SUN PARK

BY SANG-SUN PARK

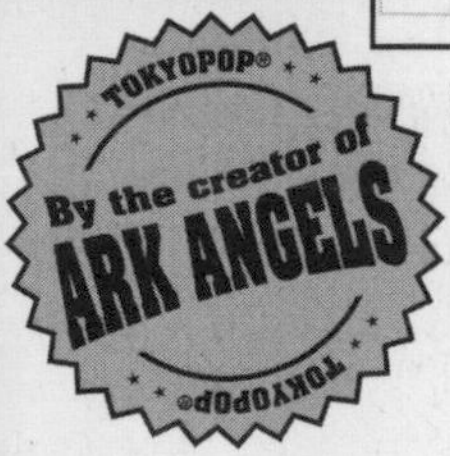
TOKYOPOP®
By the creator of
ARK ANGELS
TOKYOPOP®

THE TAROT CAFÉ

I was always kind of fond of *Petshop of Horrors,* and then along comes *The Tarot Café* and blows me away. It's like *Petshop,* but with a bishonen factor that goes through the roof and into the stratosphere! Sang-Sun Park's art is just unreal. It's beautifully detailed, all the characters are stunning and unique, and while at first the story seems to be yet another Gothy episodic piece of fluff, there is a dark side to Pamela and her powers that I can't wait to read more about. I'm a sucker for teenage werewolves, too.

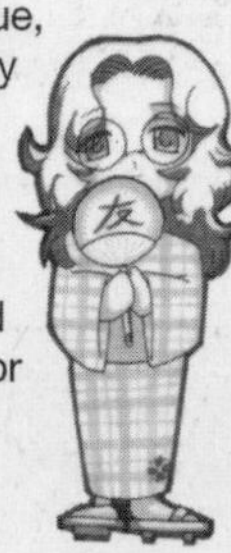

~Lillian Diaz-Pryzbyl, Editor

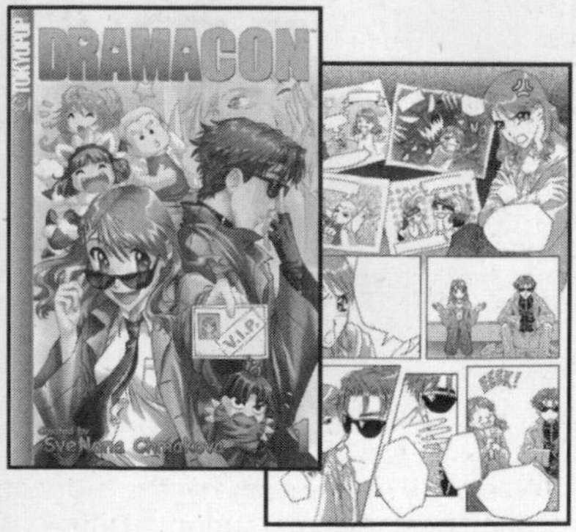
TOKYOPOP
DRAMACON
V.I.P.

BY SVETLANA CHMAKOVA

DRAMACON

I love this manga! First of all, Svetlana is amazing. She's the artist who creates "The Adventures of CosmoGIRL!" manga feature in *CosmoGIRL!* magazine, and she totally rules. *Dramacon* is a juicy romance about a guy and a girl who meet up every year at a crazy anime convention. It grabbed me from the first panel and just wouldn't let go. If you love shojo as much as I do, this book will rock your world.

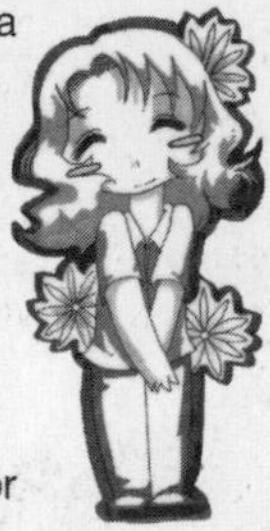

~Julie Taylor, Senior Editor

© Granger/Henderson/Salvaggio and TOKYOPOP Inc.

PSY-COMM
BY JASON HENDERSON, TONY SALVAGGIO AND SHANE GRANGER

In the not-too-distant future, war is entertainment—it is scheduled, televised and rated. It's the new opiate of the masses and its stars are the elite Psychic Commandos—Psy-Comms. Mark Leit, possibly the greatest Psy-Comm of all time, will have to face a tragedy from his past...and abandon everything his life has stood for.

War: The Ultimate Reality Show!

T TEEN AGE 13+

© Yasutaka Tsutsui, Sayaka Yamazaki

TELEPATHIC WANDERERS
BY SAYAKA YAMAZAKI AND YASUTAKA TSUTSUI

When Nanase, a beautiful young telepath, returns to her hometown, her life soon becomes more than unsettling. Using her telepathic powers, Nanase stumbles across others who possess similar abilities. On a train she meets Tsuneo, a man with psychic powers who predicts a dire future for the passengers! Will Nanase find her way to safety in time?

A sophisticated and sexy thriller from the guru of Japanese science fiction.

OT OLDER TEEN AGE 16+

© Koge-Donbo

PITA-TEN OFFICIAL FAN BOOK
BY KOGE-DONBO

Koge-Donbo's lovable characters—Kotarou, Misha and Shia—are all here, illustrated in a unique, fresh style by the some of the biggest fans of the bestselling manga! Different manga-ka from Japan have added their personal touch to the romantic series. And, of course, there's a cool, original tale from Koge-Donbo, too!

***Pita-Ten* as you've never seen it before!**

T TEEN AGE 13+

STOP!

This is the back of the book.
You wouldn't want to spoil a great ending!

This book is printed "manga-style," in the authentic Japanese right-to-left format. Since none of the artwork has been flipped or altered, readers get to experience the story just as the creator intended. You've been asking for it, so TOKYOPOP® delivered: authentic, hot-off-the-press, and far more fun!

DIRECTIONS

If this is your first time reading manga-style, here's a quick guide to help you understand how it works.

It's easy... just start in the top right panel and follow the numbers. Have fun, and look for more 100% authentic manga from TOKYOPOP®!